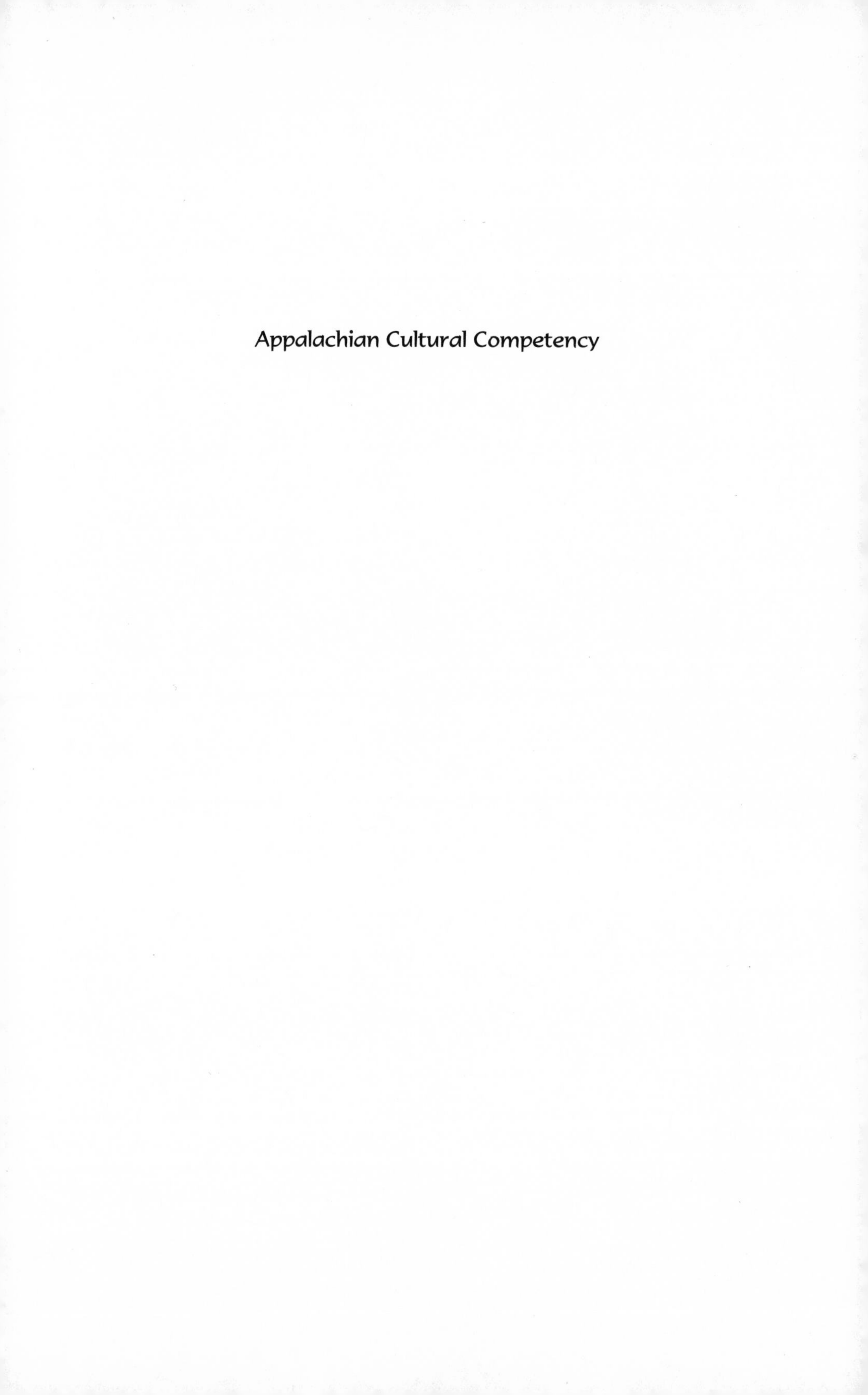

Appalachian Cultural Competency

Appalachian Cultural Competency

A Guide for Medical, Mental Health, and Social Service Professionals

Edited by Susan E. Keefe

The University of Tennessee Press / Knoxville

First Edition.

This book is printed on acid-free paper.

Library of Congress Cataloging-in-Publication Data

Appalachian cultural competency : a guide for medical, mental health, and social service professionals / edited by Susan E. Keefe. — 1st ed.

p. cm.

Includes index.

ISBN 1-57233-333-2 (hardcover)

1. Social service, Rural—Appalachian Region.
2. Human services—Appalachian Region.
3. Medical personnel and patient—Appalachian Region.
4. Appalachian Region—Social life and customs.

I. Keefe, Susan E. (Susan Emley).

HV98.A58A66 2005

361.974—dc22 2004025990

Contents

Preface

Any health and human service practitioner who has worked in the Appalachian region knows that "textbook" approaches often have little relevance. They may be confronted by behavior and values that do not conform to mainstream America and that they do not understand. They may be frustrated trying to apply approaches that have worked a thousand times before, but not in the Appalachian context. They may be required to follow bureaucratic or organizational mandates that will not work in their mountain community. They may confront criticism from their clients for practices that they did not realize were insensitive or controversial.

These lapses between practitioners' expectations and outcomes are often due to inadequate attention to the Appalachian cultural context. While the Appalachian region has received significant attention from scholars and writers in the last three decades, there is very little literature directed to helping health and social services professionals who work in the region. What exists tends to be scattered in specialized disciplinary journals. Professionals I have come into contact with are aware of the importance of understanding Appalachian culture, but, they remark, there is no single reference work that clarifies the practical relevance of a cultural approach in their particular field. This volume demonstrates the utility of a cultural approach from a variety of disciplines, including anthropology, sociology, social work, counseling, nursing, psychology, linguistics, and church ministry. Its authors, despite the diversity of their fields of expertise, share the conviction that providers of health and human services in the region often face common situations and problems that could benefit from a cultural perspective.

A cultural approach assumes, first of all, that people are intelligent actors and that peoples' beliefs and behavior reflect their understanding of the way the world works. Therefore, if a group of people acts in a way that puzzles us, the cultural perspective demands that we investigate that action from their point of view, what anthropologists refer to as the "emic" perspective. This book assists the reader in understanding this emic basis for the cultural approach. It is divided into four sections, each of which describes a key strategy in the successful professional's cultural toolbox: the reflexive stance, the acquisition of cultural competence, the avoidance of stereotyping, and the adoption of a cultural theoretical paradigm.

This collection has not been easy to assemble. In part, this is because it takes a cultural approach, one at odds with the materialist approach, dominant for decades in Appalachian studies, which explains the dynamics of Appalachia primarily in terms of economic factors independent of culture. In addition, it is relatively uncommon to find writers who are at home in the worlds of both scholarship and practice. Many of the papers emerged out of two sessions I organized for Appalachian Studies Conferences in 1993 and 1995 and one session I organized for the annual meeting of the American Anthropological Association in 1994. Others originated as conference papers which I heard and solicited at meetings of the Appalachian Studies Conference. A few were written by authors in response to my request.

What binds this collection together is the authors' grounded theoretical understanding of Appalachia based on an intimate knowledge of the region and its people and an involvement in practice and training programs. The authors provide clear and effective case studies in which the elements of Appalachian culture and their relationship to practice are made obvious. They have been encouraged to discuss the benefits of culturally appropriate practice and to make recommendations for better incorporating cultural sensitivity in agencies in the region. Taken as a whole, I hope the collection provides a wealth of wisdom and practical suggestions for those who wish to serve Appalachian people well.

I would like to acknowledge the helpful comments of a number of readers, including Diane Mines, Jeff Boyer, Dorothy Holland, Elvin Hatch, Anthony Cavender, and two anonymous readers. I also gratefully acknowledge the support of Appalachian State University over the years I have worked on this volume. Teresa Isaacs typed the manuscript and cheerfully assisted in the editing chores. Every time I open my front door, I am supremely grateful that I have had the opportunity to live and work in the mountains for the past twenty-five years. This volume is a product of that experience.

Susan E. Keefe
Blowing Rock, North Carolina

Introduction

SUSAN E. KEEFE

This volume's deceptively simple thesis, that the concept of culture is important for understanding Appalachian people and in making changes to improve their lives, carries with it significant controversy. The controversy has been at play in the field of Appalachian studies, but, more broadly, it is a controversy anchored in opposing schools of thought in the social sciences. First, the thesis raises the question of uniqueness in the Appalachian context. Are Appalachians really culturally different from other Americans? And, if so, how and to what extent? More important, the thesis calls into question basic philosophical assumptions about how human societies work. If it is assumed, for example, that human beings and their societies operate according to universal principles of rationality, then there might be some skepticism about cultural differences and their consequences. In other words, if there are cultural differences, do they matter? Both these sets of questions must be addressed before we can turn our attention to the relationship between culture and practice among Appalachian people.

Does Culture Matter?

The social sciences emerged in the Western world in the eighteenth and nineteenth centuries as modernity came to rival the earlier medieval world view emphasizing traditional forms of knowledge based on religious authority. Modern knowledge, according to Enlightenment philosophers, was based on experience, scientific method, and rational thought. While considerable internal contradictions and disputes were raised by philosophers during the Age of Reason, it is generally agreed that the central ideas of the Enlightenment included reason, empiricism, scientific knowledge, universalism, individualism, freedom, secularism, and the idea of progress (Hamilton 1992). Humans, it was argued, use rational thought as their principal way of organizing knowledge about the world around them, and humans everywhere have this fundamental capacity to apprehend empirical facts and arrive at the same conclusions. Scientific knowledge is the accumulation over time of empirical findings which produce general universal principles and laws that can be applied to situations everywhere. Individuals came to be seen as the starting point for all knowledge and action, empowering an elected government through a rational social contract assumed of individuals' own free will and assuming authority through secular institutions and structures. Society is, consequently, the product of individuals' thought and action. Finally, whereas change in the premodern era had been conceptualized as the product of God's will, the modern idea of progress implied that the human condition could be improved through the intentional application of reason and science to produce ever-increasing well-being and happiness. A sense of optimism and hope came to characterize the modern world, seen as freed from absolutist forms of power and control.

One legacy of the Enlightenment is the rational actor theory, a generalized social science framework for understanding and explaining human behavior as the result of rational thought, which is universal to all human beings (Sahlins 1976). It assumes that the world has a reality that can be objectively apprehended and understood, and that all human minds can intellectually grasp this reality. In other words, all human minds have the same mental framework and assumptions and will come to the same conclusions in similar situations. Given this, it is assumed that people everywhere will produce a single understanding of human behavior and society. Furthermore, it is assumed that people everywhere operate in their own self-interest by applying these universal principles of rationality. Thus, human society and its change over time can best be understood as the result of rational calculation producing the "one best way" to do things. Cultural differences, therefore, are believed to be irrelevant and/or unimportant because they are simply "static" in the system and over time will logically fade away. Forms of rational actor theory are found in cost-benefit analysis in economics, game theory as applied in business and political science, historical materialism as developed in certain schools of Marxist thought, sociobiological theory, and throughout the social sciences in general.

The anthropological concept of culture was developed at the turn of the twentieth century in large part in response to the theory that human behavior is simply the result of intellectual reasoning (Hatch 1973). Anthropologists began to argue that cultural meanings shape rationality and that people in different societies have different perceptions of the world and how it works. This conception of culture also developed as an alternative to racism and the belief that some human beings might be more biologically fit to develop "civilized" societies. The idea of cultural relativity, in fact, called into question the belief that certain societies have superior or inferior cultures and posited instead that there might be many kinds of equally effective cultural means of establishing lifeways. As the primary organizing principle in American anthropology, the concept of culture came to mean a set of beliefs, values, activities, practices, and symbols common to members of a society. Culture is that which is learned rather than instinctive. It is organized and integrated into a general pattern rather than consisting of unrelated bits, it is shared by members of a group, and it is transmitted through the use of language and symbols from one generation to the next (Nanda and Warms 2002). Cultures are always subject to change, as they are to some extent adaptive and created through individual agency, thus contributing to human survival. As a pattern for living, culture shapes both individuals' actions and outcomes for the group in terms of such things as social structure, economic adaptation, religious beliefs, and political organization.

Cultural theory, in other words, turns rational actor theory on its head by questioning ideas such as a universal perception of reality and a single kind of human experience with the natural world (Sahlins 1976). Instead, science itself is assumed to be a cultural system shaped by the context in which it operates (Kuhn 1962). Cultural theory asserts that culture cannot be conceptualized merely as "resistance" to class interests or an irrational impediment to progressive developments, nor is it reducible to a surface phenomenon overlaying more significant political or economic interests (Marcus and Fischer 1986). Culture becomes instead the object of inquiry, as it consists of the system of meaning by which all other things are comprehended, the lens that brings the world into focus (Peacock 1986). The cultural approach has been adopted in many subfields of the other social sciences, including cultural geography, cultural sociology, and cultural history.

So, does culture matter? The resounding answer is yes. In the case of Appalachia, as in all others, there is no aspect of life that exists without cultural meaning. Appalachian people have their own way of looking at the world and acting in it. Those who hope to work successfully with them must learn to understand and appreciate these cultural differences.

Defining Culture

Culture, as Raymond Williams has pointed out, is "one of the two or three most complicated words in the English language" (1976:76). Enlightenment philosophers used the word to refer to the general secular process of human social development which resulted in unilinear progress toward civilization (Bocock 1992). It was in this sense that, in 1870, British anthropologist Edward B. Tylor defined culture as the "complex whole which includes knowledge, belief, art, law, morals, custom, and any other capabilities acquired by man as a member of society" (quoted in Nanda and Warms 2002:72). In the late eighteenth century, the German writer Herder in *Ideas on the Philosophy of History of Mankind* (1784-91) attacked the Eurocentric claim to high culture and argued that it was necessary to speak of "cultures" in the plural. This idea of alternatives in human development was taken up by writers in the romantic movement in Germany, England, and France and was ultimately developed in American anthropology at the turn of the twentieth century by Franz Boas to refer to the distinctive ways of life, the shared values and meanings, common to different groups of people (Stocking 1968). It was this definition of culture that dominated much of twentieth century anthropology.

While this idea of culture as a way of life can be defined in many different ways, there are two main approaches that should be distinguished. The "functionalist" approach builds on the work of Émile Durkheim, which emphasizes the normative nature of culture and its function in integrating the individual into the group. In *How Institutions Think*, Mary Douglas (1986), for example, is concerned with the conceptual style of thought developed by social groupings and built into their institutions. These institutions channel individual memory and perceptions into forms compatible with the social patterns in the group. Thus, an individual's cognitive processes become shaped by social institutions, and other, more creative acts become unthinkable. According to this school of thought, the ethnographer's task becomes one of unmasking the deep-seated, "authentic" culture that dominates in society.

The second approach to culture as a way of life, called "interpretive," draws upon the work of Max Weber and puts emphasis on how culture is formed out of the interaction between individuals and society. Rather than seeing culture as a coherent system with forces of its own, culture is viewed as a set of categories of understanding by which social actors electively operate. Clifford Geertz, the most well known proponent of this approach, in *The Interpretation of Culture* (1973) argues that culture is a web of meaning spun by human actors and that there may be multiple constructions of reality sorted out by different individuals in any given setting. The ethnographer must interpret how people, as they are engaged in action, see themselves and their culture. In his classic study, Geertz (1973), for example, establishes aspects of Balinese concepts of self and culture, or identity, through his interpretive analysis of Balinese cock fights.

In the late twentieth century, the concept of culture as a way of life came to be criticized for what were perceived as its assumptions, among them the beliefs that cultures are separate bounded entities, cultures are relatively static and prescribed, cultures are relatively homogeneous, and individual agency is insignificant (Asad 1979; Clifford 1988; Marcus and Fischer 1986; Ortner 1984; Rosaldo 1989). Those writing from a postmodern perspective pointed out that this concept of culture made little sense given the fluid nature of global society, in which transnational migration, electronic mass media, and the shifting of global capital causes disjunctures rather than continuities in life (Appadurai 1996).

Another way of defining culture has emerged in response to these criticisms and out of the intellectual and social movements of the late twentieth century, including feminism, poststructuralism, and the Third World critique of the West. This approach focuses on the social practices that produce shared meaning (Bocock 1992). In other words, culture becomes a "verb" and what is significant is what culture "does" rather than what culture "is" (Street 1991). With an emphasis on process and social discourse rather than an essential set of traits, this concept of culture puts historical change, fluidity, and social interaction at the center of analysis. This model more easily incorporates multicultural diversity and situational identities, as culture is conceptualized as a highly unstable product of multiple forms of meaning (Friedman 1994). It also better ensures the analysis of power dimensions, including the "subtle mechanisms of hegemony which define non-dominant cultural practices as deviant and marginal" (Schech and Haggis 2000:25). This approach draws heavily on Bourdieu (1977) and his concept of the "habitus" or the system of lasting dispositions (habits) developed in dialectic with others, and Foucault's (1965, 1977) penetrating analyses of power relations and how shared meanings are constructed in hierarchical societies. Rather than seeing culture as a monolith, it is conceived as a battleground of contestation and struggle over the right to control the interpretation of events (Gupta and Ferguson 1997).

While these two major definitions of culture—culture as a way of life and culture as social discourse—are often presented as opposing viewpoints, Schech and Haggis point out that they are not mutually exclusive, that they each represent "distinct but related ways of approaching the study of culture" (2000:21). In a similar vein, Bocock (1992) summarizes the differences between the two as follows: (1) the first definition of culture concentrates on the meanings which a group shares while the second concentrates on the practices by which shared meanings are produced, and (2) the first definition focuses on culture as a whole way of life while the second concentrates on the interrelationships between the components making up a particular cultural practice. While the second definition of culture has received greater attention recently, some theorists have admitted that it is difficult to do without the earlier concept of a priori culture (Clifford 1988; Ortner 1995). It can be argued that both ways of conceptualizing culture offer something valuable and complimentary. Furthermore, there is no inherent reason that both cannot be applied in such a way as to incorporate change, the local-global context, power relations, multiple meanings, and the agency of individuals. As Keesing (1994) points out, a critical view of "the cultural" would take the dominant cultural forms as problematic, would examine the way symbolic production is linked to power and invested interests, and would assume that there are multiple subdominant traditions in any society. For these reasons, this volume embraces both definitions of culture as complementary ways of understanding cultural differences.

Culture and Appalachia

As "reluctant ethnics" constantly struggling to achieve status equality in American society, Appalachian residents and scholars often are unlikely to adopt a cultural approach setting themselves apart as Appalachian people (and therefore potentially inferior to others) (Keefe 1998). There is less resistance to anchoring the people to place, and Appalachian studies is commonly recognized as a particular form of regional studies. The name "Appalachia," of course, derives from the Appalachian mountain chain extending from Alabama to Canada. In defining the Appalachian region, however, scholars are likely to incorporate cultural as well as geographic, economic, and historical criteria (Raitz and Ulack 1991). In 1965, using the criterion of economic need, the federal Appalachian Regional Commission (ARC) defined the Appalachian region as consisting of West Virginia and the mountainous portions of twelve other states: Mississippi, Alabama, Georgia, South Carolina, North Carolina, Tennessee, Kentucky, Virginia, Maryland, Ohio, Pennsylvania, and New York. Those taking a more cultural approach tend to follow John C. Campbell's (1921) lead and limit Appalachia to a core area in the southern highlands consisting of West Virginia and portions of eight other states: Alabama, Georgia, South Carolina, North Carolina, Tennessee, Kentucky, Virginia, and Maryland. Even recent studies with postmodern inclinations which see place as contested and without clear boundaries must in the end locate people in a meaningful way in the world. In his recent history of the region, John Alexander Williams, for example, states, "Postmodern Appalachia is thus a zone where diverse groups have interacted with one another and with a set of regional and subregional environments over time" (2002:12). Nevertheless, in the end, Williams accepts the wide-ranging ARC boundaries while focusing on a "core region" spread over six states: Georgia, North Carolina, Tennessee, Kentucky, Virginia, and West Virginia (2002:13). Regarding Appalachia and its people solely as a regional entity, however, has problems beyond the difficulty in delimiting the region, not the least of which is that such a definition does not easily incorporate the study of out-migrants to Appalachian neighborhoods in Chicago, Detroit, and other cities outside the ARC boundaries. Cultural definitions, on the other hand, follow Appalachian people and so avoid this dilemma.

The emergence in the last thirty years of a scholarly field of Appalachian studies, two academic Appalachian studies journals, the Appalachian Studies Association, and an annual interdisciplinary Appalachian Studies Conference drawing over seven hundred attendees are indications of significant interest in what I would call a cultural group. Yet if geographic boundaries and a regional definition offer no simple markers of Appalachian people, how can we begin to understand their cultural differentness?

Appalachia's Cultural History

The emergence of any cultural way of life is based on a historical experience, which is typically open to different interpretations. Appalachia's history is no exception. Several recent histories of Appalachia, while covering similar ground, engage the topic from different vantage points, including peripheralization in a world system (Dunaway 1996) and contestation over place (Williams 2002). Richard Drake's version more clearly accepts the cultural distinctiveness of Appalachian people when he writes that the "overwhelming evidence from contemporary observers—teachers who worked with the region's youth, as well as those Appalachians who have left a record of the overwhelmingly rural society that existed before 1930—all this seems to indicate that a unique and distinctive people existed in this region" (Drake 2001:ix). The brief introduction to Appalachian history presented here condenses my own version of the common historical experience and emerging cultural consciousness of Appalachian people (Keefe 1998).

European settlement of the Appalachian mountain region occurred largely in the eighteenth and early nineteenth centuries, quickly decimating indigenous Native American populations as the result of warfare, forced labor, and disease. Immigrants moved though the ports of Pennsylvania and the settled areas in their vicinity, descending southward along the Atlantic coast into the Carolina Piedmont and southwest into the Valley of Virginia along the Shenandoah River, then pushing up to the headwaters of the smaller rivers into the Blue Ridge Mountains, and finally across the Appalachian divide into the Alleghany Mountains of Kentucky and Tennessee.

Immigrants included people of English, Irish, Welsh, German, Swiss, and French heritage, but the vast majority (perhaps four-fifths) of early European immigrants to Appalachia were Scots-Irish, an amalgam of Scottish and Irish peoples seeking religious and political freedom in America (Fischer 1989). Some immigrants brought indentured servants and slaves of African origin with them. Free people of color also moved into the mountains during this period. Ethnic diversification after this early period included emancipated slaves and, later, free blacks recruited for work in the coal mines after the Civil War, as well as eastern and southern Europeans who came to mine coal from the 1890s to the 1920s. Significant communities of Asian immigrants, Hispanic migrant workers, and white newcomers (attracted by the beautiful landscapes and rural life-style) also came to the region in the late twentieth century. Yet the overwhelming majority of the contemporary population in Appalachia, more than 80 percent, are descendants of the early northern European immigrants who arrived in the eighteenth and nineteenth centuries.

Life in the mountains was based on a rural culture with a form of farming called "forest farming," involving a combination of hunting and fishing, wild food foraging, livestock raising, and the rotation of farm plots with forested areas in order to rejuvenate the soil nutrients (Blethen 1994). Communities consisted of dispersed networks of family, friends, and neighbors living in a common geographic location (such as a hollow or along a creek) conjoined by a shared history and moral code (Beaver 1986). From this early period emerged a culture suited to the yeoman farming life-style. Mountain communities during this period were egalitarian and largely unstratified, with economic exchange based on reciprocity, that is, the exchange of goods and services between equals. Kinship was the basis for the folk society, creating a cognitive model for social relations and a real social system of people who interacted primarily with relatives. Resourcefulness and self-sufficiency were a necessity in the difficult mountain environment. With an ethnic tradition of resisting governmental authority, mountaineers prized personal freedom, pursuing "cooperative independence" through cooperation with fellow community members in order to preserve their autonomy. Attachment to the land, land symbolizing family, livelihood, and heritage, brought with it a deep loyalty to place and a sense that the mountains themselves, like the hills of Zion in the Old Testament, are sacred.

The Scots-Irish brought with them Calvinist religious beliefs, but the virtual absence of local churches and ministers in early mountain settlements led to the development of a more family-based religion fed by brief contact with circuit riders. Mountaineers were swept up in the evangelical Protestantism of the Great Awakening late in the eighteenth century. This American religious movement created a new religious order emphasizing the personal conversion experience and a literal interpretation of the Bible. The result for mountain people was a loosening of ties to their Presbyterian heritage and the emergence of independent and sectarian churches unaffiliated with national or "mainline" churches (McCauley 1995).

During the Civil War, mountain farmers, who typically had small holdings and few slaves, were split in their loyalties toward the Confederacy. Some mountain counties even became pro-Unionist (Inscoe 1989). Postbellum southern state legislatures retaliated for this disloyalty by withholding monies for schools and roads in the mountains, leading to socioeconomic deterioration in the late nineteenth century.

Industrial development in the Appalachian region, beginning with construction of the railroads about 1880, often created its own devastation. Resource extraction, in the form of mining and timbering, and the appropriation of land for the national park system created an "internal colonial economy" for much of the region (Lewis, Johnson, and Askins 1978). Stripped of their lands, disappropriated mountaineers became low-paid wage laborers in an economy controlled by external capitalists. In other areas, where mountain people retained control of their land, the mountainous landscape created natural barriers to the provision of modern transportation, communications, and utilities that slowed industrialization, manufacturing, and integration into the national economy by two or three decades compared to the rest of the nation, creating relative economic underdevelopment. The image of Appalachia as the hillbilly "Other," which emerged at the turn of the century in popular magazines, fiction, and, later, motion pictures, was thus joined with a national perception of enduring poverty and "backwardness" in the twentieth century (Batteau 1990; Shapiro 1978; Williamson 1995).

The historical experience of Appalachians has served to make a heterogeneous racial and ethnic aggregate of people into a regional group with a shared identity. The dominant religious orientation was transformed from Old World Presbyterian to evangelical Protestant American. The southern links of political and economic geography were fractured by the Civil War, after which Appalachian areas became the "untended back yards" of southern states. Perhaps most important, much of the region was transformed in a few brief decades around the turn of the twentieth century from a frontier egalitarian-oriented society to a highly stratified and peripheralized region controlled to a great extent by outside investors. These processes set the stage for an emerging consciousness among Appalachian residents as a people with a unique historical experience, a shared relationship with the outside world, and a common destiny.

Appalachia's Core Culture

Ethnographers and other social scientists studying Appalachian culture agree that a number of core values and cultural features are central to the culture. Most of this scholarship concentrates on rural areas or very small towns, but similar cultural traits are described in studies of Appalachian migrants to cities outside the region (Philliber and McCoy 1981; Schwarzweller, Brown, and Mangalam 1971). A review of the general themes of ethnographic studies over the past five decades gives some indication of the central features of mountain people's way of life: a distinctive linguistic dialect (Puckett 2000; Williams 1972; Wolfram and Christian 1976), a society based fundamentally on family ties (Beaver 1986; Halperin 1990; Keefe 1988), social structure based on kinship (Batteau 1982a, 1982b; Bryant 1981; Matthews 1966), ties to community as a source of identity and social organization (Beaver 1986; Brown 1988; Halperin 1998; Hicks 1976; Kaplan 1971; Pearsall 1959; Stephenson 1968), an independent and sectarian Protestant religious heritage (Dorgan 1987, 1989; Humphrey 1984; Jones 1999; McCauley 1995; Sovine 1983), and a strong sense of place (Allen 1990; Foster 1988; Humphrey 1984). In these studies, core values associated with Appalachian culture include egalitarianism, independence and individualism, personalism, familism, a religious world view, neighborliness, love of the land, and the avoidance of conflict (Beaver 1986; Hicks 1976; Jones 1994; Keefe 1998).

The existence of an Appalachian core culture does not imply the nonexistence of other, subdominant cultures in the region. Ethnic and racial groups such as Hispanics, the Cherokee, Melungeons, and black Appalachians are found in the region, and while they maintain their own heritage, they also take up the core culture to varying degrees (e.g., Keefe and Manross 1999; Kennedy 1994; Neely 1991; Turner and Cabbell 1985). For example, in the manner of gospel singings found throughout the mountains, the Cherokee in Cherokee, North Carolina, have a Trail of Tears Singing each June to remember through Christian music the four thousand Cherokee who died during the forced removal to Oklahoma in 1838-39 (Neely 1991). Newcomer non-Appalachians also find themselves adapting to mountain culture, sometimes reluctantly, as when seasonal residents learn through occasional vandalism that home spotlights on mountain ridges are not appreciated by local residents (Beaver 1986). More significantly, dominant social institutions such as schools, churches, and political elections are distinctively shaped by mountain culture and impose challenges for non-Appalachian in-migrants in day-to-day life (Anglin 1983).

While it is appropriate to distinguish Appalachian culture at a general level as a pattern of ideas and expectations for behavior that is coherent and distinctive, the question of Appalachian cultural differentness is more problematic. Since the dominant Appalachian culture has ethnic roots in Euro-American heritage, the cultural differences that exist between Appalachians and non-Appalachian Euro-Americans are most often differences in strength of presence of a trait or its particular iteration, rather than differences in unique kinds of traits. For example, as I have noted elsewhere, whereas "mainstream Americans interpret individualism as the right to non-conformity and equal opportunity to compete for the American Dream, Appalachians emphasize the aspects of sovereignty and self-reliance" (Keefe 1998:144). Furthermore, these cultural differences tend to take on significance due to the perceptions of the observer and the observed, rather than any inherent qualities of the traits. Mountain people are becoming adept at negotiating their ethnicity, at times electing distinctiveness and at other times disclaiming it, as they compete for resources and autonomy. Stephen Foster's (1988) study demonstrates this process of shifting ethnicity as native residents of Ashe County, North Carolina, vocally assumed a distinctive identity as people with an endangered "mountain culture" in order to stop federal authorities from damming the New River and destroying farmlands.

Nor should it be assumed that Appalachian core culture traits are evenly distributed throughout the region. Most ethnographic studies have been done in central and southern Appalachia, and one must assume that most features of Appalachian core culture are more clearly apparent in the heart of the region than in areas on the fringe. The Appalachian dialect, for example, is less evident among those speakers in the northern range of the region.

That Appalachian culture is not wholly unique is evident from our review of cultural history in which it is clear that Appalachian people have helped to shape what is American culture. Yet regional distinctiveness is still apparent, as in the particular religious experience of mountain people. Appalachian culture also shares much with the rural southern and rural agrarian life-style in general. Yet details of uniqueness can be found, such as particular mountain musical styles (e.g., dulcimer playing and claw-hammer banjo picking), the Appalachian regional dialect, and certain religious faiths, including the "No-Hellers" (Dorgan 1997). More significant at this point, perhaps, with regard to understanding cultural differentness in the region, is to move from a definition of culture as way of life to culture as social discourse. Instead of asking, Are Appalachians culturally different from other Americans? it may be more appropriate to ask, How is Appalachian culture shaped through discourse, conflict, and negotiation?

The Mistake of Reading Cultural Difference as Deficit

There is danger, of course, in speaking of cultural difference because of the ethnocentric tendency to type others not only as different but also as inferior. Stereotypes of Appalachian people continue to thrive. Each issue of the *Appalachian Journal* makes this clear in the "Signs of the Times" section, where, over the last twenty-nine years, former editor Jerry Williamson has chronicled contemporary articles making use of hillbilly stereotypes from newspapers and popular magazines. These negative images are one reason so many people with Appalachian roots resist the conceptualization of their region and their people as being unique. Even so, mountain people may be quick, when asked, to express pride in their heritage and a positive sense of peoplehood. This was true in a recent study in a western North Carolina county in which focus groups of Appalachian natives, when asked what was meant by the term "mountain people," described a people who see themselves as self-sufficient, as having a reputation for being trustworthy and morally upright, and as being embedded in personal communities with a deeply rooted heritage (Hatch and Keefe 1999). A positive identity is difficult to maintain, however, in the face of prejudice and discrimination, and the dilemma is that Appalachians are often forced to choose between two equally unacceptable identities: on one hand, that they are just like everybody else and undeserving of any special attention; on the other hand, that their culture is inferior and to blame for most of the social problems in the region.

The culture of poverty model gave legitimacy to the second of these possibilities, which sees cultural difference as cultural deficit. Originally developed by Oscar Lewis and applied to Mexicans and Puerto Ricans in poverty, the culture of poverty model proposes that a certain portion of the chronically poor develop a culture characterized by authoritarianism, fatalism, present-time orientation, suspicion of authority, a tolerance of pathology, feelings of helplessness and inferiority, and so on (Lewis 1959). According to this model, the cultural value and belief system that develops in poverty also contributes to its persistence. A number of writers applied this model to the Appalachian region in the 1960s (Ball 1968; Caudill 1962; Gazaway 1969; Weller 1965). In a recent study of poverty in the Appalachian region, Billings and Blee (2000) state that the internal colonial model, which laid blame instead on the coal companies, was in many ways a response to the culture of poverty model in explaining poverty's persistence in the region. Billings and Blee also point out that neither model has adequately described the positive traits of traditional mountain culture, especially what they call the rural agricultural society's "patriarchal moral economy," which has "a social logic distinct from those of advanced capitalist societies" and continues to contribute to these communities' survival (2000:162). Seen from this perspective, traditional Appalachian culture is not necessarily inferior to mainstream American culture but is simply an equally good and rational way of life which must be understood on its own terms.

Appalachian Cultural Identity

One result of current theoretical interest in the negotiation of cultural life has been a focus on cultural identity, which, because it is based more on perception and affiliation than on material aspects of life, is more socially sensitive and subject to rapid change than many other forms of cultural belief and behavior. The term "cultural identity" encompasses the perceptions of and personal affiliation with ethnic groups and cultures. First, the perception that there are significant differences between cultural groups must exist. If there is that perception, cultural identity forms when individuals feel an attachment to and pride in one ethnic group and cultural heritage as opposed to others (Keefe 1992). It can also incorporate the perception of prejudice and discrimination against one's own people. Cultural identity may come about through both self-motivated allegiance and forced identity due to prejudice and discrimination. These positive and negative forces may be difficult to untangle in explaining the existence and persistence of cultural identity. Nevertheless, it is increasingly clear that cultural identity, perhaps more than most aspects of cultural difference, is crucial in motivating groups to action in the public arena (Romanucci-Ross and De Vos 1995).

Appalachian cultural identity has received little attention from Appalachian studies scholars, perhaps because of Appalachians' reluctance to set themselves apart as a cultural group (for an exception, see Whisnant 1973, 1980a). Studies of Appalachian migrants have paid more attention to identity because of the more obvious presence of ethnic prejudice and discrimination in cities (Obermiller and Rappold 1994; Philliber and McCoy 1981). In either case, there is little consistency in labels of cultural identification. The term "Appalachian" is one used by scholars but only rarely assumed by members of the group. More common among southern mountain whites are identities such as "mountain people," "country people," or "mountaineer." Black Appalachians also lack an indigenous name but nevertheless carry a mountain identity along with their racial identity (Turner 1985). Regardless of the lack of agreement on an ethnic name, Appalachian natives can usually identify members of their group through the recognition of an individual's dialect and claim to a homeplace and relatives in the mountains. They are also quick to identify groups outside the mountains to which they do not belong (Keefe 1998). In any event, the absence of a name does not prevent many Appalachians from adopting a conscious pride in their cultural heritage and identification with other mountain people. This cultural identity is clearly a significant trait making Appalachian people distinctive.

The Politics of Appalachian Culture

Cultural difference is socially produced and a number of studies examine Appalachian culture in the context of contested power in the region. Many of these studies emphasize the hegemony of American national culture. Shapiro (1978) and Batteau (1990) argue that what is often recognized as Appalachian culture and identity has been a stereotypic creation by outsiders of "Otherness" that serves national interests. In *All That Is Native and Fine* (1983), David Whisnant describes the manipulation of native culture by civic workers and cultural missionaries from outside the region who established settlement schools and folk schools teaching newly invented "traditions," including, for example, imported folksongs and dances and non-native weaving patterns and woodworking styles, all in the name of "preserving" the nation's Anglo-Saxon heritage. In another study, Whisnant (1980b) examines the destructive nature of the ARC and TVA, both of which worked to impose a cultural agenda of economic development on a region inclined toward more traditional livelihoods. In his study of a coal company town in Tennessee, John Gaventa (1980) analyzes dimensions of power, including the control over values, strategies, and practices of native coal miners, as they are worked to the advantage of corporate interests, in this case British rather than American.

Other studies look more closely at the cultural forms as created by native Appalachians in the contested public sphere. In *Confronting Appalachian Stereotypes* (Billings, Norman, and Ledford 1999), the resistance is conceptualized as "back talk" in which native-born Appalachian scholars and activists "talk back to the American mainstream, confronting head-on those who would view their home region one-dimensionally" (dust jacket quote). Further developing the idea that culture is mostly a nonmaterial "space of imagination, critique, and desire," Kathleen Stewart (1996) analyzes Appalachian speakers in a marginal West Virginia holler who create a set of "ideals" that challenges America's "master narrative" of the land of progress. Conceiving culture more broadly to include practical resources and social practices, Rhoda Halperin (1990) examines the economic strategies through which rural Appalachians preserve their alternative country lifeways while adapting to the demands of urban America. Books by Stephen Fisher (1993) and Richard Couto (1999) examine the social and cultural capital specifically informing resistance and democratic action in the Appalachian region in response to market capitalism and national and global forces of modernization. While these studies of "resistance" in Appalachia have made valuable contributions to understanding social discourse in the region, there is also the temptation of imagining Appalachians as "historyless" people whose culture is but a response to outside forces (Billings and Blee 2000).

A few studies provide a close examination of both Appalachian and American perspectives in the political process of constructing and reconstructing cultural difference. For Stephen Foster (1988), Ashe County culture emerges through political conflict over the fate of land along the New River where an electrical power company wanted to build a dam. Through contestation with the power company, Ashe County residents consciously struggled to lay claim to the authenticity of their way of life and to articulate what cultural distinctiveness would be lost with the destruction done by the dam. In *It Comes from the People* (1995), Hinsdale, Lewis, and Waller examine aspects of local culture, particularly community values regarding "justice" versus "charity" and religious rituals of reunion, that become a force in community development action in a place "on the rough side of the mountain." The authors follow the dialogue between Ivanhoe community members and county commissioners as well as outside professionals in which conflict clarifies cultural differences within Appalachian society and between Appalachian natives and non-Appalachians. The study of conflict in the workplace, in voluntary organizations, and in regional decision making has also proven useful in determining how mountain people set themselves apart from others (Anglin 1993; Keefe 1983, 1994).

Culture and Practice in Appalachia

The challenge for practitioners working with Appalachian people is to ensure that Appalachian voices are included in the discourse regarding change, development, and service provision. In other words, development must be inclusive so that the process becomes one in which professionals and the people they serve work together rather than in opposition. This process requires more than an increase in financial resources. One early reader of this book suggested that it would not really matter if cultural approaches were integrated in human services because without more financial resources, things were not going to change. I would respond that more financial resources do not ensure accessibility of services. A useful model for culturally appropriate action is the one developed by Hazel Weidman (discussed in van Willigen 2002) for the provision of health services. Finding that hospital services were not equally accessible by the various cultural groups in the Miami area, she developed a research program investigating indigenous health practices among residents from Haiti, the Bahamas, Cuba, and Puerto Rico as well as southern blacks. She then designed programs and services and trained health service workers in order to attract residents from each of these cultural groups. Viewing each cultural group as a "coculture" on par with other cultures, Weidman began with the assumption that each cultural group had worthwhile cultural practices that should be recognized and become part of the discourse regarding health and illness. Her success in adapting health services to the needs of the diverse population is an excellent example of the benefits of rethinking the allocation of current resources. Cultural models of practice can develop and extend resources while models not based on culture can lead to waste and cultural destructiveness.

An example of the beneficial effects of the cultural approach in policy formulation in Appalachia is described in a study conducted by Toborg, Meyer, and Mande (1997) aimed at promoting tobacco cessation in the region, where rates of tobacco use are higher than national rates. Hoping ultimately to design culturally appropriate tobacco prevention materials, they reviewed the literature on Appalachia and identified seven criteria to assess cultural suitability. They found that successful tobacco-cessation literature

Uses an explicit or implicit appeal to family, family ties, or family loyalty
Reflects a sense of community

Uses an explicit or implicit appeal to independence, self-reliance, or empowerment

Is written at a level that most readers in the region can understand

Draws on the oral or written traditions of the region

Avoids negative stereotypes

Uses images familiar to most people within the region.

(Toborg, Meyer, and Mande 1997:38-44)

A total of 471 materials concerning tobacco prevention and control were collected from Appalachian organizations responding to their requests for materials. An evaluation of these materials found that none of them met all seven of the cultural criteria, and only 20 percent of the materials met four or more criteria. Toborg, Meyer, and Mande concluded that "many of the tobacco prevention and control materials now in use in Appalachia lack cultural congruence with the region's values, traditions, norms, and customs" (1997:51).

In conducting focus groups with men, women, and youths in West Virginia, Kentucky, and North Carolina, Toborg, Meyer, and Mande found that family is of sufficient importance to cause older family members to consider a change in health-related practices if they see a potential benefit for younger family members. Furthermore, they found that mothers are generally responsible for the health of the family, although few tobacco-cessation materials address this role. Finally, they noted that even though people were living in a tobacco-growing region, smokers were prepared not to smoke around children. Toborg, Meyer, and Mande suggest the need for development of several community kits for the prevention and control of tobacco in the Appalachian region, including a kit on secondhand smoke, a package for adults in a family context, and a package for women as wives and mothers.

This example of cultural appropriateness illustrates the orientation recommended in this book, which emphasizes the development of cultural competency in serving Appalachian people. There are a number of explicit values underlying this cultural approach.

First, local knowledge must be respected. Toborg, Meyer, and Mande began their intervention by assuming tobacco-cessation materials could be successfully designed for the region, but only if they conformed to Appalachian cultural criteria. Second, action should be designed to include diverse voices in the community, including women and ethnic minorities. Tobacco-cessation materials, for example, were specifically designed for Appalachian women as wives and mothers because mothers were generally responsible for family health in mountain communities. Third, there should be collaboration between trained professionals and local communities, groups, and individuals. This requires the involvement and participation of local people. It also assumes a relationship of relative equality between professionals and nonprofessionals in the intervention process. Toborg, Meyer, and Mande, for example, used Appalachian focus groups to assist in the creation of culturally suitable tobacco-cessation materials.

This sort of cultural approach was also adopted by Plaut, Landis, and Trevor (forthcoming) in their development of Community Oriented Primary Care for Madison County, North Carolina, in which they asked residents to identify local communities and used focus groups to help identify health problems and solutions. They put these ideas into action through the formation of a community health advisory board made up of residents and county agency representatives with backup provided by a professional staff. This kind of collaboration signals a fourth value in the cultural approach involving a commitment to empowering local people through a community-based "bottom-up" process. Power in this sense is conceptualized as people transformation and is something that can be created through work that engages local people.

The Madison Community Health Project resulted in a number of important developments, including a health fair for seniors, a diabetes education program, and the funding of a 911 emergency telephone system (Plaut, Landis, and Trevor forthcoming). Perhaps more important, the project changed the way local people worked with one another, increasing trust and expanding social networks. As a result, Plaut, Landis, and Trevor suggest that the current health consortium has the ability to set goals and confidently set out to achieve them. This marks the final explicit value of the cultural model, which is sustainability both in terms of environmental and cultural preservation. The United Nations has defined sustainable development as "development that meets the needs of the present without compromising the ability of future generations to meet their own needs" (Brundtland Report 1987:43). Development that nurtures local leadership and cultural integrity serves to sustain the community after professional intervention ceases.

Organization of This Book

This volume is organized into four parts which develop the cultural approach in depth. The introduction to each part develops theoretical ideas that are explored by authors of various case studies and analyses of particular cultural phenomena. Rather than providing complete coverage of health, social services, and cultural practice in Appalachia, the chapters are intended to illustrate the major theoretical concepts discussed.

Part I develops the concept of reflexivity as the foundation for the cultural practitioner's role. The reflexive orientation requires self-examination and the ability to step outside oneself to objectively consider how others might perceive the practitioner and the intervention. It is the self-conscious examination of one's own cultural heritage as well as the cultural heritage of others. It also involves a critical examination of the professional intervention process. Reflexivity is the first step in creating cultural awareness and sensitivity to the cultural traditions of others and openness to an adaptive cultural model on the part of the professional practitioner. The authors of the four chapters in Part I discuss aspects of this process that should be helpful for all kinds of practitioners working with Appalachian clients, focusing especially on communication and interaction styles, values, and beliefs. Once adaptation is perceived and accepted as the appropriate professional response, the next step, which involves the acquisition of cultural competence, can be taken.

Part II describes the cultural competence model, which has been developed most fully in the mental health practitioner field but also has been applied in diverse social service, public health, and criminal justice agencies. This model addresses the need for professionals to acquire specific knowledge about one's own way of life as well as that of clientele so that culturally appropriate practices can be developed. Specific suggestions are given for acquiring cultural knowledge in the Appalachian context. In Part II, authors address cultural knowledge in the contexts of the physicians' practice and in professional training programs for nurses and other health professionals. The chapters illustrate that no practitioner arena can be considered "culture free."

Part III addresses the destructive impact of Appalachian stereotypes and ways of transcending them in research and practice. Because stereotypes emerge out of a lack of reflexivity and self-awareness of one's own way of life, they can lead to ethnocentric research programs, policy making, and intervention strategies. The authors of the chapters in Part III present examples from the fields of health and wellness that demonstrate how an appreciation of Appalachian culture can lead to new and sometimes unexpected research findings and recommendations for service providers.

Continuing the theme of the appreciation of Appalachian culture and its implications for practice, Part IV examines this approach as the basis for the choice of a theoretical paradigm for research and service delivery. Using biomedicine as an example, the "value-free" rational scientific paradigm is contrasted with the cultural model as a means of understanding mental illness and the delivery of mental health care and services to Appalachian people.

The authors of chapters in Part IV examine ways in which more holistically based and culturally situated services in Appalachia might better serve the population's mental health needs.

This volume illustrates the way in which the cultural approach can be usefully applied in the health-care arena. Additionally, it is meant to provide a model for human services more generally in the Appalachian region. Healthy people develop in healthy communities, and community development of all kinds would be well served by an approach that is informed by the cultural context of residents.

References

Allen, Barbara. 1990. "The Genealogical Landscape and the Southern Sense of Place." In *Sense of Place: American Regional Cultures*, Barbara Allen and Thomas J. Schlereth (Eds.). Lexington: University Press of Kentucky. Pp. 152–163.

Anglin, Mary. 1983. "Experiences of In-Migrants in Appalachia." In *Appalachia and America: Autonomy and Regional Dependence*, Allen Batteau (Ed.). Lexington: University Press of Kentucky. Pp. 227–238.

Anglin, Mary K. 1993. "Engendering the Struggle: Women's Labor and Traditions of Resistance in Rural Southern Appalachia." In *Fighting Back in Appalachia*, Stephen L. Fisher (Ed.). Philadelphia: Temple University Press. Pp. 263–281.

Appadurai, Arjun. 1996. *Modernity at Large: Cultural Dimensions of Globalization*. Minneapolis: University of Minnesota Press.

Asad, Talal. 1979. "Anthropology and the Analysis of Ideology." *Man*, New Series, 14(4):607–627.

Ball, Richard A. 1968. "A Poverty Case: The Analgesic Subculture of the Southern Appalachians." *American Sociological Review* 33:885–895.

Batteau, Allen. 1982a. "The Contradictions of a Kinship Community." In *Holding On To the Land and the Lord*, Robert L. Hall and Carol B. Stack (Eds.). Athens: University of Georgia Press. Pp. 25–40.

———. 1982b. "Mosbys and Broomsedge: The Semantics of Class in an Appalachian Kinship System." *American Ethnologist* 9:445–466.

———. 1990. *The Invention of Appalachia*. Tucson: University of Arizona Press.

Beaver, Patricia D. 1986. *Rural Community in the Appalachian South*. Lexington, KY: University Press of Kentucky.

Billings, Dwight B., and Kathleen M. Blee. 2000. *The Road to Poverty: The Making of Wealth and Hardship in Appalachia*. Cambridge: Cambridge University Press.

Billings, Dwight B., Gurney Norman, and Katherine Ledford (Eds.). 1999. *Confronting Appalachian Stereotypes: Back Talk From an American Region.* Lexington: University Press of Kentucky.

Blethen, H. Tyler. 1994. "The Transmission of Scottish Culture to the Southern Back Country." In *Appalachian Adaptations to a Changing World*, Norma Myers (Ed.). *Journal of The Appalachian Studies Association* 6:59–72.

Bocock, Robert. 1992. "The Cultural Formations of Modern Society." In *Formations of Modernity*, Stuart Hall and Bram Gieben (Eds.). Cambridge: Polity with Open University Press. Pp. 230–268.

Bourdieu, Pierre. 1977. *Outline of a Theory of Practice.* Cambridge: Cambridge University Press.

Brown, James S. 1988. *Beech Creek: A Study of a Kentucky Mountain Neighborhood.* Berea: Berea College Press.

Brundtland Report. 1987. World Commission on Environment and Development. *Our Common Future.* Oxford: Oxford University Press.

Bryant, F. Carlene. 1981. *We're All Kin.* Knoxville: University of Tennessee Press.

Campbell, John C. 1921. *The Southern Highlander & His Homeland.* New York: Russell Sage Foundation.

Caudill, Harry. 1962. *Night Comes to the Cumberlands: A Biography of a Depressed Area.* Boston: Little, Brown.

Clifford, James. 1988. *The Predicament of Culture: Twentieth-Century Ethnography, Literature, and Art.* Cambridge: Harvard University Press.

Couto, Richard A., with Catherine S. Guthrie. 1999. *Making Democracy Work Better: Mediating Structures, Social Capital, and the Democratic Prospect.* Chapel Hill: University of North Carolina Press.

Dorgan, Howard. 1987. *Giving Glory to God in Appalachia: Worship Practices of Six Baptist Subdenominations.* Knoxville: University of Tennessee Press.

———. 1989. *The Old Regular Baptists of Central Appalachia: Brothers and Sisters in Hope.* Knoxville: University of Tennessee Press.

———. 1997. *In the Hands of a Happy God: The "No-Hellers" of Central Appalachia.* Knoxville: University of Tennessee Press.

Douglas, Mary. 1986. *How Institutions Think.* Syracuse, NY: Syracuse University Press.

Drake, Richard B. 2001. *A History of Appalachia.* Lexington: University Press of Kentucky.

Dunaway, Wilma A. 1996. *The First American Frontier: Transition to Capitalism in Southern Appalachia, 1700–1860.* Chapel Hill: University of North Carolina Press.

Fischer, David Hackett. 1989. *Albion's Seed: Four British Folkways in America*. New York: Oxford University Press.

Fisher, Stephen L. 1993. *Fighting Back in Appalachia: Traditions of Resistance and Change*. Philadelphia: Temple University Press.

Foster, Stephen William. 1988. *The Past is Another Country: Representation, Historical Consciousness, and Resistance in the Blue Ridge*. Berkeley: University of California Press.

Foucault, Michel. 1965. *Madness and Civilization: A History of Insanity in the Age of Reason*. New York: Pantheon.

———. 1977. *Discipline and Punish: Birth of the Prison*. New York: Pantheon.

Friedman, Jonathan. 1994. *Cultural Identity and Global Process*. Thousand Oaks: Sage.

Gaventa, John. 1980. *Power and Powerlessness: Quiescence and Rebellion in an Appalachian Valley*. Urbana: University of Illinois Press.

Gazaway, Rena. 1969. *The Longest Mile: A Vivid Chronicle of Life in an Appalachian Hollow*. Baltimore: Penguin.

Geertz, Clifford. 1973. *The Interpretation of Cultures*. New York: Basic Books.

Gupta, Akhil, and James Ferguson. 1997. *Culture, Power, Place: Explorations in Critical Anthropology*. Durham: Duke University Press.

Halperin, Rhoda H. 1990. *The Livelihood of Kin: Making Ends Meet "The Kentucky Way."* Austin: University of Texas Press.

———. 1998. *Practicing Community: Class, Culture, and Power in an Urban Neighborhood*. Austin: University of Texas Press.

Hamilton, Peter. 1992. "The Enlightenment and the Birth of Social Science." In *Formations of Modernity*, Stuart Hall and Bram Gieben (Eds.). Cambridge: Polity with Open University Press. Pp. 17–58.

Hatch, Elvin. 1973. *Theories of Man and Culture*. New York: Columbia University Press.

Hatch, Elvin, and Susan E. Keefe. 1999. "Exploring Mountain Identity." Paper presented at the annual meeting of the American Anthropological Association, Chicago, Nov. 18.

Hicks, George L. 1976 (reissued 1992). *Appalachian Valley*. Prospect Heights, Ill.: Waveland Press.

Hinsdale, Mary Ann, Helen M. Lewis, and S. Maxine Waller. 1995. *It Comes from the People: Community Development and Local Theology*. Philadelphia: Temple University Press.

Humphrey, Richard. 1984. "Religion and Place in Southern Appalachia." In *Cultural Adaptations in Mountain Environments*, Patricia D. Beaver and Burton L. Purrington (Eds.). Athens: University of Georgia Press. Pp. 122–141.

Inscoe, John C. 1989. *Mountain Masters: Slavery and the Sectional Crisis in Western North Carolina*. Knoxville: University of Tennessee Press.

Jones, Loyal. 1994. *Appalachian Values*. Ashland: The Jesse Stuart Foundation.

———. 1999. *Faith and Meaning in the Southern Uplands*. Urbana: University of Illinois Press.

Kaplan, Berton H. 1971. *Blue Ridge: An Appalachian Community in Transition*. Morgantown: Appalachian Center, West Virginia University.

Keefe, Susan Emley. 1983. "Ethnic Conflict in an Appalachian Craft Cooperative: On the Application of Structural Ethnicity to Mountaineers and Outsiders." In *The Appalachian Experience*, Barry Buxton, et al. (Eds.). Boone: Appalachian Consortium Press, Proceedings of the 6th Annual Appalachian Studies Conference. Pp. 15–25.

———. 1988. "Appalachian Family Ties." In *Appalachian Mental Health*, Susan Emley Keefe (Ed). Lexington: University of Kentucky Press. Pp. 24–35

———. 1992. "Ethnic Identity: The Domain of Perceptions of and Attachment to Ethnic Groups and Cultures." *Human Organization* 51:35–43.

———. 1994. "Urbanism Reconsidered: A Southern Appalachian Perspective." *City and Society* 1:20–34.

———. 1998. "Appalachian Americans: The Formation of "Reluctant Ethnics." In *Many Americas: Critical Perspectives on Race, Racism, and Ethnicity*, Gregory R. Campbell (Ed.). Dubuque, IA: Kendall/Hunt. Pp. 129–153.

Keefe, Susan E., and Jodie D. Manross. 1999. "Race, Religion, and Community: The Demolition of a Black Church." *Appalachian Journal* 26:252–263.

Keesing, Roger H. 1994. "Theories of Culture Revisited." In *Assessing Cultural Anthropology*, Robert Borofsky (Ed.). New York: McGraw-Hill. Pp. 301–310.

Kennedy, N. Brent, with Robyn Vaughn Kennedy. 1994. *The Melungeons: The Resurrection of a Proud People: An Untold Story of Ethnic Cleansing in America*. Macon, GA: Mercer University Press.

Kuhn, Thomas. 1962. *The Structure of Scientific Revolutions*. Chicago: University of Chicago Press.

Lewis, Helen Matthews, Linda Johnson, and Donald Askins (Eds.). 1978. *Colonialism in Modern America: The Appalachian Case*. Boone, NC: Appalachian Consortium Press.

Lewis, Oscar. 1959. *Five Families: Mexican Case Studies in the Culture of Poverty*. New York: Basic Books.

Marcus, George E., and Michael M. J. Fischer. 1986. *Anthropology as Cultural Critique: An Experimental Moment in the Human Sciences*. Chicago: University of Chicago Press.

Matthews, Elmora Messer. 1966. *Neighbor and Kin: Life in a Tennessee Ridge Community.* Nashville: Vanderbilt University Press.

McCauley, Deborah Vansau. 1995. *Appalachian Mountain Religion: A History.* Urbana, IL: University of Illinois Press.

Nanda, Serena, and Richard L. Warms. 2002. *Cultural Anthropology.* 7th ed. Stamford, Conn.: Wadsworth.

Neely, Sharlotte. 1991. *Snowbird Cherokee: People of Persistence.* Athens: University of Georgia Press.

Obermiller, Phillip J., and Ray Rappold. 1994. "The Sense of Place and Cultural Identity Among Urban Appalachians: A Study in Postdeath Migration." In *From Mountain to Metropolis: Appalachian Migrants in American Cities,* Kathryn M. Borman and Phillip J. Obermiller (Eds.). Westport, Conn.: Bergin & Garvey. Pp. 25–31.

Ortner, Sherry B. 1984. "Theory in Anthropology Since the Sixties." *Comparative Studies in Society and History* 26(1):126–166.

———. 1995. "Resistance and the Problem of Ethnographic Refusal." *Comparative Studies in Society and History* 37:173–193.

Peacock, James. 1986. *The Anthropological Lens: Harsh Light, Soft Focus.* New York: Cambridge University Press.

Pearsall, Marian. 1959. *Little Smokey Ridge: The Natural History of a Southern Appalachian Neighborhood.* University, AL: University of Alabama Press.

Philliber, William W., and Clyde B. McCoy (Eds.). 1981. *The Invisible Minority: Urban Appalachians.* Lexington: University Press of Kentucky.

Plaut, Thomas, Suzanne Landis, and June Palmour Trevor. Forthcoming. "Community Coalition Building in the Madison County Health Project." In *Participatory Development in Appalachian Communities,* Susan E. Keefe (Ed). Manuscript in preparation.

Puckett, Anita. 2000. *Seldom Ask, Never Tell: Labor and Discourse in Appalachia.* Oxford: Oxford University Press.

Raitz, Karl B., and Richard Ulack. 1991. "Regional Definitions." In *Appalachia: Social Context Past and Present,* Bruce Ergood and Bruce E. Kuhre (Eds.). Third edition. Dubuque, IA: Kendall/Hunt. Pp. 10–26.

Romanucci-Ross, Lola, and George A. De Vos. 1995. *Ethnic Identity: Creation, Conflict, and Accommodation.* Walnut Creek, CA: AltaMira.

Rosaldo, Renato. 1989. *Culture & Truth: The Remaking of Social Analysis.* Boston: Beacon Press.

Sahlins, Marshall. 1976. *Culture and Practical Reason.* Chicago: University of Chicago Press.

Schech, Susanne, and Jane Haggis. 2000. *Culture and Development: A Critical Introduction*. Oxford: Blackwell.

Schwarzweller, Harry K., James S. Brown, and J. J. Mangalam. 1971. *Mountain Families in Transition: A Case Study of Appalachian Migration*. University Park: Pennsylvania State University Press.

Shapiro, Henry D. 1978. *Appalachia on Our Mind: The Southern Mountains and Mountaineers in the American Consciousness, 1870–1920*. Chapel Hill: University of North Carolina Press.

Sovine, Melanie L. 1983. "Studying Religious Belief Systems in Their Social Historical Context." In *Appalachia and America: Autonomy and Regional Dependence*, Allen Batteau (Ed.). Lexington: University of Kentucky Press. Pp. 48–67.

Stephenson, John. 1968. *Shiloh: A Mountain Community*. Lexington: University Press of Kentucky.

Stewart, Kathleen. 1996. *A Space on the Side of the Road: Cultural Poetics in an "Other" America*. Princeton, NJ: Princeton University Press.

Stocking, George W., Jr. 1968. *Race, Culture, and Evolution*. New York: Free Press.

Street, Brian V. 1991. "Culture is a Verb: Anthropological Aspects of Language and Cultural Process." In *Language and Culture*, David Graddol, Linda Thompson, and Mike Byram (Eds.). Philadelphia: Multilingual Matters. Pp. 23–43.

Toborg, Mary A., Michael G. Meyer, and Mary J. Mande. 1997. *An Assessment of Tobacco Prevention and Control Materials Used in the Appalachian Mountain Region*. Landover, Md.: Toborg Associates.

Turner, William H. 1985. "Introduction." In *Blacks in Appalachia*, William H. Turner and Edward J. Cabbell (Eds.). Lexington: University Press of Kentucky. Pp. xvi–xxiii.

Turner, William H., and Edward J. Cabbell (Eds.). 1985. *Blacks in Appalachia*. Lexington: University Press of Kentucky.

Van Willigen, John. 2002. *Applied Anthropology: An Introduction*. Westport, Conn.: Bergin & Garvey.

Weller, Jack. 1965. *Yesterday's People: Life in Contemporary Appalachia*. Lexington: University of Kentucky Press.

Whisnant, David E. 1973. "Ethnicity and the Recovery of Regional Identity in Appalachia: Thoughts Upon Entering the Zone of Occult Instability." *Soundings* 56 (Spring): 124–38.

———. 1980a. "Developments in the Appalachian Identity Movement: All Is Process." *Appalachian Journal* 8 (Autumn): 41–47.

———. 1980b. *Modernizing the Mountaineer: People, Power, and Planning in Appalachia*. New York: Burt Franklin.

———. 1983. *All That is Native & Fine: The Politics of Culture in an American Region*. Chapel Hill: University of North Carolina Press.

Williams, Cratis D. 1972. "Who are the Southern Mountaineers?" *Appalachian Journal* 1:48–55.

Williams, John Alexander. 2002. *Appalachia: A History.* Chapel Hill: University of North Carolina Press.

Williams, Raymond. 1976. *Keywords: A Vocabulary of Culture and Society.* New York: Oxford University Press.

Williamson, J. W. 1995. *Hillbillyland: What the Movies Did to the Mountains and What the Mountains Did to the Movies.* Chapel Hill: University of North Carolina Press.

Wolfram, Walt, and Donna Christian. 1976. *Appalachian Speech.* Arlington: Center for Applied Linguistics.

Part 1

Preparing for Work in an Appalachian Community: Adopting the Reflexive Practitioner Role

Recognition of the significance and the value of cultural diversity is growing among professional practitioners today (Cox 1993; Cross et al. 1989; Green 1982; Kohls and Knight 1994). One outcome of this increasing cultural sensitivity is an emphasis on the need for professionals in a variety of fields to develop not only an awareness of other cultures and cultural groups, but a heightened self-awareness, the recognition that every individual, including themselves, has a cultural identity, a heritage, a set of values by which they navigate life (Lynch and Hanson 1998). With self-awareness, professionals are encouraged to develop reflective skills for lifelong professional development in a multicultural workplace (Hong, Garcia, and Soriano 2000).

Professionals might be encouraged to take one step beyond reflective thinking to "reflexivity." Meyerhoff and Ruby (1982) explore the difference between the reflective and reflexive individual. Being reflective, they note, refers to thinking about ourselves without explicit awareness of the implications of the process. Reflection is present, for example, in narcissism and the obsession with self. Reflexivity, on the other hand, necessarily involves detachment between self and others, becoming conscious of being self-conscious and considering how others might perceive us and vice versa. With reflexivity, we become both subject and object. We think about ourselves as actors and the effect that we have on others, as well as their effect on us. This heightened awareness of self is a creative act and, in general, causes an individual to think differently about the self and to alter the self. In this sense, reflexivity is a never-ending process of self-tuning in response to changing social and cultural contexts (Davies 1999).

The reflexive practitioner role requires awareness of and knowledge about the cultural practices of both the practitioner and the people they serve. The professional comes to the community she or he serves with "cultural baggage," one form of which includes his or her own personal cultural heritage and the ideas, values, beliefs, and attitudes of the ethnic group, regional culture, and social class in which she or he was born and raised. Another form of cultural baggage is the education and training received as a professional. In his book *The Structure of Scientific Revolutions,* Thomas Kuhn (1962) explores the ways in which scientific paradigms shift over time, changing how scientists think about and see the world. Professional expertise in any field, including those of applied science, is shaped by a particular way of looking at reality, one that can change over time. Reflexivity encourages the professional to carefully examine this expertise as one perspective among many in negotiating relationships with individuals in other cultural groups.

In these chapters, authors stress the importance of becoming aware of Appalachian forms of speech, interaction styles, values, and belief systems in order to become successful as practicing professionals. As a reflexive professional working in an Appalachian community, the recommended role is not one of the authoritative "expert" but more the "helpful neighbor." This requires learning local cultural patterns through careful study and adaptation to community mores. Anita Puckett, for example, advises practitioners never to give "orders" to mountain people but to express "needs" the practitioner might volunteer to fulfill. Melinda Bollar Wagner demonstrates the advantages of allowing the Appalachian informant to shape the interview in order for the practitioner to learn important but sensitive information. Implicit in these suggestions is the idea that the conceptualization of mountain people as backward, traditional, or unprogressive may be more a reflection of the lack of training received by professionals who are unprepared in some ways to work in the region than it is a true reflection of any capability or willingness for mountain people to embrace change. Uninvited "experts" tend to be regarded with suspicion in any community. The "good neighbor" role model assumes that professionals are part of and to a good extent share the same cultural values as the larger community. Good neighbors do not pry, nor do they impose on others or assume they are superior. On the other hand, good neighbors are sensitive to the needs of others and offer help when needed. If the neighbor's help is rejected, it might be because of the style or character of the neighbor who is offering rather than a lack of need. In other words, one rule of thumb for the "good neighbor" practitioner arriving in an Appalachian community might be first to ask, How must I change? rather than to ask, How should they change? The implication is that the professional whose identity is anchored in reflexive adaptation to local culture will be the one more successful in community practice in Appalachia.

This conceptualization of a reflexive and "adaptable" professional role often counters formal training practices learned at the university, many of which are better suited to more bureaucratic urban and non-Appalachian contexts. Assuming an adaptable professional role may provoke anxiety regarding "appropriate" professional behavior and ethical practice. Carol Gross, for example, contemplates the difficulties in maintaining professional standards of confidentiality as a social worker in small face-to-face mountain communities where anonymity is rare. In other instances, professional knowledge often conflicts with local conceptualizations of knowledge, creating further anxieties. Marc Sherrod discusses his reconciliation of the apparent theological inconsistencies between his Presbyterian ministry training and certain Appalachian ways of coping with death. As Lynch and Hanson (1998) point out, reflexivity does not require the wholesale adoption of another group's values, beliefs, and attitudes. However, the adaptable professional must be prepared to accommodate local knowledge while still accomplishing professional goals.

In general, then, the reflexive and adaptable professional role demands awareness, receptivity, accommodation, and flexibility. In Appalachian communities, it also assumes a degree of parity with clients. That is, just as Appalachian communities are often described ideally as egalitarian, the local practitioner will be better received if power relations are addressed as if client and practitioner are on relatively equal ground. This may seem at odds with the inherent exclusivity of professional training and expertise. On the other hand, it seems to coincide with a number of trends in practitioner fields, such as teacher/student learning communities in education, patient-involved therapeutic decision making in medicine, and participatory research in all fields. In any event, reflexive and adaptable professionalism in Appalachia requires a basic shift in professional stance to a status and identity grounded in the community rather than one step above it.

References

Cox, Taylor. 1993. *Cultural Diversity in Organizations.* San Francisco: Barrett-Koehler.

Cross, T. L., B. J. Bazron, K. W. Dennis, and M. R. Isaacs. 1989. *A Monograph on Effective Services for Minority Children Who Are Severely Emotionally Disturbed.* Vol. 1 of *Toward a Culturally Competent System of Care.* Washington, D.C.: Georgetown University Child Development Center, National Technical Assistance Center for Children's Mental Health.

Davies, Charlotte A. 1999. *Reflexive Ethnography: A Guide to Researching Ourselves and Others.* London: Routledge.

Green, James W. (Ed.) 1982. *Cultural Awareness in the Human Services.* Englewood Cliffs, N.J.: Prentice-Hall.

Hong, George K., Margaret Garcia, and Marcel Soriano. 2000. "Responding to the Challenge: Preparing Mental Health Professionals for the New Millennium." In *Handbook for Multicultural Mental Health: Assessment and Treatment of Diverse Populations,* Israel Cuellar and Freddy A. Paniagua (Eds.). San Diego: Academic Press. Pp. 455–76

Kohls, L. Robert, and J. M. Knight. 1994. *Developing Intercultural Awareness.* 2d ed. Yarmouth, Maine: Intercultural Press.

Kuhn, Thomas S. 1962. *The Structure of Scientific Revolutions.* Chicago: University of Chicago Press.

Lynch, Eleanor W., and Marci J. Hanson. (Eds.) 1998. *Developing Cross-Cultural Competence: A Guide for Working with Children and Their Families.* 2d ed. Baltimore: Paul H. Brookes.

Meyerhoff, Barbara, and Jay Ruby. 1982. "Introduction." In *Crack in the Mirror: Reflexive Perspectives in Anthropology,* Jay Ruby (Ed.). Philadelphia: University of Pennsylvania Press. Pp. 1–38.

Chapter 1

Negotiating Rural Southern Mountain Speech

Anita Puckett

One of the most frequently cited "differences" between indigenous southern mountain residents of Appalachia and others is their speech.[1] Usually negatively stereotyped as corrupt, ungrammatical, or indicative of an uneducated speaker, southern mountain speech nevertheless continues as the lingua franca of verbal communication in most of southern Appalachia. Practitioners and other professionals who live in the area but are not familiar with this speech variety must learn something about how to use it if they are to succeed in routine interactions with others, regardless of their point of view toward nonstandard varieties of English. Failure to do so will result in miscommunications, negative feelings, and, in many contexts, withdrawal from interaction.

Yet learning to use southern mountain speech is not just a question of acquiring some different words or a few variations in verb-tense construction or prepositional use. These components of speech are very important, but equally important, if not more so in routine interactions with others, is how to communicate through mastery of basic verbal interactional forms such as greetings, casual conversation, requests, and ways of obtaining information. It is by using such speech in culturally appropriate ways that we can engage in the routine, banal, and often personally fulfilling aspects of social life that take up most of our interpersonal time. Mastery of these speaking practices is a major step in our efforts at negotiating our identities within human relationships.

In this chapter, I discuss common speaking practices and their social purposes in order to assist the practitioner in integrating into professional life within a rural southern Appalachian community. I target those unfamiliar with such communities, but I also hope that those who are familiar will gain a different perspective on some of the problems newcomers may have when moving into their town or area. I assume the perspective I took when I engaged in linguistic anthropological fieldwork in a rural southeastern Kentucky community. It was as one who had moved to a community with the intention of integrating herself into community life, a stance taken by most nonlocals. One advantage I had over some was that I had grown up as the daughter of a migrant who spoke southern mountain English and was therefore familiar with this speech variety.[2] Nevertheless, local residents certainly treated me as someone "not from here" and I had to develop friendships and ties with them as would any outsider.

Southern Mountain English as a Language

The definition of "language" adopted here is that of a set of lexical and grammatical verbal patterns that accomplish the kinds of basic, universal functions of distinctly human oral communication. These include, but are not limited to, reference to events, concepts, thoughts, and entities in very precise ways that are not necessarily in the immediate context of the speaker and that allow for the transmission of such complex verbal forms as epic narratives, cultural myths, and detailed instructions on how to perform rituals or other valued activities. These communicative capacities of speech are encoded in forms and sets of relations among them that permit the writing of a grammar or documentation of the regularized patterns which permit communication to take place. Southern mountain English meets all of these requirements; it is "rule governed" in its production and is, in this sense, a language.[3]

Yet as a nonstandardized variety of the abstract and generic use of "English," it is also a "dialect," meaning a social or regional variation from whatever conventions are associated as defining this abstraction. From this perspective, the term "dialect" is used, with neutral connotation, as referring to a variety of English which has not been codified by a written grammar, accepted into formal writing, or elevated to the status of preferred use by a socioeconomic or political elite. In this sense, there is no *linguistic* reason to assume that southern mountain English is corrupt, deficient, or incapable of meeting the full range of communicative functions of any language.

As with most English dialects, in grammatical terms, southern mountain English differs in speech from standard broadcast American English (SBAE)[4] primarily in its vowel variants, its accent and stress patterns, and its lexicon (Anderson 2003; Montgomery and Hall 2004; Williams 1992; Wolfram and Christian 1976).[5] The "rhythm," to use Williams's term (1992), or intonational contours, of traditional southern mountain speech, works in concert with basic stress patterns to create distinctive phrase patterns. These patterns often affect the length and duration of vowels, intensifying a sense of speech difference.

These patterns also encourage the southern mountain English lexicon to exhibit a mono- or disyllabic stress pattern so that words of three or more syllables are truncated, treated as compounds, or simply not incorporated into daily speech. This constraint on the number of syllables means that most words of Greek or Latin origin must be modified to fit into southern mountain English. The dictionary entry for the word "medicine," for example, becomes two syllables, "med' cine," and the Latin-origin word "cemetery" is rarely used (or used in more formal contexts) while the Anglo-Saxon "graveyard" may be the preferred term in many communities. Similarly, a distinct vocabulary for illness exists in much southern mountain speech that also conforms to a mono- or disyllabic stress pattern. Examples include terms such as risin (boil), smotherin (disyllabic form of "smothering" meaning inability to breath normally), flux (diarrhea) (Cavender 2003), high blood (high blood pressure), and nerves (any nervous tremor, anxiety, or inability to concentrate). Many younger speakers, particularly working women, tend to use many more trisyllabic or tetrasyllabic words, pronouncing them close to their dictionary form, so that those intonational patterns characteristic of southern mountain speech are somewhat altered. In these speakers, vowel quality and other grammatical features index them as southern mountain English speakers (Anderson 2003).

Lexical (word) variants are numerous, requiring something of a dictionary-type treatment to capture them (see Montgomery and Hall 2004). Many are also typical of southern and African American varieties, "ain't," "youngin," "yonder," and "reckon" among them. Double modals such as "might could" and the use of "done" as a perfective (as in "done fixed it") are normative as well (Montgomery and Hall 2004:xxxv–ixv).

Grammatical differences in southern mountain English are subtle but significant. Verb tenses are the most dramatic. Most verbs form the past tense using -ed, even the so-called irregular verbs (for example, "seed," "teached," and "heared"). Prepositions often have a locative function and assist in giving directions through their geographical precision. A person "goes *over* the mountain," not across it, or "*down* to Mom's," meaning in the downstream direction, and so forth. These grammatical differences are considered progressive, meaning they simplify a grammatical process in the language or make the language more precise in its reference.

In addition, words that end in the vowels /a/ and /o/[6] in SBAE are different in southern mountain English. In much of the region, word-final /a/ as in "Sarah" regularly becomes /i/ (pronounced "ee" as in "luck*y*"), and word-final /o/ as in "yellow" almost always becomes /er/ (as in "yeller"). The plural of nouns ending in /st/ or the singular of verbs ending in /st/ is /es/ rather than just /s/ so that, for example, the plural of "post" is "postes." Likewise, nouns ending in /sp/ are pluralized by adding /ers/ so that the plural of "wasp" is "waspers".

Vowel differences center around variations in diphthongs and monothongs. The / ∈ / (short e) sound is problematic for most speakers, occurring not as a true phoneme (sound characteristic of a language) but as an allophone (a sound variation due to the influence of surrounding sounds) or as a sound unit included in a borrowed word. Consequently, words such as "kettle" and "pregnant" may sound to outsiders like /kItl/ ("I" is short i), and /praegnant/ ("ae" is the "a" in "back"). Other grammatical differences are highly variable or imprecisely studied. Subtle vowel quality differences exist, for example, between male and female speakers, marking gender differences but not necessarily language differences. While no thorough written grammar of Appalachian English has been compiled at this date, Montgomery's (Montgomery and Hall 2004:xxxv–ixv) and Wolfram and Christian's work (Christian 1978; Christian, Wolfram, and Dube 1988; Wolfram and Christian 1976) are very helpful in discussing general grammatical differences in more detail.

Educational efforts at "correction" of pronunciation to more standard forms have also introduced variability as southern mountain English speakers selectively change words in a manner that reflects differing emphases of teachers' or students' perceptions of them rather than expresses grammatical rules of either speech variety. Describing such variable features is difficult in this brief discussion because of their irregularity or subtlety. What can be said is that many of these substitutions are idiosyncratic, that is, characteristic of only a specific individual (or a small number of individuals) or based in processes of "hypercorrection" (Labov 1966) in which the speaker applies a process or rule appropriate to standard American English grammar that is not part of southern mountain English grammar to an inappropriate grammatical context. Use of "I" when "me" is the standard English grammatical form is an example, as in the sentence "Mom took Mary and I to visit Sarah." So are substitutions of expected southern mountain English words with an incorrect polysyllabic synonym representations of hypercorrection. For example, the use of "atheletic" for "epileptic" in the phrase "atheletic fit" or the widespread use of "ideal" for "idea" in a clause such as "I had me a ideal about that" are other examples of this type of language adaptation.

Consequently, when other sources of linguistic change and assimilation are also considered (television, radio, video cassette recordings, CB radios, computer networking technologies, written forms of communication, and interactions in cities due to commuting for work, business, or recreation), native speakers of southern mountain English, especially younger ones, rarely speak in a manner totally consistent with what have been described as core, definitive grammatical features of this variety. Yet very few conform to spoken versions of Standard Broadcast American English (SBAE), as they continue to maintain a preponderance of southern mountain English constructions. That is, it is often difficult to label a particular instance of verbal communication as being only southern mountain English or only Standard Broadcast American English. There will be a range of possibilities that may be fully southern mountain English, may conform to SBAE, or may be a blending of the two. This range, however, is finite and generally predictable within the framework of interactional routines, conventions, and contextual norms.

For the individual learning how to engage in routine community verbal interaction in much of the mountains, it would be impractical to try to learn southern mountain English as if it were the only English variety used; it would be equally misdirected to assume that SBAE is the lingua franca. Rather, focusing on how speakers actually use language is more productive in developing successful interactional strategies and guides the rest of this discussion.

Common Speaking Practices and Their Norms of Use

Who can say what to whom when is, in real life, guided by a number of cultural norms or conventions. Most of these are learned associations, or "indices," between a communicative form (speech form, gesture, movement, or body placement, for example) and some extracommunicative component (setting, kind of participant, emotional tone, or location, for example) present at the same time (Hymes 1974). In most U.S. urban contexts, for example, asking a stranger you meet and talk casually to on a bus or other public transportation about his or her stance on abortion is inappropriate. In this case, both the setting (public transportation) and the relationship between the interlocutors (speakers) index what are acceptable levels, types, and styles of speech. These indices, or learned associations, can, in turn, be associated with a more abstract concept or cultural norm such as rudeness or personal embarrassment. In this example, bringing up abortion would violate indices of what constitute acceptable conversational topics, which, in turn, would violate cultural norms about privacy and politeness.

Certain cultural norms of speaking apply to many situations and are therefore more general and broader in scope than others. While there are always exceptions, such general indices set up, or frame, routine, public interactions. They allow interlocutors to speak to each other cooperatively and permit the verbal exchange to be successful. For much of rural Appalachia, these general indices center around gender, age, kinship or family, personal or family "name," and "rights," "place," and "claims" relations. These are not abstract concepts to be considered intellectually but terms that apply to very real social interactions among residents on a daily basis.

Greetings and Other Public Encounters

One of the first communicative encounters in which a newcomer will engage is a greeting or other way of opening up a verbal interaction. As in many U.S. small towns or rural areas, meeting or passing someone in public in rural southern Appalachia requires some form of greeting, even when driving down a rural road. It may be as brief as the lift of a hand from the steering wheel, a nod of the head, making eye contact with a smile, or exchanging a "good day," "how are you today," "howdy," or, to use the more current and informal, "hi-dy."[7] At the same time, a woman may find that men, even men she knows, may appear to ignore her and avoid these simple greeting exchanges or are uncommonly formal and brief in greeting her. Such variation in transitory greeting behavior is an index of the most basic speaking norm: men and women rarely speak to each other except when culturally appropriate indexes of acceptability apply.

These appropriate indices are triggered when two or more speakers in a given setting create acceptable participant structures. Acceptable participant structures include speakers who are known kin (cousins, aunts/uncles and nieces/nephews, in-laws, and, of course, close family members) and fictive kin ("sisters" and "brothers" in a person's church or someone treated and addressed by family members as kin) or some other cultural category in which one interlocutor indexes a respected status (teacher, preacher, judge, or medical doctor, for example). If such indexes do not apply or are unknown to one of the participants, then it is inappropriate to exchange more than the most formal or briefest of greetings.

The separation of individuals into gendered sets extends much further than casual public encounters, of course, and, as a general rule, men and women do not engage in conversation unless the above indexical requirements are met. These norms extend to service interactions, requests for information, business exchanges of any kind, and even home interactions. Within the informal setting of homes or neighborhoods, wives and mothers may act as cultural "brokers" for their husbands to other women who will "broker" to their husbands or fathers, creating an exchange relationship of some type. And vice versa. These exchanges can become complex. For example, in one instance I observed, a woman asked another woman to ask her husband to volunteer to loan the first woman's husband a piece of heavy equipment to perform some home improvement task. The women were kin; the men were not.

One way of creating acceptable indices among interlocutors is to expand upon the usual brief greeting conventions by "placing" someone. "Place" in many rural southern Appalachian communities assigns an individual to a geographical locale (up Laurel Holler, for example) where an individual or his or her family is residing or has traditionally resided, and to "place" someone is literally to create a mental map of where someone lives within local geography. A more dominant meaning, however, which is an overlay upon the primary, geographical one, refers to one's position in a family or community network of other individuals.[8] One's place is negotiated within this network over a lifetime; younger residents have to create a place for themselves within the family or community matrix through reciprocity links and through successful social interactions. As one ages, his or her place becomes established so that it embodies certain degrees of social and political clout or value with respect to others in a referenced network.

Creating place relations is similar to building one's "name" in a community, but it is more group focused than the prestige value assigned to having a good name. If a person is a nonlocal, then he or she has neither a "place" nor a "name." Both must be created to "belong"; elaborated greeting practices assist in getting these processes started.

Commonly initiated by older residents, but not always, one common form of elaborated greeting begun after the initial "howdy" or its variants is the following basic form or something similar to it.

Example 1: Greetings

Older speaker:	Whose girl/boy are you?
Younger speaker:	I be/am [parent's full name; parent of same sex as speaker]'s boy/girl.
Older speaker then asks for clarification, such as:	
	Your daddy's from up Laurel Creek? [Or some other query that assists in "placing" the younger speaker.]

If the younger speaker can provide placing information known to the older speaker, a conversation can begin that will include some discussion of kinship relations and other residents known to both speakers. The younger speaker has been placed and a potential relationship begun. The conversation, should it continue, can be successful in terms of creating a cooperative, potentially ongoing relationship.

Nonlocals, or those who cannot respond meaningfully to these greeting queries, cannot be placed, and their ability to participate fully in community life will be compromised. It is not much of an exaggeration to claim that such individuals are undefined in cultural terms; the gates of the community will be kept fully or partially closed to them. Such greeting practices function as gate-keeping discourse (Erickson and Shultz 1981), constructing very real linguistic barriers to community membership. If a newcomer is to get past these gates, he or she must develop a place in community life through church membership, through fictive kin relations with a local, by marriage with a community member, or by performing well (in community terms) in a valued status (such as doctor, nurse, preacher, or teacher). Men can sometimes develop a place by offering a valued service in occupations such as auto mechanic or electrical equipment repairman.

Requests and Orders

One of the most widely known tropes, or sayings, attributed to mountain residents is that of "Ain't nobody tellin me what to do." "Tellin,"[9] of course, refers to the category of English constructions commonly called "orders." To the nonlocal entering many rural communities, residents' sensitivity to being directed by orders is readily apparent; workplace narratives about the misuse of them are readily told and easily available. At the same time, the use of speech that sounds like orders and elicits compliance in the addressee occurs frequently. This seeming contradiction must be unraveled and understood if a newcomer is to be successful in local verbal exchanges.

The most common grammatical form of orders is the imperative, a clause in which the verb requires a "you" or "you" deleted subject and the verb denotes an action. Clauses such as "You sit down"/"Sit down" or "You drive the car, please"/"Drive the car, please" are common examples. The use of "please" does not change the basic imperative structure. In fact, most southern mountain English speakers replace "please" with the preferred "if you don't care to." In these cases, imperatives are replaced with "would" constructions such as "If you don't care to, would you drive the car" and the potential imperative is avoided. When expressions such as "If you don't care to, drive the car," which are awkward in southern mountain speech, do occur, they are imperatives.

Among most southern mountain speakers, imperatives are readily understood as orders except in specific types of social situations, such as when the speaker cannot get to or reach an object (for example, "Pass me the beans" at the supper table) or in mixed gender contexts in which the speaker has control over the resources and is kin or in some fictive kin relationship (for example, a man can "tell" his wife to fix supper and the wife, usually, can "tell" her husband to eat it). Control over resources is not rigid but revolves around a general indexical relationship involving "rights." "Rights" are, usually, what residents consider to be biblically sanctioned justifications for engaging in purposeful actions or activities. These activities generally center around control or use of core, highly valued cultural resources. A man, for example, has the "right" to do with his land as he wishes because it is sanctioned in Genesis. Similarly, a woman can direct the education of her children because it is her "right" as a mother, again with biblical approbation. Rights cannot be proscribed, however, nor can they be approached mechanically as a set of established, finite, and specific behavioral principles. While enormous social pressure exists to affirm a central set of rights, any given speaker will have his or her own domains to which the term applies according to how this individual interprets Scripture, responds to church norms and doctrines, and/or matures within a family and community set of ideologies. Consequently, what is right for someone to do is a frequent topic of conversation, and the expression "That ain't right" is a common commentary upon others' behavior.

When two or more speakers come together within a specific setting, rights will be indexed by the configuration created and the way verbal exchanges are framed by greetings and other conversational routines. These contextual cues, in turn, determine the level and types of imperatives that can be used. Acceptable imperative uses in general revolve around women's childbearing and child-rearing activities within the home, including food preparation and consumption, household decorating and cleaning, and any activity related to the nurturance and well-being of their (or, by extension, kinswomen's) children. Men control money, activities away from the home, including political and economic ones, and most decision making. Men or women may direct a stranger's behavior if it is clearly within a their rights to do so. For example, a woman can tell any visitor to "come eat" or a man can tell someone to "pay up" at an entrance booth of a community fair. Yet these acceptable use contexts are rare and, as a rule, until one has learned those contexts in which imperatives are appropriate, it is wise *never to use them.*

The role of supervisor or boss in a work situation does not constitute a given right; other criteria falling into the broad categories discussed above must apply first before the limited contexts for using imperatives appropriately come into play. One of the most common work problems in the region revolves around the presumed authority of nonlocal management and supervisors unfamiliar with ordering discourse patterns. Using familiar corporate patterns (Ervin-Tripp 1976; Ervin-Tripp et al. 1987; Weigel and Weigel 1985), they "order" employees to perform work-related tasks. Frequently, some form of contestation or work resistance follows; employees respond verbally in a negative way, quit, slow down work, or engage in other nonproductive activities. With very few exceptions, and these will be strategic uses designed to elicit a given effect, a supervisor should avoid ordering his or her staff or crew.[10]

Under these constraints, how to ask residents for information, make requests of them, or give or receive instructions can be difficult. In general, residents engage in a series of communicative strategies to meet these needs that may seem the opposite of expected patterns to many nonlocals, particularly professionals. To be effective, these strategies must index appropriate indexes of rights and place as well as those of "claims."

With few exceptions, cultural norms require that "claims" upon each other be developed in order to make substantive demands or requests of anyone. "Claims" is a term residents often use in the expression "I/we do/don't claim him/her" and is used here in a more abstract way than is found in most southern mountain speech. It refers to an acknowledgment of a personal relationship in which an individual has access to the knowledge, skill, and resources of the other and is, in this sense, one cultural representation of the anthropological concept of reciprocity. Claims are usually, but not always, developed among members of an extended kin network, but being kin to someone does not mean that claims must exist. Claims are nurtured and negotiated over time within a preexisting or fictively created kinship network; indeed, individuals can disclaim their kin, even within the nuclear family, although this is very rare.

Claims are created by doing things for one another, from providing meals to transportation to assisting in meeting any and all needs an individual or family may have. One makes such "needs" known through a number of communicative means, but seldom by asking. With the dominance of claims relations in community life and with the lifelong familiarity many residents have about one another's lives, rarely should one have to ask for anything. In well-developed and close claims relationships, the exchange may not be verbal; the requester simply takes the desired item often with or without a verbal gloss such as "I need the saw today" or "I'm takin the vacuum cleaner." In other communicative situations in which "place" relations may be less certain, so that taking the item may not be appropriate, the listener should simply know or pick up on from verbal or other contextual indices what the speaker is likely to need and then volunteer to provide it.

Consequently, getting a listener to volunteer is one well-developed way of asking for something. The speaker engages in a conversation with the prospective provider of the good, service, or information, and then interjects a narrative, usually brief, that describes a "need." If claims (or fictive claims in some circumstances) are developed, if the listener can meet the request, and if it is "right" to do so, then he or she is likely to volunteer to provide the good, service, or information. The following is a synopsis of one such encounter.

Example 2: Volunteering Requesting Sample

[Setting: My home, a rented trailer. My landlord, who is a neighbor as well, is repairing some wiring. Another male neighbor, seeing the landlord enter, comes by to "just talk" to him. The two have been talking about the weather, the neighbor's job, home repair efforts, and other noncontestational topics (Puckett 1990).]

Neighbor:	I could get a lot more done if I had a cordless drill.
Landlord:	You can use this one when I'm done.
Neighbor:	No, no, that's all right.
Landlord:	I won't be needing this one for a couple of days; you can use it.
Neighbor:	Thanks.

In this case, the male requestor is within his "rights" to need a tool for household repairs, which is within a male domain of resources; and, as a neighbor, he has developed fictive claims relations with my landlord over time, just as I and other neighbors living on our short, dead-end road have. Nevertheless, place relations are problematic here because the neighbor is not kin and his place in community relations is not known.

Service encounters or other contexts in which the proprietor/owner is expected to provide a good or service for money or as part of their job do not generally require the same developed pattern as in informal claims requests. "Rights," "place," and "claims" indexicals must, however, be appropriate and normative. When dealing with a national chain such as McDonald's or Wal-Mart, employee verbal service interactions reflect the standardized patterns set by the companies or regional supervisors. For local businesses, encounters tend to be truncated volunteering patterns with sales personnel or clerks volunteering with "Can I help you?" or some variant. Customers will make requests in question forms, such as "Do you have air conditioners?" or "I need" forms, such as "I need an air conditioner." Again, use of imperatives, as in "Get me fifty pounds of cracked corn," are very rare.

For contexts in which a request must be made verbally and in which the narrative pattern is inconvenient or inappropriate, the "I need" or "we need" forms are most culturally normative. The use of this verb shifts the focus of the request from an ego-centered desire or want to a task or activity focus. This shift, in turn, downplays an assertion of self and, in the "we" form, creates an inclusive activity domain for those referenced. In work contexts, a request put in the form, for example, of "We need to get this section built by the end of the week" does not communicate social distance between the speaker and the listeners. It reinforces a sense of corporateness and egalitarianism. "Need" constructions, especially "we need" forms, are generally preferred and avoid the kinds of social pitfalls created by the use of imperatives and the indexical relations they create.

Making and responding to requests are universal aspects of human social life. As the same time, they are extremely sensitive in how they communicate potential compliance through the indexical relationships they create. Subtle variations in form within dialects are often culturally very significant. So it is in southern mountain speech.

Instructions

The transmission of valued knowledge and skills from one generation to the next or from one individual to another is central to the continuation of culture. For nonmembers, understanding how members of a culture construct these processes is critical to developing and maintaining relationships with them. Among most rural mountain residents, the preferred way to learn something or how to perform some task is by doing it rather than by being told about it. This preference, in turn, selects for methods which "show" someone rather than "tell" them. Showing someone how to do something involves communicative structuring different from that commonly encountered in schools and more formal organizational training sessions. Again, the problematic imperative surfaces as a potential issue in successful interaction.

For many speakers, the preferred way to learn something is to watch someone else or engage in personal experimentation and then do it him or herself. Many residents will reveal that they produced their first craft doll, woodcarving, or rebuilt car engine by simply doing it. Most of the time they are not exaggerating. Residents are frequently very good at "figuring somethin out."

Following a set of written instructions to do a task or to produce a good is rarely done, although many may consult them or a brief product description to orient themselves toward the product or service. Women are likely to consult recipes or sewing books to learn about new cooking techniques or patterns; men are much less likely to do comparable activities for appropriate male tasks.

When some training or instruction is necessary, it frequently occurs between older and younger residents, often as older relative to a child. Consequently, the verbal conventions associated with instructional speaking practices, or "showing discourse, " also index status; the one doing the instruction is indexed to be of greater status (as associated with age) than the one learning. When adult men must be shown something, they are very aware of these indexicals and therefore much prefer watching someone else do it. They can then imitate the performance of the instructor. If showing discourse cannot be avoided, it should be structured to avoid using imperatives if at all possible. The indices of social asymmetry they create simply aggravate the social ranking already indexed by the learning situation.

The following is a transcription of a tape-recorded segment from a "showing discourse" event between a local man, a whittler (woodcarver), and a local boy. The parents of the boy have brought him to the woodcarver so he would learn how to carve "right."[11]

Example 3: Instructions

[Setting: The maintenance building of environmental center about 10:00 P.M., during the night watchman's dinner break. Participants: A woodcarver (night watchman) and local boy, nine years old and distant kin to woodcarver.

Visitors: The boys' parents, a nonnative local couple, and I. We are conversing among ourselves during the boy's instruction. The woodcarver's son and daughter-in-law join us as the session continues. The carver's focus is on the boy's attempts at carving a butter knife, although the carver also has a piece he is working on in his hands. Occasionally, the carver takes the hands of the boy to show him how to hold the knife or carve. Most often, he demonstrates with his own work. WC = woodcarver; LB = local boy. Tape 8A:1986.][12]

WC: So (3.8) ya see, it's not wantin to . . . carve tha, that way.
When it gives you trouble, ya got to turn it around an (come) this way.
An too, (2.0)
if ya cut yourself,
you, you put your fist against you here,
an you're carvin out like this (3.0).
So when your knife flips off ya see your hand hits first.
So you don't hit yourself with your knife.
Because, it's, it's sort a automatic. (4.0)
Ya hold ya, you hold your arm real close to ya here. (3.0)
So usually . . . one side will carve one way,
an the other side'll carve the other. (2.5)
That's the way the grain . . . works.
So when you're carvin this way ya see ya don't see your mark here.
You carve down a little ways,
you can always glance over to see . . . where your mark is. (4.8)
Now, you make this curve. (2.0)
Put your thumb down here now,
you do everything I show you,
you won't get cut. (2.0)
Put your thumb down there ya see
an it short a shaves down like that. (2.4)
Just let that stay.
An you shave down (2.0) like,
an you back this side.
You, you'll be forgettin a lot of this stuff,
an I'll just keep showin ya. (2.0)
An you take that off.
Careful, like that ya see.

Cause ya come down against this too hard,
you'll split it off,
an then you won't cut your a,
cut your mark off. [Clears throat.] (10.0)
So when you're doin this ya see you're doin little sharp strokes. (5.8)
If ya git beyond your mark don't worry about it,
we'll uh.
There's a lot a people that change styles with their butter knives.
[All chuckle.]
Now you take this off you ya see,
You, you gone a use your thumb again for leverage. (3.0)
See there?

LB: Uh-huh.

WC: Thumb's over here.
An your knife'll come off.
An if you have it up there too high,
it'll come off when you can't stop it.
You, you make sure your thumb is down there,
below where knife comes off. (2.0)

LB: Uh-huh.

WC: An you'll never git cut,
If you, you always remember these tips.

The general approach to the process of carving in this segment is descriptive, with the woodcarver describing his own actions using a "you" form. For example, when he utters the phrase "you, you put your fist against you here," he is also putting his own fist against himself in the appropriate manner. The boy can then imitate him and continue working. One possible interpretation of this "you" form is that it is a fully expanded imperative form, but it can also be considered as a declarative in which the "you" is an indefinite pronoun meaning "one" or "anyone" and simply describes an activity. It is this ambiguity that mitigates the potential "order" status in giving instructions and allows other individuals to be directed.

While directing the boy's activities, neither looks at the other unless the woodcarver's instructions demand it. Even then, the young man looks at what the hands of the woodcarver are doing in most instances, avoiding direct eye contact. This emphasis on looking at some work in progress or, in other contexts, at something in the distance rather than making eye contact is normative and preferred, especially by older residents. Eye contact means a point has been made or a feeling communicated; continually making eye contact is rude and contradicts the strong cultural norm of focusing upon your work, which is what a person should be doing most of the time, even if it is just watching television.

Interviews

Nonlocals moving into a southern mountain community as professional practitioners frequently require interview data from residents for job-related purposes. Local residents themselves are engaging more and more in a special type of interview called the oral history to record information about earlier community events, particularly those related to coal mining and labor strikes. Both of these verbal activities establish an asymmetrical relationship between interlocutors in which one presumably has the right to ask questions of the other; the respondent is expected to provide the information asked. This presumption of control over questions and answers is not normative to southern mountain speech practices; the participant structure created by interviews creates overt indices of superiority and inferiority, violating basic cultural norms of social equality. In settings in which a woman interviews a man (and sometimes vice versa), indices of acceptable gender relations involving "rights" and "place" are also violated. Such multiple layerings of indexical misfires are bound to create at least uneasiness if not withdrawal on the part of the interviewee.

Furthermore, formal interviews usually require the interviewer to ask questions directly, using interrogatives or other direct forms of making requests for information. These conventions do not conform to requesting norms which emphasize indirectness and mitigation. All of these variations in speaking norms and indexical relations combine to make the interview an intrusive speaking practice and one that is not generally part of the local repertoire of speaking practices.[13]

As a result, those practitioners needing to obtain information from residents may find that they need to adjust their preconceptions about how interviews should take place and then develop different strategies to conduct them. "Rights," "place," and "claims" relations will certainly be factors in developing these strategies.

For a stranger, particularly a younger person, to ask questions of an older one, especially of the opposite gender, is rarely right. Nor is it the interviewer's place to do so, and it is unlikely that claims relations apply. Consequently, for the acquisition of routine information, it is generally helpful to have someone local who has established rights, place, and claims relations known by the interviewee.[14]

Furthermore, having someone the same gender as the interviewee do the interviewing is useful. If couples are interviewed as a couple, it is likely that one or the other will dominate the exchange. This expression of their interpersonal relationship may or may not affect the accuracy of the interview, depending upon the kind of data sought. Asking for individual interviews may be offensive; it may be better to ask a trusted local who can function as a cultural broker for assistance. If couples are interviewed, it is helpful to have a pair of interviewers, one male and one female, to compensate for variation in gender.

Whether the interviewer is known or unknown to the interviewee, mountain speaking practices for obtaining knowledge or information assume that the interviewee has the right to control how the communicative exchange should be structured and what constitutes acceptable content. The following is a segment from a 1984 oral history interview initiated by a community college professor for an Appalachian studies class.

Example 4: Oral History Interview

[Setting: Interviewee Amy's (OW) own home. Interviewer (YW): A neighbor who lives up the hollow from OW. YW is a younger woman in her late twenties to early thirties who is using a standardized set of questions provided by her instructor. The two women regularly visit, and OW is known in the community as a woman of excellent reputation, even and kind temper, and solid Christian beliefs. OW is in her early eighties, married (husband living), with four to six children and numerous grandchildren. She lives with her husband, also in his eighties, and one daughter in a well-kept, traditional country home which they rent from a logging corporation in a now sparsely populated holler. She seldom leaves home and gardens assiduously with her husband to make money. Her husband reported picking sixty bushels of beans one day during the same year as this interview. YW is married and also has an excellent reputation, but she interacts infrequently with local people, staying at home with her three young children or driving to town to take two of them to a private Christian school or to attend class at the area community college. Both OW and YW are local Ash Creek women.]

YW:	Well when you had your youngins at home, how soon did ya have to start gittin up n takin care of m agin?
OW:	JIst in a few day:s.

YW:	A few days?
OW:	Well when I had Sue that's my first n, I hoed ta:, I had her one mornin hoed taters next e:vnin.
YW:	O:h law Amy [chuckles] I don't see how you could do that, oh goodness.
OW:	I sure did Hoed taters out in the garden I left her in the house Hoed taters.
YW:	Didn't that about kill ya?
OW:	Didn't hurt me a bit I: s jist as strong as I ever was I felt so good.
YW:	Well that's wonderful that you could feel that good after having a baby I sure never did [chuckle] after mine.
OW:	Well most of mine I didn't ei:ther.
YW:	[cough]
OW:	But, b, I did after she was born I didn't have another pai:n an I felt so good.
YW:	Huh Jist glad to be rid of all that weight I guess [aspirated chuckle].
OW:	yEUh.

The younger woman asking for information about an older woman's life history is well known to the older woman. They are of the same gender, are neighbors, and have distant kin ties. When the younger woman indicated that she "needed" the information for a class, the older woman was quite willing because she was "helpin out" the student. "Helpin out" is an expression that refers to the willingness of individuals to assist a kinsperson or neighbor in performing a task or meeting a "need." It refers to a specific type of claims-forming relation and to a type of reciprocity (Puckett 2000).

In this example, the repetitions and giggles of the younger woman indicates that she is deferring to the knowledge of the older woman and allowing her to control the flow and direction of the interview. While the student has a set of interview questions to ask, it is clear that the interviewee can shape and direct the flow of talk as she feels is important. This speaking pattern is common among local residents. It gives the speaker the right to construct narratives and tell the "story" as he or she remembers. It also requires a shift in verbal interaction expectations for those with preconceptions of more formal and directed-type interviews.

Conclusion

Some common threads weave through the preceding discussions of common, daily life speaking practices in much of rural southern Appalachia. Among them is the use of speech itself to reproduce central social relationships among individuals. This is done primarily through the creation and recreation of indexical relationships signaled by the context and form of a speaking practice itself. Although the actual speech is ephemeral, uttered to the air by a speaker to be heard by a listener, its effect is palpable and can be long lived. Relationships created by indexical meanings are critical to creating these effects. Within conventional and often stylized verbal exchanges such as greetings, requests, and instructions (or ways of *not* directly requesting or instructing), these indexical meanings can become strongly patterned. These patterns, in turn, have an enormous impact on how sociocultural relationships are continued in rural Appalachian communities. Those not familiar with these patterns will, through intuition or formal study, find that, as one nonlocal put it, "something is off" in routine, daily communications with locals.

Despite warm and pleasant verbal exchanges with local residents, nonlocal professionals often find themselves wondering what went wrong after a few months or a couple years as they encounter problems in their professional work with clients or customers. Many leave, often citing reasons other than language-based ones. During three years of my residence in southeast Kentucky, I counted seventeen nonlocals out of twenty I knew who left the region after a maximum of three years. These individuals were educators (5), educational administrators (5), social service practitioners (2), or allied health practitioners (5). Citing various reasons, most noted that they had problems in exercising the professional role that they had been trained to do. Some reasons given were people did not listen, they would not recognize their professional ability, or they had some type of run-in with a resident or a family. In response, residents might comment that a given nonlocal told them what to do, thought he/she was better than they were, or did not understand "our ways." Regardless of whether a local or nonlocal was attempting to explain the problem, the tendency was to become personal, passing judgment on the other individual or individuals.

As discussed in this chapter, many of these reasons can be reconsidered as problems in using language and in understanding the ways in which it functions. Such awareness will assist in opening windows of membership in communities and provide a more objective understanding for why individuals respond the way they do. The meanings given to the ways we talk to each other really do matter.

Notes

1. The term "southern mountain speech" is used in this discussion to refer to the everyday speech of most native-born, rural residents of that region of the eastern United States commonly called "Appalachia." "Southern mountain" is a more indigenous term than "Appalachia" and has been used historically to designate the region addressed in this article (e.g. Williams 1992). I am also using the term "southern Appalachia" to refer to that portion of the southern Appalachian Mountains where this variety of spoken English occurs. In general, this area includes much of the southern Appalachian coalfields and other rural areas of the upland South.

2. Data for this presentation comes from seven years of ethnographic fieldwork as a linguistic anthropologist and local community college teacher, and from subsequent data collection accessible through my position in the Appalachian Studies Program at Virginia Tech, located in Appalachian Virginia. Since I am a woman anthropologist, data is skewed toward a woman's understanding of how southern mountain speech is constructed and used, but access to male speech was frequent. It is often possible for women to simply listen in on men talking, where the opposite is less culturally normative.

3. I prefer to use "southern mountain English" or "southern mountain speech," which is more consistent with residents' own labeling of their speech and conforms to Williams's (1992) usage, rather than a dialect designator coined by sociolinguists (e.g., Wolfram and Christian 1976) in keeping with preferences in linguistic anthropology to recognize indigenous linguistic usages. Nevertheless, anyone researching this speech variety should keep in mind that much of the scholarship on it uses the label Appalachian English.

4. Standard Broadcast American English (SBAE) is that form of spoken American English which is commonly adopted by television news broadcasters. It is generally considered to be the least dialectal variety of spoken American Englishes and conforms more closely to written standard American English than other spoken varieties. Linguists generally consider standard American English to refer to a written form of American English which conforms to standard grammars on the language. Few speakers of American English consistently conform to standard American English when they speak informally or among peers, regardless of educational level or locale. SBAE is one of a few speech varieties which approximates standard American English closely.

5. Southern mountain English overlaps with varieties of English, including prestigious ones, in many, if not most, of its grammatical and phonological (sound) features. It is most similar to southern English and exhibits many of the stigmatized features associated with African American Vernacular English (AAVE) as well. One distinction separating it from Southern English is its retention of intervocalic /r/ in words such as "pork" and "horse." It would be tempting to classify it as a variety of Southern English, Midlands English, or some other

variety encompassing a larger region, but when the full set of grammatical, prosodic (stress and intonation), and phonological features are considered, it becomes distinct as its own variety of English. For discussions of issues surrounding classification, see Carver 1987; Christian, Wolfram, and Dube 1988; Feagin 1979; Kurath 1972; Montgomery 2004; Wolfram and Christian 1976; Wolfram and Clarke 1971; and Wolfram and Schilling-Estes 1998. This discussion emphasizes speaking practices within the region and is therefore not focusing on the extremely complex and intertwined issues related to defining and classifying dialects.

6. It is standard linguistic notation to include an abstract representation of a language's sounds or words in slashes. This notation indicates how a sound or word is pronounced rather than how it is spelled.

7. "Hi-dy" is clearly a merger of "hi" plus the frequently used "howdy" and is used extensively by younger residents.

8. The process of "placing" people, as discussed here, is found throughout much of the southern Appalachian region (see, for example, Allen and Schlereth 1990; Kingsolver 1992; Puckett 2000). The concept of "place" as a central organizing principle guiding ethnology and impacting cultural theory is discussed in such works as Feld and Basso (1996) and Rodman (1992).

9. When representing southern mountain speech in this discussion, I use a transcription system that captures regularized sound differences that vary from American English dictionary pronunciations. I do not use the stereotyped impressions of speech found in comic strips and some fiction. These renderings (e.g., "dawg," "pappy," or "purty") constitute an "eye dialect" rather than an attempt at an accurate representation of how someone said something. Therefore, I write the "ng" at the end of present participles as "n" in keeping with a distinct sound difference between more standard American speech and southern mountain speech as I encountered it in the communities I have observed.

10. One example of a strategic use occurred when I was living in a rural eastern Kentucky area. A supervisor of a work crew who was from the region, although not local, "ordered" an employee to perform a task after the employee indicated that this task was something he did not want to do. The supervisor got his expected response, which was a resignation from the employee. Hard feelings followed, and some sabotage of company equipment was attributed to the employee.

11. This speech segment also appears in Puckett (1998, 2000) under different transcription styles for different argumentative purposes.

12. Recorded speech is transcribed into "lines" rather than sentences and paragraphs with the natural speech units uttered in actual instances of talk. How an individual constructs the rhythm, or intonational contours, of their speech usually conforms to a finite number of patterns that are characteristic of their language variety. These patterns of stress and non-stress, or pause and run-on speech, can affect how the listener interprets an utterance. Therefore, transcription into lines on the basis of these rhythms and pauses is a more accurate way of capturing the meaning of southern mountain speech.

In addition, the following notations are used in transcribed speech segments:

(1) A period before the end of a line indicates a slight pause that does not indicate a line break. It indicates a pause of about half a second. Two periods would indicate a pause of about one second.

(2) A period at the end of a line indicates falling intonation corresponding to the end of a sentence in English.

(3) A question mark at the end of a line indicates rising intonation corresponding to the end of a question in English.

(4) A colon indicates that the sound associated with the preceding letter was spoken longer than in normal speech.

(5) Comments in brackets indicate a glossing of co-occurring action.

(6) Comments in parentheses indicate a paralinguistic activity such as laughing.

(7) Numbers in parentheses at the end of lines indicate that the length of the pause at the end of the line was longer than normal for that speaker. In general, end-of-line pauses are about two or three seconds for men and about one or two seconds for women in the communities I've observed.

(8) The use of /I/ instead of /i/ in words such as "get" or "just" represents use of the standard linguistic symbol of a short /i/ sound. I do this to avoid evoking eye dialect stereotyping of southern mountain speech. The short /i/ in these words is expected in southern mountain speech and represents a phonemic difference (cf. Williams 1992).

13. For a comprehensive discussion of the interview as a culturally loaded speaking practice, see Briggs 1986.

14. Having someone conduct the interview whom the interviewee knows may backfire if he or she is someone disliked by the interviewee. Nevertheless, the benefits to be gained by using someone local, especially if the interview is to be long or involve obtaining detailed responses, outweigh this possibility. Of course, as the nonlocal becomes aware of interpersonal relations or is assimilated into community "place" relations over time, this caveat may no longer apply.

References

Allen, Barbara, and Thomas Schlereth (Eds.). 1990. *Sense of Place: American Regional Cultures.* Lexington: University of Kentucky Press.

Anderson, Bridget. 2003. "An Acoustic Study of Southeastern Michigan Appalachian and African American Southern Migrant Vowel Systems." Ph.D. Dissertation, University of Michigan.

Briggs, Charles. 1986. *Learning How to Ask: A Sociolinguistic Appraisal of the Role of the Interview in Social Science Research.* New York: Cambridge University Press.

Carver, Craig M. 1987. *American Regional Dialects: A Word Geography.* Ann Arbor: University of Michigan Press.

Cavender, Anthony. 2003. *Folk Medicine in Southern Appalachia.* Chapel Hill: University of North Carolina Press.

Christian, Donna. 1978. "Aspects of Verb Usage in Appalachian Speech." Ph.D. dissertation, Georgetown University.

Christian, Donna, Walt Wolfram, and Nanjo Dube. 1988. *Variation and Change in Geographically Isolated Communities: Appalachian English and Ozark English.* Tuscaloosa: University of Alabama Press.

Erickson, F., and J. Shultz. 1981. *The Counselor as Gatekeeper: Social Interaction in Interviews.* New York: Academic Press.

Ervin-Tripp, Susan. 1976. "Is Sybil There? The Structure of Some American English Directives." *Language in Society* 5:25–56.

Ervin-Tripp, Susan, A. Strange, M. Lampert, and N. Bell. 1987. "Understanding Requests." *Linguistics* 25:107–43.

Feagin, Crawford. 1979. *Variation and Change in Alabama English: A Sociolinguistic Study of the White Community.* Washington, D.C.: Georgetown University Press.

Feld, Steven, and Keith Basso (Eds.). 1996. *Senses of Place.* Santa Fe, N.M.: School of American Research Press.

Hymes, Dell. 1974. "Models of the Interaction of Language and Social Life." In *Directions in Sociolinguistics,* John Gumperz and Dell Hymes (Eds.). New York: Holt, Rinehart and Winston. Pp. 35–71.

Kingsolver, Ann. 1992. "Contest Livelihoods: 'Placing' One Another in 'Cedar,' Kentucky." *Anthropological Quarterly* 65:128–36.

Kurath, Hans. 1972. *Studies in Area Linguistics.* Bloomington: Indiana University Press.

Labov, William. 1966. *The Social Stratification of English in New York City.* Washington, D.C.: Center for Applied Linguistics.

Montgomery, Michael. 2004. "English Language." In *High Mountains Rising: Appalachia in Time and Place.* Richard A. Straw and H. Tyler Blethen (Eds.). Urbana: University of Illinois Press. Pp. 147–64.

Montgomery, Michael, and Joseph Hall. 2004. *Dictionary of Smoky Mountain English.* Knoxville: University of Tennessee Press.

Puckett, Anita. 1990. Unpublished field notes.

———. 1998. "Rights, Claims, Orders, and Imperatives in Rural Eastern Kentucky Task-Focused Discourse." In *More than Class: Studying Power in U.S. Workplaces,* Ann. E. Kingsolver (Ed.). New York: SUNY Press. Pp. 96–123.

———. 2000. *Seldom Ask, Never Tell: Labor and Discourse in Appalachia.* New York: Oxford University Press.

Rodman, Margaret. 1992. "Empowering Place: Multilocality and Multivocality." *American Anthropologist* 94(3):640–56.

Weigel, M., and R. Weigel. 1985. "Directive Use in a Migrant Agricultural Community: A Test of Ervin-Tripp's Hypotheses." *Language in Society* 14:63–80.

Williams, Cratis. 1992. *Southern Mountain Speech.* Berea, Ky.: Berea College Press.

Wolfram, Walt, and Donna Christian. 1976. *Appalachian Speech.* Arlington, Va.: Center for Applied Linguistics.

Wolfram, Walt, and Natalie Schilling-Estes. 1998. *American English: Dialects and Variation.* Malden, Mass.: Blackwell.

Wolfram, Walt, and N. H. Clarke (Eds.). 1971. *Black-White Speech Relationships.* Arlington, Va.: Center for Applied Linguistics.

Chapter 2

Connecting What We Know to What We Do: Modifying Interview Techniques for the Collective Self in Appalachia

Melinda Bollar Wagner

"Why didn't we learn about that *before* we interviewed?" lamented a student some weeks after she had confronted a less than successful interview experience. This chapter is the progeny of her comment. Interviews are a common tool employed by anthropologists to learn about a culture and by practitioners to learn about their clients. A successful interview sometimes requires that the interviewer has some knowledge of the culture of the interviewee (the very thing he or she is trying to learn about via the interviews) before the interview even begins. Because interviewees' ways of communicating affect interview style and tempo, in this chapter, I will describe ways of communicating considered typical of people who are native to the Appalachian region.

Following the description of various communication styles, the student quoted above and the project she participated in will provide examples of a range of interviewing modes. Practitioners may deduce guidelines for their own interviewing endeavors from these examples. The student's interview was part of an ongoing project undertaken with undergraduate students that combines basic research, applied anthropology, and pedagogy.

The Project

In the spring of 1993, my Appalachian Studies seminar class studied a controversy between a utility company and citizens' protest organizations concerning a proposed 765,000-volt power line. This project served as an entree into a symbiotic relationship with the citizens of the affected county. After our principal resource person viewed and positively evaluated the mock town meeting the students had created, he requested that we undertake an ethnographic study that could be used as a supplement to an environmental impact statement. Particularly, he asked us to study cultural attachment to land in the county.

Three recent graduates, three continuing students, and I became the founding members of the County Research Team and tackled this major project. The research question was, "Is there cultural attachment to land in the county, and if so, on what is it based?" It was at this point, then, that we clearly began doing applied anthropology, specifically in the field of cultural conservation.

In the summer and fall of 1994, we interviewed ninety-eight residents in interviews lasting half an hour to six hours. We used the information collected in a report documenting the relationship between the county residents and their environment. The data revealed a cultural attachment to land that was based on sentimental, aesthetic, moral-religious, and, to a lesser extent, economic ties. The residents' knowledge of the history of their families and homeplaces, their neighbors, and the county was vast. For them, culture and nature were intertwined. They carried a cultural knowledge of their natural surroundings that was both broad and deep; their knowledge covered a wide variety of topics in great detail. They lived in a "genealogical landscape" where history, current culture, and nature were inextricably joined (Allen 1990). They saw their families' futures as tied to the land. They had forged links of reciprocity with kin and neighbors that enabled continuing agrarian use of the land in economically challenging times. They used metaphors to describe their bond to the land, such as "The land is like another member of the family" and "It may not be heaven but it's close." Our report was cited in the official environmental impact statement and has figured in subsequent efforts by residents and anthropologists to assure that good ethnographic research methods are used when discussing cultural attachment to land and other aspects of living culture (see Howell 2002; Wagner 2002).

In a follow-up study, we called upon thirty-six more students who were enrolled in my Anthropology 411 Appalachian Cultures classes. As a class project, each student was given the name of a county resident to interview. Most of these students had not taken the Ethnographic Research Methods course. So a team of the previous year's students, who had taken both Ethnographic Methods and Appalachian Cultures classes, became the teachers and coordinators for the efforts of the current Appalachian Cultures class.

After the deadline for submitting transcribed and analyzed interviews with county residents had long passed, the student quoted above asked her question: "Why didn't we learn about that *before* we interviewed?" The "that" the student was referring to are the "implicit personality theories"—alternative views of the self—that we were learning about in the Appalachian Cultures anthropology class. These views of the self have an impact on communication styles, and certainly on any applied work within the Appalachian region.

The Sense of Self: Alternative Cultural Possibilities

At the risk of oversimplifying the world's diversity, let us start with a dichotomy between societies that have an "individualistic" versus a "collective" sense of self. The categories should be seen as "ideal types" which serve to broadly characterize various cultural forms; remember that there is actually much variation among Appalachian cultures. Permit me to make comparisons to other cultures, for this is the way anthropology shines a light onto cultural form. A look at alternatives, at what might be, throws into relief what is.

American society is said to be an "individualistic" one (e.g., Bellah et al.1985; Hsu 1972; Luckmann 1967; Marsella 1985; Tocqueville 1969 [1835–40]). Our society has reified the self. The manifestations of an individualistic sense of self are numerous. Take competition, for example, which begins with Vic Braden's Tennis for Two Year Olds, continues to T-Ball and Little League, then moves into the adult corporate world. Individual achievement is prized and is cause for pride and reward from early on. A visit to the house of a friend who has a child is likely to be an exercise in watching the child "performing"—doing whatever it is the child is doing at its particular developmental stage. Our legendary movie lines, repeated over and over, reflect individualism: "Frankly, my dear, I don't give a damn," says Rhett Butler egotistically (in response to Scarlett O'Hara's own egotism). Self-actualization is a way to find meaning in life, and problems in self-actualization are considered mental illness. We Americans are familiar with this individualism that characterizes modern Western societies, but it is said to be exceptional among the world's cultures (Dumont 1985, 1986; Marsella 1985; Wikse 1977).[1]

A less familiar alternative sense of self is found in "collective" cultures. For examples, we can look to some of the North American Indian groups, peoples of the Pacific, and people closer to home, such as the Hutterites, the Amish, and cultures within Appalachia.[2]

Let us look at various aspects of these two "ways of being" in order to clarify the dichotomy. In individualistic societies, there is a "task orientation" as opposed to the "person orientation" common in collective societies, where there is an overriding concern with making things go smoothly within the group. What this means is, if you are confronted with the choice between accomplishing a task *and* hurting someone's feelings, versus *not* accomplishing a task *and not* hurting someone, you will tend to choose the former if you are a member of an "individualistic" society.

The latter choice can be exemplified by anecdotes from the Appalachian Mountains region. For example, a Presbyterian minister tells of wanting to fix the road to his newly assigned church. With the elders of the church, he discusses getting slate, a byproduct of coal mining, from the coal companies free of charge. Subsequently, he has the slate laid onto the road, and on the first rainy day, it turns to a slimy, slippery mess which eventually has to be bulldozed away. Only then did the church committee "come forward with the fact that they had known all along what would happen, [but] they had said nothing because they were afraid" that the minister would think they were opposing him (Weller 1965:47). In effect, their explanation for not telling him would have been, "Well, Reverend Weller, you seemed to want to do it, and we didn't want to hurt your feelings."[3]

The modes of "identity" associated with these two orientations differ as well. Middle America, especially in recent years, has been noted for its expressions of "selfhood." Political theorist John Wikse (1977:1, 2, 6, 9) describes the American ideology as viewing "the self as private property." We see ourselves as "private, separate persons," he notes. "We can think of ourselves as self-sufficient, self-reliant, self-actualized, and self-possessed." It is "a mode of self-consciousness" which celebrates the "freedom of the solitary, private man" and which "emphasizes extreme individuality as the genuine foundation for being oneself." "In the extreme it is the fantasy of the self-sufficiency of the individual, the project to complete and contain all meaning within the separate self" (see also Rappaport 1976).

In collective societies, on the other hand, one's identity is ultimately bound up with the community; the self is a product of the collectivity. Kai Erikson discusses the self as embedded in the collectivity in Appalachia: "One's stature in the community as well as one's inner sense of well-being is derived largely from the position one occupies in a family network [and in peer groups] and to step out of that embracing surround would be like separating from one's own flesh" (Erikson 1976:86). People invest much of themselves in the commonality and become "absorbed by it." "The larger collectivity around you," Erikson states, "becomes an extension of your own personality, an extension of your own flesh" (1976:191).

Dorothy Lee (1986:12) would label this the "open self." She notes that in "such societies, though the self and the other are differentiated, they are not mutually exclusive. The self contains some of the other, participates in the other, and is in part contained within the other." The difference between the individualistic and collective identities has been likened to the difference between eggs hard-boiled together in a pan and eggs fried sunny side up. The (egg white) identity stays separate in the first case and becomes one in the second. (Although, just as the egg yolks remain separate in both cases, so both kinds of societies do recognize each person as a separate entity.)

A whole passel of traits goes with a society's mode of identity. For example, in collective cultures, it is not desirable to step out, to be recognized, to set yourself apart as different from—perhaps better than—your group. Philosophy professors have noted that it is difficult to teach philosophy in the traditional way to Appalachian students, because causing them to criticize one another's thinking is like searching for the philosopher's stone (Acquaviva 1980; Bogert 1980; Humphrey 1980). Competition among individuals is hardly compatible with the collective mode. The inhabitants of the Trobriand Islands, near New Guinea in the Pacific Ocean, are so noncompetitive that although missionaries easily taught youngsters to play basketball, they could not teach them to keep score. The children had no reason for wanting to learn; they did not care who won (Lee 1959). When I relate this example to my middle American students, they ask, "Then why did they want to play?"

Mental illness in cultures such as these is not likely to be defined as a lack of self-actualization. More common is "separation anxiety," which can occur when members of the collectivity are separated for some reason, or "running amok," which sometimes occurred in Inuit cultures when closeness to people and repression of hostile feelings seemed to combine to produce a type of short-lived hysteria.

Obviously, cultures with these differing views of the self manifest different goals in their child-rearing. Hence, it is not surprising that American children meet with challenges, competition, rewards for individual achievement, and opportunities to make decisions early on.

It is probably necessary to convince the American reader that it is possible to have children who are *not* individualistic and competitive. Taking a cross-cultural perspective, we see that examples abound. Edward T. Hall (1976) comments that culture has always dictated where to draw the line separating one thing from another. The cultures we label individualistic "cut the apron strings" from the child's nurturing group. The collective cultures do not; people grow away from childhood, but not away from the group. Hall's collective examples are China, Japan, traditional Jewish families of central Europe, Arab villagers, the Spanish of North and South America, and Pueblo Indians of New Mexico.

How are children raised to have a "collective" consciousness? They are rarely alone; often they can find refuge with any adult in the group as a momentary surrogate mother or father. They do not have "things" of their own. It is only in modern Western or Westernizing cultures that newborn babies are brought home in their own car seat, in their own clothes, and put to sleep in their own beds, in their own room, surrounded by their own toys. A mother among the !Kung San, hunters and gatherers of southern Africa, does give her baby some beads; when the baby grows to a toddler, she is encouraged to give them away, settling her into her culture's lifelong pattern of sharing and reciprocity.

Child-rearing styles which "produce" or encourage the rugged individualist as opposed to the collective adult are well depicted in Margaret Mead's film series *Four Families,* portraying farm families in India, Canada, Japan, and France. Each of the families had a one-year-old baby with one or two older siblings. At the time, in the 1950s, only one of the four families' babies, the Canadian, had her own bed in her own bedroom, with her own toys. Scenes of the mothers bathing their babies showed that the Indian mother washed her baby as if he were a rag doll or an extension of herself. The baby was not expected to resist his mother's motions with his own little arms and legs, and he did not. The Canadian baby, on the other hand, had to be persuaded to put her toys in her box and come away to take her bath. While she was in her little plastic tub, she grasped the washcloth. Her mother entreated her, "Give me your washcloth; please give it to me. Now give me your washcloth." She finally relinquished the washcloth when asked nicely by her mother, and as her mother tugged on it. The Canadian baby was not being bad; she was asserting her individuality and ownership, as she was expected by her culture to do. The Canadian mother recognized a legitimacy to the baby's actions, and her entreaties reflect that the washcloth (and many other things) belong to, and are under the control of, the baby. (I am reminded of working mothers who tell of impatiently waiting while their toddlers decide what to wear to day care.)[4]

Within the collective mode, an indirect style of communication, which anthropologist George Hicks (1976) calls the "ethic of neutrality," accompanies the collective orientation. In parts of Appalachia, a person may not directly ask, "How much did that new car cost?" Instead, he might say, "I bet a car like that cost a right smart" or "You can't get a car like that for $200." And the owner of the car can answer, "Yep," or "Nope," or "It cost ——— dollars" or not answer at all. The same ethic applies to controversial subjects and to verbal confrontation in general. It is a "'round Robin Hood's barn" circumlocutious way of communicating, letting the person questioned have his head, leaving reply up to him.

Applying Cultural Knowledge: Connecting What We Know to What We Do

Do I live by this knowledge of varying views of the self, connecting it to my life and work? I have sometimes forgotten it when talking to my neighbors or students. For example, a student who had written an extensive ethnography about horse show culture for my Practicing Ethnographic Methods course came to my office to chat and to tell me that she had sold her horse. Surprised, I exclaimed, "You did? How much did you get for him?" Standing in front of my desk, she drew herself up to her full height and replied, "Enough."

But I have not asked questions in the course of fieldwork that have breached the preferred indirect communication mode. However, I have sometimes not sufficiently restrained student interviewers from doing so. In the County Cultural Attachment to Land Study, our charge was to discover whether cultural attachment to land exists in the county, and if so, on what that attachment is based. To answer these questions, the study utilized the ethnographic method. Ethnography, which has been described as a "disciplined attempt to discover and describe the symbolic resources with which members of a society conceptualize and interpret their experience" (Basso and Selby 1976), seeks to elicit from the people themselves the bases for the cultural significance of, in this case, elements of their environment.[5]

In the county study, each researcher was given a standardized set of interview questions. The questions we asked were designed to elicit talk from the residents, talk that would replicate as closely as possible the way natives talk to each other. This gives us the insider's/native's (anthropologists call this "emic") point of view.

A student from the original County Research Team coordinated the linking of residents with students and handled the trouble shooting that inevitably attends acquiring interviews from a preset sample of people. The original team came to the class to teach anthropological principles for good interviewing and to role play interview situations. They offered themselves as support personnel. Shannon Scott describes this aspect of being a County Research Team member: "We went into the class and explained that they would be helping us by going into the County and interviewing residents for us. Because many of these students had not done an ethnographic interview before, it was our job to teach them how to do an interview—which questions to ask, which questions to avoid and how to present themselves" (Wagner, Scott, and Wolfe 1997:114; Scott 1995).

Analysis of the text of each interview discovered what is salient to people by finding (1) what they talk about *first,* (2) what they talk about *often,* (3) what *kinds* of things they talk about, (4) what things they talk about with much *detail,* and (5) what kinds of things they *could* talk about but *do not.* The analyst is seeking themes and patterns.

The interview questions were meant to be used when necessary to encourage talk and make this analysis possible. Sometimes it was not necessary to rely on the questions. For example, if a person shows you her home, pointing out family photographs and describing who all the people in her family are and where they live, it is not necessary to then ask, "How many members of your family live nearby? Where else do members of your family live?"

That is the key: the questions were meant to serve as a guide, to help "direct" the flow of the interview if it strayed way off course. The researchers were to have a deep familiarity with the questions so they could ascertain whether the questions were being addressed. But if the student relied on the questions too heavily, they could be taken as overly "direct" in communication mode and negative feelings could result.

The students from the original team recommended not asking "why" questions. "Why did you move back here?" can be rendered less threatening if it is phrased, "How did you make the decision to move back here?" They also advised the interviewers to "not be afraid of silences," to not interrupt or fill silences with their own talk. It would have been well if they had added, "Take your time; do not be in a hurry."

One piece of advice some of the students took too literally was the admonition that an ethnographic interview is not like a regular conversation. A conversation is balanced, with each participant taking a roughly equal part, questioning, answering, and commenting on each other's answers in turn.

An ethnographic interview, on the other hand, is purposely unbalanced, with the interviewee doing the lion's share of the talking and leading (Spradley 1979). Some students took this to mean that they could not say anything other than to ask the relatively standardized questions. However, rapport building requires that the interviewer reveal some things about herself that the interviewee will want to know: Where is she from? Who are her kin? Is she familiar with farms? What is this class she is taking? What will this interview be used for? What else is she doing in school? Does she like this area? Rapport building is certainly necessary in any culture, but it might possibly be more so within some Appalachian cultures.[6]

The most successful students were open to their interviewees' questions about them and then followed the advice of one of their student colleagues, who said, "If a fellow tells you a story about a dog, you're not supposed to then tell him about *your* dog. But you could say, 'What else has your dog done?' or 'Have you had other dogs?'" This student was giving two pieces of excellent advice at once: direct the conversation away from yourself and stay alert so you can ask follow-up questions. Fieldwork demands, as Dorothy Lee (1986:83) says of motherhood, "full commitment to the situation, with all one's senses and other capacities *there,* alive and straining and alert."

An example of eventually asking a follow-up question is in this excerpt from one of my interviews in the county. Remember that these interview excerpts show the actual, unedited talk (as opposed to the vastly trimmed versions that eventually appear in ethnographic analyses). "RES" stands for resident, and "INT" denotes the interviewer. As is typical in anthropological reports, the names of people and places have been omitted; blanks are used for proper names.

> INT: Is there anything else, you know, that you'd like to say, that you think would, you know, help us out?
>
> RES: It's just, you know, it seems like the county is different from any other county. There was a piece in the paper the other day, uh, we saw the piece in there about ——— on the, um, porch up there. Wasn't that somethin'?
>
> INT: Yeah.
>
> RES: Last Sunday there was a piece in there about a man like ——— in a place like this county.
>
> INT: Was that in Sunday's ——— paper?
>
> RES: Um-hm.
>
> INT: I missed that.
>
> RES: You want it?

INT: Yeah. I've, you know, got it somewhere recycled, but—

RES: Uh-huh.

RES: But I want you to go and see ———.

INT: I will.

RES: For a family that is just this county. And go back off—in the back of the old house. It is so neat, I just love it.

INT: I've got to get into her kitchen, you say.

RES: Yeah, get into her kitchen. [Both laugh.]

INT: But you know, now you've said somethin' here that's important when you've said that the county is different, and so it might be good to, uh, to talk about that a little bit. In other words, how you would describe it to somebody. You know, [describe it to] somebody who never—maybe who had never been here—how it's different. We didn't know anything about it. Assume we didn't know anything about it. How would you describe it to somebody, you know, in Washington, D.C., or whatever. How would you say how it's different?

It might be said that this interview "went off on a tangent" about the piece in the paper and the tip on another family to interview. But the original essence of the interviewee's speech—"It seems like the county is different from any other county"—was plumbed eventually.

Our teaching partner in the county, a resident who teaches my class about the history of the county and helps locate interviewees, noted another attribute that student interviewers would need to take into account.[7] She said that because standing out and talking about oneself are not generally acceptable, residents would tell students they had nothing of importance to say and would need to be frequently reassured that this is certainly not the case.

Since the purpose of an ethnographic interview is to discern what the *natives* think is important, ethnographers are careful not to ask leading questions or make leading comments. (For example, questions and comments such as "Would you say you loved your land?" or "I'll bet you love your land" would never be used.) There were no answers implied in the questions that we asked; there were no multiple choice answers supplied. One of the interviewers forgot this rule when asking this question: "If you had a day when you could do anything you wanted to—nothing needed to get done—where would you go? How would you describe this place to someone who couldn't go there?" The original objective of this question was to elicit descriptions of places. Actually, the answers to this question taught us much about how county residents spent their time. One of the interviewers transposed the question into "If you had a day when you could do anything you wanted to—nothing needed to get done—where would you go, to the Mall?" Fortunately, the informant did not feel compelled to follow the interviewer's lead and described instead how she spent her time on her own homeplace.

It also is not good practice for the interviewer to interject her opinions. Fortunately, in this interview, the interviewee was sufficiently strong-minded to counteract the interviewer's leading:

> RES: Another thing that I find interesting is that we've been hearing recently and reading in the paper about ——— project and how they're pumping millions of dollars into the ——— project.
>
> INT: I'm glad to see that, aren't you?
>
> RES: Well, I think it's very interesting, but I think it is very interesting that our state is trying to create what we—what already exists here in the county!

The most potentially threatening question on our list was "How much land do you have here?" One reason we asked this question was to obtain demographic data that would enable us to compare our sample of interviewees to the population of the county at large. The question also became an important indicator of one of our findings. We found that the residents of the county knew an enormous amount of detail about their environment—its flora, fauna, and geological characteristics. They also knew exactly how much land they owned, sometimes down to the tenth of an acre, even in this mountainous hard-to-survey area.

In each of the excerpts from interviews reproduced below, land ownership is being discussed. The excerpts contrast interviewers who heeded the advice of their predecessors with those who did not. Note the degree of directness or indirectness and the page number of the transcription, an indicator of how much time has elapsed before the topic is discussed.

In the first excerpt, I had the good fortune to be along for the ride when a resident showed another resident and me his land. Thus, I could hear how residents talk to one another. The two residents are indicated by RES A and RES B. At transcript page 23:

> RES A: Now the whole back side of this mountain is ———.
>
> RES B: [Pointing, to direct my gaze.] The marker.
>
> INT: Oh, from that marker down that way.
>
> RES A: Yeah, and all the way out to the mountain just about. They come to the top, but there are two or three places out here that was the old homeplaces went down on the side. And Mr. ——— gathered together all together about seven old homesteads up here and he gathered them up over a

period of twenty-five or thirty years. And there was seven tracts of land when I bought it. There was seven different tracts of land up here.

INT: You put together seven tracts.

RES A: No he did. Just like the ———. He bought the ——— tract for a silver dollar. It wasn't but two acres.

Six pages later:

RES A: It's what they call the frost line, just like ——— Mountain. I don't see any [trees] on that one. A few.

RES B: A lot of times it will be warmer up high. And usually I can tell at my house. If I'm warmer than ———, it's usually going to rain.

RES A: She [interviewer] lives in ——— so she's up high, too. Do you see any apples on that one? It's a few.

INT: Yeah.

RES A: Boy, those deer go crazy over them. Now here, ———, is where you go to the ———'s house. It goes down there a good ways, there's forty acres; more than two acres in that tract.

RES B: Do you own it?

RES A: Yes. He bought twice. He bought off ———; he bought off two or three ——s. He bought off old man ———.

And eight pages later:

RES A: This is where they took this picture. See when I first mowed out here there was none of those trees there. And these people bought this place there and they just let it grow up. So in the summer time I can't see through, but as soon as the leaves fall you can see right on.

RES B: Now do you own down here?

RES A: To that fence right there.

RES B: Now who owns on the other side?

RES A: That was ———.

RES B: Okay, so you don't own up until you get here?

RES A: Right here and go to the corner. See I bought fifteen and a half acres off ——— back in 19—. See there was no right-of-way to this place except over them. And there was another road went over to the ———. But they stopped that; they locked that up after ——— moved. And so ——— and ——'s line is a little dab of it right through here and cuts between here. But they sold it.

RES B: So it's up to your fence.

RES A: And then it goes in a wedge shape about five thousand feet way out the mountain.

RES B: You'll have to draw it on a topo for me.

RES A: It's an odd thing.

INT: How big is it all total?

RES A: There's about three hundred acres total. [Showing a window pane.] If you'll look, this glass is squiggly; see all the squiggles in it.

Thus the potentially threatening question was not asked until well into the interview (about an hour had elapsed) and until the residents themselves were pointing out land boundaries. Notice, too, that the researcher's contributions to the "purposeful conversation" are slight. Students who have analyzed my interviews have teased that my contributions are mostly "Uh-huh" and "Yeah." I tell them that their observation is a complement.

The next excerpt is from an interview conducted by a talented and sensitive anthropology student who was chosen to be an original member of the County Research Team. At page 38 of the interview, she is being shown around the resident's property:

RES: And so, our property—on the back side of the mountain lays—I'll have to get a map—kinda this way.

INT: Oh, you have property on the *back* side?

RES: We've got about ninety-four or ninety acres on the back side. It's just a disjointed piece that I think is wonderfully pristine because it's just a nice little rectangle sittin' back there that's got a super great neighbor that you never even hear from on the lower side surrounded by ——— on the other three sides which I think is just great. It's nice. It's real rugged and cannot be developed, I don't guess.

Here, the researcher gained this information without asking, in the context of being shown the property and its boundaries.

The following is an excerpt from page 3 of a student's interview. He has included in parentheses his thoughts about his uneasiness about asking the question (which he reworded):

INT: I understand. Okay, do you commute to work, obviously?

RES: Ahh, yeah I do.

INT: And how far is that?

RES: Ahh, about thirty miles.

INT: Okay, given that you still live here, let's say you got a job transfer or something but you still wanted to live here, how far would you be willing to commute to work?

RES: Well, as far as I could do it within reason, an hour's commute each way.

INT: I wouldn't want to give up your house, I like it out here. Uhh, how much land do you own? [I was hesitant at first about asking this question but I felt that he was open enough so I asked him.]

RES: Uhh [He becomes a little uneasy when I asked him this. He shifted from a relaxed position to a more rigid position in his chair.], that's a question that you usually don't ask people; it's like asking how much money do you have in the bank.

INT: Oh, I'm sorry.

RES: That's alright, I understand the people that make up these don't understand that. [He said this while pointing to the plus pack with the interview questions.] I'm surprised that they may not tell you but for one good reason, and it's eighty acres because I've always felt that, and many people feel that way, too, that a family can't take care of more than eighty or roughly that number and still keep it in good shape for the next generation. It's very hard to do.

The "dropped in" question, a sensitive one at best, mitigated against the rapport the student may have built with the resident by this point in the interview.

The last excerpt is from an interview between a very direct communicator and a more indirect communicator, both very bright. It is this student who lamented that learning about the differences between individualistic and collective cultures in advance of the interview could have afforded her a happier experience. This is the beginning of the interview:

RES: Mrs. ——— wanted me to tell you we're having our one hundred and twenty-fifth anniversary of our ——— Methodist Church.

INT: Where is the ——— Methodist Church?

RES: It's—you came by it as you came up ———.

INT: Oh, oh at the turn off at ———?

RES: At ———.

INT: One hundred and twenty-five years.

RES: It's going to be ———.

INT: That's my birthday.

RES: Is that right?

INT: But I'm not one hundred and twenty-five.

RES: You know, that I saw in the paper, I mean the TV, a church in ——— County that celebrated, a Methodist church.

INT: I saw that. Mrs. ——— would you tell me your age?

RES: Yes, I'm ———.

INT: ———. And, your father was born in ——— County, and you also?

RES: Yes, my father and my grandfather.

INT: And you've lived here all your life?

RES: Well, I didn't stay here all my life but I was born here, yes.

INT: When did you decide to leave?

RES: Well, I went to college, and then I taught in ———. And then after that I got another position at ———, from there to somewhere else and . . . and that took me elsewhere.

INT: When did you decide to come home?

RES: After my father died.

INT: Had your father left you your farm, your home?

RES: My mother had the place. This is really not, I think that's, huh, our personal business.

INT: OK, I'm sorry. Uh, you see, kinda the point of what me and the classmates are trying to discover is your relationship with your home.

At page 4:

INT: Uh, I have a schedule of questions. I'm perfectly willing to not use them. Uh, one of the questions is how much land you have.

RES: That's a personal question and I don't think that they're necessary for you.

When faced with very direct questioning, the offended resident, usually indirect in communication style, becomes very direct in turn.

Certainly these vignettes show that ethnography is not an "efficient" means of collecting data. Ethnography is, of course, renowned for its ability to take an in-depth look at a relatively bounded arena. It takes much time and many interview pages to achieve rapport, and to learn what people think is significant in a culture, from their point of view and with them leading the way. The best interviews were the longest ones; they contained data relating to the questions, eventually. In the bargain, they amassed many stories and other information that contributed clues to what the residents deemed important in their environment.

Conclusion

I have assumed that practitioners desire, as ethnographers do, to obtain information from their clients/informants that is as close as possible to the native way of thinking, information that is filtered or translated for us as little as possible. Perhaps the essential lesson to be learned here is that the interviewer should let the interviewee take the lead, not only in the *kinds* of information she thinks are important in her culture but also in the *ways of asking and talking* about that information.

In the case of people who hail from cultures where the collective self is valued over an individualistic one, allowing time to become acquainted (not just you with the client, but the client with you) and asking in a more indirect, less strident way may help meet the ultimate goal. Letting the client know who you are while foregoing inserting your opinions or "multiple-choice" answers is a challenging but rewarding skill. Teachers have noted that their student/teacher conferences were more fruitful when they took the time to orient themselves in the parents' world (i.e., answered the "Who are you?" that was in the parents' minds). Nurses have described carefully observing patients and taking notes that are both "subjective" and "objective" in form.

Good interviewers are made, not born. The same is true for health practitioners, educators, and community planners. In the important and worthwhile endeavor of learning from the natives what you should know, it helps to take time to know your clients, to listen more than talk, to reassure them that you are interested in learning what they have to teach you, and to let them lead in the careful dance that is the essence of anthropological fieldwork and an essential element in applied practice.

Notes

1. For more about the concept of self and the degree to which the Western self is unique, see Ewing 1990; Goldschmidt 1995; Murray 1993; Shanahan 1992; Shweder and Bourne 1984; Spiro 1993; and Taylor 1989.

2. See also Wagner (1994, 1995) concerning the collective characteristics of one of Appalachia's ancestral cultures, that of Scotland.

3. See also Dumont (1986:106, 160, 260) for discussion of the primacy of relations between human and human in collective societies, versus between human and objects in individualistic societies.

4. See Coles 1971; Looff 1971; and Abbott-Jamieson in this volume for more on childhood in the Appalachian region.

5. See also Wagner 1997 for more about using the ethnographic method.

6. See Looff 1971 concerning an extended "warm-up period" he observed.

7. The label "teaching partners" to accurately describe the relationship between a university teacher and community residents was devised by my colleague, Mary LaLone.

References

Acquaviva, Gary J. 1980. "Teaching Philosophy in Appalachia: An Existential Approach." Paper presented at the Appalachian Studies Conference, East Tennessee State University, Johnson City.

Allen, Barbara. 1990. "The Genealogical Landscape and the Southern Sense of Place." In *Sense of Place,* Barbara Allen and Thomas J. Schlereth (Eds.). Lexington: University Press of Kentucky. Pp. 152–63.

Basso, Keith H., and Henry A. Selby. 1976. *Meaning in Anthropology.* Albuquerque: University of New Mexico Press.

Bellah, Robert N., Richard Madsen, William M. Sullivan, Ann Swidler, and Steven M. Tipton. 1985. *Habits of the Heart: Individualism and Commitment in American Life.* New York: Harper and Row.

Bogert, Frans van der. 1980. "The Cultural Context of Philosophic Criticism." Paper presented at the Appalachian Studies Conference, East Tennessee State University, Johnson City.

Coles, Robert. 1971. *Migrants, Sharecroppers, Mountaineers.* Vol. 2 of *Children of Crisis.* Boston: Little, Brown/Atlantic Monthly.

Dumont, Louis. 1985. "A Modified View of Our Origins: The Christian Beginnings of Modern Individualism." In *The Category of the Person,* Michael Carrithers, Steven Collins, and Steven Lukes (Eds.). New York: Cambridge University Press. Pp. 93–122.

———. 1986. *Essays on Individualism.* Chicago: University of Chicago Press.

Erikson, Kai T. 1976. *Everything in its Path.* New York: Simon and Schuster.

Ewing, Katherine. 1990. "The Illusion of Wholeness: Culture, Self, and the Experience of Inconsistency." *Ethos* 18(3):251–78.

Goldschmidt, Walter. 1995. "An Open Letter to Melford E. Spiro." *Ethos* 23(2): 244–54.

Hall, Edward T. 1976. *Beyond Culture.* Garden City, N.Y.: Doubleday.

Hicks, George L. 1976. *Appalachian Valley.* New York: Holt, Rinehart, and Winston.

Howell, Benita J. 2002. "Appalachian Culture and Environmental Planning: Expanding the Role of the Cultural Sciences." In *Culture, Environment, and Conservation in the Appalachian South,* Benita J. Howell (Ed.). Urbana: University of Illinois Press. Pp. 1–16.

Hsu, Francis L. K. 1972. "American Core Values and National Character." In *Psychological Anthropology,* Francis L. K. Hsu (Ed.). Cambridge, Mass.: Schenkman. Pp. 209–30.

Humphrey, Richard. 1980. "Academic Philosophy and Appalachian Culture." Paper presented at the Appalachian Studies Conference, East Tennessee State University, Johnson City.

Lee, Dorothy. 1959. *Freedom and Culture.* Englewood Cliffs, N.J.: Prentice-Hall.

———. 1986. *Valuing the Self: What We can Learn from Other Cultures.* Prospect Heights, Ill.: Waveland Press [orig. 1976].

Looff, David H. 1971. *Appalachia's Children: The Challenge of Mental Health.* Lexington: University of Kentucky Press.

Luckmann, Thomas. 1967. *The Invisible Religion: The Problem of Religion in Modern Society.* New York: Macmillan.

Marsella, Anthony J. 1985. "Culture, Self, and Mental Disorder." In *Culture and Self,* Anthony J. Marsella, George DeVos, and Francis L. K. Hsu (Eds.). New York: Tavistock. Pp. 281–308.

Murray, D. W. 1993. "What Is the Western Concept of the Self? On Forgetting David Hume." *Ethos* 21(1):3–23.

Rappaport, Roy A. 1976. "Liturgies and Lies." *International Yearbook of Sociology and Religion* 10:75–104.

Scott, Shannon T. 1995. "Cultural Attachment to Land in County." Paper presented at the Southern Anthropological Society Annual Meeting, Raleigh, N.C.

Shanahan, Daniel. 1992. *Toward a Genealogy of Individualism.* Amherst: University of Massachusetts Press.

Shweder, Richard A., and Edmund J. Bourne. 1984. "Does the Concept of the Person Vary Cross Culturally?" In *Culture Theory: Essays on Mind, Self, and Emotion,* Richard A. Shweder and Robert A. LeVine (Eds.). Cambridge: Cambridge University Press. Pp. 158–99.

Spiro, Melford E. 1993. "Is the Western Conception of the Self 'Peculiar' Within the Context of the World Cultures?" *Ethos* 21(2):107–53.

Spradley, James P. 1979. *The Ethnographic Interview.* New York: Holt, Rinehart and Winston.

Taylor, Charles. 1989. *Sources of the Self: The Making of the Modern Identity.* Cambridge: Harvard University Press.

Tocqueville, Alexis de. 1969. *Democracy in America,* George Lawrence (Trans.); J. P. Mayer (Ed.). New York: Doubleday [orig. 1835–40, *De la démocratie en Amérique*].

Wagner, Melinda Bollar. 1994 and 1995. "The Cross-Cultural Study of Ethno-personality." *ALCA-LINES,* Journal of the Assembly on the Literature and Culture of Appalachia, National Council of Teachers of English, 3(1): 6, 16 and 4(1): 16–17, 23.

———. 1997. "The Study of Religion in American Society." In *Anthropology of Religion: A Handbook,* Stephen D. Glazier (Ed.). Westport, Conn.: Greenwood. Pp. 85–102.

———. 2002. "Space and Place, Land and Legacy." In *Culture, Environment and Conservation in the Appalachian South,* Benita J. Howell (Ed.). Urbana: University of Illinois Press. Pp. 121–32.

Wagner, Melinda Bollar, Shannon T. Scott, and Danny Wolfe. 1997. "Drawing the Line Between People and Power: Taking the Classroom to the Community." In *Practicing Anthropology in the South,* James M. Tim Wallace (Ed.). Athens: University of Georgia Press. Pp. 109–18.

Weller, Jack E. 1965. *Yesterday's People: Life in Contemporary Appalachia.* Lexington: University Press of Kentucky.

Wikse, John. 1977. *About Possession: The Self as Private Property.* University Park: Pennsylvania State University Press.

Chapter 3

To Listen Is to Learn: The Social Worker in Rural Appalachia

Carol Gross

A good many years ago, when I was a college student in the Northeast, I applied for a summer internship with a rural health program based in Berea, Kentucky. When told I had not been chosen, the program director succinctly stated the reason for the rejection: "You talk too fast." The true meaning of that trenchant phrase did not become significant until I moved to western North Carolina to teach social work practice at a local university. Immediately apparent was my awareness that I was a stranger, an alien, an unknown, and, if not a threat, then certainly different.

What did I need to know, to be, and to do to find a place in this rural Appalachian environment, to be a relevant teacher, and to become an accepted part of this community, both personally and professionally? How could I integrate the roles of teacher/social worker and my own person? Furthermore, what are the attributes needed for a social worker in a rural community? In what ways is the Appalachian rural community similar to and different from rural communities across the United States?

Social Work: Two Views

The concept that rural social work (like health and mental health services) may be different from the more familiar urban model is not a new one, but the focus is heightened by a new insight into, and concern for, understanding and acceptance of diversity and difference. Rural populations are now seen as one in a group of populations/cultures which have unique features and require special knowledge, skills, and understandings. In the 1930s, Josephine Brown published *The Rural Community and Social Case Work,* which was promptly forgotten as the profession moved toward a focus on psychotherapy and on "adjusting" clients to their surroundings, concepts considered irrelevant or not applicable to rural communities. As the profession comes full circle, it is discovering that Brown's concepts appear as relevant to contemporary rural communities as to the farm communities about which she wrote (Davenport and Davenport 1984). A new body of literature is emerging which realizes that to treat everyone the same is to discriminate against some, and that rural populations, which are unique in many aspects, must not be written off.

Characteristics of the Rural Community

Ruralness is both a statistical definition and a geographical description. Specifically, a rural area is generally defined as a nonmetropolitan area of under fifty thousand persons by the Bureau of the Census. After decades of outmigration to urban areas, rural areas are increasingly retaining larger numbers of the population as well as attracting migrants from urban areas. While population figures provide a context for the definition of rural, many writers suggest that there are other factors to be considered. Waltman writes that "it connotes a way of and an outlook on life characterized by a closeness to nature, slower pace of living and a somewhat conservative life-style that values tradition, independence and self-reliance, and privacy" (1986:467).

No longer is it viable to believe that rural areas are necessarily homogenous. In North Carolina, for example, "rural" may identify coastal or mountain areas or used-up and worn-out mining and timbering communities. Within each of these areas are diverse cultures, social classes, and races which mingle to a greater or lesser degree. Rural communities are not static, unchanging entities; they are influenced by both in- and out-migration. Currently, in western North Carolina alone, several "newcomer groups" can be identified: Hispanics (both migrant farm workers and well-to-do Cubans who buy or rent second or vacation homes); "Floridians" who flee to the mountains to escape tropical heat and crowded cities; immigrant populations from a variety of Asian countries; and, most recently, "telecommunicators" who have discovered that their business can be successfully managed far from the urban areas (Hanson 1966).

However, statistics alone do not suffice in presenting a true picture of any community. Many writers suggest (Sheafor and Lewis 1995; Anglin 1983; Devore and Schlesinger 1998) that to truly understand a rural community it is necessary to consider, at a minimum, the factors of land, the economy, the people, and relevant historical and political factors. Failure to take these factors into account can make the newcomer vulnerable to misunderstanding and being misunderstood. People who live in rural communities cherish their roots. Many residents are tied not only to their own land but also to the history of that land. They know or knew the people for whom every ridge or crossroads is named, they have personally participated in the development and growth of commercial or residential systems, they are related to the local governing officials, and they perpetuate history (e.g., a road near where I live is named Milton Bass Heirs Road).

Cherishing the land, many people eligible for services from governmental systems (Medicaid, Food Stamps, etc.) reject these services if access to them entails selling any portion of their land, even though that land lies idle and nonproductive (Beaver 1986; Ginsberg 1998). Land and its use is one of the more heated points of friction between local residents and in-migrating populations. Newcomers and home builders have transformed the landscape through "fencing off" their property, limiting access to the woods and hills that formerly were open territory for hunting, fishing, and camping. Roads have been carved out of the hills with no awareness of the impact of snow and floods, stream run-off, and contamination. Two-lane "highways" are expanded to four, five, and six lanes. In what appears to be a need to recreate the environment from which they fled, in-migrants have demanded (and received), for example, highly specialized medical services, limiting the provision of less lucrative (but essential) services to outlying, underserved populations and placing demands on the infrastructure that rural communities, especially in rural Appalachia, are hard pressed to meet. Locally owned businesses give way to chain stores, and local eateries lose out to franchised restaurants familiar to the in-migrants. One consequence of this increased pressure is that land values have risen sharply, and families who have owned their land for generations often struggle to pay the increased taxes assessed against their property. In one of the "mountain" counties of North Carolina, 23 percent of available housing is classified as "seasonal," increasing pressure on available land by second-home in-migrants and raising taxes for local, long-time landowners (Daw et al. 1992). At the same time, 147 families in the county are on the waiting list for low-income housing.

In-migrants

Past history puts its mark on current perceptions and attitudes. The rural community was and is wary of strangers, variously identified as "familiar outsiders" (Daley and Kobek 1990) or "back-to-the-landers" (Beaver 1986; Ginsberg 1998). These terms were initially used to describe the activists of the 1960s, who saw themselves as escaping from urban materialism to a less complex and more "pure" environment. These in-migrants, the "familiar outsiders," had no intent to change the rural populations but a desire to "replace that selfish and hurtful individualism with commitment and service to a 'community'" (Daley and Kobek 1990:248). Even with their benign goals and the desire to become a part of the rural community, they were perceived as well-intentioned outsiders, substantively different from the local populations. Usually from urban backgrounds and with college educations, the familiar outsiders were not totally dependent on the local economy for subsistence and had cultural and social connections to the "outside." As Beaver has pointed out, despite their attempts to merge into and be seen as the same as the local inhabitants, it never quite came off. She suggests that their presence was often disruptive to the community, that they were "representative of economic changes in the nation [and] cultural changes as [local] children were exposed to drug use in the public schools, women moved into the public labor force, unemployment rose, and the economy placed greater strain on the family" (1986:137).

Many more recent in-migrants have come bearing skills and/or money, anticipating that the "depressed" areas will welcome both with open arms. As Anglin points out, this "problem (of acceptance) is particularly acute for those functioning in a professional capacity . . . which highlights other aspects of their lives—such as educational background, salary, personal power—setting them apart from other members of the community" (1983:230ff). As it was explained to me, "You're not considered a member of the community until no one remembers a time before you were here."

Social Problems and Rural Appalachia

Lynn Morris (1995:2070) finds that "during the 1980s the poverty rate in rural areas remained consistently higher than the poverty rate in urban areas" and suggests that the factors contributing to this include economic restructuring, high unemployment rates, relocation of manufacturers to overseas, government policies, and historical patterns of oppression and inequality. Like many urban areas, rural communities now have single mothers, increasing substance abuse, family violence, and pockets of substandard housing.

The rural areas of North Carolina exhibit many of the characteristics of rural communities across the United States. (The state is the second most rural area in the United States in absolute numbers.) These characteristics include poverty, vulnerable populations, and scarcity of social services.

In examining the eleven North Carolina counties that border the spine of the Blue Ridge Mountains, we find that the population ranges from 3,800 to 17,000 in nine of these counties, and from 16,000 to 28,000 in the other two counties. Eight of the counties have a density per square mile of 9 to 44 persons, while three have population densities of 45 to 106 persons. The county poverty rates range from a low of around 13 percent in four counties to two with a poverty rate from 16 to 18 percent. Unemployment rates range up to almost 15 percent in the most rural counties to a low of 2–3 percent in the most "urban" county, which is also the seat of a state university. Supporting Morris's findings, table 3.1 demonstrates that the poverty rate and children in poverty rate are higher than the state average in almost all counties, and the unemployment rate, abuse/neglect rate, and birth to teens rate are higher than the state average in the majority of counties.

Table 3.1. Poverty and Child Risk Factors in Selected North Carolina Rural Counties

	Poverty Rate (%)	Unemployment (%) (2002)	Abuse/Neglect Substantiated (Rate/1,000)	Infant death (Rate/1,000) (1996–2000)	Birth to Teens (Rate/1,000) (2002)	Children in Poverty (%)
Alleghany	13.9	8.1	16.4	.01	76.4	23.6
Ashe	14.2	11.4	11.6	8.4	67.1	22.5
Avery	14.9	5.6	30.6	4.9	34.3	22.6
Cherokee	14.7	10.4	27.6	8.4	77.8	23.5
Graham	16.6	12.3	30.2	21.7	100.4	25.3
Haywood	12.8	8.2	33.1	8.5	48.2	22.1
Madison	15.4	6.2	22.8	8.9	31.5	22.4
Mitchell	13.1	11.9	21.7	12.5	44.7	20.8
Swain	18.0	14.9	11.1	28.2	92.6	31.3
Watauga	13.1	2.8	6.8	8.0	12.2	15.4
Yancy	14.9	14.1	31.5	20.6	62.9	23.7
N.C. rates	12.3	6.8	16.6	9.1	58.5	19.4

SOURCES: North Carolina Child Advocacy Institute, *The Children's Index . . . ; a Profile of Leading Indicators of the Health and Well-being of North Carolina's Children* (Raleigh, NC: North Carolina Child Advocacy Institute); United States Bureau of the Census, 2000, *Simple Demographic Profiles, Current Population Survey* (Washington, D.C.: U.S. Government Printing Office).

The Rural Social Worker

A major role of the social worker, rural or urban, is to provide services to generally underserved populations, to assess needs and resources, and to act as an advocate, an enabler, and an activist. Generally, in urban areas, these roles are usually differentiated and specialized. Not so for rural areas. In some rural areas, the social worker may be "the only game in town" and must be prepared to function in all of these roles, sometimes within the same day. An additional rural role is that of providing information to rural clients and communities, making services accessible (i.e., bringing services to the participants, providing transportation, etc.), and, perhaps most important, legitimizing the utilization of services by those in need.

Many social workers who have grown up in urban communities tend, as do other voluntary migrants, to look at rural areas through rose-colored glasses. Coupled with this idealized vision is its counterpart, the view that locating to, and working with, a rural community is somehow less prestigious than to be part of a complex, "professional" urban environment. Neither of these views is accurate. The rural area is no Garden of Eden, nor is rural social work less "professional." Rather, it is often described as more demanding of creativity and providing greater challenges. Rural areas furnish an unparalleled opportunity for innovations in service delivery to those persons in rural areas who need and are seeking help with a myriad of social problems.

Davenport and Davenport (1998b) present suggestions for helping human service professionals attain competencies for working with diverse individuals and groups and remind us that it is often forgotten that rural (and other) communities have cultures and social characteristics that will enhance or limit the effectiveness of help that is being offered. Rural communities tend to evaluate social workers and other human service professionals by the help they deliver rather than their professional credentials. It is critical for the worker to understand and respect the power of informal relationships that "must be understood and used appropriately" (Davenport and Davenport 1998b:47). This demands a knowledge beyond that of the textbook, the necessity to become culturally competent as an individual and a helper.

Many writers have presented suggestions for cultural competency which can be applied to and utilized in working in rural Appalachian communities (Sue and Sue 1990; Devore and Schlesinger 1999; Morales and Sheafor 2002). Paramount among them is the need for individual self-awareness of one's person and ethnic identity and how this may influence the development of relationships and provision of professional services. Sue and Sue (1990) specifically identify as critical characteristics of the culturally competent, skilled worker an awareness of one's own values and biases and a level of comfort with differences that exist between self and others in terms of belief systems. The authors go on to state that it is critical to understand the world view of the client and community, to have a grasp of the sociopolitical system influencing the group, and to obtain specific knowledge and information about the particular client, group, and community.

The social worker who moves into a rural area to practice his/her profession is often perceived as an outsider and is accepted with considerable hesitation. The social worker may be perceived as intrusive, disruptive, threatening, and disdainful of the local norms and cultures while at the same time representing "the system" (government). Yet many social workers (and other helping professionals) have succeeded in establishing a reasonably successful role within the rural community. This does not happen quickly or easily.

Characteristics of the Effective Rural Social Worker

To be effective as a rural social worker in Appalachia, or in any rural setting, the social worker must pay attention to and learn about the community, its residents, and him/herself in the context of being a rural helper. In addition, the social worker must be able to identify not only the limitations of service delivery to rural, isolated populations but also the multiple strengths of the residents and the many opportunities available for creative, enhancing, and supportive services (Davenport and Davenport 1998a).

Barry Lopez (1986) has quoted an Eskimo informant as stating, "When you come into a new country, listen a lot." Listen, observe, learn. Listen to who speaks. Listen to speech patterns as well as to content. Listen for the emotions behind the words. How is information passed on? What is the appropriate interaction between young and old? How does one learn that "fall out" means to faint, that "public" work means any work outside the home for pay? What are the prescribed roles of men and women? The dress norms?

In most rural communities, and notably in Appalachia, *who* you are may determine what you are able to do. Very few interpersonal transactions are cut and dried. Nearly all are preceded by general discussion of weather, who is where, how the crops/trees are coming along, and so on. Hurrying this interaction is perceived by rural Appalachians as rude, and it can lead to cutting off important sources of information and the perception that you are *not* a person of value but merely someone doing a job. And this interaction demands reciprocity—a willingness to share personal information and to become "involved."

The social worker is seen by many as a representative of a distrusted governmental force, an outside and imposed bureaucracy whose rules and regulations fail to take into account community norms and expectations. However, a change is taking place. With the increase in numbers of undergraduate social work programs located in rural areas or small towns, it is becoming somewhat more likely that the rural social worker may be a member of a local or nearby community, familiar with the local customs and cultures, and able to be easily identified as "one of us." While it is true that increasing numbers of educated professionals are returning to rural areas, the numbers are still small.

Social workers often move to rural areas for the same reasons as do other professionals, back-to-the-landers, and other newcomers, imbued with the same myths of a more leisurely and community-based experience than they feel is possible in urban areas. Often educated to work one-on-one with dysfunctional individuals and families, they are initially uncomfortable with the multiple roles and demands of the rural social work professional. They will need to learn not to be threatened by the lack of "resources," to cherish the leisure afforded by the realities of distance, to be excited about learning the norms and expectations of the community, the many strengths of the residents, and the opportunities available for creative, enhancing, and supportive professional and personal experiences that abound in rural areas.

Adaptability and creativity are the most useful skills the social worker can bring into her or his professional repertoire, coupled with what might be called "personalism" and the ability to listen and learn. He or she will learn ways to reinterpret the social service system, often only visible as "interfering in the way families bring up children" (i.e., intervention in child abuse and neglect and removal of children from homes to foster or institutional care).

Many factors that appear to limit the effectiveness and receptivity to intervention in this area are a reflection of a more conservative (as compared to urban areas) attitude. Factors limiting intervention include a perceived threat to parental rights and family privacy, a lack of knowledge about and reluctance to report child abuse and neglect, the perceived political consequences of deviating from "the norm," a fear of becoming known as the "reporter," and the geographical distances that separate families and community. The rural social worker will find it productive to emphasize the less visible and probably more acceptable social services that assist with services to aging, housing, community action and development, in-home services to children, and so on.

The helping professional who moves into a designated role in an unfamiliar environment may often assume that the inhabitants are "just the same" as he or she is, with similar values, world views, and personal history. The different emphases on values of self-sufficiency, personal responsibility, and self-determination of residents of rural communities may initially limit the ability of the social worker to effect either personal or social change. The values of place, history, family structure, and family relationships, the role of extended family and kin, and the emphasis on religion/spirituality may contradict professional social work values emphasizing individual responsibility and the positive value of change. The tendency of rural inhabitants to resist radical change may be mistaken for fatalism. Rather, the rural community is better conceptualized as carefully considering, over time, the consequences of change—believing that decisions should not be made in haste.

The family remains the central social institution in rural society, and family-centered activities take high priority. Mutual misunderstandings can easily arise. When, in the classroom, I comment on how odd it is that most students I teach talk by telephone to their families daily and return home each weekend, I'm perceived as coming from the planet Mars. When I describe my college experience as going home (ninety miles) only for Thanksgiving, Christmas, and spring break, and indicate that my family would have been concerned if I had come home more often, I am amazed to receive a group response that suggests I must come from a totally dysfunctional background. When, as a practicing social worker in southern Indiana, I suggested to my poverty-level clients that for financial reasons they should forego trips to Kentucky or Tennessee, these family-comes-first folks received my suggestion in stony silence and totally ignored my (naïve and alien) recommendation.

An important rural emphasis is religion and the church. In the Appalachian region, churchgoing and church activities rival the emphasis on family (often they are one and the same). Small churches dot the landscape; others are hidden down winding roads. Often families have their own cemeteries, where several generations of family members are buried and where the upkeep and maintenance of these burial sites is a familiar and cherished ritual. In-migrating social workers will find that acknowledgment of their own religious affiliations and practices will indicate proper respect for a significant local institution.

The "Person" of the Social Worker

Professional social work culture holds that the helping process includes a body of skills, knowledge, and values that can be utilized to promote change (individual and/or group/community), to assist in optimum development of the identified unit, and is somewhat separate and apart from the person providing the services and resources. This concept is counterproductive in rural areas. Who you are, what kind of person you appear to be, may be more convincing than all the degrees attached to you. Are you willing to conform to the norms of the community? Do you live in the community, shop at the local stores, become involved in community rituals, attend the parades, participate in the community fund-raising suppers? Will you take the time to chat about the weather and the local elections before "getting down to business"? Are you willing to learn about the importance of "names" and understand that a family name can often tell you about the socioeconomic status of a family and the family's reputation within the community (Harper and Lantz 1996)? Do you read the local newspaper; know who has had a baby or who is in the hospital or who has died?

Professional confidentiality and the personal privacy of the worker are transparent in rural communities. How can you explain confidentiality to your children when you meet clients in the local Kroeger's, and when your high school son comes home and tells you, "Mom, Mary says you're a really neat social worker"? Or protect your privacy when, careful not to distribute your phone number widely, you find that clients can easily locate you by telephoning all the last names like yours in the phone book?

Is the child who is playing with your children also the client of your agency? Are you a room mother to several children from client families? Is the waitress at the luncheonette receiving public assistance and moonlighting illegally? What is your responsibility when, on a Saturday night, you are in a local "hangout" and see a client whose probation orders are to refrain from inhabiting this establishment and to avoid contact with former friends (with whom he is playing pool)? And what about your own life? Whose car is in front of your door? Are you a part of the community Monday through Friday, gone to "the city" for the weekend? How well is your property kept up? And how do you feel knowing that your children's behavior as well as yours are public knowledge?

In an urban area, most of these issues are nonexistent; in the rural area they are part of everyday life and both add to and confound the complex role of the rural social worker. An example of this occurred recently in an Appalachian community when the local battered women's shelter was unable to utilize the services of an expert plumber because he was the abusing spouse of one of the residents (and this information was something "everybody" knew).

Newcomers to rural areas are often surprised and troubled by the myriad social problems they encounter. With in-migration and improved communication and transportation, many "city" problems are cropping up in rural areas, and such problems are compounded by the more limited resources of rural areas. The very distances that must be traveled by social workers and health professionals to provide even basic services is unexpected. A local, western North Carolina truism is that distance is not only measured in actual miles traveled but must be measured in "mountain miles"—those minutes or hours it takes to get from "here to there." And often, the formula "You can't get there from here" is a reality. Roads are often snow covered and impassable in winter and muddy, rutted, flooded, and equally impassible in spring or fall. The saying "The good Lord willing and the creeks don't rise" is not a poetic idiom but an expression of reality.

Most funding formulas for providing social services are based on direct client interaction. The time necessary to provide these services (i.e., transportation time, telephone) is rarely reimbursed by state or federal monies. Since it is as difficult for clients to get to an agency as it is for staff to go to them, more often than not effective delivery of services becomes the outreach responsibility of the agency.

The relative scarcity of services is another factor the social work practitioner must confront. Rural areas are notoriously underserved in terms of child welfare, health, mental health, educational, and training resources. The assumed ability of the rural social worker to provide service linkage is severely handicapped by the nonexistence of formal services. Yet many informal and effective services are already in place and can be accessed merely by "the asking." A major task for both the new and the experienced rural social worker is to locate the "natural helpers" in the community and to work toward developing linkages between these persons and the formal agencies. Natural helpers may best be described as those members of the community who are personally motivated to help, have natural helping skills, and are accepted and respected members of the community. One of the most amazing natural helpers I have ever encountered was a lifelong resident of a black community in southern Illinois. A minister with her own church in an isolated rural area, she not only knew each member of her community but also was connected by knowledge, experience, and expertise to the formal helping systems. When she asked an agency for assistance, she knew the problem, the client, the family, the community, and the agency system far better than most of the professional staff. Her call essentially would be "Here's what's needed; do it." And we did. And this worked reciprocally—she was the person the agency called for advice, information, and problem solving. Every rural community has people like this. It is the role of the formal helping systems to find and learn from them.

Other informal helpers available in the rural community are the "gatekeepers" and "opinion leaders." Family and friends must come to be perceived by the social worker not as part of the problem but as allies in finding solutions to problems. Neighbors can provide information and support, and most pastors are intimately involved with the lives of members of their congregations. Many of these people know the local resources, know what is needed and/or missing, and can help to provide the essential linkage between the formal (and somewhat forbidding) services and the informal (and more welcoming) systems.

The social worker who is moving into a rural community must come to that community ready to listen and learn. He or she must enter with few set notions about specific solutions to problems to be encountered. If social workers can be flexible, they are less likely to find resistance to their services. Many professionals have dutifully read about their new locale, and most have developed preexisting ideas about what the people and life will be like. However, a stereotype is neither an individual nor a community. There is the same range of diversity within identified groups as between groups. The group history, length of time in an area, the extent of interaction with outside groups, all play into individualizing the person within his community and culture.

My Journey

In my journey, I have thought of Lopez's Eskimo informant and the need to listen a lot. I have listened to neighbors, storekeepers, longtime residents, and students from the region. I have enrolled in classes dealing with local culture and history, which have been invaluable in providing a foundation for understanding and a forum to think through how to integrate professional knowledge and ethics with community values in a way that will do no violence to either. I have found out what people value and the accepted style of introduction and interaction. Moving into a rural home, I became aware of the care that was lavished on the upkeep of property. I began cosmetic repairs on outside areas long neglected, cleared brush and trash, and planted flowers. Inadvertently and luckily, I had stumbled into a functional entry to the community because working outside made it possible for people to look me over without appearing to do so and to decide, without pressure, the level of interaction they wished.

I began to learn the dialect and the importance of place. I smiled when, after a few years, one of my neighbors said, "You know, you're getting to be a real southerner."

I continue to listen, to ask, to participate, and to learn and share. Perhaps this, as much as birthplace alone, is what makes an Appalachian.

References

Anglin, Mary. 1983. "Experiences of In-migrants in Appalachia." In *Appalachia and America*, A. Batteau (Ed.). Lexington: University Press of Kentucky. Pp. 227–38.

Beaver, Patricia. 1986. *Rural Community in the Appalachian South.* Lexington: University Press of Kentucky.

Daley, Nelda, and Sue Kobak. 1990. "The Paradox of the 'Familiar Outsider.'" *Appalachian Journal* 17(3):248–60.

Davenport, Joseph, and Judith Davenport. 1984. "Josephine Brown's Classic Book Still Guides Rural Social Work." *Social Casework* 65(7):413–19.

———. 1998a. "Rural Communities in Transition." In *Social Work in Rural Communities* (3d ed.), Leon H. Ginsberg (Ed.). Alexandria, Va.: Council on Social Work Education. Pp. 39–54.

———. 1998b. "Economic and Social Development and Rural Social Work as a Model of the Generalist Approach for the 21st Century." In *Preparing Helping Professionals to Meet Community Needs,* Shirley J. Jones, and Joan Levy Zlotnik (Eds.). Alexandria, Va.: Council on Social Work Education. Pp. 45–58.

Daw, Jonathan, Neal Lineback, Arthur Rex, and Mark Heglin. *The 1990 Census Atlas of North Carolina.* Boone, N.C.: Appalachian State University

Devore, Wynetta, and Elfriede G. Schlesinger. 1999. *Ethnic-Sensitive Social Work Practice.* 5th ed. Boston: Allyn & Bacon.

Ginsberg, Leon H. 1998. "Introduction: An Overview of Rural Social Work." In *Social Work in Rural Communities* (3d ed.), Leon H. Ginsberg (Ed.). Alexandria, Va.: Council on Social Work Education. Pp. 3–22.

Hanson, K. 1966. "The Joy of a Working Vacation." *U.S. News and World Report,* June 10, 89–90.

Lopez, Barry. 1986. *Arctic Dreams: Imagination and Desire in a Northern Landscape.* New York: Scribner's.

Morales, Armando, and Bradford W. Sheafor. 2002. *The Many Faces of Social Work Clients.* Boston: Allyn & Bacon.

Morris, Lynn C. 1995. "Rural Poverty." In *Encyclopedia of Social Work* 3:2068–85. Washington, D.C.: NASW Press.

North Carolina Child Advocacy Institute. 2002. *The Children's Index . . . ; a Profile of Leading Indicators of the Health and Well-being of North Carolina's Children.* Raleigh: North Carolina Child Advocacy Institute.

Sheafor, Bradford, and Robert Lewis. 1995. "Social Work Practice in Rural Areas: Appalachia as a Case Example." In *Social Work: A Profession of Many Faces* (7th ed.), A. Morales and B. Sheafor (Eds.). Needham Heights, Mass.: Allyn and Bacon. Pp. 403–30.

Sue, Derald W., and David Sue. 1990. *Counseling the Culturally Different.* 2d ed. New York: John Wiley & Sons.

United States Bureau of the Census. 2000. *Simple Demographic Profiles. Current Population Survey.* Washington, D.C.: U.S. Government Printing Office.

Waltman, Gretchen. 1986. "Main Street Revisited: Social Work Practice in Rural Areas." *Social Work* 66(8):467.

Chapter 4

Remembering the Dead, Comforting the Living: Adapting Christian Ministry to Appalachian Death Practices

Marc Sherrod

A couple of weeks after the death of her father, I visited Mary in her home. A native of Avery County, as had been her father before her, Mary was part of an extended family with enduring roots in the mountains of western North Carolina. She did not seem particularly distraught since he had been sick for some time. She asked me, "Do you want to see the pictures that we took of Daddy?" She got up, and when she returned, she sat down beside me and opened a family photo album, turning to the page displaying pictures of her daddy—that is, the corpse of her daddy—lying in his casket at the local funeral home. As we looked at those pictures, I sensed that they served as a mourning catalyst, helping Mary to express love for her father as well as her own feelings of grief and loss. She spoke of how her young son and daughter would one day treasure those final photographs even as she treasured them now.

Blanche's middle-aged son had died tragically in an automobile accident not long before I talked with her about his death. "If you watch someone go out of sight, you'll never see him again—alive," she said to me as we sat in her kitchen.

> I know it's true 'cause I saw my son go beyond the Social Services building the night he was killed. I've heard people say, "Don't watch people go out of sight." . . . I did put my housecoat on and watch[ed] him cross the road and go by Social Services out of sight and next day I saw him, he was dead. . . . I watched him by the streetlight—it was 1:00 A.M.—I started to follow him. . . . My mother and grandmother always told me, "Don't watch someone go out of sight. . . ." I wanted to go after him—I could have reversed it—but what would people think of me going out towards the pool hall [with a housecoat on at 1:00 A.M.]. . . . I'd give anything in this world if I had.

Blanche shared this folk belief—her trust in "them old things," as she put it, passed down through several generations of her family—as a way to cope with her son's untimely death. She voiced her remorse and anxiety by turning to a "superstitious belief" in order to come to terms with the mysterious and perplexing nature of a death in her family.

The pastoral obligation to care for the dying and the bereaved and to officiate during funeral and burial ceremonies meant listening carefully to stories like those of Mary and Blanche, for they narrated important truths about the human experience of grief, anguish, and ambivalence when death occurs. Both women's families had been residents of the southern mountains for many generations. Mary was a Presbyterian and regular participant in the mountain chapel I served as pastor; Blanche grew up as a "Hardshell Baptist" in nearby Carter County, Tennessee and sometimes attended a Christian (Disciples of Christ) Church in Newland, North Carolina. My seminary training for ministry in the Presbyterian Church (USA) had not prepared me for the diverse and unusual approaches to death taken by many of the mountain Christians in my community.[1] Mary's pictures and Blanche's use of a folk belief were not ways of coping with mortality that I had previously encountered, either during my adolescence in the rural South or in preparation for the ministry as a young adult. On the one hand, I knew that photographing the dead and explaining a sudden death by resort to a folk belief were not practices that necessarily represented the habits of everyone under my spiritual care. On the other hand, these practices did strike me as unusual and deserving of theological reflection. Was the photographic preservation of a "memory picture" of the loved one's dead body (and the underlying mortuary "arts" of embalming and cosmetic facial restoration that helped make the corpse presentable for the photograph) a practice that trivialized the Christian doctrine of the resurrection (see Crissman 1994; Ruby 1995)? Did this kind of memory making constitute a form of reverence for one's family (or even ancestor worship) that could potentially diminish one's primary allegiance and devotion to God? Did relying upon a "superstitious" belief to interpret death's mystery make sense as an explanation for an event whose immediate cause was medically known? Or, from the perspective of Christian theology, what was I to do with an interpretation of death's timing that suggested no familiarity with the traditional language of the church (e.g., trust in God's providence, sovereignty, or grace)? Issues such as these loomed large for me as I sought to reconcile my own sense of pastoral vocation with the religious and cultural context of ministry in the southern mountains.

Gradually I realized that authentic ministry called for a deepened pastoral understanding of mountain death practices without compromising the integrity of practical theology. Building on the work of Paul Irion in his groundbreaking book *The Funeral and the Mourners* (1954) and Paul Connerton's *How Societies Remember* (1989), Thomas G. Long recommends in his essay "The Christian Funeral in American Context" that the first task of practical theology during the hour of death is to describe "the complex constellation of ritual activity set into motion by a death, all of [which is] embedded in a matrix of cultural attitudes, traditions, fashions, and conventions" (1999:87). By observing, studying, describing and reflecting upon my regular interfacing with mortality and grief, I could be empowered to come to terms with the cultural and theological world view and ethos that death practices "performed" in the lives of the people with whom I shared a pastoral care relationship.

Appreciating the Lived Religious Experience of Mountain People

My reflexive turn to contemplate the purpose of ministry turned into the pursuit of a style of practical theology that honored both the church's faith tradition and the cultural particularities of bereaved individuals and their families. Put differently, the challenge was to figure out how to mingle the principles of practical theology gained from training in a mainline Protestant seminary with the reality that some death practices in the mountainous region of North Carolina were foreign to my experience and outside the orthodox theological scope of the church. How should I balance the teaching of correct doctrine with the formation of meaningful pastoral care relationships based on respect for the life situation of those who trusted me as an agent for the healing of grief? I had been taught to model a non-anxious presence with the grief-stricken, to listen to each particular story of sorrow. But what should I do with my own theological angst as I encountered death practices that seemed to contradict certain theological categories for organizing the practice of ministry?

The nervous voice of the apologist for orthodoxy gradually softened. I realized that embedded within the narratives I heard and the practices I observed was the teller's own particular stance of faith and confidence in God—even though their words and customs seemed, at times, "superstitious" or even unusual or quaint. In other words, culturally sanctioned or conditioned beliefs and practices for contending with death did not necessarily lessen the relevance and authenticity of an individual's or a family's commitment to Christianity. The stories and practices representing the struggle of mountain folks to come to terms with death reflect what I have come to call their experience of "lived religion" (see Orsi 1994; Hall 1998). This understanding of religion is less concerned with describing religious institutions, leaders, creeds, doctrines, or codes of conduct than it is with unfolding the reality of what religion means for people in their everyday life and experience. What spiritual resources do people utilize as they negotiate their way through times of change, crisis, or uncertainty? What strategies for coping with feelings of anger or loss "make sense" to individuals and families as they confront death, experience grief, or recall memories of a loved one? I came to realize that such practices as cemetery decoration days, telling folk beliefs, or memorializing loved ones through a published tribute in the county newspaper were particular ways people "lived" their religion on a daily basis.

The vitality of a "non-institutional" dimension of religion for mountain folks does not negate the importance many of them would attach to correct belief and behavior, particularly as doctrine and ethics are taught in the Bible, interpreted by the minister and other church leaders, or function as an unspoken code regulating actions and declaring pervasive moral truths. Conversion, salvation, eternal life, grace, Scripture, and so forth remain critical doctrinal categories viewed as essential dimensions of religious faith and practice in the southern mountains. American religious historian Catherine Albanese in *America: Religion and Religions* offers a helpful distinction between "extraordinary" and "ordinary" religion in the regional religion of the southern mountains. Thus, in Appalachia, an "organized and extraordinary religion [that is] mostly Protestant and, in large measure, Calvinistic" coexists with a more ordinary religion that emphasizes the role of "the family as the most important religious and social institution" (Albanese 1981:242, 235). In her chapter "Regional Religion: A Case Study of Tradition in Southern Appalachia," Albanese's analysis paralleled my own observations about a distinction in mountain religiosity between more institutional or "churchly" forms of religion and the "lived religion" of ordinary time and space. In fact, many of those approaches to dealing with death that I found surprising or unusual were expressions of familial and personal religious experience not necessarily connected with the extraordinary dimension of religious knowledge or the practice of churches. A series of observations across the cultural landscape of my community illustrate the vitality of ordinary religion as the bereaved shape religious memory through the material cultures of death and social practices for coping with grief.

Consider, for instance, the memorial tributes that the bereaved publish in the weekly county newspaper, the *Avery Journal* (*AJ*), often in conjunction with important calendar celebrations within the family, such as Christmas, Mother's Day, a wedding anniversary, or the deceased's birthday.[2] These printed tributes and commemorations appear weekly, conveying familial sorrow and reminding the reading public of the dynamics of grief and the need to revitalize the memory of the dead. The granddaughter of Delana Cooke memorialized her grandma, on what would have been her eighty-seventh birthday, by remembering her skills as a quilter:

> But the greatest quilt with love she pieced together,
> Is the family she made that will love her forever.
> For her love has lasted longer than any thread known,
> To hold together any quilt she had cut out and sewn.
> So now when I see the quilt lying there,
> I think of her joy and the love she has shared.
> Her flowering love that will never wilt,
> And will hold together Grandma's Greatest Quilt.
> (*AJ*, Dec. 22, 1994)

Similarly, on what would have been the seventy-sixth birthday of W. B. "Short" Gragg, his family pictured him taking the hand of Jesus in the promised land, standing at heaven's picture window as though preaching to the living: "Family and friends through the blood of Jesus is the only way" (*AJ*, Sept. 1, 1994). A mother grieved the death of her baby daughter by describing her divine vision of an incomparably beautiful rose that became covered with snow only to reappear when the sun later came out and melted the snow away: "So now at last I realize, yes, Noell, I know, the grave holds not bitter pain and sorrow, just a rose . . . beneath the snow" (*AJ*, Aug. 24, 1994). The anniversary of death brings anxiety and the renewed pursuit of consolation. As the years pass, inevitably, the memory of the deceased slips out of communal awareness. The publication of a memorial tribute calls newspaper readers to remember what the bereaved will never forget. On the anniversary of her son's death, Cloe Hartley Stewart remembered March 12 as "the saddest of the year. . . . Only those who have lost a child / Can tell the pain of parting with one so dear." This mother, however, took solace in the fact that "as I was saying 'Goodbye' / Jesus was saying 'Hello'" (*AJ*, Mar. 15, 1994). The retention of the child in memory hinged on the eschatological exchange of an earthly goodbye for a heavenly hello. The memorial of death's anniversary coincided with a reminder that the memory of this mother's "lost" child had not passed into oblivion.

Connecting evangelical religious experience and the memory of loved ones with the material objects and reality of everyday life is an important link evident in many of these newspaper memorial tributes. Quilts, roses, and looking out picture windows are but a few of the ways in which memory becomes intertwined with the embodied actions of daily life. D. R. Young's family imagined him as now having "a weedless garden to stroll through, grown by the Master's own hand" (*AJ*, Nov. 3, 1994); the friends and family of Jacque Hughes Childress remembered her birthday by comparing her love for walking along the beach with their testimony that "now you walk the streets of gold" (*AJ*, Nov. 30, 1994). These tributes also commemorate the "good" death of a gentle dying. In a "Tribute to a Mountain Man," a daughter holds the hand of her father, who "is sick and silently dying." She recalls their walks along Roaring Creek and the chirping of bluebirds. As her father "falls asleep," she believes that "his soul ascended the mountain—straight into the arms of God." She constantly feels his presence, even though her father is gone, for "the creek still echoes his voice, and the bluebird sings his song" (*AJ*, Nov. 16, 1989). A natural theology, evident in a profound reverence for the mountains, becomes, for this grieving daughter, a way of coming to terms with the fact that, yes, the life of her deceased father continues, but in a remembered sort of way that will be quite different from her previous experience. His journey into the afterlife has not left her fatherless because of her own religious trust and the natural signs of his continuing presence in the sounds and sights of the southern mountains. For many mountain folks, the publication of memorial tributes represents a way to mingle grief and faith, personal reminiscences and the desire for communal memory. The *Avery Journal* is one "site" coalescing the personal and the communal search for resolution to grief. More concrete as sites of religious memory are the cemeteries that dot the landscape of the county.

American cemeteries and graveyards endure as ubiquitous locations to "read" the ordinary or lived religion of personal, familial, and communal devotion. This is no less true in Avery County. The epitaph "Gone but not forgotten," the single most common tombstone phrase in the county, suggests that the space of burial in the southern mountains represents an important sacred space of memory. End-time beliefs among more conservative Appalachian Christians concerning the body's reconstitution at the second coming of Christ, the grave as the place for the final rite of the dead separating from the living, the proximity of family and kin who are "asleep in Jesus" (another ubiquitous gravestone phrase) alongside one another in the "beds" of their interment, and the ritual activity of loved ones visiting the grave, either privately or on a family's cemetery decoration day—all of these beliefs and practices turn the grave into a site for healing grief, affirming core religious beliefs, and maintaining the memory of the dead. Hallowing and sentimentalizing the home as the locus of devotions is a common way religious experience and death become intertwined in the space of mountain cemeteries. A familiar gravestone motif, for instance, depicts several people walking on a road lined with Fraser fir trees leading toward a cabin with smoke coming out of its chimney, framed by snow-capped mountains. Gravestone commemorations of the mountain cabin and a regional identity are reminders of the particularity of death's intersection with the ideals and hopes of survivors. The gravestone of a contemporary Avery County resident, buried in the Daniels' Family Cemetery, illustrates the vitality of a lived religious outlook. In this case, the family has resorted to the use of Scripture as a way to remember and sacralize the deceased's favorite recreational activity, hunting. This particular headstone contains the etching of a bear's head, hunting dogs, a hunter firing a gun, and a quotation from the first book of the Bible: "He was a mighty hunter before the Lord" (Gen. 10:9). Here, the world of the Bible and the world of the deceased as remembered by the living are fused into one world, identifying the remote time of a biblical past with the ordinary or everyday activity of this "mighty hunter." As the anthropologists Elizabeth Hallam and Jenny Hockey note in their study of the material cultures of death, "Objects and images are infused with a bittersweet quality evoking that which they cannot replace and providing touchstones for inchoate feelings of grief" (2001:19). From live and artificial flowers with words and emblem messages left at grave sites, to elaborate etchings on tombstones, to decoration days at local burial grounds, the mountain cemetery reflects a symbolic universe that stages the "performance" of the "ordinary" religious experience of individuals, families, and kin groups.

Sometimes, as mountain folks draw near to death, language that describes the "extraordinary" dimensions of religious faith and experience merges with the impulse to root devotion in the ground of a sacred place. Ed, a lifelong resident of the western North Carolina mountains, lying on his deathbed, used doctrinal language to draw upon the assurance of God's providential and electing activity in his life. Just before he died, he testified that nothing could divert the sovereign intentions of his transcendent Creator, who orchestrated death's timing. The act of dying also became an occasion to exhort his family to bury him in the particular soil of the Mount Pisgah United Methodist Church Cemetery. "Bury me on top so I can look out and see the Grandfather [Mountain]," he told them. Ed's religious outlook, anchored by doctrine and God's transcendent character, was never acknowledged as at odds with an everyday natural theology that identified God with the intimacies of nature. Even in death, his desire was to remain connected—indeed, to become one with—the sacred quality of the mountainous landscape that had contributed so much to his identity as a Christian and a "mountain man," as he liked to call himself.

Some of the mountain families suffering loss couched their performance of beliefs about mortality and the afterlife by referring to Scripture and the teachings of Christian tradition. I remember, for instance, going with an elder of one of the county's Free Will Baptist churches to visit his small family cemetery adjacent to his house. As we stood beside the grave of his teenaged son, who had died in an automobile accident many years earlier, I remarked about a picture of his son inside a locket that had been inserted into the gravestone. This image of his son in the fullness of youth prompted a verbal reference to 1 Thessalonians 4:16: "The Lord himself shall descend from heaven with a shout, with the voice of the archangel, and with the trump of God: and the dead in Christ shall rise first." This elder then added, "I hope the Lord comes back before any more have to die." The citation of Scripture on gravestones remains the single most convincing proof of the vitality of the Christian cosmology that unites extraordinary and ordinary religious experience. Gravestone etchings of praying hands, lambs, roses, the cross, or an open Bible add to the religious aura cast over the southern mountains.

Less conventional from the perspective of extraordinary religion is the practice of telling a folk belief to explain death's timing. These stories, often featuring a sign in nature that, in retrospect, predicted the arrival of death, represent acts of bereavement that facilitate the healing of grief and point to divine providence. "If a bird flies into your window, it's a sign that somebody in your house is going to die" was an often repeated folk belief. Several widows related this folk belief as an entry point for renewing the memory of their husbands' final months on earth and for reencountering their own struggles with the meaning of his death and their grief. What became clear during the course of my pastoral visits was that a reliance upon such an event in nature to predict a forthcoming death was not intended to contradict faith in God; rather, the bird flying into the window was a divinely appointed sign sent to signal an approaching death in the household. Only in retrospect, these widows told me, were they able to discern that God had, in fact, been preparing them for the despair of death's separation. But there was clearly in their minds a correspondence between this event in nature and the unfolding of a husband's divinely determined destiny. The recollection of this event from daily life resourced memory's healing power and confirmed knowledge of God's continuing care.

The practice of healing grief comes in many forms, like these narratives that feature a folk belief. Many variations of folk beliefs used to explain aspects of death have been documented across North Carolina through the monumental study *Beliefs and Superstitions from North Carolina,* in particular, the section of volume 7 titled "Superstitions: Death and Funeral Customs" (Hand 1961). More common as a way of coping during the immediate aftermath of death are the formal and informal ritualized practices undertaken to demonstrate solidarity with the bereaved. In the southern mountains, because of the importance of familial networks and neighborliness, contending with death and engaging in the process of grief and healing are rarely experienced in isolation. The liminal or transitional time between the separation brought by death and the reincorporation of the bereaved back into the world of the living is the critical moment when the community of friends, family, church members, and neighbors attempt to make their presence palpably present to the bereaved.[3] Often, gestures of consolation express a "lived religion." Gift giving at the time of death is a simple and time-honored way that one's "religion" becomes visible during the crisis of sorrow. Preparing and delivering a cooked dish to the bereaved involves sharing the highly symbolic gifts of time, love, and, most important, feelings of mutual sympathy and compassion; it is a tangible way to enact and (often) nonverbally to communicate a stance of religious support and trust. One who shares his or her religious faith through the gift of food (or flowers, cards, etc.) can likely count on the generous reciprocity of others at the giver's future time of need. Sometimes, of course, explicit references to the value of prayer or Scripture accompany the gift as a further expression of the giver's religious commitments: the simple yet richly suggestive words "Just remember, I'm praying for you," "Jesus never forgets his own," or "He never gives us more than we can handle."

As Tom Long argues in his previously mentioned article, no longer is there uniformity in the meaning of the religious rituals American Protestants use to dispose of the dead body. Yet Appalachians, as with most rural whites in the United States, generally enact the root metaphor of death as inaugurating the journey into the afterlife (as opposed to urban Protestants, who view funeral rites as primarily for the transformation of the mourners). The mourners in the southern mountains who attend funeral and burial rituals are the ones who "perform and reenact the conviction that the deceased is traveling from this world to the next accompanied from the deathbed to the grave by the faithful." Everything from a reluctance to leave the body unattended, repeated viewings of the corpse made to look lifelike by the mortician, "dressing up" the body for its journey, gifts of food to the family, and walking in procession with the body to the space of interment illustrate the centrality of this journey motif for mountain people. Thus, the preferred mountain pattern dictating the body's movement is always from home, to church or funeral home, to the cemetery, and thence into heaven. And thus the growing popularity in American society of the memorial service in which the body would be cremated or buried first in a private ceremony, followed then by a celebrative gathering of remembrance as a therapeutic alternative for the mourners—this pattern for funeral and burial rites would be rejected by longtime mountain residents (Long 1999:98).

Members of kin, community, and church circles who respond to the crisis of death typically do so out of a spontaneous sense of a personal faith. The visitation at the funeral home, usually the night before the funeral service, puts an emphasis on ordinary religion freed from the control of church and clergy. The ritualized display of the cosmetically restored corpse becomes a public occasion in which the bereaved can "feel" the supportive presence of the prayers and concern of others who have come to "give their respects" to the family. Survivors derive spiritual comfort and emotional equilibrium by means of their participation in this ceremony of viewing the corpse and visiting with others; indeed, having a prescribed role to perform during this liminal period between death and burial provides survivors with a memorable counterbalance to the threat of death to shatter enduring familial and social relationships.

In summary, then, the human confrontation with mortality—as death approaches, as the dead are buried and remembered, as the living grieve—offers a unique perspective for viewing the particular shape and substance of what a "lived religion" looks like among residents of the southern mountains. Everything from newspaper memorial tributes and photographs of the dead to gravestone markers, death bed requests, folk beliefs, the practice of giving gifts, and the funeral home visitation exemplify the manner in which the bereaved and other mourners face the "problem" of death. For many of the people to whom I ministered and with whom I interacted at death, the primary concern was less on what the deceased believed about God or even whether he or she had been "saved" than on what resources the living could call upon in order to relieve the burden of the survivors' anguish and suffering.

After a couple of years of ministry in Avery County, I discerned an array of practices that empowered the bereaved to cope with death. Various rituals and practices brought religious assurance and emotional stability to the bereaved that appeared to be as meaningful as whatever words from Scripture or the Christian tradition I might offer in my official status as pastor. Or maybe, as I began to surmise, although doctrinal formulations and ecclesiastical positions were not without relevance in people's lives, theological concepts and definitions often failed to resonate with the everyday experience of living with loss. Folk beliefs and mountaintop burial grounds, the reciprocity of gift exchange, and the ritualized words spoken during a funeral home visitation were spiritual resources that cultivated an everyday context for remembering the dead and claiming faith.

For my ministry to have value and meaning in people's lives, it was crucial for me to interpret mountain death practices such as folk beliefs and funeral rituals in a pastoral light. On the one hand, I knew that many of these practices were unique neither to western North Carolina nor to the Appalachian region in general. On the other hand, at times they did suggest some persistent features and characteristics of a regional religiosity. Over time, reflection on an "Appalachian way of death" helped to bridge my own faith commitment and preparation for the pastorate with a deeper appreciation of my context for ministry.

Understanding the Appalachian Way of Death

The pastoral practice of giving spiritual care to the dying and the bereaved and officiating during funeral and burial rites entailed a sensitivity to the life situation of the grief-stricken as well as bearing witness to the Christian response to death and the search for hope. If I, nonetheless, neglected to grasp the "world" mountain folks inhabited as they encountered mortality and remembered the dead, could ministry be authentic and relevant? I needed a broader perspective to connect the theology and practice of ministry with the particular dynamics of my cultural setting and the distinctive pastoral care issues rising from that setting. Stated differently, I needed to learn how to "listen" to the ways in which members of my church and community contended with death in the context of their everyday lives as well as their familial strategies for achieving stability in the wake of death's disorienting presence.[4]

A consideration of the anthropology of funereal customs and practices in America was one way to ponder the varied ways people confront their mortality. The authors of *Celebrations of Death*, for instance, argue that the rites of passage associated with funerals embody a system of symbols "that express the core of life values sacred to the society at hand" (Huntington and Metcalf 1979:19).[5] In other words, to comprehend the central values and religious commitments of a particular group of people, it is important to reflect on their attitudes toward the dead, the particular complex of narrative, symbols, and ritual practices that they rely upon in order to bring order and meaning out of the chaos left in the wake of death. What is more, to borrow a phrase from a recent study of cremation in America, I came to realize that, although mountain death practices are conservative in nature, there is an underlying impulse toward "ritual improvisation" that animates the encounter with mortality and grief (Prothero 2001).

If the first step of practical theology is descriptive—"What's going on here?"—then I had to pay attention to mountain death practices in all of their variation and ritual complexity. What function, for instance, in religious ritual improvisation, does the decoration day ceremony play in the expression of religion as a cultural system of meaning? This annual practice of cleaning the cemetery of brush and debris, placing freshly cut flowers on the graves of loved ones, participating in a time of prayer, Scripture reading, or hymn singing, and sharing in the conviviality of food and fellowship is an important symbolic gesture that lends insight into the intersection of religious values and cultural practices. The various "cults of piety" evident in the care of the cemetery are ways to honor ancestors, express communal devotion to the past, reinforce the bonds of group solidarity, and affirm the Christian belief in the continuing existence of the faithful in heaven (Jeane 1989:107–36). Mountain kin groups typically celebrate this event separate from the presence of nonmountain families. The decoration day ceremony, therefore, seems to be a rich and significant ritual moment in which mountain folks establish a boundary that symbolically declares their "difference" from other residents of the mountains who do not share a similar traditional orientation or disposition to revere a remote past. This practice—along with others mentioned earlier, such as images celebrating the mountainous landscape on gravestones or newspaper memorial tributes—points to persistent attitudes, beliefs, and practices that help people to orient and anchor themselves in the face of death's threatening presence.

Ceremonies and ritualized practices that help the living to remember the dead are not the only expressions of religiosity contributing to a regional view of death. Two anthropologists who made a comparative study of communities in the eastern and bluegrass regions of Kentucky have argued for the distinctiveness of Appalachian bereavement practices. Thomas Garrity and James Wyss (1980) found that in the mountainous areas of eastern Kentucky, death had a more visible, familiar reality than it did in the bluegrass region of the state. For example, family and kinfolk seemed to surround the dying in greater numbers in Appalachian Kentucky, and there seemed to be a greater preference in eastern Kentucky for audible crying at funerals and for displaying bodies in homes and churches. Their study suggests that people of eastern Kentucky "have greater intimacy and contact with death, the dying and the bereaved, before, during and long after the actual occurrence of death" (Garrity and Wyss 1980:108). Throughout my time of ministry, Avery County continued to receive an influx of new residents, mainly wealthy retirees and part-time summer residents. I began to realize that even within my own church setting, noticeable differences regarding death attitudes and practices persisted between mountain families and newer residents in the community who became participants in the life of our church.

My observations and pastoral experiences hinted at a contrast between the approach to dying and bereavement practiced by those having deep roots in the mountains ("natives") as juxtaposed with those not having long ties to the region ("foreigners").[6] One part-time summer resident from Florida, for instance, could not understand why children, grandchildren, nephews, nieces, and cousins would line the halls of a local hospital in a kind of all-night vigil or death watch for the matriarch of their family. To this "foreigner," such a practice and its accompanying noise and disrespect for other patients, seemed an intrusion on the medical community's space of authority and expertise. Another new resident thought the custom of "parading" before the public's eye one's feelings of grief and sadness in newspaper memorial tributes inappropriate and something only "uneducated people would do." In general, I noticed a contrast between "natives" and "foreigners" regarding the values and meanings they attached to such ritualized practices as funeral home visitations or the ways they would choose to memorialize a loved one. There did, however, seem to be a substantial common affirmation of an evangelical ethos based upon beliefs such as salvation through commitment to Jesus Christ as Savior and Lord, a coming divine judgment for all, the authority of Scripture, and so forth.

Certain discernible cultural differences regarding beliefs, attitudes, and practices about death still left me wondering if it was either wise or possible to think in terms of a regional view of death. Many of the customs and behaviors concerning human mortality that I had encountered were, in fact, consistent with approaches for dealing with death present in the rural South or in American culture generally. The methods lifelong residents use to dispose of the body are really not much different in the southern mountains than they are across the United States, especially among rural populations, the same methods that have dominated American mortuary practices since the late nineteenth century: rapid removal of the deceased from the site of death, embalming the corpse, applying the mortician's cosmetic arts to give the appearance of sleep, the ritual display and "last gaze" of the cosmetically restored body at the funeral home, a service led by clergy in the funeral home chapel or some local house of worship, and earth burial, including a brief committal service also led by a member of the clergy.[7] According to Gary Laderman's cultural history of the twentieth-century funeral home, it is the temporary preservation of the corpse through the art of embalming that took center stage in American mortuary arts until the closing decades of the century: "Embalming allowed survivors an opportunity to look death square in the face and, in its still silence, recognize life's finality without experiencing the destabilizing terror and dread typically associated with corpses and the processes of dying (2003:104). The morticians at the local funeral home in Newland report that on rare occasions, a mountain family of Avery County might still hold a traditional all night wake at the deceased's home or church; generally, however, the manner for handling the dead follows the larger pattern present throughout rural white American society. As already described, the mountain decoration day ceremony is a time for kinfolk to gather each summer at the family cemetery to clean the graves, remember the dead, and celebrate the ties that bind (Beaver 1986). Yet this practice clearly has affinities with southern practices for remembering the dead, such as those identified by Gwen Kennedy Neville in her book *Kinship and Pilgrimage: Rituals of Reunion in the American Protestant South* (1987).[8] The mountain approach to death, then, shows continuities with social, cultural, and religious patterns that were certainly not restricted to the southern mountains.

In one sense, the boundaries between my Appalachian context for ministry and the broader contours of American society were permeable and fluid. Members of my church and community approached death largely from the perspective of evangelical Protestant Christianity, the rural South, and, more broadly, the general disposition toward death evident in American culture as a whole. In another sense, however, the geography and history of the region and the persistence of certain folk elements suggested to me that there was something distinctive about the ritual improvisation and local response to death that called for my continuing reflection and attention. Part of that distinctiveness related to the various particularities of the practice of a "lived religion" described earlier in this chapter; another aspect focused on the geography and landscape of the region and the symbolism of the mountains for residents. Is it possible to talk about something as nebulous as a "religion of place" for a people whose family history, occupations as shrubbery and Christmas tree farmers, or sense of the rhythm and flow of time are so tied to the particular space in the southern mountains?[9] What does it mean when members of an extended kin group, for example, attending their annual cemetery decoration day, conclude their time together by joining hands around a large tree in the center of the cemetery and sing, "God Be with You Till We Meet Again"? In what ways does communion between the living and the dead get reinforced in mountain churches which celebrate their annual homecoming in the summer in conjunction with the decoration of graves in the nearby cemetery? What roles do memory, honoring the past, and a sense of place play for those ascending a hill to visit the grave of a loved one? Discerning answers to questions such as these would extend our understanding of those beliefs and customs that contribute to the mountain perspective on death. Similarly, attention to the memorializing practices of particular church groups, such as those discussed by Howard Dorgan in *Giving Glory to God in Appalachia* (1987), would provide additional layers of insight into a regional perspective on the intersection between religion and death.

Although she does not address mortuary attitudes and practices in Appalachia, the book on mountain religion by Deborah Vansau McCauley (1995) has confirmed many of my suspicions about the history of Christianity in the region. That is, that there are two major strands of Protestant Christianity there, one more "homegrown" and the other the product of historical forces from outside the region. McCauley recognizes the importance of distinguishing between Appalachian mountain religion and religion in Appalachia. The former is more closely identified with the matrix of land, family religiosity, and a particular church history rooted in a regional past; the latter is that which bears more similarity with "mainstream" Protestantism, particularly those currents of evangelical Christianity that dominated the late-nineteenth- and early-twentieth-century attempts to missionize Appalachians. Richard Humphrey's (1984) description of mountain religion is also useful, since he recognizes that the dominant ethos of evangelical Protestant Christianity actually coexists with a "religion of Zion" consciousness, a vital undercurrent that has a pronounced influence on the mountain view of death and the afterlife.

In Avery County, an evangelical world view dominates the religious landscape, particularly through the high visibility of Baptist, Methodist, and Presbyterian churches that dot the county. The holiness or Pentecostal influences that McCauley (1995) identified in the southern mountains are also prominent religious traditions whose influence we are only just now beginning to appreciate. As I thought about beliefs and attitudes related to human mortality during my time of ministry in the southern mountains, it seemed that the lifelong mountain residents who attended the various churches of the county lived in two worlds simultaneously: one, a world of mountain religion with particular patterns of memory and regional identity related to the dead, and the other, a world of evangelical Christianity that shared in transregional patterns of American religiosity and perspectives on death. While it was rarely easy to separate what was "Appalachian" from what was "American" or to discern at what points the two merged and coalesced, I became convinced of the reality of "something different" as I sought to listen and learn from the particular nuances and inflections that mountain folk gave to their Christian faith as it intersected with the way they coped with death.

Suggestions for the Minister as Giver of Pastoral Care

Many demands compete for the time and attention of ministers as they carry out their various roles and functions, including the tasks of preaching, teaching, church administration, counseling, and providing pastoral care. As early as the 1840s in pastoral care handbooks published in America, mentor ministers warned protégés to be careful how much time they would give as pastors to preparing funeral sermons and spending time with the bereaved (Humphrey 1842:224). The question of how a minister is to allocate his or her time and energy with the dying and the bereaved remains a contested issue as models for ministry shift in response to changes in practical theology and cultural context. To reflect on the meaning of death for members of one's religious community, especially the connection between death and the people's lived religious experience, might get "lost" among all the ever-expanding list of pastoral obligations and time constraints. Nonetheless, a willing commitment to meet with the dying and grief-stricken is critical to the formation of relationships with church or community members and their widening webs of family and kinfolk. The same people who will often forgive a pastor's shortcomings as a church administrator or teacher, for example, will be less likely to pardon a pastor who never seems to have time to hear their story of loss and sadness. Pastoral insensitivity to the spiritual needs of the dying, an inability to hear the family's struggle for meaning and purpose, or an unwillingness to attend to the many dynamics of the grief process can all translate into a sharply reduced relationship of trust between minister and people. In order to enhance the pastor's capacity to bring understanding and healing to the pain and anguish experienced by those encountering death, there are several steps he or she can take to evaluate, intervene, and help bring resolution with those experiencing feelings of anger or abandonment that death often brings.

First, education about the particular dimensions of one's ministerial context must be ongoing. This is especially crucial for those who are "natives" neither by birth nor by an extensive time of residence in the mountains. Familiarity with the literature describing the milieu of the southern mountains and narrating aspects of the region's distinctive religious history can ease the pastor's transition into the world of practices and customs that might at first appear unusual, quaint, or even "backward."[10] In addition to McCauley's fine book on Appalachian religion and a study of death and dying customs in central Appalachia by James Crissman, recent publications by Bill Leonard (editor) and Loyal Jones frame important religious matters in their mountain context. Jones, for instance, notes that in the southern uplands, an "organic and natural relationship with the cycle of life and death, seeing it always around them, ordinary folk talk more frankly of death than do those who may feel that dwelling on death and tragedy is somehow unsophisticated" (1999:48). Oral history projects with church members or others in the local community can certainly lend credibility and sensitivity to one's overall ministry, perhaps especially with regard to the issues and context for death and dying. Having said that, however, grasping this context can be an elusive project; there are few written resources to consult, and even mountain culture itself is not homogenous, as variations in death practices and customs are evident as one moves from place to place in the southern mountains. In fact, the absence of homogeneity is a sure sign that the plural practices of ritual improvisation put Appalachians squarely in the American mortuary mainstream. The pastor's time spent gaining local knowledge is, I think, the most instructive, efficient, and fruitful way to ponder this intersection of death and life. To analyze and appreciate the people's experience of "lived religion" is the crucial first step for coming to terms with the distinctive spiritual resources that mountain folk evoke to negotiate their passage through times of transition, crisis, change, and uncertainty.

Such "listening" to the local culture entails developing at least a few of the ethnographer's skills: developing a keen sense of observation, learning how to evaluate one's "data" in a nonjudgmental fashion, making comparative analysis, and so on. Keeping one ear "tuned" to the world of ethnography became, for me, an ally and friend. The cultivation of these ethnographic skills were not, however, ends in themselves but served the larger purpose of enriching my own pastoral sensitivity and presence with those whose lives had been profoundly shaken by death. The pastor who makes an effort to meet people on their own terms and to respect their views and practices is probably a pastor who, in the long run, will have the greatest rapport and trust at those crucial moments of life crisis and passage when those who feel bewildered or forsaken desire some word of comfort and hope. Similarly, the pastor who studies and appreciates the particular dynamics of a region's religious history can come to a deepened understanding of the beliefs and attitudes that shape regional expressions of Christian faith. The pastor who grapples with history can also begin the (often painful) process of critical reflection on his or her denomination's ambivalent record of involvement over time in a particular geographic area. In my case, I had to acknowledge that the Presbyterian Church in the past—sometimes with good intentions yet often blind to the reality of the authenticity of mountain religious faith and practice—had often been paternalistic and self-serving with regard to its history of home missions in the southern mountains (Sherrod 1993).

Second, a part of developing healthy and supportive relationships with members of one's church and community, especially at the time of transition such as that brought about by death, is to be aware of what ideas and expectations the people have of the minister's role and function. The minister as "family chaplain" was the most commonly held image that the mountain folk I lived and worked with seemed to have of the pastor. While I never heard anyone actually use this term to describe me or my ministry, it is a descriptive term that captured what many lifelong residents of the mountains understood to be my essential function or purpose. As a hospital chaplain makes regular visits to patients, so a large part of my expected role was that of spending time with families and kin groups: visiting in their homes on a frequent basis; taking part in their celebrations of life cycle events such as birthdays, weddings, and, of course, the rituals and practices associated with funerals; and in some ways simply acting as the always present (and friendly) neighbor to the family groups who formed the extended church family. Such a strong emphasis on the pastor's expected presence with family and kin relationships is not surprising given, for example, the anthropological literature that identifies the dominant position of family and the kin network throughout many sections of the southern mountains (Keefe 1988).

My understanding of family dynamics, especially the minister's role in life cycle events, was greatly enhanced by a book on the family systems approach to pastoral care by Rabbi Edwin Friedman. He argues for a three-layered approach to counseling and pastoral care that considers the families within one's congregation, the congregation as a family system, and the personal families of the clergy. Friedman, furthermore, recognizes that rites of passage, a funeral for instance, is a time of passage not just for the deceased but also for the whole family. He writes that "death is the single most important event in family life," and the potential of funerals to either help resolve family problems or to create new ones can have enormous implications for generations to come. The clergy person or other professional who is assisting the family in their time of passage has the potential to effect change in that family structure as no one else does (Friedman 1985:168). Death, in other words, is often a crucial moment when entire family groups can experience alienation or reconciliation, guilt or forgiveness, fear or hope.

In as much as mountain folk often expect the minister to take on the role of a "family chaplain," he or she regularly receives a level of trust, respect, and confidence normally afforded a wise and trusted member of the family. This status as an "insider" within the mountain family often offers a unique entree for helping individuals, families, and kin groups experience healing as they contend with issues of grief and bereavement and sort out the meaning of the deceased's life and death in the midst of ongoing family ties and dynamics. My position as "family member" led to many powerful experiences in the context of issues around dying and death. One particularly memorable moment involved a lifelong resident of Avery County—with whom I had a long pastoral care relationship—who asked that I stand in the receiving line during the funeral home visitation for her deceased husband. Her desire, specifically, was that I "fill the void" left in her family by the death of her son who had died many years earlier. While I both honored this request and recognized the impossibility of honoring it entirely, this "double role" represented an important reference point during future pastoral visits. On an almost daily basis during my ministry in western North Carolina, reflecting on the expectations of me as "family chaplain" facilitated and enriched my ability to serve and to help the families of my church and community.

Third, the minister who takes seriously his or her role as one who can intervene and facilitate healing should realize the high value individuals and families place on prayer and Scripture reading. These time-honored practices within the Christian faith, especially as they are shared by the minister during the hour of death, are crucial conveyors of the message of salvation and the hope of eternal life. Part of the importance of the Bible and prayer is intertwined with people's lived religious experience, devotional piety, rootedness in a Protestant evangelical ethos, and participation in the work and ministry of a local congregation. The aural nature of Scripture read aloud and prayers spoken during a pastoral visit represent essential resources for assisting the sick, the dying, and the bereaved to regain their equilibrium and to enable them to voice what they perceive to be the larger divine purpose or meaning being revealed in their lives. To rehearse the story of salvation through explicit reference to the life of Jesus and the events of the cross and resurrection, or to recall the various visions of heaven contained in Scripture, is both a theologically and pastorally appropriate act as well as one that invites the bereaved to incorporate their own "narrative" into the faith community's unfolding story that transcends time. The widows who spoke of their loss by referring to a folk belief featuring a bird flying into a window for instance, identified with stories such as the accounts of Jesus raising Lazarus from the dead or the sorrow of Jesus' mother at the cross.[11] Since doctrinal issues for many of those encountering death are less important than discovering resources to aid them in their time of "existential" crisis, the devotional writings of the Psalmist, Jesus' encounters with the diseased or the dying during his earthly ministry, or the events surrounding the cross, resurrection, and ascension of Christ can grant powerful insights into human ambivalence in the face of death.

At the same time, the pastor should not neglect listening to the bereaved's own voice as it merges with that of Scripture. I sat in the kitchen with a lifelong resident of Avery County whose only surviving relative, a daughter, I had recently helped bury. "You know where Jesus says, 'My God, my God, why hast Thou forsaken me?'" she said. "That's how I feel right now. That's how I feel." Locating the points at which human experience intersects with the world of Scripture enables the minister to assist the bereaved in fathoming the depths of their pain, thus enhancing the process of healing and recovery.

The pastor should also ponder the symbolic power of the "family Bible" as a sacred object and as something that bonds families together over generations. Not only did many mountain families in my community continue the old practice of entering births, baptisms, weddings, and deaths as a genealogical accounting of their family history, but they also often stored within the pages of the Bible obituaries, funeral home memorial cards, newspaper tributes, and pressed flowers from a loved one's casket spray. Incorporating memory-provoking items such as these into the sacred world of Scripture was one way to affirm the living's love for the deceased and to testify to the commitment to perpetuate their sacred memory. In addition to its teaching about spirituality, theology, or ethics, the Bible thus has an iconographic status that nurtures the human encounter with the divine even as it enriches the desire to remember deceased loved ones by inspiring and renewing the bereaved's communion with the dead.

Yet another aspect of why the pastor should remain sensitive to the importance of Bible and prayer is the persistence and importance in the southern mountains of extraordinary religion. Time-honored religious beliefs and values practiced and affirmed in church worship services, prayer meetings, hymn sings, baptisms, and decoration days shape the living's search for meaning, order, and resolution during and after the time of death. The pastor, for example, should not fail to appreciate the powerful stimulus to memory, the possibilities for the transformation of suffering, and the enduring connection with a regional religiosity represented by old hymns such as "Beulah Land," "Amazing Grace," "Sweet Hour of Prayer," "What a Friend We Have in Jesus," "In the Garden," or "If I Could Hear My Mother Pray Again." Of all the elements of extraordinary religion, hymns seem to have the greatest capacity to recreate a sense of the past while striking the chords of memory, nostalgia, and hope. Time and time again as I visited with the bereaved on the anniversary of a loved one's death, the music from the funeral service was that which was most vividly remembered—not the prayers, sermon, or Scripture readings.

The reality of human mortality often confronts the living with unavoidable, painful, and perplexing dilemmas. Why does God allow suffering? Is there an afterlife and, if so, is that a realm where *my* loved ones continue to exist? In what ways should I try to perpetuate a loved one's memory? For how long should mourning and bereavement continue following the death of a spouse? At what point does honoring the dead become a way of living in the past and denying life in the present? These and many other questions challenge the minister to take seriously his or her pastoral responsibilities to bear the presence of reconciliation and hope to those whose lives have been disrupted by death. Certainly, Christians have a particular perspective on the transitory nature of life and death as well as the endurance of the soul beyond mortality and oblivion. Nonetheless, the need to remember the dead and to experience relief for the emotional distress and turmoil of grief is, perhaps, the glue that binds all of humanity together in a common condition, regardless of the presence or the absence of a religious preference. Understanding the particular ways that Christians in Avery County, particularly the lifelong mountain residents among them, cope with death was essential for my practice of ministry and the reflexive act of facing my own mortality.

Notes

Some of the material in this essay is taken from my Appalachian studies master's thesis, "Asleep in Jesus: Death Rituals in Southern Appalachia," Appalachian State University, 1990. I would also like to thank Maria Braswell for her assistance in gathering data for this chapter. The names of the informants mentioned herein are pseudonyms.

1. For background information on Reformed Theology and the particular beliefs of the Presbyterian Church, see Leith (1981).

2. See the front page article on Charles Spraker of Craig County, Virginia, a local man known for his writing of obituaries, who began writing them because of his "heartfelt observations on the old-time mountain people." "In Tender Prose, He Honors Lives Passing," *Roanoke Times and World-News,* May 30, 1994; for a discussion of death notices in a very different context, see Davies (1994:24–39).

3. The interpretation of the tripartite movement from one status to another (separation, transition or liminality, and reincorporation) was originally articulated by Arnold Van Gennep (1960); see also Turner (1969).

4. The importance of ministers and theologians "listening" to their local culture is suggested by Schreiter (1985).

5. See also Geertz (1973).

6. These labels are applied by the lifelong residents as a way to distinguish themselves from those whose wealth, life-style, and values often contrast sharply with traditional mountain ways and customs. More than one "native" shared with me their anger and disdain for "foreigners" who placed No Trespassing signs on their property.

7. While cremation is gaining in popularity in the United States, this option for disposal of the body seems less widely accepted among mountain people, who prefer traditional earth burial. The traditional practice of neighbors and family digging graves for the deceased continues for many of Avery County's lifelong residents. For a good overview of the literature and recent issues regarding perspectives on the dead body, see the twin study of Laderman (1996:1–11 and 2003:119–69); on the "last gaze" and its connection with embalming and the rise of the funeral home industry in the late nineteenth century, see Laderman (1996:174); on cremation, see Stephen Prothero, *Purified by Fire: A History of Cremation in America* (2001).

8. See also Crocker (1971).

9. See Humphrey (1984:122–41).

10. Assumptions about Appalachians' "backwardness" have often dominated writing on the region by ministers and mission workers who have come to live in the region; see, for example, those of Presbyterian minister Jack Weller (1965).

11. For a contrasting use of biblical narrative in more of a prophetic than a pastoral context, see Hinsdale, Lewis, and Waller (1995:175–208).

References

Albanese, Catherine L. 1981. *America: Religion and Religions.* Belmont, Calif.: Wadsworth Press.

Beaver, Patricia D. 1986. *Rural Community in the Appalachian South.* Lexington: University of Kentucky Press.

Crissman, James K. 1994. *Death and Dying in Central Appalachia: Changing Attitudes and Practices.* Urbana: University of Illinois Press.

Crocker, Christopher. 1971. "The Southern Way of Death." In *The Not So Solid South,* J. Kenneth Moreland (Ed.). Athens: University of Georgia Press. Pp. 114–29.

Davies, Jon. 1994. "One Hundred Billion Dead: A General Theology of Death." In *Ritual and Remembrance: Responses to Death in Human Societies,* Jon Davies (Ed.). Sheffield, Great Britain: Academic Press. Pp. 24–39.

Dorgan, Howard. 1987. *Giving Glory to God in Appalachia: Worship Practices of Six Baptist Subdenominations.* Knoxville: University of Tennessee Press.

Friedman, Edwin H. 1985. *Generation to Generation: Family Process in Church and Synagogue.* New York: Guilford Press.

Garrity, Thomas, and James Wyss. 1980. "Death, Funeral and Bereavement Practices in Appalachian and Non-Appalachian Kentucky." In *Death and Dying: Views from Many Cultures,* Richard Kalish (Ed.). Farmingdale, N.Y.: Baywood Publishing. Pp. 108–28.

Geertz, Clifford. 1973. "Religion as a Cultural System." In *The Interpretation of Cultures.* New York: Basic Books. Pp. 87–125.

Hand, W. D. (Ed.) 1961. *Popular Beliefs and Superstitions from North Carolina,* Vol. 7. Durham, N.C.: Duke University Press.

Hall, David D. 1998. *Lived Religion in America: Toward a History of Practice.* Princeton: Princeton University Press.

Hallam, Elizabeth, and Jenny Hockey. 2001. *Death, Memory and Material Culture.* New York: Oxford University Press.

Hinsdale, Mary Ann, Helen M. Lewis, and S. Maxine Waller. 1995. *It Comes from the People: Community Development and Local Theology.* Philadelphia: Temple University Press.

Humphrey, Heman. 1842. *Thirty-Four Letters to a Son in the Ministry.* Amherst, Mass.: J. S. & C. Adams.

Humphrey, Richard. 1984. "Religion and Place in Southern Appalachia." In *Cultural Adaptation to Mountain Environments,* Patricia Beaver and Burton Purrington (Eds.). Athens: University of Georgia Press. Pp. 122–41.

Huntington, Richard, and Peter Metcalf. 1979. *Celebrations of Death: The Anthropology of Mortuary Ritual.* New York: Cambridge University Press.

Irion, Paul. 1954. *The Funeral and the Mourners: Pastoral Care of the Bereaved.* Nashville: Abingdon Press.

Jeane, D. Gregory. 1989. "The Upland South Folk Cemetery Complex: Some Suggestions of Origin." In *Cemeteries and Gravemarkers: Voices of American Culture,* Richard E. Meye (Ed.). Ann Arbor: UMI Research Press. Pp. 107–36.

Jones, Loyal. 1999. *Faith and Meaning in the Southern Uplands.* Urbana: University of Illinois Press.

Keefe, Susan Emley. 1988. "Appalachian Family Ties." In *Appalachian Mental Health,* Susan Emley Keefe (Ed.). Lexington: University of Kentucky Press. Pp. 24–35.

Laderman, Gary. 1996. *The Sacred Remains: American Attitudes Toward Death, 1799–1883.* New Haven: Yale University Press.

———. 2003. *Rest in Peace: A Cultural History of Death and the Funeral Home in Twentieth-Century America.* New York: Oxford University Press.

Leith, John H. 1981. *Introduction to the Reformed Tradition: A Way of Being the Christian Community.* Atlanta: John Knox Press.

Leonard, Bill J. 1999. *Christianity in Appalachia: Profiles in Regional Pluralism.* Knoxville: University of Tennessee Press.

Long, Thomas G. 1999. "The Christian Funeral in American Context." *Papers of the Henry Luce III Fellows in Theology* 4:87–106.

McCauley, Deborah Vansau. 1995. *Appalachian Mountain Religion: A History.* Urbana: University of Illinois Press.

Neville, Gwen Kennedy. 1987. *Kinship and Pilgrimage: Rituals of Reunion in American Protestant Culture.* New York: Oxford University Press.

Orsi, Robert. 1994. "'Have You Ever Prayed to Saint Jude?': Reflections on Fieldwork in Catholic Chicago." In *Reimaging Denominationalism: Interpretive Essays,* Bruce Mullin and Russel Richey (Eds.). New York: Oxford University Press. Pp. 134–61.

Prothero, Stephen. 2001 *Purified by Fire: A History of Cremation in America.* Berkeley and Los Angeles: University of California Press.

Ruby, Jay. 1995. *Secure the Shadow: Death and Photography in America.* Cambridge: MIT Press.

Schreiter, Robert J. 1985. *Constructing Local Theologies.* Maryknoll, N.Y.: Orbis Books.

Sherrod, Marc. 1993. "The Southern Mountaineer, Presbyterian Home Missions, and a Synod for Appalachia." *American Presbyterians: Journal of Presbyterian History* 71, no. 1 (Spring): 31–40.

Turner, Victor. 1969. *The Ritual Process: Structure and Anti-Structure.* Chicago: Aldine Press.

Van Gennep, Arnold. 1960 [1909]. *The Rites of Passage,* Monika Vizedom and Gabrielle Caffee (Trans.). Chicago: University of Chicago Press.

Weller, Jack. 1965. *Yesterday's People: Life in Contemporary Appalachia.* Lexington: University of Kentucky Press.

Part II

Acquiring Cultural Competency: Understanding and Respecting the Appalachian "Difference"

In Part I, authors identified several distinctive aspects of Appalachian culture, such as rural southern mountain speech patterns and certain death practices. Whenever cultural differences are identified by an outside reference group, it is common for those differences to be misunderstood and judged deficient in some way. In Part II, authors explore ways of not only increasing awareness of cross-cultural similarities and differences but also understanding their meaning within the Appalachian frame of reference and developing acceptance of and respect for those differences.

The approach to working with culturally diverse peoples recommended implicitly by the authors in Part II has been developed most fully in the emerging field of "cultural competency." The cultural competence model was first elaborated in 1989 in the field of children's mental health by Cross et al. in *Towards a Culturally Competent System of Care.* A continuum of negative to positive positions was identified categorizing transcultural approaches of individuals and institutions, including (1) "cultural destructiveness," in which racist and ethnicist attitudes, beliefs, and behaviors do damage to other cultural groups; (2) "cultural incapacity," in which discrimination is reduced but prejudice continues to be culturally destructive to individuals and groups; (3) "color blindness," which claims to treat all people equally and seeks to ignore diversity thereby threatening adequate service delivery; (4) "cultural precompetence," which recognizes cultural differences and the need to increase awareness and skills in working with members of other cultural groups; (5) "cultural competence," which values diversity and adopts the process of developing cross-cultural knowledge; and (6) "cultural proficiency," which recognizes advanced competence, contributions to the knowledge base of culturally competent practice, and the promotion of culturally appropriate services to clients. The cultural competence model has had a significant impact on services because it can be applied to both individuals and institutions and because it incorporates not only cultural sensitivity to values and attitudes but also programmatic attention to behaviors, structures, and policies (Mason, Benjamin, and Lewis 1996). In the 1990s, federal grants and initiatives have developed requirements for addressing cultural competency in applications, and many state grants and agencies also have begun to require attention to these issues (Hernandez and Isaacs 1998). Agencies far beyond mental health have been and likely will be affected by the cultural competence model, including maternal and child health, public health, education, substance abuse services, child and family welfare, employment training, and criminal and juvenile justice (Hernandez and Isaacs 1998; Mason, Benjamin, and Lewis 1996).

The cultural competence model has been applied most commonly to people of color, in particular to four major American ethnic categories: African American, Latino, Asian American, and Native American (Isaacs-Shockley et al. 1996). However, authors stress that there is considerable cultural diversity within these ethnic categories, such as the overlap of race and ethnicity among black Hispanics and the range of less acculturated to more acculturated Asian Americans. Furthermore, authors recognize that the model can also be applied to other cultural groups, including Euro-American subgroups such as Jewish Americans and Appalachians, as well as to nonethnic categories of diversity, including gays and lesbians, the homeless, the handicapped, and the working poor (Mason, Benjamin, and Lewis 1996). It should be noted that these cultural categories do not include mainstream Euro-American culture because it is assumed that this is the culture of most practitioners and the dominant institutions in America, a point which relates to the introduction to Part I, which encourages reflexivity and the understanding of one's own culture and personal background in the context of practice.

The cultural competence model addresses several domains of competence, including (1) an "awareness level" that involves the process of developing an awareness of one's own cultural heritage and cultural stereotypes about others and an ability to recognize and learn to respect cultural differences in other groups; (2) a "knowledge level" that actively seeks to acquire specific knowledge about one's own culture as well as the cultures of clientele through self-study, professional training, and the pursuit of cross-cultural experiences; (3) a "skills level" that involves learning specific culturally appropriate skills for assessment, intervention, and evaluation; and (4) an "institutional level" that addresses changes in institutional policies and structures in order to ensure cultural competence is activated at the societal level (Campinha-Bacote 1994; Hong, Garcia, and Soriano 2000; Mason, Benjamin, and Lewis 1996).

The chapters in Part II address the second domain of cultural competence, issues of "cultural knowledge" in the Appalachian context. In order fully to understand and appreciate a cultural group, it is necessary to learn how its members see the world, in other words to grasp their "emic" perspective. In order to do this, one must understand the concept of culture, that it is learned and patterned in predictable ways. It also requires setting aside preliminary judgments, adopting a reflexive role, and taking an interest in how others understand the nature of things. Cultural knowledge can encompass many things, a number of which may be discipline-specific for different professionals. Minimally, a practitioner ought to seek to learn about the following aspects of cultural knowledge with regard to Appalachians:

Language, dialect, and nonverbal communication
Cultural values
Phases of the life cycle
Gender roles
Intercultural heterogeneity (races, ethnic groups, rural/urban differences, geographic subregions)
Cultural history
Family organization and child-rearing patterns
Social organization (household, community, institutions)
Religious orientation
Regional economic and political organization
Social change and social problems

Several excellent resources with extensive bibliographies with regard to Appalachia are available on these topics (e.g., Ergood and Kuhre 1991; Higgs, Manning, and Miller 1995; Obermiller and Maloney 2002).

In Part II, Susan Abbott-Jamieson's chapter introduces the reader to the Appalachian pattern of parent/child co-sleeping. She points out that, in a family-centered society, this practice serves as a means of cementing the child's later interdependence with parents. She also points out that this behavior is common cross-culturally and that it is the American pattern of infant/child sleeping-in-isolation that is, in fact, more outside the "normal" range. Meanwhile, she situates the intolerance of American medical practitioners for the Appalachian practice in the cultural context of American mainstream values of independence and the primacy of the marital couple. Finally, she describes her application of this understanding of the Appalachian "difference" in intervention efforts aimed at reshaping the perceptions of both medical professionals and Appalachian mothers with regard to co-sleeping, by encouraging professionals to increase their tolerance and reassuring mothers about the normalcy of their behavior. Thus, Abbott-Jamieson's chapter actually moves from stimulating awareness of an Appalachian cultural difference, through an understanding of its meaning within the cultural context, to the application of this cultural knowledge and intervention.

Chapters by Charlotte Chase and Anne Blakeney describe the development of training programs that aim to produce cultural competence among practitioners working in the Appalachian region. They summarize methods by which they were able to develop these professional training programs and help trainees acquire cultural knowledge, including grantsmanship, research and publication, curriculum development, and continuing education opportunities. Both mention that these techniques successfully enabled students to identify their own and others' stereotypes about mountain people and culture. Both also point out that native Appalachians are no more likely than non-Appalachians to have developed a consciousness of their culture and are just as likely to have learned to be intolerant of the Appalachian difference. Blakeney, in particular, suggests that one important outcome of these training programs is that they serve to increase pride among native Appalachian professionals in their own Appalachian heritage and to improve their sense of self-worth, promoting self-healing as well as an abstract appreciation of Appalachian culture.

Both Chase and Blakeney juxtapose two models of professional training, one that emphasizes "culture-free" (i.e., "color-blind") professionalism and another that emphasizes culturally competent as well as technically competent professionalism. The vignettes presented by Blakeney generously illustrate the pitfalls of the "culture-free" technical competence model that potentially may not only fail to solve but also aggravate the problem.

References

Campinha-Bacote, Josepha 1994. "Cultural Competence in Psychiatric Mental Health Nursing: A Conceptual Model." *Mental Health Nursing* 29(1):1–8.

Cross, T., B. J. Bazron, K. Dennis, and M. R. Isaacs. 1989. *A Monograph on Effective Services for Minority Children Who Are Severely Emotionally Disturbed.* Vol. 1 of *Towards a Culturally Competent System of Care.* Washington, D.C.: Georgetown University Child Development Center, National Technical Assistance Center for Children's Mental Health.

Ergood, Bruce, and Bruce E. Kuhre (Eds.). 1991. *Appalachia: Social Context Past and Present,* 3rd ed. Dubuque, Iowa: Kendall/Hunt.

Hernandez, Mario, and Mareasa R. Isaacs (Eds.). 1998. *Promoting Cultural Competence in Children's Mental Health Services.* Baltimore: Paul H. Brookes.

Higgs, R. J., A. N. Manning, and J. W. Miller (Eds.). 1995. *Appalachia Inside Out.* Knoxville: University of Tennessee Press.

Hong, George K., Margaret Garcia, and Marcel Soriano. 2000. "Responding to the Challenge: Preparing Mental Health Professionals for the New Millennium." In *Handbook of Multicultural Mental Health: Assessment and Treatment of Diverse Populations,* Israel Cuellar and Freddy A. Paniagua (Eds.). San Diego: Academic Press. Pp. 455–76.

Isaacs-Shockley, Mareasa, Terry Cross, Barbara J. Bazron, Karl Dennis, and Marva P. Benjamin. 1996. "Framework for a Culturally Competent System of Care." In *Children's Mental Health: Creating Systems of Care in a Changing Society,* Beth A. Stroul (Ed.). Baltimore: Paul H. Brookes.

Mason, James L., Marva P. Benjamin, and Sarah A. Lewis. 1996. "The Cultural Competence Model: Implications for Child and Family Mental Health Services." In *Families and the Mental Health System for Children and Adolescents: Policies, Services, and Research,* Craig Anne Heflinger and Carol T. Nixon (Eds.). CMHS Vol. 2. Thousand Oaks, Calif.: Sage. Pp. 165–90.

Obermiller, Phillip J., and Michael E. Maloney (Eds.). 2002. *Appalachia: Social Context Past and Present,* 4th ed. Dubuque, Iowa: Kendall/Hunt.

Chapter 5

Mediating Perceptions of Parent/Child Co-sleeping in Eastern Kentucky

Susan Abbott-Jamieson

In the late 1980s, I began a new ethnographic field research project whose focus was to be family life and child-rearing patterns in an eastern Kentucky county. Not long into this work, I became aware of a conflict between local child-rearing practices and pediatric practice as it was embodied in two young pediatricians, New Yorkers doing their two years of postgraduate national service in a medically under-served area—the area where I was conducting my research. They expressed surprise that so many children slept with their parents. They also expressed concern. In their professional opinion, babies should sleep alone. These young doctors' reactions to local, culturally based practices in child rearing were, and continue to be, reflective of the most widely accepted recommendations in pediatric practice: it is best for infants and children to sleep alone (e.g., Shelov 1993; McKenna 2001). This chapter presents my attempts to educate professionals who treat children from the region who may be concerned about parent/child co-sleeping and to reassure local residents that their preferred cultural practices are not abnormal or "questionable."

The cultural competence model (Cross et al. 1989), as Keefe describes it in the introduction to this section of the book, provides a useful way to frame both the typical response of physicians caring for mothers and their children in Appalachian Kentucky and my efforts to educate current and future regional medical practitioners. I will return to this point later.

The Research

Based on several months' fieldwork living in an eastern Kentucky county, I have published a detailed account of the practice of parent/child co-sleeping (Abbott 1992a).[1] The following summarizes my findings reported in that earlier publication.

Perhaps the best way to review local cultural practice is with a table. Table 5.1 presents the responses of 107 mothers to three questions: What was the child's first sleeping location? When you moved the child, where did she/he sleep? What is the child's current sleeping location? Mothers reported that 36 percent of the children started out their lives in their parents' bed, and an additional 47.7 percent occupied their own crib or bed in their parents' bedroom. In other words, 84.1 percent of the children started out their lives in close proximity to their parents, sharing their bed or bedroom.

Considerable movement in sleeping locations subsequently occurred. Some who started out in the parental bed/bedroom were moved out, while others were moved in. These moves were made at various ages and for diverse reasons. The overall trend, however, was that with increasing age, children got moved into their own beds/bedrooms or were shifted into rooms shared with siblings.

Table 5.1. Children's Sleeping Locations as Reported by Their Mother (N = 107)

	Parents' Bed	Parents' Room	Siblings' Room	Own Room
First sleep location	36.4%	47.7%	1.9%	14.0%
Second sleep location[a]	23.4%	21.5%	18.7%	36.4%
Current sleep location[a]	15.0%	20.6%	23.3%	41.1%

[a]Those moved plus those not moved.

The most common age for shifting children out of the parental bed or bedroom was near the end of the first year. Others were shifted later, however; the oldest was nine years old. Among those who were moved at older ages, 31 percent of those who were between two and five years of age continued to co-sleep. A minority, 10 percent, stayed in the parental bed or bedroom into middle childhood, moving out between six and nine years of age.

In addition to age, other factors were examined to see if they helped explain the preferred parent/child co-sleeping pattern. The size of the house was shown to be a factor in initial sleeping location. Those with very large houses (eight or more rooms) were most likely to put their child in its own room from the beginning, but nearly as many persons with large houses kept their infant with them in their own room (three vs. four). No relationship could be demonstrated between children's initial sleeping locations and the number of household residents, the marital status of the parents, or the mother's occupation. On the other hand, persons with university education were least likely to co-sleep with their children in general, and particularly with their sons.

Finally, the birthplace of the mother (but not the father) was shown to be related to children's initial sleeping location. Locally born women were the ones most likely to have their infants and young children in bed with them. This suggests that the high rate of co-sleeping is a regional cultural pattern under the mother's control. The few mothers in the sample who had grown up in Michigan, Ohio, and California were not co-sleeping.[2]

Responses to other questions in the interviews supported the interpretation that mothers seem to be the more important parent in both initiating and maintaining co-sleeping. Mothers spoke about the practice as a two-person event—that is, "I sleep with my child" or "I never slept away from my babies when they were little, never slept alone"—never mentioning the father. Upon further questioning, it was learned that the father was also typically present, but no mother ever said, "We sleep with our baby." Only five married women said their husband slept in another bed.

One of the most commonly discussed features of Appalachian families is the degree and depth of family solidarity (e.g., Brown 1952; Hicks 1976; Bryant 1981; Batteau 1982; Beaver 1986). No one, however, documents the specific socialization mechanisms used by parents now and in the past that result in young adults retaining powerful emotional motivation to remain close to parents and extended family throughout their lives. The interpretation I present in my 1992 article sees parent/child co-sleeping in the eastern Kentucky context as part of an ongoing complex of behaviors and values that are designed to socialize adults toward greater family interdependence. This notion has not escaped at least one contemporary Kentucky writer, an elderly woman now, who comments in her memoir *Common Folks:*

> I don't care what doctors say, I believe it best for the mother and child to be together. . . . These new mothers are losing two of the greatest blessings that God gave mothers—the pleasure of sleeping with your child, and letting it nurse. A closeness that cannot be understood unless you have experienced it. How can you expect to hold onto them later in life if you begin their lives by pushing them away? (Slone 1978:60)

Historical and Cross-cultural Comparisons

Parent/child co-sleeping in early childhood has a venerable history in the region based on available oral history and related material. This literature is fully reviewed in my earlier article (Abbott 1992a:36–37), but to communicate its flavor I will quote from Montell's work based on oral histories describing the period prior to the First World War:

> Another narrator stated that she and her sister slept in the same room with their parents until the sisters were married. A male informant observed that he slept with his mother until he was thirteen years old; his brother, four years older, slept with their father. I asked him if he ever felt a need for privacy during those years. "Well, not too much," he responded. "You see, if you ever take off from home, you'll crave it. It's just what you grow up with." (Montell 1986:29)

This may seem problematic to the North American reader with little or no experience of alternative organizations of family life, who has no knowledge of patterns other than that portrayed in our popular media as the usual and expected. Parent/child co-sleeping as practiced in contemporary eastern Kentucky is not common in urban, middle-class, white U.S. populations based on my review of other studies of Americans' sleeping practices (Abbott 1992a:39–40). There, depending on the study, the percentage of co-sleeping varies from 0 to 11 (Madansky and Edelbrock 1990; Lozoff, Wolf, and Davis 1984; Litt 1981; Rosenfeld et al. 1982). Interestingly, community studies of African Americans in the urban upper Midwest and New England regions report that co-sleeping ranges between 46 and 55 percent (Madansky and Edelbrook 1990; Lozoff, Wolf, and Davis 1984; Litt 1981), placing that population midway between urban, middle-class whites and the eastern Kentuckians in my study. Mosco, Richard, and McKenna (1997) and McKenna (2000), in their more recent reviews of infant sleeping practices in the United States, suggest that infant/parent co-sleeping is underreported. Since it is a highly contested cultural practice in our society, they believe parents have been reluctant to report it. To better understand this pattern, we next turn to the cross-cultural comparative literature on sleeping practices.

Several studies have documented the near-universal practice of mother/child co-sleeping in infancy, which is usually defined as birth to two years of age (Whiting 1964; Barry and Paxson 1971; Konner 1981; McKenna 1986; McKenna 2000). These studies have emphasized the sleeping practices of non-Western peoples, including those who live in rural farming communities or make a living as nomadic hunters and gatherers. Co-sleeping in middle childhood is also reported, although the most frequent pattern is that, upon the birth of the next child (children being spaced two to three years apart when no artificial birth control is available), the toddler is replaced at its mother's side by the new baby. The toddler then sleeps next to siblings. In many of these cultures, the father sleeps elsewhere in his own room or house, or with other adult men in a men's house or on a men's sleeping platform. In many cultures, siblings will be separated into sex-based sleeping groups sometime in mid-childhood.

Perhaps more interesting for us in this context are studies of other industrial, complex societies. The child-rearing practices and patterns of family life in Japan, for example, have been extensively described by both Japanese and American anthropologists interested in Japanese culture. Among the ethnographic sources by Americans is the well-known work by Caudill and Plath (1966) that states that the Japanese continue co-sleeping throughout childhood, with age eleven the age of transition (the process is not completed until age fifteen or sixteen). Subsequent literature continues to corroborate this earlier work for contemporary, urban Japanese (Caudill and Weinstein 1969; Norbeck and DeVos 1972; DeVos 1973, 1983).

We can begin to see that eastern Kentucky sleeping location preferences for infants are similar to the most common practice described in the ethnographic literature. It should be noted that it is highly unusual to separate an infant from its mother in a nightly ritual of solo sleeping. It should further be noted that the eastern Kentucky age of transition away from co-sleeping varies such that 31 percent of children between two and five years of age continue to co-sleep with their parents, while 10 percent are co-sleeping to as much as nine years of age in my sample. This places these Kentuckians somewhere between those urban Americans reported in the literature cited above and the Japanese with their more extended practices.

Japan is a highly successful urban-industrial society, but the Japanese do not value American-style self-reliance and independence (Christopher 1983; LeVine 1990:471; Morelli et al. 1992). The literature typically links Japanese co-sleeping with an emphasis on high levels of family interdependence, as I suggest it is linked to an emphasis on family interdependence in eastern Kentucky (Abbott 1992a). While the Kentuckians do not continue the practice as late as the Japanese, they certainly engage in co-sleeping much more extensively than other white Americans described in the literature.

The Literature on Children's Sleeping Locations

We live in a literate society in which we tend to turn to experts for advice on how to do any number of things, including how to rear our children. Many new parents feel insecure about their new role. Many new mothers have limited experience with newborns because they grew up in a family with few children, far from any extended family that might have provided experience with infants and young children as well as adult advice from their own mothers or other female relatives. Babysitting experience in early adolescence may have provided some experience, as it did for this author, but that experience is also of a circumscribed nature.

In the twentieth century, particularly in the years after World War II, the creation of advice manuals to help insecure, struggling parents cope emerged as a significant industry. Today, the authors of these parenting manuals include social workers, psychologists, and pediatricians, among others. Pediatricians, family practitioners, and psychologists are also available for consultations, provided parents have the financial resources. The pediatrician and family practitioner are probably the most common experts or professionals that a broad spectrum of parents in this country consult on a recurring basis about how they should be caring for their infants and children.

To give some sense of the parental advice literature prior to World War II, U.S. government publications produced by the Children's Bureau are a good place to start. The first publication in the bureau's Care of Children series was concerned with prenatal care of the mother; the second was titled *Infant Care* (West 1972, orig. 1914). These works were a distillation of the standard literature at the time on the care of infants as well as consultation with experts of the day, including physicians, nurses, and other specialists. The intended audience was every mother in the country. The Children's Bureau felt these mothers had the right to know what the best authorities advised so that they could care for themselves and their infants and children in the best possible way. By the time the seventh edition appeared in 1963, nearly forty-eight million copies had been distributed—truly a best seller by anyone's standard!

The collective professional opinion in 1914 was clear: the infant "should always sleep in a bed by himself, and whenever possible in a room by himself" (West 1972:56). West goes on to warn mothers that "not a few babies are smothered while lying in the same bed with an older person, some part of whose body is thrown over the baby's face during heavy sleep" (56). The 1929 edition of *Infant Care,* authored by Martha M. Eliot, repeated the advice to place babies in their own rooms (22, 38) but then expanded discussion of sleep issues with infants by stating:

> Parents must not start the habit of coaxing a baby to sleep by rocking, walking, or holding him, lying down with him, or holding his hand after he is put in bed. He should not be put to sleep with his bottle. He should never be given a nipple to suck or anything else to put in his mouth. (57)

The Children's Bureau continued to publish its successful booklet through several more editions. The 1963 seventh edition written by Laura Dittman was an expanded, redesigned, and rewritten product for a changed America. The introduction gives more attention to fathers, to the need for emotional development in the infant, and to the baby's impact on parents. The list of experts consulted in its preparation expanded to include child psychiatrists and psychologists and parent educators—paralleling the elaboration of specialized knowledge in the culture and expert roles in the society at large.

The advice remained the same, the baby should have its own bed and room (24–25), but there is more elaboration about the reasons for making this recommendation. A special warning is issued that "it may be tempting to take the baby to bed with you, when you are feeding or calming him at night, but it is unwise to do so" (25). The list of reasons provided for avoiding co-sleeping included both problems seen to primarily affect the parents and those seen to primarily affect the babies. Those affecting the parents include the idea that noisy babies disturb parents' sleep, the baby is an intrusion between a married couple which parents will resent, and babies wet beds—"a pest" for parents (25). Those affecting the baby include the danger of smothering, the danger of being hurt by a parent rolling on the baby, and the concern that babies like being near their mothers so much they will decide "to move in" (25). Other than possible physical damage to the infant, the reasons are weighted toward concern with maintaining a particular kind of relationship between the parents. The emphasis on this last point should be noted.

Another influential advisor on child care after World War II was Dr. Benjamin Spock, whose books of advice went through multiple editions. Two of his books, *Common Sense Book of Baby and Child Care* (1957, orig. 1945) and *Dr. Spock Talks to Mothers* (1961, orig. 1954), were examined to see what advice he offered on infants and children's sleeping locations. In *Common Sense*, Spock clearly recommends that babies should have their own beds and their own rooms "at least by the time any 3-month colic is over" (163). A bit further on, he heads a chapter subsection "Out of the parents' room by six months if possible" (164) to emphasize the need for the child's own room. In this section, he explicitly warns that "the young child may be upset by the parents' intercourse, which he misunderstands and which frightens him" (165). He warns in another chapter subsection, "*Better not let the child in your bed*" because "he is apt to cling to the security of his parents' bed" (165). He continues, "I think it is a sensible rule not to take a child into the parents' bed for any reason (even as a treat when the father is away on a business trip)" (165). In his 1961 publication addressed to mothers, he only discusses sleeping locations in regard to two year olds (171). He opposes the practice for this age group, even if the parents do not mind; he further states that parents should not lie in the child's bed with children of this age.

The two overriding concerns for Spock are fear of encouraging dependency on parents and fear that the child may be disturbed by his or her parents' sexual activity. Although almost certainly aware of other cultures' approaches to the sleeping location issue, since he was pediatrician to the daughter of noted anthropologists Margaret Mead and Gregory Bateson and was present for her birth in a New York Hospital, itself an important innovation in its time, he makes no mention of other cultures' practices.

Another pediatrician who today enjoys wide influence both within professional circles and as a prolific writer of advice books for parents is T. Barry Brazelton (1969, 1974, 1992). Unusual among medical writers, he is not only aware that other cultures prefer that mothers and infants sleep together, but he comments on this at some length in two of his publications reviewed for this chapter (1974, 1992).

Brazelton's continuing, overriding concern centers on the issue of the way sleep training in infancy and early childhood is important in encouraging the child's development toward appropriate autonomy and independence. In his view, parent/child co-sleeping is a behavior that will retard this development. In his 1974 book, which appears to be written for both a lay and professional audience, he states flatly, "In our culture, sleeping in bed with a parent is too threatening" (73). He discusses other cultures in which norms allow co-sleeping but ends by saying, "I am sure that no parent in our culture can allow (or encourage) a child to sleep in his or her bed without feeling guilty and ambivalent about it" (73). Brazelton's continued emphasis on pushing for autonomy and independence in early childhood is in part based in his theoretical allegiance to neo-Freudian theory as represented by Erik Erikson's general theory in *Childhood and Society* (1963, orig. 1950), the only work he cites.

Most books of general parenting advice reviewed for this chapter repeat the recommendation against co-sleeping (Shelov 1993; Smith 1996). The American Academy of Pediatrics (Shelov et al. 1991) has prepared its own authoritative advice book, *Caring for Your Baby and Young Child,* which can stand for these books. They want the babies out of the parents' bedroom by four months and recommend against taking a child into one's bed to comfort him or her.

A new literature devoted exclusively to curing children's sleep problems has emerged during the past fifteen years. It seems to be the product of the invention and institutionalization of a new research and medical specialty devoted to studying sleep and treating its disorders (Ferber 1985; Guilleminault 1987; Huntley 1991). Sleep experts such as Ferber (1985) are unconvinced by any cultural argument about the benefits of co-sleeping and, bolstered by their experience in their sleep labs, state, "We know for a fact that people sleep better alone in bed" (38). Ferber reiterates the same points made by Brazelton on independence training for the child and potential effects of the practice on the relationship between the parents (38–40). McKenna (2000, 2001) provides a thorough review of this literature, grounding it in an analysis of the historical patterns of European and American history and Western medical practice.

The overwhelmingly negative attitude toward parent/child co-sleeping is counteracted by one group of advice writers whose work is summarized in a parental advice book written by Rebecca Huntley (1991) titled *The Sleep Book for Tired Parents.* This is a "how to" book for parents who have a child who keeps them awake at night. In an even-handed way, Huntley, who is a psychiatric social worker and parent educator, reviews four strategies for getting children to sleep, each with a distinctive underlying philosophy. The first is the "family bed approach," in which parent/child co-sleeping is the norm.

This approach is associated with the La Leche League in the United States (La Leche League 1987), but is also promulgated by others (Thevenin 1977), including the pediatrician Sears (1987).

Huntley, relying heavily on Sears (1987), points out that there are significant cultural pressures militating against the practice of the whole family sleeping together, but she goes on to delineate more advantages than disadvantages in using this strategy as a way to get one's children to sleep through the night (1991:47–51). Among the specified advantages is the encouragement to be gained from stronger bonding among all family members, not just the mother/infant pair. She also notes among the disadvantages that parents will have less time alone, and that if one has sleeping alone as an ultimate goal, this may be made more difficult to achieve.

Based on the review of advice books for parents, many written by pediatricians, one expects that professional writing will also share the general view that babies and children should sleep alone. The five pediatrics textbooks and specialized works in pediatric sleep disorders covering the past thirty years examined for this chapter conform to this expectation (Brazelton 1974; Levine et al. 1983; Klackenberg 1987; Sheldon, Spire, and Levy 1992; Hoekelman, Friedman, and Wilson 1997). They either assume separate sleeping without commenting on it (Levine et al. 1983; Hoekelman, Friedman, and Wilson 1997), specifically mention co-sleeping but recommend against it (Brazelton 1974; Sheldon, Spire, and Levy 1992), or seem neutral after reporting co-sleeping as an inconclusive factor in certain sleep disturbances of childhood (contradicting other research that cites co-sleeping as a contributor to sleep disturbances; see Klackenberg 1987).

The accepted medical wisdom, then, is that if one wants to promote successful psychological separation from parents (i.e., the mother), one begins the process by requiring the infant and young child to sleep separately, preferably from birth. As one pediatric textbook phrased it,

> Brief, predictable physical separations from the parent facilitate successful psychological separation for young children. The first such separation occurs when the infant is put to bed alone at night. . . . Most parents are uncomfortable with these first separations. (Levine et al. 1983:83)

Further, if one wants to prevent sleep problems, avoidance of co-sleeping is important because it is tagged as one of the five factors that research has identified to distinguish sleep-problem children from other children (Sheldon, Spire, and Levy 1992). Pediatric sleep specialists state that "children should learn to sleep alone, without parental intervention" (Sheldon, Spire, and Levy 1992:76), as one of the basic principles of sleep hygiene in childhood.

In summation, the majority of parental advice books, professional textbooks, and specialized works on children's sleep recommend against parent/child co-sleeping. A few moderate their position by appearing to accept the fact that very young infants—birth to six months or so—may be kept in the parent's bedroom in their own crib. The only exception are the proponents of the family bed concept, who are regarded by many as extreme because they suggest that the whole family should sleep together (Huntley 1991).

Here is a case where two general cultural preferences are being actively rationalized and promoted as based in scientific opinion. First, it is our culture's emphasis on individualism and self-reliance or autonomy that drives a demand that parents send infants to sleep by themselves; better to start training new members of society as soon as possible to avoid any unfortunate "dependence" on parents. This concern is glossed as "fostering autonomy" in the pediatric and parental advice literature. Publications going back many years have discussed the American commitment to core, linked values of individualism or rugged individualism and self-reliance. Older examples include works by Margaret Mead (1942), Geoffrey Gorer (1964), and Francis Hsu (1970, 1972), while more recent work includes Bellah et al.'s (1985) widely read assessment of contemporary middle-class Euro-American values, *Habits of the Heart.*

Second, it is commitment to a family organization that emphasizes the marital pair over other family relations that raises such intense concern about the reduction of intimacy and privacy in the marital relationship (Hsu 1983). In general American culture, the privileging of the marital pair over other family relationships is symbolized in the provision of a separate, private space reserved for their exclusive use. Comparison with the Japanese case clearly highlights both these points, as does a recent study by Shweder, Jensen, and Goldstein (1995).

Shweder and his colleagues have become intrigued by the growing discussion surrounding co-sleeping, which they see as a symbolic action with intimate ties to a cultural community's moral ideals. They present the results of their own comparative research exploring cultural preferences for sleeping arrangements in a middle-class Euro-American sample in the Chicago area and a sample of high-caste families, the Oriyas, in Bhubaneswar, Orissa, India. In both cases, study participants completed a sleeping-arrangements task sorting a hypothetical seven-person family into sleeping locations under diverse resource constraints, then evaluated and ranked the deviant sleeping arrangements that were produced for relative seriousness of breach of moral rules. Among their results are different, ordered preferences for sleeping arrangements for the two sets of respondents.

The Oriyas arrange their sleeping locations according to the four moral preferences of incest avoidance, protection of the vulnerable, female chastity anxiety, and respect for hierarchy. Three moral preferences were implicit in the Euro-American's choices: incest avoidance, what these researchers labeled "the sacred couple," and autonomy. Though both cultural communities shared the incest avoidance principle, they differed in the ages at which it must be applied. While the Oriyas would never let an infant or young child sleep alone because that would violate their moral principles surrounding protection of the vulnerable, nor rarely let sexually mature, unmarried daughters sleep alone because of female chastity ideals, the Americans preferred to put both these categories of family members in separate spaces for sleep because of their different moral commitment to autonomy. The Americans felt the sacred couple principle so strongly they always wanted to place the married pair in a space separate from the rest of the family. This was a rare choice for an Oriya.

So long as those seeking advice from our society's experts participate fully in the same general culture, the advice will probably be experienced as congruent with their own experience and expectations and thus seem "right" and "correct" advice, although they may find it "uncomfortable," as noted by one of the pediatric textbooks cited earlier (Levine et al. 1983:83; also see McKenna's 2001 discussion of the intertwining of American cultural folk assumptions in the construction of the scientific research literature on infant sleep). But what happens when the advice is at odds with the culture of the recipient of the advice?

The Conflict between Local and Professional Practice

In the course of my research on eastern Kentucky child rearing and sleeping arrangements, I noted that many mothers were aware of the professional disapproval of local sleeping practices. Several times mothers commented to me that they knew their doctor did not approve of babies sleeping with their parents. Although made uncomfortable by their doctor's remarks, they did not change their practice. These comments were as often made by middle-class mothers, including professionally trained nurses and schoolteachers, as they were by working-class mothers. These mothers sometimes offered that they had read that it was not a good idea to sleep with your baby.

The mothers did not comment about co-sleeping's impact on their sexual relationship with their spouse, nor did they comment on their husbands' attitudes with one exception. One mother did offer that her husband had been very supportive of their infant co-sleeping with them.

The issue of the potential for incest is often raised by persons who have heard me talk about local sleeping practices. At least one mother in my sample raised the issue while being interviewed. She said she knows incest occurs but she thought it uncommon and an intensely disapproved of behavior. She added that her children had all shared her and her husband's bed and that they had turned out alright—one is now a practicing physician in the region—so she saw no problem with the practice.

Fear of smothering or injuring an infant while it and its parents sleep in the same bed was never mentioned as a concern by these mothers. A few said that they put their newborns in a bassinet or crib next to their bed when they were very young, but when they were a few months older they moved them into their bed next to them. This strategy may have been motivated by concerns about smothering or injuring their baby when it was very young, although they did not say so.

At the conclusion of my formal interviews, I made a point to share with these mothers information about the nearly universal practice of mother/infant co-sleeping. I also told them it was common around the world for young children to sleep within sight and sound of their parents, a pattern produced by culturally mediated housing layouts and sleeping preferences. I would conclude with a description of Japanese practices, pointing out that they often extended co-sleeping into late childhood and early adolescence. This always interested them. They often expressed relief to learn about others' patterns which appeared similar to theirs.

On completing the analysis of my data, I decided to use the knowledge I gained to attempt to influence attitudes and possibly change practice among pediatricians, child psychiatrists, and other practitioners likely to treat or interact with children in the region. I also wanted to find ways to communicate to the general public within the region a positive message about their historic and preferred sleeping practices. At the time, I was a member of the anthropology faculty at the University of Kentucky and held a joint appointment in the Department of Psychiatry in the Medical School.

In terms of the Cross et al.'s (1989) cultural competence model mentioned earlier, my research was located at the "knowledge level"; it described one aspect of local cultural practice that diverges from the cultural folk assumptions of dominant American pediatric practice. I now hoped to push this understanding into the "skills" level of the model through educating future regional medical practitioners so that they could adopt culturally appropriate assessment, intervention, and evaluation skills.

In my efforts to influence medical practitioners, I was able to use the forum provided me by my joint appointment in the Department of Psychiatry. The University of Kentucky hospital serves as a tertiary referral medical facility for the state's entire eastern region, including the area where I conducted my research, and so the medical staff frequently encounters patients and their families from eastern Kentucky. Both medical students and residents as well as faculty come from diverse regions of the United States as well as other countries.

At the time, I presented an annual series of lectures to medical students doing clerkships and newly trained physicians doing residencies in general psychiatry. I also presented a recurring series of lectures to residents training in the Department of Psychiatry's joint residency program in pediatrics and child psychiatry. I devoted one-third of my time to discussing the practice of co-sleeping in the region and situating it within a broader national and international context. Information presented in these forums resulted in spontaneous comments from some residents that they intended to look differently at this practice when they encountered it in their patients.

One psychiatry resident of Indian ethnicity remarked to me after one of these presentations that co-sleeping was the common practice in India; it is the way she had been reared. She added that she had never said anything about this when the issue came up in her classes or in discussion of treatment recommendations for her and others' patients, but now she felt freer to talk about alternatives to the dominant medical view. She personally had never seen co-sleeping as problematic.

I have given psychiatry grand rounds on the theme of co-sleeping whenever invited. In general, my presentations have been well received and have usually provoked lively discussion. I have also been asked to give talks and lead small group discussions on aspects of Appalachian family life and child rearing relevant to medical practice at other medical schools in the region, most recently at the West Virginia School of Osteopathic Medicine in Lewisburg, West Virginia.

Is this approach working? It is hard to say if physicians who are exposed to an alternative way for viewing parent/child co-sleeping in the region change their attitudes in the treatment room. I have not surveyed local pediatricians, family physicians, and child psychiatrists on the topic. I do know, however, that at least one local physician has been convinced, because she presented a public service program on a local radio station based on my published article in *Ethos* (1992a). She was trained at our medical school and did her residency in the Department of Psychiatry.

I also made an effort to communicate the results of my research to both the community within which I did the research and the larger regional public. To accomplish this, I first distributed copies of drafts of the original paper, and later copies of the published version of the paper, to selected opinion leaders in the county where the data were collected. Those who received these materials included the directors and staff of the clinics where I was permitted to interview mothers bringing their children for treatment. I also distributed the materials to the staff at the local church who were most supportive of my general research and the principal of one of the local elementary schools where I conducted some interviews.

I have published a short popular article (Abbott 1992b) in *Across the Ridge,* the newsletter of the Appalachian Civic Leadership Project, which was widely distributed. That article produced a letter from a nurse in an eastern Kentucky practice thanking me for the article. She wrote that she had always felt conflicted and perhaps a bit guilty or bad about sleeping with her babies because medical dogma had led her to believe it was probably a bad practice. Now she felt justified in her practice.

I continue to give talks in the region whenever possible. For example, I gave a talk on the topic at the Annual Meeting of the Anthropologists and Sociologists of Kentucky when it was held in Pikeville, which is situated in eastern Kentucky. This organization attracts a membership from across the state, primarily faculty from the regional universities, small private colleges, and community colleges, as well as some state employees. Undergraduate and some graduate students also attend. Local residents with no particular professional identity may come as well. Following my talk, I was approached by some local women who wished to share their experiences with me and thank me. One commented that she had said to herself, "Oh no, another talk about how we are doing something else wrong," when she saw the title of my talk in the program. Once I began speaking, however, she realized that my message was not the expected condemnation. She thanked me and went on to share her own experiences growing up. She had slept with her parents into middle childhood, and as a parent she had slept with her own babies.

Conclusion

The Appalachian region and its people have been the object of outsiders' commentary and advice for several decades. The region's residents are often ambivalent if not hostile about all this free advice on how they can change and, by implication, improve their patterns of living, their economic well-being, their educational systems, or their religious practices. Additionally, certainly in Kentucky, there is ongoing lively discussion among the region's intellectuals and other concerned, aware citizens about the literary and sometimes academic portrayal of themselves in stereotypes as ignorant and violent people. This discussion once again reached a national audience through the award of a Pulitzer Prize to Robert Schenkkan for his play *The Kentucky Cycle,* which ran for two months at the Kennedy Center in Washington, D.C.

Bobby Ann Mason, herself a Kentuckian and a nationally recognized novelist, discussed Schenkken's portrayal of Kentuckians as violent, greedy, and ignorant, and Kentuckian sensitivity to such portrayals, in an essay appearing in the November 1, 1993, *New Yorker.* She used the mechanism of counterpoint interviews with Schenkkan and Gurney Norman, another Kentucky writer, best known for his 1971 novel *Divine Right's Trip* and *Kinfolks: The Wilgus Stories,* a short-story collection originally published in 1977 and still in print. The Wilgus stories are set in the area of eastern Kentucky where I have conducted ethnographic research, the area where Norman grew up. Norman comments, "Schenkkan may not realize he's written into a living situation. People here resent it, and they feel used" (Mason 1993:60).

Norman's comments are sufficient reason for all of us to be cautious in dispensing advice about how folks can improve themselves. It is a caution that was clearly in my mind when I wrote and distributed my article on local sleeping practices in the community where I had collected the information. I was acutely aware that I had "written into a living situation," and there was a risk that people would "resent it" and "feel used" when I published my articles. For that reason, I have been gratified that reaction at the local and regional levels has been so positive. I feel secure in my efforts to, on the one hand, educate care givers in the Appalachian region about local family and child-rearing practices and patterns, and on the other, to find ways to disseminate information to people in the region that helps them understand and appreciate their child-rearing practices within both their own cultural context and a wider world context. I believe this to be the most important outcome of any research, whatever the reasons for engaging in it in the first place.

Notes

1. In the original study, an opportunistic sample of ninety-seven mothers in pediatric clinic waiting rooms was interviewed regarding their children's sleeping locations throughout childhood. They were also queried about changes in sleeping locations over time and about their feelings at the time. An additional quota sample of twenty mothers, selected on the basis of social class (one-third each lower, working, and middle/upper middle class) and the sex of their child who was the focus of the interview (50 percent mothers of a son, 50 percent mothers of a daughter), was added to the total sample. This second sample of mothers participated in a detailed, open-ended interview focused on one of their children. A wide variety of child-rearing issues and household division of labor were explored in this interview; most lasted at least two hours. They were tape-recorded in their homes.

2. These women had married local men returning to their husband's home community to live.

3. McKenna has devoted many years to research on infant's and mother's sleep practices. He has been particularly interested in the relationship between SIDS (sudden infant death syndrome) and these patterns (McKenna 1986), but his work has grown beyond this initial concern to documenting the complexity of the mother/infant co-sleeping relationship, including patterning of sleep architecture, exchange of gasses, touch, and so on. A discussion of this extensive literature by McKenna and many other researchers, most of it in the medical and psychological research literature, is beyond the scope of this chapter. The reader is referred to McKenna 2000 for a thorough review of the literature.

4. It should be noted that I asked no direct questions about the husbands' attitudes toward co-sleeping, nor about the mothers' sexual relationship with their husbands. This is a limitation of the research being reviewed here. Local cultural norms likely militated against spontaneous disclosures of husbands' or partners' attitudes toward co-sleeping, particularly toward anything about its impact on the pairs' sexual relationship.

References

Abbott, Susan. 1992a. "Holding On and Pushing Away: Comparative Perspectives on an Eastern Kentucky Child-rearing Practice." *Ethos* 20:33–65.

———. 1992b. "Sleeping Arrangements and Family Solidarity." *Across the Ridge* 3:4–5.

Barry, Herbert, III, and Lenora M. Paxson. 1971. "Infancy and Early Childhood: Cross-Cultural Codes 2." *Ethnology* 10:466–508.

Batteau, Allan. 1982. "The Contradictions of a Kinship Community." In *Holding On to the Land and the Lord*, Robert L. Hall and Carol B. Stack (Eds.). Southern

Anthropological Society Proceedings, No. 15. Athens: University of Georgia Press. Pp. 25–40.

Beaver, Patricia D. 1986. *Rural Community in the Appalachian South.* Lexington: University Press of Kentucky.

Bellah, Robert N., Richard Madsen, William M. Sullivan, Ann Swidler, and Steven M. Tipton. 1985. *Habits of the Heart: Individualism and Commitment in American Life.* Berkeley and Los Angeles: University of California Press.

Brazelton, T. Berry. 1969. *Infants and Mothers: Differences in Development.* New York: Delacorte Press.

———. 1974. *Toddlers and Parents: A Declaration of Independence.* New York: Delacorte Press/Seymour Lawrence.

———. 1992. *Touchpoints: Your Child's Emotional and Behavioral Development.* Reading, Mass.: Addison-Wesley.

Brown, James S. 1952. *The Family Group in a Kentucky Mountain Farming Community.* University of Kentucky Agricultural Experiment Station Bulletin 588. Lexington: University of Kentucky.

Bryant, F. Carlene. 1981. *We're All Kin: A Cultural Study of an East Tennessee Mountain Neighborhood.* Knoxville: University of Tennessee Press.

Caudill, William, and David W. Plath. 1966. "Who Sleeps by Whom? Parent-Child Involvement in Urban Japanese Families." *Psychiatry* 29:344–66.

Caudill, William, and H. Weinstein. 1969. "Maternal Care and Infant Behavior in Japan and America." *Psychiatry* 32:12–43.

Christopher, Robert C. 1983. *The Japanese Mind: The Goliath Explained.* New York: Linden Press/Simon and Schuster.

Cross, T., B. J. Bazron, K. Dennis, and M. R. Isaacs. 1989. *A Monograph on Effective Services for Minority Children Who Are Severely Emotionally Disturbed.* Vol. 1. of *Towards a Culturally Competent System of Care.* Washington, D.C.: Georgetown University Child Development Center, National Technical Assistance Center for Children's Mental Health.

DeVos, George. 1973. *Socialization for Achievement: Essays on the Cultural Psychology of the Japanese.* Berkeley and Los Angeles: University of California Press.

———. 1983. "Dimensions of the Self in Japanese Culture." In *Culture and Self: Asian and Western Perspectives,* Anthony J. Marsella, George DeVos, and Marcelo Suarez-Orozco (Eds.). New York: Tavistock.

Dittman, Laura L. 1972. "Infant Care. Children's Bureau Publication No. 8. 1963." In *Child Rearing Literature of Twentieth Century America,* David J. Rothman and Sheila M. Rothman (Eds.). New York: Arno Press.

Eliot, Martha M. 1972. "Infant Care. Children's Bureau Publication No. 8. 1929." In *Child Rearing Literature of Twentieth Century America,* David J. Rothman and Sheila M. Rothman (Eds.). New York: Arno Press.

Erikson, Erik H. 1963. *Childhood and Society.* New York: W. W. Norton [orig. 1950].

Ferber, Richard. 1985. *Solve Your Child's Sleep Problems.* New York: Simon and Schuster.

Gorer, Geoffrey. 1964. *The American People.* New York: Norton.

Guilleminault, Christian (Ed.). 1987. *Sleep and Its Disorders in Children.* New York: Raven Press.

Hicks, George L. 1976. *Appalachian Valley.* New York: Holt, Rinehart and Winston.

Hoekelman, Robert A., Stanford B. Friedman, and Modena E. H. Wilson. 1997. *Primary Pediatric Care.* 3d ed. St. Louis: Mosby.

Hsu, Francis L. K. 1970. *Americans and Chinese: Two Ways of Life.* New York: Doubleday.

———. 1972 . "American Core Value and National Character." In *Psychological Anthropology,* F. L. K. Hsu (Ed.). Cambridge, Mass.: Schenkman Publishing. Pp. 241–62.

———. 1983. "The Effect of Dominant Kinship Relationships on Kin and Non-Kin Behavior: A Hypothesis." In *Rugged Individualism Reconsidered: Essays in Psychological Anthropology,* Francis L. K. Hsu (Ed.). Knoxville: University of Tennessee Press. Pp. 217–47.

Huntley, Rebecca. 1991. *The Sleep Book for Tired Parents.* Seattle: Parenting Press.

Klackenberg, Gunnar. 1987. "Incidence of Parasomnias in Children in a General Population." In *Sleep and Its Disorders in Children,* Christian Guilleminault (Ed.). New York: Raven Press. Pp. 99–113.

Konner, Melvin J. 1981. "Evolution of Human Behavior Development." In *Handbook of Cross-Cultural Human Development,* R. H. Munroe, R. L. Munroe, and B. B. Whiting (Eds.). New York: Garland. Pp. 3–52.

La Leche League International. 1987. *The Womanly Art of Breastfeeding.* New York: New America Library.

Levine, Melvin D., William B. Carey, Allen C. Crocker, and Ruth T. Gross. 1983. *Developmental-Behavioral Pediatrics.* Philadelphia: W. B. Saunders.

LeVine, Robert A. 1990. "Infant Environments in Psychoanalysis: A Cross-Cultural View." In *Cultural Psychology: Essays in Comparative Human Development,* J. W. Stigler, R. A. Shweder, and G. Herdt (Eds.). Cambridge: Cambridge University Press. Pp. 454–74.

Litt, Carole J. 1981. "Children's Attachment to Transitional Objects: A Study of Two Pediatric Populations." *American Journal of Orthopsychiatry* 51:131–39.

Lozoff, Betsy, Abraham W. Wolf, and Nancy S. Davis. 1984. "Cosleeping in Urban Families with Young Children in the United States." *Pediatrics* 74:171–82.

Madansky, Deborah, and Craig Edelbrock. 1990. "Cosleeping in a Community Sample of 2- and 3-Year-Old Children." *Pediatrics* 86:197–280.

Mason, Bobby Ann. 1993. "Recycling Kentucky." *New Yorker* 69(36):50–62.

Mead, Margaret. 1942. *And Keep Your Powder Dry.* New York: William Morrow.

McKenna, James J. 1986. "An Anthropological Perspective on the Sudden Infant Death Syndrome (SIDS): The Role of Parental Breathing Cues and Speech Breathing Adaptations." *Medical Anthropology* 10:9–53.

———. 2000. "Cultural Influences on Infant Sleep". In *Sleep and Breathing in Children: A Developmental Approach,* J. Loughlin, J. Carroll, and C. Marcus (Eds.). New York: Marcell Dekker. Pp. 199–230.

———. 2001. "Part 1: Why We Never Ask 'Is It Safe for Infants to Sleep Alone?' Historical Origins of Scientific Bias in the Bedsharing SIDS/SUDI 'Debate.'" *Academy of Breast Feeding Medicine News and Views* 7(4):32, 38.

Montell, William Lynwood. 1986. *Killings: Folk Justice in the Upper South.* Lexington: University Press of Kentucky.

Morelli, G. A., B. Rogoff, D. Oppenheim, and D. Goldsmith. 1992. "Cultural Variation in Infants' Sleeping Arrangements: Questions of Independence." *Developmental Psychology* 28:604–13.

Mosco, S., C. Richard, and J. McKenna. 1997. "Maternal Sleep and Arousals During Bedsharing with Infants." *Sleep* 20(2):142–50.

Norbeck, Edward, and George DeVos. 1972. "Culture and Personality: The Japanese." In *Psychological Anthropology,* Francis L. K. Hsu (Ed.). Cambridge, Mass.: Schenkman Publishing. Pp. 21–70.

Norman, Gurney. 1977. *Kinfolks: The Wilgus Stories.* Frankfort, Ky.: Gnomon Press.

———. 1990. *Divine Right's Trip: A Novel of the Counterculture.* Frankfort, Ky.: Gnomon Press [orig. 1971].

Rosenfeld, Alvin A., Anne O'Reilly Wenegrat, Diane F. Haavik, Brant G. Wenegrat, and Carole R. Smith. 1982. "Sleeping Patterns in Upper-Middle-Class Families When the Child Awakens Ill or Frightened." *Archives of General Psychiatry* 39:943–47.

Sears, William. 1987. *Nighttime Parenting: How to Get Your Baby and Child to Sleep.* New York: Plume.

Sheldon, Stephen H., Jean-Paul Spire, and Howard B. Levy. 1992. *Pediatric Sleep Medicine.* Philadelphia: W. B. Saunders.

Shelov, Steven P. (Ed.) 1993. *Caring for Your Baby and Young Child: Birth to Age 5.* American Academy of Pediatrics. New York: Bantam Books.

Shweder, Richard A., Lene Arnett Jensen, and William M. Goldstein. 1995. "Who Sleeps by Whom Revisited: A Method for Extracting the Moral Goods Implicit in Practice." In *Cultural Practices as Contexts for Development,* No. 67, Jacqueline J. Goodnow, Peggy J. Miller, and Frank Kessel (Eds.). San Francisco: Jossey-Bass Publishers. Pp. 21–40.

Slone, Verna Mae. 1978. *Common Folks.* Pippa Passes, Ky.: Alice Lloyd College.

Smith, Lendon H. 1996. *How to Raise a Healthy Child* . New York: M. Evans.

Spock, Benjamin. 1957. *The Common Sense Book of Baby and Child Care.* New ed. New York: Duell, Sloan and Pearce [orig. 1945].

———. 1961. *Dr. Spock Talks to Mothers.* Boston: Houghton Mifflin [orig. 1954].

Thevenin, Tine. 1977. *The Family Bed: An Age-old Concept in Childrearing.* 2d ed. Minneapolis: Thevenin.

West, Mrs. Max. 1972. "Infant Care. Care of Children Series No. 2. Children's Bureau Publication No. 8. 1914." In *Child Rearing Literature of Twentieth Century America,* David J. Rothman and Sheila M. Rothman (Eds.). New York: Arno Press.

Whiting, John W. M. 1964. "Effects of Climate on Certain Cultural Practices." In *Explorations in Cultural Anthropology,* Ward H. Goodenough (Ed.). New York: McGraw-Hill. Pp. 511–44.

Chapter 6

Creating Cultural Competence among Appalachian Nursing Students

Charlotte F. Chase

This chapter focuses on three components of an introductory course for an RN-BSN nursing program in central Appalachia which enable students to become more culturally competent. The principal activities of the program are designed to enable a successful student transition from technical to professional practice, to implement active learning strategies, including small group work, to improve critical thinking and clinical decision making, and to enhance the educational experience in the clinical lab (Johnson 1997). Current nursing literature points to the importance of increasing the knowledge, attitudes, and skills of health-care professionals about cultural competence (Lipson, Dibble, and Minarik 1996). Description and analysis of student reactions to these three experiences demonstrate the impact they have had on changing student attitudes and behavior as well as furthering their understanding of themselves as individuals, of their group identity, and of their ability to provide culturally competent care.

Program Site

Southwestern Virginia, part of central Appalachia, has been designated a health professional shortage area (HPSA). The bachelor of science in nursing program described here is located at a public university branch campus in a rural liberal arts college three hundred miles from the main campus. Once the program was approved and funded, classes began in fall 1993. The first students graduated in 1995, and the program received national accreditation in October 1996. The program was organized to meet the needs of adult students in a rural area, many with family responsibilities and most already holding full-time positions in health care. Over one-third of the students travel one or more hours one way to attend class.

A needs assessment was conducted prior to program approval. Responses to the questions were taken into consideration in the program design. Six hundred sixty-nine (37 percent) out of 1,811 mailed questionnaires were usable. Of the 610 active (not retired) respondents, 371 (60.8 percent) expressed interest in the program being developed. Of these, most were working in critical care (22 percent) or medical-surgical or adult nursing (63 percent), while only 15 percent were in community health. The survey included questions about the educational efficiency of the clinical laboratory. While it cannot be assumed that every student entering the nursing major is competent, it also cannot be assumed that they lack basic skills. Submission of a record of positions since graduation, proof of state board licensure, and a letter of reference and check sheet from their present employer helps establish the student's level of practice; the faculty is responsible for further validation. The primary goal of the baccalaureate program is the development of intellectual skills that enable the student to carry out technical skills at the right time and make appropriate judgments about nursing care. The program is based on the recent emphasis on expert practice in nursing (Benner 1984) as opposed to the more typical nursing programs that emphasize lengthy clinical laboratories patterned after routine work assignments.

The American health-care system is currently undergoing dramatic reform. This reform includes a shift away from a sickness model to one that emphasizes wellness and universal health coverage, especially in rural areas such as the one described here. The nursing program that I have been involved with was primarily developed to address the shortage of professionally trained nurses. It targets occupational nurses who have been practicing in this area for some years. As nursing positions become more difficult to find in this economically depressed area, it is imperative for experienced nurses to complete their BSNs—the minimum level of training for professional nurses. In addition to the program goals mentioned earlier, the curriculum is designed to provide these nurses with additional skills required in the practice of community health nursing. Gerberich and her colleagues, in particular, have stressed the importance of BSN students acquiring experience in the conduct of community needs assessments (Gerberich, Stearns, and Dawd 1995).

In the overall philosophy of the program, nursing is concerned with promoting, maintaining, and enhancing health in individuals, families, and communities (see American Association of College Nursing 1986). Nurses emphasize primary health care and promote healthy life-styles recognizing the importance of health promotion and disease prevention. Nurses and the recipients of their care share responsibility for assessing, planning, and evaluating health care. The role of the nurse evolves in response to changing expectations and demands in the marketplace. Nurses provide holistic health care that includes health education, advocacy, and a committed, caring relationship. They are responsible for participating in discussions and seeking solutions for health-care issues locally, regionally, and nationally.

The curriculum is grounded in characteristics and needs of students, traditional health-care and nursing practices, and a community-based health-care system. Faculty and students share custodianship for learning goals, learning outcomes, and participatory learning activities. Teachers select and guide learning experiences consistent with student knowledge, skills, and experience. Teachers interact with community and health-care professionals to provide disciplinary and interdisciplinary learning activities and practice opportunities. It is presumed that students learn best in an active, stimulating, and exciting environment that encourages inquiry, curiosity, critical thinking, and insight. Faculty believe that students in such an environment achieve at a higher level and gain tools and aspirations for continuing their education.

In keeping with this philosophy, the program is designed to make the clinical lab experience an opportunity for students to be as creative as possible. Their diverse clinical background experiences encourage the beginning of a shift in thinking and attitudes from technical to more professional nursing.

Since the program began in 1993, there have been twenty-three graduates, seven of whom have gone into nurse practitioner master's programs. Sixty-three nurses are currently enrolled and taking courses in two different locations, Wise and Abingdon. Wise, Virginia, is situated in the mountains on the border of Kentucky, while Abingdon, Virginia, is a small city on Interstate 81, the main north-south route through the state. The region as a whole shares many of the problems of rural America: unemployment and underemployment, racism, poverty, poor health, and so on. All but two of the students have been Caucasian, and there have been only eight men in the program. Students range from twenty-two to sixty years of age, but the majority are in their late thirties.

Program Components

While enrolled in the introductory course in the curriculum, titled "Nurse, Patient and Health," students are asked to conduct five required exercises and two optional ones. Required exercises are completed by both individuals and groups. Individual exercises include making a life-style change, assessing one's health roots, teaching for health, and outreach health care. The group project requires conducting a mini-community assessment. Optional individual projects include folklore medicine, exploring community resources, writing a critique of two articles on health care from popular literature, and, finally, a student-designed activity. An in-depth description of three of these exercises (assessing one's health roots, folklore medicine, and the group community assessment project) will illustrate the benefits of engaging student interest and creativeness in this first course of the program. The students seem to especially enjoy these three exercises. Class discussions were filled with illustrations of how these projects enhanced their understanding of individual, family, and community values and change in values over time. Moreover, the exercises provided particularly rich material for exploring concepts of stereotyping and cultural identity and the importance of these in providing culturally competent health care.

Assessing Personal Health Roots

This program component asks nurses what they know about their own health genealogy. Each student completes a health-roots chart based on information from parents, siblings, grandparents, aunts, and uncles (see table 6.1). Information collected for each individual includes (1) year of birth, (2) death, date, cause of death (if applicable), (3) occupation, (4) major health events (number of pregnancies, number of live births, surgeries), (5) chronic illnesses, (6) weight assessment (overweight, underweight, or ideal weight), and (7) abuses (food, tobacco, alcohol, drugs). Completion of this exercise is generally easy, for most students have direct access to an extended family or, as is often the case, live in extended households. Extended family households, in fact, enable students to find time to enroll in the program, because other members of the

Table 6.1. Health Roots Chart Produced by a Typical Female Student

DENISE (Female Student)	
1. Year of birth	1963
2. Death/date/cause	N/A
3. Occupation	RN/critical care nurse, BSN student
4. Major health events	0 pregnancies; 6 surgeries
5. Chronic illnesses	N/A
6. Weight assessment	Ideal weight
7. Abuses	None
Female sibling	**Male sibling**
1. 1960	1. 1970
2. N/A	2. N/A
3. Housewife and mother	3. Police officer
4. 3 pregnancies: 2 miscarriages, 1 live birth	4. 3 surgeries
5. Diverticulitis	5. GERD, ulcers
6. Ideal weight	6. Ideal weight
7. Tobacco, coffee	7. None

PARENTS	
Mother	**Father**
1. 1941	1. 1937
2. N/A	2. Deceased 1985; myocardial infarction
3. Supervisor of garment factory	3. Disabled veteran
4. 3 pregnancies: 3 live births, 3 surgeries	4. 5 surgeries
5. Hypothyroidism, back problems	5. Cardiac disease
6. Slightly overweight	6. Ideal weight
7. None	7. Tobacco up to 7 years before death, coffee

AUNTS	
Maternal	**Paternal**
Aunt #1	**Aunt #1**
1. 1938	1. 1920
2. N/A	2. N/A
3. Housewife and mother	3. Housewife and mother
4. 7 pregnancies: 3 miscarriage, 4 live births	4. 3 pregnancies: 1 miscarriage, 2 live births
5. Kidney stones	5. Diabetic, cardiac disease
6. Overweight	6. Overweight
7. Food	7. Food
Aunt #2	**Aunt #2**
1. 1939	1. 1935
2. N/A	2. N/A
3. Housewife and mother	3. Housewife and mother
4. 9 pregnancies: 2 miscarriages, 1 stillbirth, 6 live births	4. 2 pregnancies: 2 live births
5. Allergies	5. Diabetic, pulmonary disease
6. Overweight	6. Underweight
7. Food	7. Tobacco, coffee

Continued on next page

Aunt #3

1. 1943
2. N/A
3. Hair dresser
4. 3 pregnancies: 1 miscarriage, 2 live births
5. None
6. Underweight
7. None

Aunt #4

1. 1947
2. N/A
3. Housewife and mother
4. 3 pregnancies: 3 live births; 2 surgeries
5. None
6. Overweight
7. Food, tobacco

Aunt #5

1. 1952
2. N/A
3. Housewife and mother
4. 1 pregnancy: 1 live birth, 2 surgeries
5. None
6. Ideal weight
7. None

Aunt #6

1. 1954
2. N/A
3. RN MSN
4. 2 pregnancies: 2 live births; numerous surgeries
5. None
6. Underweight
7. None

UNCLES

Maternal

Uncle #1

1. 1936
2. N/A
3. Coal miner, owner/operator
4. N/A
5. High blood pressure, kidney stones
6. Ideal weight
7. None

Paternal

Uncle #1

1. 1922
2. N/A
3. Retired coal miner
4. 5 surgeries
5. Side effects of pituitary tumor
6. Overweight until past year, ideal weight at present
7. None

Uncle #2
1. 1945
2. N/A
3. Coal miner
4. None
5. High blood pressure, kidney stones, allergies
6. Ideal weight
7. Tobacco, alcohol

Uncle #3
1. 1950
2. N/A
3. School teacher, Ph.D.
4. Kidney stones
5. None
6. Ideal weight
7. None

Uncle #4
1. 1956
2. N/A
3. Disabled
4. 1 surgery
5. Blind in left eye from birth, back problems, kidney stones
6. Underweight
7. None

Uncle #2
1. 1925
2. N/A
3. Retired veteran and school teacher
4. Cerebral vascular accident
5. High blood pressure, diabetic
6. Overweight
7. Food

Uncle #3
1. 1929
2. Deceased 1951; accident
3. Carpenter
4. None
5. None
6. Ideal weight
7. Alcohol

Uncle #4
1. 1931
2. N/A
3. Retired coal miner
4. None
5. None
6. Ideal weight
7. None

GRANDPARENTS

Maternal Grandmother
1. 1901
2. Deceased 1979; congestive heart failure
3. Housewife and mother
4. 7 pregnancies: 7 live births
5. Diabetic, cardiac disease, chronic congestive heart failure
6. Overweight
7. Food, tobacco

Grandfather
1. 1900
2. Deceased 1972; pneumonia
3. Farmer
4. Cerebral vascular accident
5. High blood pressure
6. Underweight
7. Tobacco

Paternal Grandmother
1. 1914
2. Deceased 1986; pneumonia
3. Housewife and mother
4. 13 pregnancies: 11 live births, 2 still births; 2 surgeries
5. Cardiac disease, high blood pressure
6. Ideal weight
7. None

Grandfather
1. 1915
2. Deceased 1975; myocardial infarction
3. Farmer
4. High blood pressure
5. Cancer, seizures, cirrhosis of liver
6. Overweight
7. Food, tobacco, alcohol

family are available to assist with child care. Students typically have at least one family member who already has an interest in genealogy and who volunteers to assist with development of a health-specific family roots chart. In the words of one nurse, "My mother has always been the historian and storyteller of the family. She was eager to discuss her family roots." Family Bibles are also cited as key resources, and the deep religiosity of the region is often evident in student papers describing their personal health-roots chart. For example, one student noted,

> In March 1969, God blessed my parents with the gift of conception. Little could I realize how important these roots could be. This is the moment during which a child can inherit any outstanding characteristics, any predisposition to diseases, or any undesirable features. (S.M.)

This student went on to describe the faith of her grandparents:

> In talking with my grandmother, I learned that my grandparents were very enduring people. They suffered through many hardships and illnesses. My grandmother was moved to a sanitarium in the 1950s when diagnosed with tuberculosis. Treatment was not far advanced, and the outlook was poor. Patients were isolated and medical treatment was limited to support and comfort measures. Once, after my grandfather had visited her, she lay praying. The Lord impressed upon her that it was time to leave (the sanitarium). My grandfather was on the road home and he, too, received an impression from God to return to the hospital. Upon entering her hospital room, my grandfather was surprised to find my grandmother packed and ready to leave. The doctors were amazed by the handiwork of God. She no longer had signs of tuberculosis, and all tests were normal. I found faith and enrichment during my conversations with my grandmother. (S.M.)

Another story about her grandfather provides further insight into the depth of this family's faith in God:

> He had a heart attack, and the family met many obstacles in their attempt to reach a health-care facility. One of which was a train that had stopped and blocked the tracks. Once he arrived at the hospital, it was learned that he had a hole in the bottom of his heart. The doctor bluntly looked at my grandmother and explained, "By all medical terms, your husband should not even be alive now." My grandmother smiled as she said, "You apparently don't know the God I know." (S.M.).

This student concluded her report by stating that her faith is the most important characteristic of her being since her conception in 1969.

Student papers often address substance abuse, homicide, spousal abuse, and, occasionally, violence as a cause of death:

> Three of my father's six sisters died before they reached fifty. His oldest sister was killed in a car accident. Two of his younger sisters were killed by their husbands. The older one's husband bludgeoned her with a hammer and then committed suicide with a handgun. The other sister's body was found in a river. She was addicted to pain killers and had a history of alcoholism. She had been treated for depression and codependency. Writing this paper has been depressing. I have a strong family history of chemical dependency. (M.J.)

Completed genealogies also reveal the extent to which students in this program are frequently the first in their families to pursue higher educations. Their papers also indicate how many of the students come from families where husbands, brothers, fathers, and uncles are employed in the mines. Students point out that illness among family members may often be attributed to difficult life-styles associated with occupations such as mining and compounded by heavy smoking. One student's comments illustrate this:

> All the men on my father's side are coal miners with the exception of the oldest son, who works in a factory. All of the men in my family at one point have been in more than one mine cave in. My grandfather was killed in a cave in before I was even born. My father, brother, and one uncle are permanently disabled as a result of mining accidents. Seventy-five percent of the females on both sides of the family are nurses. It is the men that have no interest in college and tend to work odd jobs. (A.R.)

The frequency with which tobacco is linked to high morbidity and mortality in the region is readily observable in these exercises. Apart from King Coal, tobacco is the most important product of this region, and nicotine abuse is widespread. Farmers in the area are extremely sensitive to government intervention in local decisions about this crop. For example, I attended a small-town parade in the middle of tobacco country. One float was decked out as a funeral barge carrying a skeleton holding a forked spear. Signs draped along the sides of the float cautioned against outside interference by the U.S. Department of Agriculture (USDA). The float implied that a recent USDA decision to implement policies to discourage tobacco production was actually leading to the economic death of their community. Students often make the connection between life-style practices and health consequences in their studies:

> In years past and into the present, most of the men in my family smoked tobacco. The majority of the men worked hard in the coal mines or farming the land. The women canned food in the summer so that their families could eat in the winter. I remember my grandmother telling me as a child about my aunts and uncles having rickets as children. This project brought back a whole lot of memories. (B.W.)

Other student papers carry a common theme of how hard the lives of people have been in the region and some of the health consequences:

> A few in my immediate family suffer from health problems. My mother recently quit smoking and is healthy except for a chronic cough due to a long history of cigarette smoking. As for myself, I have rheumatoid arthritis for which I take medication. My father, who died last year at the age of seventy-three, was a lifelong smoker, retired coal miner, retired army sergeant, and was afflicted with many illnesses. He had black lung, arthritis, and was diagnosed with leukemia one week before his death. (D.S.)

One nurse quantified the afflictions of her family:

> After tabulating totals for numbers of persons afflicted with individual diseases, I learned that my descendants and I are predisposed to several illnesses and conditions. Of those blood relations on the paternal side of the family tree, five persons had cardiac disease, four had hypertension, two were anemic, one had diabetes mellitus, two had chronic obstructive pulmonary disease, and eight had cancer—six due to lung cancer. Four children died in infancy. On the maternal side of the family tree, two out of six had strokes, two had diabetes mellitus, three had arthritis, three had hypertension, two had emphysema, two had chronic obstructive pulmonary disease, two had strokes, one had cardiac disease, one had asthma, one had cancer, one had anemia, and one had an adrenal tumor. The result of this study makes one aware that there is great need for a healthy life-style and awareness of wellness.

Concern with regard to links between environmental degradation and health is another common theme in student descriptions accounting for disease patterns prevalent in both their families and in their communities. A number of community assessments (discussed below) directly addressed this ecological perspective.

Conduct of these exercises leads to student recognition of the health-care context and the difficulties that might be encountered when trying to change life-styles. For example, one student concluded:

> This exercise taught me not to be judgmental when interviewing a patient and their families about their life-styles. It has also taught me to have patience, understanding, and compassion when assisting anyone in changing a life-style that may have been in operation for generations. (C.W.)

The exercises also prompt students to assess how their behaviors in the clinical setting might be altered:

> I was very careful to convey an optimistic view to the person I interviewed. I also had to consider their strengths and convey a tolerance of their weaknesses. I also had to be empathetic, recognizing their feelings without criticism. The person had my complete attention. I listened carefully. Their comments were my sole concern. I provided optimal conditions in order to conduct a smooth interview by inviting members of my family to my home. We sat over a cup of coffee as I conducted this interview. I was able to provide privacy and was not interrupted during the interview. (S.H.)

The need for improving clinical skills in history taking is a recurrent theme as students summarize their individual experiences with this family roots exercise. They also acknowledge the importance of good history taking and subsequent patient teaching. Attitudinal changes are often evident as students become more aware of the roots of their own values and attitudes about health and make vows to modify negative life-style behaviors in themselves and in their children. Decreasing fast food intake is one particularly worrisome and recurrent example.

In summary, the health-roots exercise enables our students to learn much about themselves as well as further their knowledge about their families. Obstacles to health-care access are repeatedly mentioned in the personal histories. Group discussion about the genealogical exercise has led to recognition that many students come from large families and that childbirth at home had been common in the recent past. Students recognize that early prevention of illness is critical to reversing the negative trends detected in their family roots. Common illnesses in the health charts include hypertension, stroke, and congestive heart failure, all associated with life-style behaviors. The nurses priorities are to improve the chances of a better quality of life for their children. Most students demonstrate that they are strongly motivated to change health-related behaviors which they address in another exercise devoted to making life-style changes.

Folklore Medicine

A second component of the program examines the relationship of folklore medicine and health care. Alternative or folklore medicine has long been traditional in Appalachia. However, as Cavender (2003), Couto, Simpson, and Harris (1995), and others point out, the persistence of folk healing practices such as herbal medicine and religious faith healing do not necessarily pose barriers to accessing the benefits of scientific medicine. My colleague and I have taught this introductory course eight times since the beginning of the program, and we have never encountered any evidence that folklore medicine has impeded access to scientific medicine among student nurses or their families.

In this component of the program students develop a questionnaire to guide interviews with senior citizens. Students seem to enjoy this exercise in particular. They identify elderly relatives, neighbors, and friends who readily share with them their memories of what folk remedies were used in the area in the past when health services were not as readily available as today. A number of students are especially interested in herbal remedies. They bring to class herbal samples they have gathered in the fields or purchased in local health food stores. They also use reference books and cite them in their presentations. One student pointed out that while folklore medicine may be dying out, knowledge of it contributes to improved patient care today.

The interviews often give nurses an improved appreciation of health-care changes in the region. The following is one student's summary of her interviews with two elderly women (ages sixty-eight and seventy-four):

> It is hard for me to imagine before talking with these individuals how much things have changed over the years concerning health care. These days the government has become more involved with everyone's life, especially in health care. Today insurance companies are placing time limits on how long a person can be hospitalized before they quit paying. This in many cases is sending patients home before they are physically or mentally prepared to go. Back when these two ladies I interviewed were growing up, there was no such thing as insurance, and the doctors made house calls on a regular basis. I can't think of any doctor that makes house calls today, and if they did, it would cost a fortune. My experience with this exercise has made me realize as a nurse, how much the older generation depended on these home remedies. I figure some of these are still being used today by some people. I don't see anything wrong with trying these as an alternative to other medications, as long as it doesn't cause harm. (S.H.)

One student interviewed a retired physician born in 1919:

> This doctor recalled that as a child there had been a doctor in his community, but he was rarely called upon. Health care mostly consisted of home remedies used by mothers and local midwives. The midwife traveled for miles and was the closest form of medical help or advice. She had no formal medical training, just the notions and potions that were handed down from generation to generation. He shared the philosophy that had shaped his career and that he still abides by: "Medicine is an art, not a trade; Medicine is a calling, not a business; a calling in which you use your heart as much as your head; Medicine begins with the patient, continues with the patient and ends with the patient." (S.H.)

Interviews for this exercise teach students much about the area in which they are living. A high percentage of people living in Appalachia have no health-care coverage. Although professional health care is more accessible than it used to be, it is still "too expensive."

Faith healing is frequently mentioned in the interviews students conducted for this exercise. According to one student,

> This neighbor took off my brother's big wart, right in the middle of his hand. He asked my brother for a coin. He (the brother) had a fifty-cent-piece which he just gave to him and then was told to just go about his business and forget about it (the coin). A month later he (the brother) was playing baseball, and his hand didn't hurt. Usually he would always hurt his wart when he'd catch the ball. He just stopped and said, "Hey it's not hurting," running to Mom and showed it to her and it was gone. We wished that we had talked to him (the neighbor) more, he was Christian, he believed in God, he said (for us to) just go on and be good, God is going to take care of it. (D.W.)

Another student reported that when she asked, "What type of remedy was used to treat wounds or bleeding?" her seventy-year-old mother replied, "We would go to Grandma and she would quote a verse from the Bible (Ezekiel 16:6) which states: 'And when I passed by thee, and saw thee polluted in thine own blood, I said unto thee, when thou wast in thy blood, live, yea, I said unto thee, when thou wast in thy blood, live.' And the bleeding would stop, just like that" (T.S.).

This folklore medicine exercise also stimulates students to evaluate their current attitudes toward clinical nursing. One nurse concluded that her interviews had taught her how important it was to listen to the individual's story as a whole: "If the individual is clearly aware of what you need to hear at the beginning, then the story will unfold in its own unique way. Nurses must become avid listeners because there is so much to learn."

Another student concluded, "I will keep in mind that these were ways of life that were taken very seriously, therefore tread lightly because if you think it is funny, they probably do not because they have had to rely on this as their source of medical treatment for years."

In group discussions, students state that they feel a lot of the folklore medicine traditions described to them by elderly relatives are disappearing. They attribute this to out-migration by young people and to the fact that older folk are no longer teaching such traditions to the young. The students describe a resurgence of interest, however, in herbal remedies. One student said, "I bought a book hoping that it would tell me the purposes of the herbs I collected last spring. I want to know how it (the tea) works physiologically."

In summary, students gain considerable knowledge about the historical evolution of health-care practices and barriers to health-care access in the region in this component of the course. They appreciate the important role of folklore medicine in the past and the persistence of beliefs about faith healing in those people they know and interview. They further recognize the importance of being good listeners and they implement these attitudes, values and skills in subsequent clinical interviews.

Community Health Assessment

A third component of the course is a group exercise devoted to conducting of mini-community assessments. As mentioned previously, only 15 percent of the respondents in the needs assessment were working in community health, while the remainder were still employed in acute care settings. Therefore, our program has particularly emphasized the importance of students conducting their clinical laboratory experiences in community-based facilities or in association with community-based health coalitions.

The mini-community assessments are particularly helpful for students in identifying cultural diversity within the region, a region often stereotyped as overwhelmingly white. Students often conclude at the end of their assessment experience that they are actually "different" and that this recognition evolved during the course of conducting the mini-assessments. Students in the program come from a wide array of cultural backgrounds, although they may not have acknowledged or previously appreciated a cultural identification with these backgrounds. Students of mixed ancestry with American

Indian, African American, and Melungeon backgrounds were eager to explore cultural heritages that they had long since forgotten or ignored.

One student group researched the history of Melungeons in the region reporting that they have been subjected to equal parts of prejudice and legend. Prejudice has excluded them from the surrounding community and left them economically isolated, educationally segregated, and socially outcast.

Other students conducted a mini-assessment of the health needs of Hispanic migrant farm workers who are employed in the tobacco, apple, and Christmas tree industries of the Abingdon area. Student activities included outreach to the farmers who employ migrants, visits to the places where migrants live or frequent (including laundromats and corner grocery stores), providing assistance in a newly established health clinic, and providing health education to migrants in ESL classes offered by local college students.

One nurse, a farmer herself, contacted friends and relatives who employed migrants in their orchards in order to advertise a volunteer health clinic. However, as her network extended beyond close friends, farmers became less cooperative. This student also wrote:

> The farmers that I talked to were reluctant to show me the migrant homes. Each farmer was quick to state that "they don't stay here, they just do the work and move on." Each of the farmers was also quick to disown any responsibilities that employers might have for their workers. No mention is ever made of Social Security benefits, accident insurance, or time off for illness. The farmers are passing the buck just like the government. (C.W.)

The student also shared her personal feelings about this: "Clearly, the migrant worker's plight needs to be addressed. Discovering this form of discrimination was an unexpected outcome of my investigation."

This student also volunteered in the clinic and shared her concerns about that experience:

> My anticipated area of difficulty concerning this activity centered around the language barrier, which, to my surprise, was not that much of an obstacle. During the time I volunteered at the migrant clinic, the migrant worker had a Spanish language data sheet and I had the English version, and communication was possible. The experience at the clinic was very enlightening. Relaying information based on little language comprehension was difficult, but with lots of facial expressions and hand signals, it became an authentic eye opener. It is disheartening to comprehend discrimination that is practiced at my own doorstep. (C.W.)

Other students reported how they had conducted health education for farm workers in a weekly volunteer-run clinic. One wrote:

> I spent a few minutes at the end of their (the farm workers') English class telling them a little about oral care. I was surprised at how interested they seemed to be. The most valuable part of this learning activity was the research I did on this group of people. I was never very familiar with the migrant farm workers until now. Before I had done this research, I would run into migrants from time to time in the grocery store and never really paid much attention to them. After researching their background, I find myself being more observant. I know that in the future, if I ever have the chance to be involved in the care of migrant farm workers, I will definitely treat them with respect (the way I expect others to treat me). They are proud of who they are and what they do. Their hard work brings food to your table. (C.W.)

One student recalled a clinical laboratory experience she had as a student in her associate degree training:

> My prior clinical experience at the local health department while I was in nursing school showed me that the staff there are very unfeeling and unfriendly toward people who utilize this agency's services. The agency staff often display an attitude that the patient is inferior. Perhaps one day when new employees are hired, this attitude will change and people will more readily utilize the agency's services. (S.A.)

Another group of students conducted an assessment of the needs of the elderly in their community. They recognized the acute need for medicine for the very elderly on their case load. This group took the class project a step beyond assessment by organizing and raising funds to acquire pharmaceuticals for the elderly in their community who might otherwise not be able to afford medication.

Summary and Implications for Nursing Education

In this chapter, I have described how faculty in a nursing program have involved students in exercises designed to familiarize them with community-based nursing practice. The different components of the program include a series of well-integrated exercises designed to enhance critical thinking. The findings of one exercise easily leads into the questions addressed in subsequent exercises. Both attitudinal and behavioral changes have resulted from student involvement in this introductory course. Student participation in these exercises contributes significantly to heightened awareness of their own culture and the recognition of stereotypical thinking in themselves and the workplace, as well as in the community.

Students in the program come to recognize their own attitudes and how these attitudes shape their behaviors. Many resolve to change behaviors, particularly in clinical settings, as a result of such recognition. For example, students reporting on activities related to the health-roots exercise frequently point out how this activity causes them to realize both the importance of taking family health histories and the fact that such interviews must be conducted with patience, understanding, and compassion. Students also make the link between attitude changes and requisite changes in clinical practice. Some point out the need for conveying an optimistic frame of mind while interviewing clients about their health histories. Many vow to become better listeners in their communications with patients and family. The mini-community assessments lead students to appreciate the level of discrimination against outsiders that exists in the communities in which they live and work. This exercise leads many students to become active in a variety of community-based health coalitions. In several cases, groups of students have been instrumental in organizing communities around particular health needs, such as the Migrant Health Network and the organizing of medications for needy elderly.

Evaluation of these exercises has been done by students in connection with both individual and group learning experiences. In addition, we as faculty have been engaged in regular discussion and evaluation of these exercises. Both student and faculty evaluations indicate the significant lessons that may be learned by involving students in the exercises described here. Assessment of the curriculum indicates that there is much that can be done through training programs to improve the delivery of culturally competent health care in Appalachia.

References

American Association of Colleges Nursing. 1986. *Essentials of College and University Education for Professional Nursing.* Washington, D.C.

Benner, Patricia. 1984. *From Novice to Expert: Excellence and Power in Clinical Nursing Practice.* Boston, MA: Addison-Wesley Publishing.

Cavender, Anthony. 2003. *Folk Medicine in Southern Appalachia.* Chapel Hill: University of North Carolina Press.

Couto, Richard A., Nancy K. Simpson, and Gale Harris. 1995. *Sowing Seeds in the Mountains: Community-Based Coalitions for Cancer Prevention and Control.* Washington, D.C.: National Institutes of Health, National Cancer Institute.

Gerberich, S. S., S. J. Stearns, and T. A. Dawd. 1995. "A Critical Skill for the Future: Community Assessment." *Journal of Community Health Nursing* 12(4): 239–50.

Johnson, Betty M. 1997. Personal communication. Clinch Valley College of the University of Virginia, Mar.

Lipson, Juliene G., Suzanne L. Dibble, and Pamela A. Minarik. 1996. *Culture and Nursing Care: A Pocket Guide.* San Francisco: University of California, San Francisco, Nursing Press.

Chapter 7

Educating Culturally Sensitive Health Professionals in Appalachia

Anne B. Blakeney

The literature describes several specific issues that make recruitment and retention of health professionals difficult within rural areas. Doctors and nurses often cite the following reasons for leaving rural practice: high case loads, little professional support, few continuing education opportunities, and large distances traveled with poor road conditions (Clevett and Maltby 1992; Crandall, Dwyer, and Duncan 1990).

Allied health professionals are also in high demand in both rural and urban areas. Occupational therapists, physical therapists, speech and language pathologists, respiratory therapists, and physician's assistants historically have been very difficult to recruit within rural areas. Those who have been recruited successfully into rural practice sometimes report "burn out." Some of these professionals cite specific difficulties related to rural service delivery: chronic personnel shortages, lack of specialized training available locally, inadequate continuing education opportunities, professional isolation, lack of supervision, large case loads, poor travel conditions, and inadequate preparation for working in rural areas (Kohler and Mayberry 1993). It is the last point, regarding preparation for working in rural areas, that educators in the health professions throughout Appalachia especially need to address.

As people began to study the rural recruitment of health professionals, several authors suggested that individuals tend to work where they are trained (Gesler and Rickets 1992; Lutz 1991; Rabinowitz 1993; Roberts, Davis, and Wells 1991; Roberts et al. 1993). Thus, one recruitment strategy has been to offer at least a portion of the health professional's training within rural areas.

Others have argued that recruitment is only half the battle. Retaining health professionals in rural areas remains a persistent challenge. Therefore, some authors have argued that we should draw students into the health-care fields who are originally from underserved rural areas (Crandall, Dwyer, and Duncan 1990). This strategy is based at least in part on the assumption that those who have experienced a rural life-style previously will be more likely to return to rural areas to live and work.

Significant attention has been given to both of these recruitment strategies in past decades. However, neither of these approaches specifically addresses the inclusion of cultural information as an integral part of the health-care provider's education.

As an educator with extensive experience in preparing health professionals to work within Appalachia, I would argue that including content about Appalachian culture within the educational curriculum is absolutely critical for the success of any recruitment or retention strategy. Without an informed cultural context within which to interpret actual clinical experiences, students cannot achieve the maximum benefits of their training whether they are themselves natives of Appalachia or those coming into the region for the first time.

Observations from the Field

Eighteen years ago, I obtained a faculty position in the department of occupational therapy at a state supported university within Appalachia. As in many academic departments, the occupational therapy faculty were drawn from around the nation. Having grown up in a nearby state, I was the only faculty member in the department who was also a native of Appalachia.

Unlike my previous teaching experiences, this university is not affiliated with a major medical center. Thus, students travel extensively into various communities in order to complete their clinical training courses.

A major portion of the faculty's teaching responsibility is to precept students in their clinical courses. While in various hospitals, community clinics, nursing homes, rehabilitation centers, and public schools, students are exposed to a wide range of health-care providers. Some of these health professionals interact with Appalachian patients in large, urban hospitals that serve as major referral centers. Others interact with mountain people in small, rural, community-based settings.

One of my early observations was that the majority of these health professionals appeared to possess very good clinical skills. For example, they displayed current rehabilitation techniques for stroke patients or traumatically injured individuals. They knew how to break down complicated, disabling problems and deal with them step by step in the clinical setting. Technically, they demonstrated state of the art clinical practice. In this regard, they were very good professional role models for the students.

At the same time, these health professionals often made very derogatory comments about mountain people. This was particularly true if patients were from rural communities or if they were perceived to be poor or working-class individuals. These Appalachian patients were frequently described as ignorant, uncooperative, difficult to manage, and unwilling to communicate. Their religious beliefs and family relationships were labeled as "weird." Often they were judged as failing to follow through on treatment goals established "in their best interest." Patients were sometimes even discharged prematurely because some health professionals simply did not want to bother with people who "weren't motivated to improve themselves."

The accent and speech patterns of mountain people were a favorite topic of humor during the professionals' lunch hours. Many times, there was a very real failure in communication, as health professionals from outside the region attempted cross-cultural interaction with their patients. For instance, one physical therapist who was originally from New York related the following episode.

Every day, this young therapist entered a hospital room to do bed mobility and range-of-motion exercises with an elderly mountain woman. After introducing herself to her patient and asking if it would be alright to do the exercises the doctor had ordered, the patient would respond, "Well, I don't care to." Day after day , the therapist immediately left the room and officially recorded that the patient had refused therapy. It was not until weeks later that she discovered from a colleague that she should have been interpreting "I don't care to" as "I don't mind" doing those exercises now. This young woman was technically a very competent physical therapist, but she had no knowledge of local culture, particularly as it influenced patterns of speech.

Another technically competent therapist at a major urban medical center told a group of students that all of her Appalachian patients were either very rich coal miners or lazy, unemployed welfare recipients. During a formal lecture in a regional hospital, a physician told the students that all mountain patients were uneducated, unmotivated, uninformed, unemployed, and uninsured. In his judgment, these patients were personally very frustrating to treat and a particular "drain" on the hospital's resources.

I was initially puzzled and offended by the extreme judgments and demeaning comments which otherwise clinically competent health professionals made about their Appalachian patients. As I supervised the students clinically and interacted with their mountain patients, I did not find them to be much different from the majority of people I had known as I was growing up. Yet the negative attitudes toward these patients were pervasive, and most people appeared to hold them automatically. Furthermore, it seemed no one challenged these perceptions. All in all, there was generally nothing positive about Appalachian people that was being conveyed to students as they carried out their clinical courses.

What were the images of Appalachia that were being conveyed to students while they were on campus? Regrettably, things were not much better in the classroom than they were in the clinics. Several Appalachian students reported accounts of being publicly ridiculed and shamed by professors or classmates because of their accents or the particular expressions that they used. That this continues to happen even today in a public institution which is committed to serve Appalachia and its citizens is particularly appalling.

Eighteen years ago, the general atmosphere in which students were being educated as health professionals did not reflect an informed perspective on Appalachian culture. At that time, very few of the Appalachian students identified themselves as natives of the mountain counties surrounding the university. Those who did so tended to be outgoing, gregarious students who were often the leaders among their classmates. Others worked very hard to disguise their accents and carefully guarded the true identities of their home communities. They were often very quiet students who carefully observed what was happening around them but did not share their thoughts openly unless pressed to do so. They were often criticized by faculty for their lack of assertiveness.

Non-Appalachian students accounted for slightly more than two-thirds of the student body. They typically encountered very little information while on campus that would have challenged some of their preconceived stereotypes of rural mountain people which they brought to the campus with them. At times, there was clearly a lack of mutual respect between the two groups of students.

The Catholic priest at the campus Newman Center in the early 1980s was very sensitive to the pressures mountain youth faced. He once stated that the main message the university conveyed to Appalachian students was this: "Here's your degree; it's your ticket out of Appalachia. Take it and don't ever look back." In this atmosphere, it is little wonder that very few students ever sought out employment within the Appalachian region, despite the fact that some of them were Appalachian natives who had received many hours of clinical training in rural communities throughout the mountains.

Increasing the Awareness of Appalachian Culture

To address the stereotypical perceptions of Appalachians both in the clinical and the university environments, I pursued four different strategies. First, I wrote an article dealing with culturally appropriate health-care services for Appalachians, and it was published in a professional journal (Blakeney 1987). This article was intended to challenge some of the worst stereotypes and to convey the complexity of cross-cultural interactions. It was also important as a first step toward introducing information about Appalachian people into the occupational therapy literature, as nothing about Appalachia had been published previously within this professional literature. Occupational therapy students are now required to read this article during one of the introductory courses in their professional curriculum.

Second, I planned and carried out a series of annual continuing education conferences for health professionals over an eight-year period. The topics focused on various aspects of Appalachian culture. The goal was to demonstrate the relationship between culture and behavior so that the health professionals who served as role models for the students during their clinical training could better understand their Appalachian patients. Many of the faculty for these conferences were drawn from the membership of the Appalachian Studies Association. In addition to the scholars in the region, some of the poets and authors of fiction were also invited to participate. Film resources from Appalshop were also utilized. The intent was to tap into as many different avenues for learning about Appalachian culture as possible.

Very few physical or occupational therapists ever attended these conferences. When surveyed, they responded that they would have attended if the focus had been on technical treatment innovations. However, they did not perceive a need to learn anything about culture and failed to see how doing so might enhance their clinical practice.

Nurses, social workers, and hospital chaplains did attend the conferences in large numbers. On their evaluation forms, at least half of the nurses stated that they were tired of attending technical skills training and were looking for a change of pace in their continuing education offerings. These conferences offered them the opportunity to gain a more informed perspective on the cultural context of their work. They responded positively to the inclusion of content from the humanities, commenting particularly upon the value of the poetry and films.

Conference evaluations revealed that the most positive benefits of these sessions seemed to be gained by those nurses who were themselves natives of Appalachia. These individuals accounted for approximately 75 percent of conference participants. None of them had previously been presented with a balanced perspective on their own culture. Their most consistent feedback was that, for the first time in their lives, they no longer felt ashamed of being Appalachians. They frequently purchased tapes and books at the conclusion of the conferences to continue to study independently once they returned home. Thus, they may have begun a process of becoming more reflexive clinicians.

In addition to health professionals, a total of twenty-eight faculty from various departments in the university also attended these conferences over the eight-year period. None of these individuals were from Appalachia, but they were interested in hearing the visiting poets and scholars who came to the campus to deliver their presentations. Approximately 25 percent of faculty participants reported a willingness to consider learning more about Appalachia as a means to enhance their understanding of the university's student population.

The third strategy involved teaching a new course on delivering health care in Appalachia. I was approached by the department chair and asked to design a course that would fit a rural health emphasis for a newly proposed master's degree program in occupational therapy. The chair agreed that Appalachia could reasonably serve as the emphasis of such a course. I subsequently designed and implemented a course that is offered at both the graduate and undergraduate levels. Several faculty and students have enrolled in the course over the past twelve years. The readings are drawn from the scholarship within Appalachian studies. Topics include social, political, economic, and historical information about the region. The goal is to give the students a broader context in which to analyze many issues so that they may become more reflexive practitioners. For example, they begin to see how health care is influenced by the political economy throughout Appalachia. They learn how to examine the social and cultural capital of communities in the region.

For their course projects, several students have pursued an in-depth life history of one or more elderly Appalachians. In doing so, they have placed individual life stories within the broader context of the historical forces that have shaped the region. Issues such as labor conflicts, out-migration, lack of health care, and episodic unemployment become more than abstract facts when viewed from the perspective of individuals who have experienced them personally.

Finally, the fourth strategy that was implemented to challenge the stereotypical notions of Appalachian people involved obtaining grant monies. The department chair secured a grant from the state in order to expand training opportunities for students in rural locations throughout the mountains. A colleague and I each volunteered to precept students in two separate clinical courses off campus. Each year we traveled with approximately twelve students more than one hundred miles into the university's service region. We lived in a rural mountain community for one month. Under our supervision, the students completed a required clinical course while simultaneously providing health-care services to underserved populations. During the first ten years in which these service-learning courses were offered, a total of 114 students completed them.

As part of these courses, students were required to complete additional readings about Appalachia while they were interacting with mountain people on a daily basis. This course was both an intensive clinical and cultural educational experience in which students were encouraged to reflect upon their experiences and record their perceptions. To date, one-third of those students completing these courses have returned to mountain communities to live and work professionally. The majority of those returning were themselves natives of Appalachian communities.

The clinical training of occupational therapists continues to be provided in an increasing number of rural communities. This training is now enhanced by information on the cultural context of Appalachia which students receive before they leave the campus. Students no longer assume that all of their clinically competent role models are also culturally informed health professionals. Rather, they now know enough to question the cultural knowledge of their supervisors when presented with stereotypical judgments.

Not all of the faculty in the university are convinced that studying and understanding culture is beneficial for future health professionals. Some faculty and clinical supervisors still hold to the perspective that technical skills are "culture free." From this perspective, if students master technical skills to a level of proficiency, they should become competent health-care providers wherever they live and work. Individuals who assume the "technical competence" viewpoint continue to engage in the same stereotypical judgments about mountain people that they previously did. Therefore, Appalachian students who encounter these individuals sometimes still struggle with the judgments that are made about them and their mountain patients.

Nevertheless, students now have a broader context in which to sort out such issues for themselves. The overall atmosphere on campus and in the clinics has been altered. The result has been that an increasing number of students have become sensitized to the need to consider the cultural background of any patient whom they might encounter in the future. Thus, initial steps have been taken toward encouraging students to become reflexive practitioners. There is also an understanding of the ongoing need to continue to focus upon Appalachia as faculty come and go from the university.

Recruiting Health Professionals in Appalachian Communities

As more faculty and students gained an informed perspective on Appalachian culture, there was a simultaneous expansion of job opportunities within many rural communities throughout the mountains. For years, hospital administrators had been unable to attract enough qualified allied health professionals willing to work in rural Appalachia. In the 1980s, however, the job market expanded beyond the hospital settings into nursing homes, public schools, home health agencies, and child development centers. This was the result of rapid changes within the health-care delivery system itself and shifts in patterns of reimbursement for health-care services (Rabinowitz 1993; Clevett and Maltby 1992; Couto 1988; Denham 1996).

The combination of more culturally informed learning experiences within rural Appalachia and the expansion of job opportunities within the mountains has resulted in a growing number of graduates who are now going into Appalachia to provide health care. The majority of these health professionals are themselves Appalachian natives. Many have gone back to their home communities to live and work. These health professionals have a lot to teach us about how we might better prepare future students for working successfully in Appalachia.

The following vignettes are presented to illustrate the effect of educational preparation on health professionals in Appalachia. Pseudonyms have been used in each example. The information is drawn from a series of in-depth interviews with ten graduates of the program described above. Of the interviewed graduates, eight were females and two were males, nine were Appalachian natives, and one was from outside the region. Six additional interviews were conducted with Appalachian students enrolled at the university during the past year. All six of the currently enrolled students were females. Information was also obtained from the journal entries of approximately forty-five students enrolled in the course on providing health services in Appalachia over the previous twelve years.

The individual vignettes below are composites of information from each of these sources. The information has been compiled into fictionalized case vignettes in order to illustrate the most common experiences of students. None of the cases is meant to reflect any single individual.

Allison: An Individual Loses Her Identity, and Appalachia Loses a Health Professional

"Allison" graduated from the university in 1980. Her educational history reflects the period at the university prior to any significant efforts toward challenging the dominant, negative perspective of Appalachian culture. As a member of a large family and a native of a very small, rural Appalachian community, Allison came to the university following several of her older siblings. She decided to become a health professional after coming to college. Later she returned to the same university to earn a master's degree. It was during her graduate education in the class on providing health services in Appalachia that she began to reflect upon her earlier experiences.

As an undergraduate, Allison's adjustment to the university was initially very difficult. She was homesick and went home every weekend. Her older siblings who had completed college urged her to return to school every week during that first year. Without their support, she feels that she would have given up and dropped out of college.

As a freshman, Allison remembers being encouraged by some faculty members to alter her accent. Her impression at that time was that being an Appalachian person was viewed by others as a negative thing. She remembers trying to develop a specific speech pattern and a life-style similar to her perceptions of the non-Appalachian students in her classes. She also remembers one professor specifically complimenting her for her progress in making these changes in herself.

When she completed her undergraduate degree, she considered going home to work so that she could live near her family. The local hospital had job openings. But she was not encouraged by anyone to apply for a position at home. People at the university and even some people in her home community urged her to "think bigger" than the local hospital. In addition, she stated that some people in her home community felt that the local hospital had a poor reputation. Many of the health professionals who worked there were foreign nationals. It was not perceived as a place in which a promising young professional would want to begin a career.

After considering everyone's advice, Allison reluctantly chose to go to work in a large, urban area in a major medical center. She quickly advanced within her department and was soon in a supervisory position. She often encountered Appalachian patients, but she never thought much about where they had come from or where they would be going once they left the medical center. She rarely spoke about her community of origin and continued to think of it as an embarrassment. Most of the staff who worked for her had no idea that she had grown up in the mountains, nor that she counted very powerful politicians in the state among her relatives.

When she returned to graduate school, she hesitated before enrolling in the class on providing health services in Appalachia. As the Appalachian course progressed, Allison began to get a more informed perspective on her past. For the first time in her professional life, she felt affirmed as an Appalachian woman. She wondered what it would be like to go home and work.

However, Allison had accumulated significant benefits and promotions within her job. She had established a life for herself in the urban community where she lived and worked. To leave now and return home did not appear to be a feasible choice for her. In one journal entry, she described herself as "old Allison, finally out of the closet as an Appalachian." She stated that she felt better about herself. She wondered if she were not able to provide better health care to others as a result, especially those patients whom she encountered who were also from the mountains.

Allison's experiences appear typical for several of the students who were her peers as an undergraduate. In addition, some of the current students report the same initial homesickness and the negative perceptions of Appalachians on the campus which Allison faced two decades ago. While Allison reported never talking about these experiences with others on campus, current students state that they do seek out other Appalachian students for socialization and support.

In the same year in which Allison chose her first job in an urban area, the hospital in her local community was recruiting health professionals from the Philippines in order to fill all of their positions. Although Appalachian natives were graduating from the university annually, it would be more than ten years before any of them began to apply for positions such as the one that Allison briefly considered for herself and then rejected in 1980.

Jennifer: A Rural Appalachian Goes to the City then Finds Her Way Home

"Jennifer" graduated from the university in 1984. She also recalls negative impressions of Appalachians on campus and within the clinical settings where she received her training. Unlike Allison, however, Jennifer never moved to the campus as a residential student. She was an older, married student when she began her studies. Therefore, she chose to commute to school.

Jennifer never had the opportunity to enroll in a course on Appalachian health care. However, she did attend some of the annual conferences on Appalachian culture that were offered to health professionals. She eventually served as a speaker at one conference and shared her own experiences with others.

In reflecting upon her educational experiences, Jennifer feels that it was beneficial to her to be an older student with a more firmly established cultural identity. She had attended college previously. She had married and worked in various capacities. She returned to the university specifically for training as a health professional after a member of her family became ill.

Jennifer was very aware of the negative stereotypes of Appalachians that many people conveyed to her while she was at the university. However, she also knew that she would never leave her home community. Therefore, she ignored much of what she heard on the campus. She returned home daily and joked with her own family about the various misperceptions of mountaineers. She took the stereotypes that she heard at the university and turned them on their heads, often poking fun at the same people who had criticized her accent only hours earlier.

When she graduated, Jennifer felt initially that she needed contact with other health professionals in order to gain confidence in her own clinical skills. Therefore, she took her first job in an urban medical center and continued to commute several hours per day to and from work. She often encountered mountain patients in her case load and always felt comfortable working with them. She agreed to serve as a clinical supervisor for students and served as an excellent culturally informed role model for them.

Jennifer's ultimate professional goal was to return home to work independently. Working for a large health-care corporation had never appealed to her. After gaining almost four years of solid experience, she began to track the development of jobs in the mountains. As the trend toward home health care grew, she made her move into that market. She formed her own business and began to obtain contracts for service delivery in home health and in the public schools delivering services to handicapped children. She was still commuting daily, but now she was traveling into other mountain communities providing services in underserved areas. She soon had more work than she could handle. Faced with this dilemma, she hired additional staff. As some of these therapists began to join her and then leave over time, she gradually cut her business back and returned once again to individual private practice.

When interviewed about these decisions, Jennifer revealed some of the difficulties that she faced as an employer within a close-knit mountain community. Her primary problem was finding culturally sensitive health professionals who could work effectively with Appalachian people. For example, one of her employees was given directions by a family to their rural mountain home. The therapist was told to "turn left just beyond the tipple." Knowing nothing about coal mining and having no idea what a "tipple" was, the therapist assumed that the individual had mispronounced "temple." She spent hours driving though a very rural mountain community looking for a synagogue before stopping to ask for directions a second time.

Another employee considered the close attachments that families demonstrated toward their handicapped children to be problematic. This therapist appeared to resent the presence of mothers while she was attempting to provide therapy to children. She felt that the strong attachments that many Appalachian children displayed toward their mothers interfered with her therapy sessions. She was never able to see the mothers as potential partners with her in their children's care because she saw them as overly protective and uneducated. As a result, she was often irritable with the children and tended to blame the mothers for any lack of progress in their children's development.

A third therapist claimed to enjoy her work in the mountains. However, she perceived communicating with Appalachian patients and their families to be a major problem. She frequently complained about how difficult it was to educate patients and their families. She often said that she tried her best to "simplify things" and to "talk down to their level of understanding," only to find that her patients failed to follow her directions. This therapist considered her rural patients to be either intellectually limited and unable to follow "basic directions" or "unwilling to listen" even when she tried her best "to tell them what to do." She was never able to view cross- cultural communication as an equal exchange of information between herself and her patients. She viewed her rural mountain patients as unable to communicate with an "educated" person.

As Jennifer summarized her struggles with these staff members, she commented:

> The worst thing is getting someone who has never taken the time to learn anything about the region or someone who has learned a little bit and thinks that they know everything. They will piss people off every time, and the very first call you'll get after sending them out to work is "Don't ever send that person back here again." They fail to comprehend how complex personal communication is here, and they insult people all over the place and never even know it. They need someone to go along with them and translate for them. By the time you run around and put out all the fires that they've started, you really haven't gained very much by hiring some of these people.

Jennifer lived and worked in a community where most people knew her well and many people were her relatives. When her employees insulted people, she felt personally responsible for their behavior. People who had known her family for years were shocked that she would hire such insensitive health professionals. From her perspective, having technically proficient but culturally insensitive health-care providers was worse than being unable to provide enough services to fulfill all the needs. Coping with the disappointment of people whom she was trying to serve was very hard for her emotionally. "You all didn't cover how to handle this when we were in school," she said.

Jennifer's ultimate solution to her dilemma has been to encourage others to go into private practice for themselves and to refer her overflow work to them. Although she still receives calls from people who would prefer that she provide services to them, she now feels better about her own reputation.

Another dilemma which she has not solved is obtaining more work for herself closer to her home. As her children have grown, Jennifer would rather not commute such long hours each day. She could obtain more local contracts if her family were well connected to the local political power structure. She has not been able to break into the tightly controlled school system in her own county. Handicapped children in the public schools have frequently gone without services which she could have provided had the school board been willing to hire her. But her family has been a member of the minority political party for generations. "I just don't have the right politics," she said.

Jennifer's experience is similar to others who have gone home to work in Appalachia. Some of the other health professionals in the region are well connected to their local power structures. For these individuals, the path is cleared for easier access to patients, whether it is in the public schools or in the local hospitals whose boards also control access to jobs. But for Jennifer, there is little that she can do to change the historical legacy of her family's position in her home community. Everyone knows the political stance that her relatives have held for generations.

Paula: An Entrepreneur Goes Home

"Paula" completed her degree in 1993. She was on the university campus after the environment began to shift and more faculty were becoming aware of the need to learn about Appalachian culture. Paula came to school with the goal of becoming a health professional and returning home to her mountain community to work. Energetic, bright, and extremely motivated to succeed, Paula was both a single mother and an outstanding academic student. By the time she enrolled in the professional phase of her education, some of the hospitals throughout the mountains had shifted their recruitment strategies and begun to offer traineeships to local students. Paula received such a financial aid package from her local hospital.

When Paula returned home and began to work for the hospital, she felt pressured to produce a certain amount of income. Her supervisor often overbooked her for home health visits. In order to see all of the patients for whom she was scheduled, she often worked fourteen-hour days. "You know what it's like to get behind a coal truck going up some of these mountains. You just can't get anywhere very fast," she stated. In addition, she was often scheduled to see too many handicapped children in public schools that were spread too far apart to visit within one day.

When Paula complained to her administrator about this work schedule, she was told to deal with the problems on her own. It was suggested that she reduce treatment times to the minimum in order to cover all of the patients who were assigned to her case load. Gradually, her own health began to suffer as she struggled to meet the demands of an unreasonably large case load while trying to provide quality health care. Her home life suffered, too. "I hardly ever saw my baby," she said.

Paula eventually perceived a true ethical dilemma for herself. She felt that she was being pressured to provide less than adequate health care while the hospital billed for the maximum reimbursement of her services. "You all didn't train me to behave unethically," she stated. After struggling with this dilemma for several months, she sought the advice of a trusted local businessman. With his backing and support, she borrowed a very large sum of money, paid the hospital for her scholarship, and resigned her job. She then went into business for herself so that she could begin to repay the money she had borrowed.

Like Jennifer, Paula quickly had more work than she could handle by herself. With a large debt hanging over her head, she also felt that she needed to earn as much as she could. Thus, she chose to hire additional staff. After advertising broadly, Paula was still unable to find another health professional from Appalachia. However, her first new staff member had graduated from her own alma mater. She came into Paula's business from a major urban area on the West Coast. Paula quickly began to struggle with the same problems that Jennifer had experienced with culturally insensitive staff.

Determined to pay off her debt quickly, Paula explored several alternatives to cope with her staffing problems. She hired one of her younger relatives to accompany her new staff member. In essence, her relative served as a culture broker between the local people and this health professional (van Willigen 1993). While this did not eliminate all of the embarrassing moments, it did provide a local person who could smooth things over on behalf of Paula as soon as a problem arose.

Paula also hired an old friend as an office manager in order to ease some of her paperwork burden. Although some of her days were still quite long, she felt more in control of her own schedule. She also felt confident that she could remain ethical as a health professional and still earn enough money to repay her debt.

Privilege or Problem: Perceptions of Working in the Mountains

Both Paula and Jennifer perceive similar constraints and benefits in their work. Their constraints include poor travel conditions, large case loads, a sense of professional isolation, and chronic personnel shortages. Their most critical constraint remains the lack of culturally sensitive health professionals available to work with them in Appalachia.

When young Appalachian health professionals go home to the mountains to work, they often return to communities in which personal relationships exist within a complex social web. When a health-care provider inadvertently insults another person, everyone within this web eventually knows about it. Both Paula and Jennifer reflected the sentiment that "your reputation is everything here." The success of their businesses hinged upon their abilities to maintain their reputations as sensitive, caring individuals. When those who worked for them insulted the people who had known them all of their lives, they were faced with a dilemma for which none of their health-care education had prepared them. How they chose to negotiate this dilemma reflects two different strategies.

One of the problems that both Jennifer and Paula expressed was that health professionals from outside the region did not truly enjoy their daily interactions with mountain people. Both of these women perceived sharing an outlook on life and a sense of humor with other Appalachians as a particular reward of their work. They looked forward to each day's interactions.

Jennifer was particularly disappointed that the health professional with whom she had shared some of her original contracts did not appear to appreciate them. The woman who assumed some of Jennifer's public school contracts struggled with cross-cultural communication. She did not perceive that parents and teachers were eager to work with her, nor that they listened to what she suggested. Jennifer reflected sadly:

> She just gave those school contracts to her paid staff to cover. I couldn't believe it. I loved going to those places, even with the long hours of driving. They were always so glad to see me when I got there. They did everything that I suggested. They were so eager to learn. I hated to give up those contracts. I felt like I was giving her rare jewels or something, and it meant nothing to her.

Whether or not one perceives working with Appalachian people as a problem or a privilege apparently depends upon one's cultural perspective.

Implications for the Future

While these few vignettes point out some of the complexities of health-care delivery in Appalachia, they barely begin to scratch the surface of what we as educators need to know in order to better prepare future students. A series of in-depth ethnographic studies would be helpful in detailing more of the complex issues that both native and nonnative Appalachian health professionals currently face. In addition, much more research needs to be done to document and describe the miscommunication that occurs as those from outside the region attempt cross-cultural communication during health-care delivery.

The addition of the cultural context into a university curriculum for health professionals appears to have been very significant, especially for Appalachian students. With an informed perspective on their cultural heritage, they are affirmed and feel positive about going home to work. Additionally, an informed cultural context during training has been important in encouraging more nonnative students to enter the region to work as health professionals. The clinical practice among both groups of students may be enhanced as they move toward more reflexive clinical decisions.

However, when non-Appalachians work with Appalachian health-care providers, their failure to communicate well with local mountain people may create problems. The differences in communication patterns may be subtle. But it is apparently the subtleties that make all of the difference in whether or not one is viewed as a competent, contributing member of a health-care team or as a problem requiring additional staff to serve as culture brokers. If we are to increase the effectiveness of people working in the mountains in the future, we will have to begin to address the issue of cross-cultural communication patterns much more effectively than we have in the past.

References

Blakeney, Anne. 1987. "Appalachian Values: Implications for Occupational Therapists." *Occupational Therapy in Health Care* 4(1):57–72.

Clevett, Debbie, and Rycki Maltby. 1992. "Recruiting for Outlying Nursing Stations." *Nursing Management* 23:124–28.

Couto, Richard. 1998. "The Political Economy of Appalachian Health." *Health in Appalachia: Proceedings from the 1988 Conference on Appalachia.* Lexington: Appalachian Center at the University of Kentucky. Pp. 5–16.

Crandall, Lee, Jeffrey Dwyer, and R. Paul Duncan. 1990. "Recruitment and Retention of Rural Physicians; Issues for the 1990's." *Journal of Rural Health* 6(1):19–38.

Denham, Sharon A. 1996. "Family Health in a Rural Appalachian Ohio County." *Journal of Appalachian Studies* 2(2):299–310.

Gesler, William, and Thomas Rickets (Eds.). 1992. *Health in Rural North America: The Geography of Health Care Service and Delivery.* New Brunswick, N.J.: Rutgers University Press.

Kohler, Elizabeth, and Wanda Mayberry. 1993. "A Comparison of Practice Issues Among Occupational Therapists in the Rural Northwest and the Rocky Mountain Regions." *American Journal of Occupational Therapy* 47:731–37.

Lutz, Sandy. 1991. "Family Matters on Rural Recruiting." *Modern Healthcare* 21:43, 13.

Rabinowitz, Howard. 1993. "Recruitment, Retention and Follow-up of Graduates of a Program to Increase the Number of Family Physicians to Rural and Unserved Areas." *New England Journal of Medicine* 328:934–39.

Roberts, Allan, Laurence Davis, and James Wells. 1991. "Where Physicians Practicing in Appalachia in 1978–1990 Were Trained and How They Were Distributed in Urban and Rural Appalachia." *Academic Medicine* 66:682–86.

Roberts, Allan, Robert Foster, Margaret Dennis, Laurence Davis, James Wells, Mary Bodemuller, and Carolyn Bailey. 1993. "An Approach to Training and Retaining Primary Care Physicians in Rural Appalachia." *Academic Medicine* 68:122–25.

van Willigen, John. 1993. *Applied Anthropology: An Introduction.* Rev. ed. Westport, Conn.: Bergen and Garvey.

Part III

Transcending Stereotypes in Research and Practice: Examples from Health and Wellness

The chapters in Part III begin by addressing stereotypes regarding people in the Appalachian region. Some might argue that this is misguided. They suggest that it would be better to begin a study of Appalachian practice without rehashing destructive stereotypes. As one reviewer of this manuscript said, "Perhaps it is time to let that whole set of issues drop." Yet the fact that many of the authors in this volume feel the need to examine the phenomenon of Appalachian stereotypes as they affect their area of interest must be taken seriously. Negative stereotypes are imposed from outside a cultural group and they are the product of a history of oppression and inequality. They create general misunderstandings of peoples and cultures that are pervasive and persuasive. They lead others to lower their expectations regarding the cultural group, and their internalization reduces self-esteem among cultural group members. Moreover, they become part of the cultural context in which academicians set research agendas and policy makers create public policy. These consequences are very real, and instead of dropping the issue of stereotypes, we might better begin by heightening our sensitivity to various aspects of stereotypes in the Appalachian context and examining their impact on research and practice.

It is typical for discussions of stereotypes in Appalachia to begin with Jack Weller's book, *Yesterday's People* (1965). The fact that this book, written almost forty years ago, is still among the University Press of Kentucky's bestsellers testifies to its significance in the Appalachian literature and in the popular mind. As McKinney and Parrish (2000:3) note in an obituary about Weller, *Yesterday's People* "remains one of the best known and most important books ever written about Appalachia." It has been used as a handbook and "indispensable guide" (according to the book jacket) by generations of practitioners concerned with social welfare in the region, including Vista workers, social workers, psychologists, health-care workers, community development specialists, and those training for the ministry.

Short and readable, *Yesterday's People* continues successfully to engage readers from outside the region because it interprets and evaluates Appalachian culture through the mainstream American lens, and not surprisingly, Appalachia comes up short. In an appendix to the book, for example, Weller provides a comparative summary of southern Appalachian versus "middle-class American" traits, which lists mostly pejorative terms to characterize southern Appalachians, including such things as "fatalism," "individualism; self-centered concerns," "no interest in long-range careful planning," "little concern for job security or satisfaction," "ambivalence toward education," "fear of doctors, hospitals, those in authority," and "suspicion and fear of outside world" (1965:161–63). Meanwhile, the traits ascribed to middle-class Americans include "self-assurance," "oriented to progress," "desire and ability to plan ahead carefully," "striving for excellence," "attachment to work," "emphasis on education," and "acceptance of the world."

Little wonder Appalachian natives respond as they do to literature like *Yesterday's People.* Stereotypes are painful, and readers must be as willing to allow for the expression of anger and disbelief at these characterizations as they are willing to allow the characterizations to be expressed in the first place. In *Confronting Appalachian Stereotypes* (Billings, Norman, and Ledford 1999) a number of native-born Appalachian scholars explore their personal reactions to these stereotypes, and chapters in several parts in the volume at hand contain personal reactions to stereotypes as well. In chapter 7, for example, Appalachian native Anne Blakeney is passionate about her dismay at the stereotypes expressed on her campus and among medical professionals and her concern that these often go unassailed. In chapter 10, Carol Stephens notes that cultural stereotypes often serve as the only basis for decisions made by health-care professionals regarding Appalachian patients, a concern motivated not only because of her position on a nursing faculty but also because of her marriage to a native of the region.

Having recognized the persistence of cultural stereotypes, how do we find new orientations from which to approach research and practice in the region? The chapters in Part III suggest possibilities from the field of health and wellness. Susan Keefe and Paul Parsons, for example, began their research determined to collect comparative data on health behavior. By designing their research to gather survey data from both Appalachian and non-Appalachian respondents, they avoided making unwarranted assumptions about either group. Alternatively, Carol Stephens designed her study as an ethnographic description of preventive health practices, and her intention was to identify the Appalachian emic perspective rather than to assume the outside observer's perspective. Lisa Lefler turned to indigenous Cherokee healing specialists and asked about both traditional *and* new healing practices, recognizing the need to address the evolution of native Cherokee belief systems in a changing world.

The authors' recommendations for practice draw from these participant-centered approaches to research. Lefler, for example, admonishes practitioners to look for the persistence and revitalization of cultural traditions, such as native healers among the Cherokee, but also to be aware that they may have changed significantly, as have the "traditional" healers, in this case, who have expanded their repertoire to incorporate Christian and non-Cherokee traits. In her interviews with rural white mountain people, Stephens discovered local traditions not previously identified, such as religious resources and a "tradition of self-care," that should be recognized as significant indigenous health prevention practices by practitioners. In the same vein, Keefe and Parsons identify religious beliefs and practices, particularly prayer, that have been overlooked as resources in the literature on health assessment in the Appalachian region. In constructing their survey, Keefe and Parsons originally created a list of "alternatives for health care" by looking at other research questionnaires, none of which included religious alternatives. The alternative "prayer" was added only after reflection based on Keefe's ethnographic experience in the region, an alternative her students who helped construct the survey at first found odd and somewhat humorous. This example reminds us that health, like any cultural concept, must always be situated in its cultural context, which for both the Cherokee and southern mountain whites includes a significant spiritual dimension.

References

Billings, Dwight B., Gurney Norman, and Katherine Ledford (Eds.). 1999. *Confronting Appalachian Stereotypes: Back Talk from an American Region.* Lexington: University Press of Kentucky.

McKinney, Gordon B., and Thomas Parrish. 2000. "Yesterday's Author?" Berea College *Appalachian Center Newsletter* 29, no. 3 (Summer):3.

Weller, Jack. 1965. *Yesterday's People.* Lexington: University Press of Kentucky.

Chapter 8

Health and Life-style Indicators in a Rural Appalachian County: Implications for Health-Care Practice

Susan E. Keefe and Paul Parsons

Studies of health in southern Appalachia tend to focus on special subpopulations such as the poor or the elderly (Pearsall 1962; Steinman 1970), or to examine the use of traditional folk medicine (Lang et al. 1988), or to make assumptions without comparative data about what are characterized as suspicious and fatalistic health attitudes and behaviors of the Appalachian population (Loof 1971; Polansky, Borgman, and DeSaix 1972). These studies often produce findings that reinforce stereotypes regarding Appalachian people. On the other hand, very little research has been done on health attitudes and behavior in the general population of the southern mountains (for exceptions, see Couto, Simpson, and Harris 1995 and Plaut, Landis, and Trevor 1992). Likewise, there is little research examining differences in health attitudes and behavior between Appalachian natives and non-Appalachian newcomers, migrants into the region whose numbers have increased significantly since 1970 (an exception is Keefe 1988).

This chapter examines data from a Health and Lifestyles Survey conducted in Watauga County, North Carolina, in 1994–95. Watauga County is a rural county with a population of almost thirty-seven thousand, approximately one-third of which resides in the county seat of Boone. Appalachian State University is located in Boone, and the town is also a tourism center and a regional shopping and professional/medical services magnet area for surrounding counties. Newcomers have been attracted in large numbers to the county, many of them retirees or summer residents who have decided to live in the mountains year-round. In 1990, 37 percent of the county's population was made up of these recent non-Appalachian in-migrants. There is considerable tension between the Appalachian natives, most of whom live in the rural areas of the county, and the non-Appalachian newcomers, who more often live in and around the town of Boone. Differences between the groups are also apparent in cultural heritage, language and dialect, cultural identity, social networks, and socioeconomic status (see Keefe, Reck, and Reck 1989). Results from the Health and Lifestyles Survey are examined for differences between the Appalachians and non-Appalachians who were interviewed. The results indicate the need to reexamine common assumptions about Appalachian health behaviors and health-care needs.

Research Methods

A survey instrument was created after reviewing several existing questionnaires, including the Carter Center of Emory University Health Risk Appraisal Form (ND), the Heart Chec Plus Questionnaire (1987), and forms used by the Wellness Center at Appalachian State University. The final version of the instrument covered a variety of health and life-style indicators, including (1) definitions of health, (2) tobacco and alcohol use, (3) diet and nutrition, (4) exercise and relaxation, (5) exposure to hazards, (6) personal health status, and (7) the use of health-care alternatives. The survey contained a total of sixty-one mostly close-ended questions and could be administered in about ten minutes.

A systematic random sampling procedure was used to identify respondents. Two sections of the Watauga County telephone directory were selected for sampling: Boone (covering the urban county seat) and Sugar Grove/Watauga (covering the rural western part of the county). Using a random number start on every three pages, telephone numbers were selected using an interval of N = 10. A total of 225 telephone surveys were administered. The response rate was 65 percent.

Appalachian identity was established by asking the respondent his/her county of birth and classifying the county according to the list of southern Appalachian counties identified by the Appalachian Regional Commission (1974). These counties include all those in West Virginia and portions of Alabama, Mississippi, Georgia, Tennessee, Kentucky, South Carolina, North Carolina, and Virginia. This means of establishing cultural identity in Appalachia has been usefully employed in a number of recent studies (Dunst, Trivette, and Cross 1988; Keefe 1988; Keefe, Reck, and Reck 1989).

Surprisingly, only 36 percent of the sample is classified as Appalachian. This probably reflects, to some extent, the significant county in-migration rate in the last twenty-five years. University students who reside in the county (and who make up 20 percent of the sample) are also primarily non-Appalachians. On the other hand, the low proportion of Appalachians in the sample probably also reflects difficulties in administering a telephone survey. Appalachians, who are more likely to be lower in socioeconomic status, may be less likely to have a telephone or more likely to work evening jobs when many of the telephone calls were made. There may also have been group difference in the likelihood of volunteering for the interview once telephone contact was made; the refusal rate was somewhat higher, for instance, in the rural Sugar Grove/Watauga area of the county.

Respondents average forty-two years of age. Fifty percent of the sample is female, and 99 percent are classified racially as white. Forty-eight percent of the respondents are married, 34 percent are single, and 18 percent are either separated, divorced, or widowed. Fifty-seven percent live in a rural nonfarm setting, and 33 percent live in town, while only 10 percent live on a farm. The average length of residence in Watauga County is eighteen years.

The average household size is 2.4 persons, with 29 percent of the households consisting of parents and children, 22 percent married couples, 22 percent single individuals, and 19 percent individuals living with unrelated persons. Respondents tend to be Protestant (75 percent), and the most common denominations are Baptist (35 percent) and Methodist (14 percent). Twenty percent of the sample claim no religious affiliation. The majority (75 percent) of the sample have had one or more years of college; 21 percent have completed a graduate degree. Fifty-one percent of the sample have a white-collar job. Sixty-two percent of the respondents make less than thirty-five thousand dollars per year in family income.

The Appalachian respondents are overwhelmingly from North Carolina, where 90 percent say they were born. They have lived in Watauga County an average of thirty-three years. Non-Appalachians are most frequently from North Carolina as well (43 percent), but twenty-nine other states and three other countries were also named as places of birth. Most non-Appalachians were born in the South (71 percent), as opposed to the Northeast (19 percent), Midwest (7 percent), and West (2 percent). Non-Appalachians have lived in the county for an average of ten years.

There are significant differences between Appalachians and non-Appalachians in the sample with regard to background data. Appalachians in the sample are older on average (forty-eight vs. thirty-nine mean years of age) and are more likely to be female (60 vs. 44 percent). Appalachians are somewhat more likely to have married; only 26 percent of Appalachians have never married, in contrast to 38 percent of non-Appalachians. Appalachians are also somewhat more likely to live in a household with related family members (69 vs. 54 percent). With regard to residence, Appalachians are less likely to live in town (25 vs. 38 percent) and are more likely to live on a farm (18 vs. 5 percent) than non-Appalachians. Very few Appalachians claim no religious affiliation (9 vs. 23 percent). Furthermore, compared to non-Appalachians, most Appalachians in the sample are Baptist or Methodist (62 vs. 40 percent).

Socioeconomic differences also differentiate the two groups. Appalachians have less education, averaging 13.5 years as opposed to 15.4 years for non-Appalachians. The majority of non-Appalachians have a college degree or graduate studies (53 percent), compared to only 33 percent of the Appalachians. These group differences are mirrored in occupational status and income. Non-Appalachians are somewhat more likely to have white-collar jobs (72 vs. 64 percent), and non-Appalachians are much more likely to report family incomes of over thirty-five thousand dollars per year (47 vs. 22 percent).

Differences in Health and Life-styles

Group comparisons reveal a number of significant differences in all but one of the health and life-styles content areas. Table 8.1 summarizes data on tobacco and alcohol use in the sample. Thirty-two percent of the respondents use tobacco; most of these are cigarette smokers averaging thirteen cigarettes per day. About half of the nonsmokers have used tobacco in the past, and most of these quit more than ten years ago. There are no statistically significant differences between the Appalachians and non-Appalachians in tobacco use. It is interesting to note, however, that non-Appalachians are somewhat more likely than Appalachians to use chewing tobacco.

Table 8.1. Tobacco and Alcohol Use

	Appalachian (N=80) (%)	Non-Appalachian (N=144) (%)	Total (N=225) (%)
Tobacco Use			
Uses tobacco	34	31	32
cigars	0	2	1
pipes	4	2	3
chewing tobacco, snuff	15	24	21
cigarettes	85	82	83
#cigarettes/day	16	11	13
Nonsmoker ever used tobacco	48	52	51
Quit more than 10 years years ago	68	59	62
Alcohol Use			
Drinks alcoholic beverages	46	75[a]	65
Drinks 5+ drinks/session	19	14[b]	15
2+ drinking sessions/week	38	48	45

[a]Significance level: .001.
[b]Significance level: .05.

Alcohol use is much more characteristic of non-Appalachians than Appalachian natives (75 percent vs. 46 percent). While consumption rates are not significantly different among drinkers in the sample, the data seem to support the common assumption that Appalachians who drink are more likely to be binge drinkers since those in this sample are somewhat more likely than non-Appalachians to drink only once a week and to consume more alcohol when drinking.

Diet, exercise, and relaxation data are reported in table 8.2. Only two significant differences appear in the diet and nutrition indicators. Appalachians are more likely to report using shortening (a saturated fat) and whole milk (higher in fat and cholesterol than skim milk), both of which may contribute to coronary heart disease. Interestingly, Appalachians are no more likely than non-Appalachians to say they consume fruits and vegetables, despite this rural county's ubiquitous gardens and farms. Dietary practices in Appalachia have changed considerably in past decades as convenience foods and fast-food chains have become commonplace in the region.

Differences emerge on a number of exercise and relaxation questions. Appalachians are less likely to report engaging in vigorous aerobic exercise than non-Appalachians. Appalachians are more likely than non-Appalachians to respond that they sometimes experience severe nervous tension so that it

Table 8.2. Diet, Exercise, and Relaxation

	Appalachian (N=80) (%)	Non-Appalachian (N=144) (%)	Total (N=225) (%)
Diet and nutrition			
Snack several times a week	63	61	51
Shortening is primary fat	28	12[a]	18
Butter is primary spread	40	33	35
Use whole milk	35	15[b]	22
Use whole grains	79	85	82
Eat salty foods	39	40	40
Average servings per week:			
Red meat	3.2	3.0	3.1
Desserts	3.3	2.8	3.0
Fish or fowl	3.6	4.2	4.0
Eggs	3.4	2.5	2.8
Deep fried foods	2.7	2.6	2.6
Fruits and vegetables	12.2	12.4	12.4
Exercise and relaxation			
Job requires vigorous exercise	35	26	29
Vigorous exercise 3+ times a week	51	65[a]	59
Often experience stress	37	30	32
Sometimes experience severe tension	36	19[a]	24
Often take time to relax	54	71[a]	66
Get 7–8 hours sleep	65	69	68
Have close friends/relatives for help	94	97	96
Have group activities/hobbies	79	89[c]	85

[a]Significance level: .01.
[b]Significance level: .001.
[c]Significance level: .05.

Table 8.3. Exposure to Hazards

	Appalachian (N=80) (%)	Non-Appalachian (N=144) (%)	Total (N=225) (%)
Always wears seatbelt	71	78	76
Exposed to dust at work	21	11	14
Exposed to chemicals at work	19	11	14
Exposed to chemicals at home	16	11	13

disrupts their normal activities (36 vs. 19 percent). Appalachians are less likely to say they often take time to relax, and they are less likely to report participating in group activities (such as church or community activities) or in hobbies they enjoy.

As indicated in table 8.3, no differences appear in the questions regarding exposure to hazards in this particular sample. Only three significant differences are evident in the health status data in table 8.4. Appalachians are more likely to report having had arthritis, depression, and peptic ulcer.

Table 8.4. Health Status

	Appalachian (N=80) (%)	Non-Appalachian (N=144) (%)	Total (N=225) (%)
Overweight[a]	34	26	28
Normal blood pressure	66	67	67
Had one or more of the following diseases	80	66	71
Average number of diseases	1.8	1.3	1.4
Had following diseases:			
Allergies	45	42	43
Asthma	8	9	8
Emphysema	0	1	0
Lung disease	0	1	0
Tuberculosis	0	0	0
Cirrhosis	0	0	0
Diabetes	5	3	4
Kidney disease	3	1	1
Thyroid disfunction	5	5	5
Tumor or cancer	13	6	8
Epilepsy	0	1	0
Gout	1	5	4
Arthritis	34	18[b]	24
Nervous breakdown	4	1	2
Depression	21	9[c]	13
Stroke	3	1	1
Hypertension	11	6	8
Heart disease	6	3	4
Intestinal trouble	10	12	11
Jaundice/hepatitis	1	3	3
Peptic ulcer	9	1[c]	4

[a]Established by asking height and weight of respondent and comparing to height/weight standards for men and women issued by the Metropolitan Life Insurance Company (Gershopff 1990).

[b]Significance level: .01.

[c]Significance level: .05.

Table 8.5. Alternatives for Health Care

	Appalachian (N=80) (%)	Non-Appalachian (N=144) (%)	Total (N=225) (%)
Has health insurance	72	87[a]	82
Has dental insurance	24	52[b]	42
Used in past year:			
Dentist	59	81[b]	73
Chiropractor	8	11	10
Physician	79	81	80
Prescription medicine	76	69	72
Over-the-counter drugs	93	94	93
Home remedies	43	47	46
Folk medicine	13	20	17
Prayer	78	48[b]	58
Average number of health care alternatives used	4.5	4.5	4.5

[a]Significance level: .01.

[b]Significance level: .001.

Finally, table 8.5 summarizes data on health-care alternatives utilized by respondents. Appalachians are significantly less likely to have either medical or dental health insurance. This is probably the result of employment in jobs which often do not carry these benefits, such as seasonal, part-time, farming, and self-employed occupations.

Respondents are likely to seek help from a wide variety of health-care alternatives, averaging 4.5 sources of help in the last year. Group differences are evident in the use of only two of eight alternative sources for health care. Appalachians are much less likely to have seen a dentist, and they are much more likely to have prayed about their health in the last year. Interestingly, while the difference is not statistically significant, non-Appalachians are slightly more inclined to report using home remedies and folk medicine than Appalachian natives.

To summarize, the Appalachian respondents have significantly lower rates of alcohol use, rigorous exercise, group activities, time to relax, dental visits, and dental and medical insurance. On the other hand, the Appalachian respondents have significantly higher rates of use of shortening and whole milk, higher rates of severe tension, arthritis, depression, peptic ulcer, and are more likely to use prayer as an alternative for health care. Statistical analysis in the following section is used to further isolate the impact of cultural identity and background as opposed to socioeconomic status on these differences between Appalachian and non-Appalachian respondents.

The Salience of Cultural Identity

Significant differences between Appalachians and non-Appalachians appear throughout the data on health and life-styles. However, cultural identity is also significantly intercorrelated in this sample with other independent variables, including age, gender, rural/urban residence, education, and income, and these variables also have an impact on health and life-styles (table 8.6). Regression analysis was employed to test the relative significance of cultural identity (using birthplace as a marker) as compared to these other variables in determining health and life-style behaviors.

Appalachian birthplace contributes to an explanation of the variance in seven of the fourteen variables tested: alcohol use, dental insurance, peptic ulcer, severe tension, vigorous exercise, whole milk use, and prayer for health (table 8.7). Appalachian birthplace is the primary factor identified in explaining the variance in the first five of these variables.

Table 8.6. Correlation Coefficients of Fourteen Dependent Variables and Six Independent Variables

Dependent Variables	Appalachian Birthplace	Education	Income	Age	Male Gender	Urban Residence
Alcohol use	–.36[a]	.18[b]	.20[b]	–.30[a]	.18[b]	.24[a]
Dental insurance	–.27[a]	.23[a]	.24[a]	–.27[a]	.06	.14
Peptic ulcer	.21[b]	–.12	–.05	.15	.04	–.12
Severe tension	.19[b]	–.18[b]	–.14	.08	–.08	.03
Vigorous exercise	–.17[b]	.12	.11	–.05	.09	.13
Whole milk use	.22[b]	–.30[a]	–.13	.00	.18[b]	–.12
Prayer for health	.29[a]	–.09	–.12	.29[a]	–.14	–.10
Use of dentist	–.22[b]	.40[a]	.36[a]	.04	–.08	.17[b]
Shortening use	.23[a]	–.30[a]	–.18[b]	.06	–.04	–.14
Group activities	–.12	.24[a]	.14	–.10	.09	.11
Time to relax	–.20[b]	.25[a]	–.01	–.03	.07	.04
Arthritis	.19[b]	–.25[a]	–.11	.42[a]	–.02	–.16
Medical insurance	–.16	.24[a]	.21[b]	.00	–.02	.19[b]
Depression	.16	–.06	–.18[b]	.14	–.11	.07
Independent Variables						
Appalachian birthplace	1.00	–.36[a]	–.27[a]	.22[a]	–.17[b]	–.20[b]
Education		1.00	.34[a]	–.13	–.02	.21[b]
Income			1.00	.05	–.01	.12
Age				1.00	–.09	–.24[a]
Male gender					1.00	.09

[a]Significance level: .001.
[b]Significance level: .01.

Table 8.7. Results of Regression Analysis

Dependent Variable	Significant Predictor Variables
Alcohol use	Birthplace, age, income, gender, residence
Dental insurance	Birthplace, age, income
Peptic ulcer	Birthplace
Severe tension	Birthplace
Vigorous exercise	Birthplace
Whole milk use	Education, gender, birthplace
Prayers for health	Age, birthplace
Use of dentist	Education, income
Shortening use	Education
Group activities	Education
Time to relax	Education
Arthritis	Age, education
Medical insurance	Education, residence
Depression	Income, age

Measures of socioeconomic status (education and income) are more important in explaining the variance in the remaining seven variables tested: use of a dentist, shortening use, group activities, time to relax, arthritis, medical insurance, and depression (table 8.7). Socioeconomic status is the only factor contributing to an explanation of the variance in the first four of these variables.

Thus, Appalachian cultural identity is of importance in determining at least seven health and life-style indicators. These indicators cut across almost all categories of health and life-style that were surveyed, including alcohol use, diet and exercise, personal health status, and the use of health-care alternatives. The results indicate impressive cultural differences between Appalachian natives and in-migrants that have significant implications for health status and health services. These are explored in the conclusion.

Conclusion and Implications

This survey demonstrates that Appalachian cultural identity significantly shapes health and life-style factors. It is especially significant in determining alcohol use, aspects of diet, exercise and relaxation, and access to dental insurance. Certain stress-related illnesses (peptic ulcer and severe nervous tension) are also significantly related to Appalachian birthplace.

Given the strong correlation between Appalachian identity (as measured by birthplace) and lower socioeconomic status, those health and life-style factors determined more by SES also have a significantly greater impact on Appalachian natives as a group than on non-Appalachians. Thus, the additional health and life-style factors concerning diet, exercise and relaxation, access to medical insurance and dental care, and occurrence of arthritis and depression contribute to the health problems experienced more by Appalachians than non-Appalachians.

It is notable that several stereotypes concerning Appalachian health and life-style are not supported by the data. Appalachians are not significantly more likely to chew tobacco, eat farm-generated products and garden produce (such as fruits and vegetables and red meat), or use folk medicine and home remedies. Nor do Appalachian respondents indicate any suspicion of physicians and modern medicine, as the vast majority have seen a doctor and used prescription medicine in the last year.

Instead, Appalachians appear culturally distinctive in the survey primarily due to strong reliance on religion and prayer and abstinence from drinking alcoholic beverages, probably due mostly to religious sanctions. While numerous studies of Appalachian people pay attention to religious beliefs and practices and their impact on an Appalachian way of life (Dorgan 1987; McCauley 1995), little discussion of the significance of this appears in the literature on health in the Appalachian region (for exceptions, see Humphrey 1988; Keefe 2003; Simpson and King 1999). Another aspect of Appalachian lifestyles, a "multiple livelihood strategy," consists of a combination of economic strategies, such as gardening and the cultivation of small-scale cash crops (such as tobacco), performing odd jobs and seasonal work, relying on self-maintenance for household and machine repair, and commuting to factory jobs (Halperin 1990). It is likely that a multiple livelihood strategy, while creating economic stability for Appalachians, also contributes to the lack of access to medical and dental insurance benefits associated primarily with full-time large-industry employment. Finally, there are several indications that Appalachians, particularly those of lower socioeconomic status, must deal with greater levels of stress and experience a higher incidence of stress-related illnesses than non-Appalachians (see also Greenlee and Lantz 1993). Reasons for this cultural difference may be varied and could include the difficulty for Appalachians in juggling multiple livelihoods, the burden of extended family responsibilities, the relative lack of a safety net of insurance benefits and entitlement programs, and the strain of adapting to rapid sociocultural change in the mountains.

The results of this study challenge many preconceptions about Appalachian health behaviors. The results also indicate significant health-care needs of Appalachian natives, including dental care and the prevention and treatment of stress-related illnesses. Those concerned about health in the southern mountains are urged to increase efforts to provide health-care practitioners with a realistic appraisal of health status and practices in the region and health service needs.

Acknowledgments

We would like to acknowledge the assistance of the Appalachian District Health Department, especially Director Carl D. Tuttle, who first suggested this topic and its significance. Carl Jackson deserves special thanks for his assistance in the data analysis. Research support by the Department of Anthropology at Appalachian State University is gratefully acknowledged. Members of Keefe's Methods in Anthropology classes in spring 1994 and spring 1995 assisted in creating the survey instrument and interviewed half the respondents, while the remaining respondents were interviewed by Parsons and Sonya Little. Parsons was responsible for most of the data entry and much of the analysis. Keefe was responsible for designing the study and writing the results.

References

Appalachian Regional Commission. 1974. "The New Appalachian Subregions and Their Development Strategies." *Appalachia* 8(1):11–17.

Carter Center of Emory University. ND. *Healthier People: Health Risk Appraisal.* Atlanta: Carter Center of Emory University.

Couto, Richard A., Nancy K. Simpson, and Gale Harris (Eds.). 1995. *Sowing Seeds in the Mountains: Community-Based Coalitions for Cancer Prevention and Control.* Appalachian Leadership Initiative on Cancer. Washington, D.C.: National Cancer Institute.

Dorgan, Howard. 1987. *Giving Glory to God in Appalachia.* Knoxville: University of Tennessee Press.

Dunst, Carl J., Carol M. Trivette, and Arthur H. Cross. 1988. "Social Support Networks of Families with Handicapped Children." In *Appalachian Mental Health,* Susan Emley Keefe (Ed.). Lexington: University Press of Kentucky. Pp. 101–21.

Gershopff, Stanley. 1990. *The Tufts University Guide to Total Nutrition.* New York: Harper and Row.

Greenlee, Richard, and James Lantz. 1993. "Family Coping Strategies and the Rural Appalachian Working Poor." *Contemporary Family Therapy* 15:121–37.

Halperin, Rhoda H. 1990. *The Livelihood of Kin: Making Ends Meet "The Kentucky Way."* Austin: University of Texas Press.

Heart Chec Plus Questionnaire. 1987. Clackamas, Oreg.: Wellsource, Inc.

Humphrey, Richard A. 1988. "Religion in Southern Appalachia." In *Appalachian Mental Health,* Susan Emley Keefe (Ed.). Lexington: University Press of Kentucky. Pp. 36–47.

Keefe, Susan Emley. 1988. "An Exploratory Study of Mental Health Service Utilization by Appalachians and Non-Appalachians." In *Appalachian Mental Health,* Susan Emley Keefe (Ed.). Lexington: University Press of Kentucky. Pp. 145–58.

———. 2003. "Religious Healing in Southern Appalachian Communities." In *Southern Heritage on Display: Public Ritual and Ethnic Diversity within Southern Regionalism,* Celeste Ray (Ed.). Tuscaloosa: University of Alabama Press. Pp. 144–66.

Keefe, Susan E., Gregory G. Reck, and Una Mae Lange Reck. 1989. "Measuring Ethnicity and Its Political Consequences in a Southern Appalachian High School." In *Negotiating Ethnicity: The Impact of Anthropological Theory and Practice,* Susan Emley Keefe (Ed.). NAPA Bulletin 8. Washington, D.C.: American Anthropological Association. Pp. 27–38.

Lang, Forest, Dana Thompson, Brock Summers, Wesley Hanson, and Michael Hood. 1988. "A Profile of Health Beliefs and Practices in a Rural East Tennessee Community." *Journal of Tennessee Medical Association,* Apr., 229–33.

Looff, David H. 1971. *Appalachia's Children: The Challenge of Mental Health.* Lexington: University Press of Kentucky.

McCauley, Deborah Vansau. 1995. *Appalachian Mountain Religion: A History.* Urbana: University of Illinois Press.

Pearsall, Marion. 1962. "Some Behavioral Factors in the Control of Tuberculosis in a Rural County." *American Review of Respiratory Diseases* 85:200–210.

Plaut, Thomas, Suzanne Landis, and June Trevor. 1992. "Enhancing Participatory Research with the Community Oriented Primary Care Model." *American Sociologist* 23(4):55–70.

Polansky, N. A., R. D. Borgman, and C. DeSaix. 1972. *Roots of Futility.* San Francisco: Jossey-Bass.

Simpson, Mary Rado, and Marilyn Givens King. 1999. "'God Brought All These Churches Together': Issues in Developing Religion-Health Partnerships in an Appalachian Community." *Public Health Nursing* 16(1):41–49.

Steinman, David. 1970. "Health in Rural Poverty: Some Lessons in Theory and from Experience." *American Journal of Public Health* 60:1813–23.

Chapter 9

Culturally Relevant Preventive Health Care for Southern Appalachian Women

Carol C. Stephens

Prevention and health promotion are major focuses in the contemporary health-care environment. In recent years, a shift in emphasis from *treating* disease to health promotion and *preventing* disease has occurred, and with it an emphasis on the individual as bearing the primary responsibility for his or her own health (Laffrey, Loveland-Cherry, and Winkler 1986). The major emphasis of health promotion is focused on the individual, and the responsibility for health change is placed solely on the individual (Wallack and Winkleby 1987).

A widely held misconception about southern highlanders is that they are poor candidates for health promotion and preventive health care. This misconception is informed, to some extent, by the literature on Appalachian health, and it is further supported by widely held negative characterizations of southern Appalachian people.

Relatively few studies have investigated the health beliefs and practices of southern Appalachians, and even fewer studies have been conducted of their preventive and health-promoting behaviors (Stephens 1994). In fact, some writers have argued that Appalachians are not interested in preventive care (Stekert 1970; Weller 1965). Other writers, such as Rowles (1991), maintain that economic barriers and limited geographic access are major impediments to preventive care for mountain people. Some writers have implied that the health problems of mountain people can be attributed to Appalachians themselves. Simon (1987) and Tripp-Reimer and Friedl (1977) attribute health problems of Appalachians, in part, to the value and behavioral systems of mountain people. For example, Tripp-Reimer and Friedl write that in "Appalachia, acute health needs result from an internally reinforcing feedback system consisting of an illness-promoting environment, inadequate medical care, and the value and behavioral systems of the mountaineers" (1977:43).

Studies of preventive health behavior among Appalachians have frequently developed from the etic or professional point of view and have a highly specific focus, such as contraceptive use (Gairola, Hockstrasser, and Garkovich 1986), nutrition knowledge (Halverson 1987), tuberculin testing (Nickerson and Hockstrasser 1970), or the utilization or effectiveness of medical services (Cowan et al. 1978; Femea 1981; Fisher and Paige 1987; Jarvis et al. 1966). Although valuable, these studies have made little contribution to the understanding of indigenous preventive health patterns among southern highlanders.

The notion that preventive and health-promoting knowledge may be part of southern Appalachian culture is one which has received very little attention in the literature (for an exception, see Burkhardt 1992). A limited number of studies of Appalachian preventive health behavior have been conducted from the emic or native point of view rather than an etic perspective (Hansen 1985; Hansen and Resick 1990; Hardin 1990; Riffle, Yoho, and Sams 1989; Stephens 1994). Some researchers, including Boyle and Counts (1988), Hansen (1985), and Hardin (1990), have focused on Appalachian culture as it relates to preventive health beliefs and behavior. A few studies have researched health attitudes and behaviors among the general mountain population (Couto et al. 1995; Plaut et al. 1992). Most of these studies, however, did not specifically examine aspects of the traditional Appalachian cultural pattern which were health enhancing.

The views held of Appalachians by members of mainstream middle-class culture are often informed more by stereotypes than by accurate cultural description (for discussion, see Batteau 1990; Shapiro 1978; Whisnant 1980). These conditions promote misinterpretation of Appalachian health beliefs and behaviors, as well as ethnocentrism on the part of health-care professionals.

Ethnocentrism is not limited to health-care professionals whose origins are from outside the Appalachian region. Health professionals who are native to the mountains may also develop ethnocentric biases since most are educated within the middle-class value system of mainstream culture (Hansen and Resick 1990). Branscome (1971) and Clark (1974) have argued that education of Appalachian students in middle-class institutions has the effect of alienating them from their native culture. Batteau and Obermiller (1983) describe the recent emergence of a socially dominant professional class in Appalachia, including health-care professionals, which serves to perpetuate perceptions of the inferiority of mountain people and their culture.

Southern Appalachians have been subjected to powerful and pervasive negative stereotyping for decades. Writers such as Caudill (1962) and Weller (1965) have a role in perpetuating the stereotype of the ignorant, stoic, and unmotivated mountaineer. Belcher has noted that "the stereotype of the 'mountaineer' which is so firmly fixed in many minds bears little resemblance to the reality of today—or, indeed of any other time" (1962:37).

Negative stereotypes about Appalachians also appear in nursing and medical literature. On the basis of a study conducted at the West Virginia University School of Medicine, Goshen (1970) categorized southern Appalachians as being either cultural primitives who have traits like those seen in schizophrenia or traditional farmers having a character more parallel with neurotic psychopathology.

Flaskerud (1980), a nurse researcher, is one of several writers who has characterized Appalachians as being fatalistic and resistant to change:

> They are guided by traditionalism and resistance to change as opposed to the emphasis on progress and development that guides the rest of the United States. They are passively resigned to their situation in life and have been characterized as fatalistic in opposition to the dominant culture which stresses achievement, competition, and mastery over one's environment (1980:142).

Flaskerud's description of Appalachians was undoubtedly not intended to be pejorative; however, "fatalistic" and "resistant to change" are characterizations that continue to appear in the literature, and they have become associated with the negative stereotyping of Appalachians.

Misconceptions about Appalachian health behavior together with widely held cultural stereotypes have profound implications for the interactions of health professionals with Appalachian clients and the quality of health care these clients receive. In order for nurses and other health-care professionals to provide effective, culturally competent care, it is essential that they be knowledgeable about the cultural context of client health beliefs and behaviors.

The purpose of the study described in this chapter was to develop knowledge about southern Appalachians and their health attributes, which can be used to inform the practice of nurses who work with this population. This study describes health beliefs and practices of rural working-class southern Appalachian women from the emic perspective.

Methodology

An ethnographic study of health beliefs and practices of rural southern Appalachian women in western North Carolina was conducted in rural areas of one of the westernmost counties of North Carolina. The study sample consisted of ten women who were wives and mothers, ages twenty-five to eighty-three, living in working-class families.

Informants were considered to be Appalachian based on their having met a three-generational depth criterion. They, along with their parents and grandparents, were from the Blue Ridge Mountains of southern Appalachia, with no generation having lived outside the region for longer than two years. A purposive sampling method was used, and informants, with one exception, were nominated by public health nurses. Additional selection criteria included the following: no known substance abuse, being a reliable informant, being white southern Appalachian, and speaking from a native frame of reference, that is, not translating into a professional or middle-class perspective.

Data were collected using observation and in-depth interviews. An interview guide based primarily on Leininger's (1978) culturologic assessment domains was developed. The modified domains used to develop the guide included (1) general cultural life patterns of life-style, (2) social network, and (3) cultural values and norms. Each of these domains was explored as they related to preventive health practices. All the informants were interviewed once, and four women, identified by the researcher as key informants, were subsequently interviewed two to four more times. Interviews were primarily conducted in the informants' homes, although one woman was interviewed at her place of business. Ethnographic strategies were used to analyze interview transcriptions and field notes.

Description of Informants

Susie

Susie is an erect, slim woman of eighty-three whose energy is readily apparent in her quick movements, lively talk, and easy laughter. She trots instead of walks, and she always manages to keep herself busy. She and her husband of sixty-nine years live in a small wood-frame house located fifteen minutes from the nearest town.

Susie and her husband had eight children, five of whom are still living. The other three died in infancy. The living children range in age from forty-eight to sixty-six, and they all live nearby and visit regularly. Susie's children and their families take turns coming for Sunday dinner; she has twelve to fifteen people for dinner every Sunday, and she does all the cooking.

Susie's activities include caring for the pedigree animals she raises to sell, refinishing furniture, piecing quilts, making Irish needlework pieces, mowing the yard on a riding mower, gardening (which includes everything except plowing), canning and filling two freezers, and doing all her own cooking and housework. She cared for her parents and her mother-in-law in her home during their advanced age until their deaths.

Birdie

Birdie is a fifty-eight-year-old woman whose household also includes her disabled husband. At one time, she was the caretaker for five generations, including her husband's sick grandmother, who moved in with them. She owns and manages a small shop on the outskirts of town, while the family lives in the countryside.

Birdie describes her day as beginning at 6:00 A.M. with breakfast, followed by an hour of devotional time during which she reads the Bible, thinks, and prays. After her devotional time, she showers and straightens up her house. She carries out many different types of activities during the course of the day in the store. Her husband owns a portable toilet business and she handles all the billing and bookkeeping for him out of her store. She works with customers, manages details of her own business, and serves as a kind of resource network for friends and neighbors. People frequently come by asking about where to go to obtain various kinds of services or information.

Birdie is a soft-spoken woman who speaks thoughtfully and easily. She has very strong health beliefs based on her belief that her body is the temple of the spirit and that her body tells her what it needs. She believes in the wisdom of the body, and she seems very attuned to the nature of her own bodily needs and responses.

Gerri

Gerri is thirty-three years old and the mother of three children: a twelve-year-old son, a two-year-old daughter, and a three-month-old son. She is moderately overweight, and she dresses plainly and wears no makeup. She described herself as being very country and honest. Her presentation of herself was shy and self-conscious, but she was very genuine and thoughtful in talking about herself.

She and her family were the least prosperous of the informants, and they live in a very rural, isolated section of the county. Their home, located at the end of a dirt road by a creek, is a two-story log house which they built themselves. They grow all their own food in the garden and they rarely eat meat.

Gerri's focus in life is her children and making a good family life for them. Her typical day includes child care and some work around the house. The only other person she sees is her husband's mother. She describes not having anyone to turn to when she has a problem. She leaves home only to go to the health department or the grocery store. Even then, her children are her focus, and she makes careful preparations in order for the children to be well fed and rested ahead of time.

Antique

Antique is forty-four and the mother of two sons and three daughters whose ages range from six to twenty-six. She selected her code name because she loves old things. The household consists of Antique, her husband, who is a minister and carpet layer, their fourteen-year-old son, and their six-year-old adopted daughter.

Their house, a mobile home which has added on permanent rooms, sits on a small rise deep in the countryside. The house is located on a large sprawling property which includes a large, old unpainted barn and several outbuildings set in rolling hills dotted by very large old trees.

Antique does not work outside the home, but she works all day. Much of her day is spent cleaning and cooking, gardening and canning and freezing in the summer, and caring for her children and her elderly father, who lives alone. Her husband is between churches, but she takes an active role as the preacher's wife when he does have a church. Her fourteen-year-old son raises hound dogs and she helps him with that. She said there were two things she would not tolerate in her children: being backward or being lazy.

Maggie

Maggie is a seventy-five-year-old widow who lives alone. She is thin and fairly erect, despite a chronic illness which causes her to have a great deal of weakness and fatigue. She is retired after working as a secretary for a well-published author. Her three children, grandchildren, and great grandchildren live nearby and she sees them often.

Her house is a moderate-sized wood-frame house which her husband built over fifty years ago. It sits back from the road on a small rise surrounded by enormous oak trees. She lives in a rural area about twenty-five minutes from town. Maggie is a warm, gregarious woman who has a large number of friends, many of whom check on her often.

Maggie does not drive, but friends come take her out, often to church or the community center. She still attends church on a regular basis. Unlike the other women, she is no longer in a care-giving role. She values her independence, but she asks for and accepts help.

Alicia

Alicia is twenty-five and she lives in a mobile home with her husband and their five-year-old daughter. Their home is on a very small, cramped piece of property in the bend of a dirt road. The home and yard are modest and show signs of neglect. Alicia's husband is a tree trimmer, and she has periodically worked in local factories when their daughter's health permitted.

Most of their money, and almost all of Alicia's time, is devoted to her little girl, who was born with a birth defect and has severe chronic respiratory disease. The child almost did not survive, and she has been able to do so only with her mother's care and expensive medical intervention. They have taken her several times to a medical center down state, and more recently to a specialty center in the western part of the United States.

Alicia acknowledges that her life is hard, but despite that and the fact that they have severe financial problems, she is cheerful and optimistic. She values her family more than anything in the world, and she thinks her child has a special reason for living. She talks about how much her daughter has grown up in the last five years. Alicia is both very loving and strict with her daughter. She insists on enforcing limits with her and expects her to be considerate of others.

Lucille

Lucille at sixty-eight is very short and stocky, deeply tanned, and deeply wrinkled. She is the mother of one son, "Rooster," who was present for the first interview. Lucille's husband had a massive stroke five years ago, and she has cared for him at home since he left the hospital.

Rooster quit his job as a long-distance trucker five years ago in order to come home and help care for his daddy, who is bedridden and incoherent. Lucille said they were told that her husband needed institutional care and that he would not survive at home. However, he has gained weight on the tube feedings and he has never had a bed sore.

Their home is a small, modest wood-frame house which, though in a rural area, is part of a cluster of like houses. The living room contains a large oil space heater. The room is dark, sparsely furnished, and the air is stale. Lucille's husband is visible in a hospital bed in an adjacent room.

Brooke

Brooke is thirty-four and the mother of four young children, the youngest of whom is a year-old infant. Her husband is an electrician, and Brooke taught primary school, but she left teaching five years ago in order to be home with the children full time.

Her home is a mobile home, and they are gradually building a house around it. Their home is set far back from a two-lane country road at some distance behind her parents' home. Her family raises beef to eat. They also have a large garden which provides much of their food.

Brooke does a lot of the outdoor work and the finishing work on the construction of their new home. Her mother takes care of the children during large parts of the day so that Brooke can do this work. Her days are very full, and they are spent almost exclusively at home or with relatives nearby.

Tammy

Tammy is thirty-seven, and she works part time as a nursing assistant on two different jobs. She is the mother of three adolescent children, and she is the caretaker of several other members of the family. Her father and her mother-in-law live nearby on the property, and she helps care for them. Her husband is disabled as the result of an occupational injury, and though he is alert and talks with her, he needs a great deal of physical care. In addition, she has a brother who is depressed and unemployed and she is a primary care giver for him. She was also involved in the care of other elderly relatives, some who were seriously ill.

Tammy's health pattern differed from that of the other informants. She said she only gets between three and five hours of sleep each night and she eats on the run and drinks over a gallon of iced tea each day. She was an extreme example of taking care of others and not taking care of herself. There did not appear to be anyone available to provide care for her, since the people in her immediate circle are either children or adults with serious health problems.

Ann

Ann was the only informant who lived in the city limits. She and her husband had grown up in the country, and they had raised their family there. They had come to the city only upon retirement. They retained the patterns associated with rural living, and they were considered rural for the purposes of the study. Ann had worked at various times in her life, including a few years in a school cafeteria, as a beautician in her home, and at some factory jobs.

She and her husband continued to work hard, to stay in close contact with a large number of family, and to maintain a garden. She continued to can, clean, and cook, including Sunday family dinners and the Christmas meal for thirty-one family members. Ann suffered a heart attack, and she died before the study was completed.

Findings

The following three findings of the study are ones which have not been previously reported in the literature: (1) traditional Appalachian culture includes health-maintaining and preventive health practices, (2) determination is a cultural trait of the informants, and (3) intuitive knowing is an important source of insight and guidance for health-related problem solving. The remaining findings of the study were supported by findings from previous studies. The following discussion of findings is organized according to the six themes which emerged from the data.

The following themes emerged from intensive analysis of the data: (1) health is life, (2) healthy living is the way to have a healthy life, (3) family is the most important thing, (4) the mother is at the center of the mountain family, (5) determination is a mountain trait, and (6) intuitive wisdom and "the Lord told me" are important sources of insight and guidance for health-related problem solving. These themes will be described in detail.

Health Is Life

When asked to define health in her own words, Susie said, "Let's see, it is life. Health, I think, it's happiness, and what else? Happiness and thankfulness, feel good and not have a dread on you [being worried]." Later on she added, "Well, when you are healthy, you are happy and looking forward to life, and so I think that's it."

Informants defined health both in terms of feeling good and being able to work, and their responses were equally divided between the two types of definitions. Informants' descriptions of the former type included "Feeling good," "Feeling strong," and "Having energy." Descriptions related to being able to work included "Being able to do what you want to," "Being able to do what you need to," and "Being able to take care of yourself." The importance of work as a source of, and a manifestation of, health was mentioned several times. The meaning of health, then, was embedded in the life context.

Antique's values about work are similar to the values expressed by other informants in the study:

> That's the way we was raised up. When you do something, you do it right. And you don't quit on anything. And I've tried to bring that over to the kids like when they were playing ball. They were half way through the season and they'd want to quit. I'd make them finish it out. I guess that's more or less what we were taught by our parents. My dad stresses hard work. I mean, that is the way we were brought up. When you do it, you do it right. You don't goof around, you work.

Healthy Living Is the Way to Have a Healthy Life

Nine of the informants reported health practices related to having a healthy life. These practices included preventive as well as health-maintaining and health-promoting activities.

The most frequently reported health practices were diet related. Nine of the informants emphasized the importance of a balanced diet in relation to good health.

There was, however, variability in the informants' definition of a balanced diet. Nine reported that they emphasized vegetables in their diet. Eight of the informants included meat in their diet, but five reported avoiding excess sugar, meat, fat, and salt in their diet. Seven of the informants reported avoiding or limiting their intake of processed foods, and they emphasized the importance of home-cooked food and eating a variety of foods. A commonly expressed concern was the negative health effects of food additives. All except two of the informants raised their own food in gardens, and their families provided garden vegetables to them. Antique's description of her family's diet is typical of the informants' responses:

> We don't eat things like other families do. Like TV dinners and things like that. We don't eat a lot of prepared foods. I prepare it. We might open two or three cans here a week, you know, store-bought cans. But they just don't eat it. I guess it's the way I brought them up from the start. TV dinners and things like that, there is no way. Any of those frozen dinners, the Banquet frozen—I tried those and you can forget that, too. They just pretty much eat things from scratch, like vegetables and potatoes and stuff that is cooked, instead of stuff that has been precooked.

Two informants did not have gardens; Maggie has myasthenia gravis, and she does not have the stamina to garden. Alicia does not have her own garden, but she works in her parents' garden. They both have home-grown vegetables available to them.

The importance of exercise and activity to good health was described by eight of the informants. Nine of the informants reported engaging in outdoor activity, and five described the importance of getting activity outdoors in fresh air. Over half of the women described the importance of staying busy to good health, and four of the women reported using activity to energize themselves or to moderate their moods. These women used activity or staying busy to overcome fatigue, avoid worrying, or improve depression.

Self-care is a strong pattern among informants in the study. Half of them reported going to the doctor as little as possible, relying on prevention and self-care instead. Three of the informants believed that a person's body would let its needs be known if one would only listen. The informants, with one exception, demonstrated acceptance of responsibility for their own health.

Seven of the women described the importance of spiritual activities to their well-being. The spiritual practices included prayer, meditation, quiet time, Bible reading, and attending church services.

Six of the women described participating in activities to cope with or to modify stress. The most frequently reported activities were the spiritual activities just described. Other practices included looking to the future, consciously deciding not to worry, talking to someone, turning worries over to the Lord, and talking to oneself.

The informants were consistent in their belief that rest is important to health, however, three of the women reported getting less than seven hours of sleep each night. Two of these were mothers of small children who stayed up late either to have her own quiet time or to do chores when the children slept. None of the three reported being dissatisfied with the amount of sleep obtained.

Five informants reported specific safety practices which were intended to prevent injury. Examples of these practices included taking care when using machinery, precautions taken to avoid falls, and protecting children from poisoning or drowning. There was no consistent pattern of seat belt or smoke detector use.

Most of the informants engaged in some practices designed to promote family health. One such practice was that of taking care of their own children, and giving their children opportunities and the resources to grow healthy and strong, such as lots of fresh air, good food, time for their own interests, clear limits, and a harmonious family life.

Only two of the informants reported the current use of herbs for health reasons. Gerri and Susie reported using catnip tea to promote rest and sleep. Gerri gives the tea to her children as well.

Several of the informants described health practices historically used by mountain people which were preventive or health maintaining in nature. According to the informants, there was a traditional emphasis on a varied diet, which included little sugar and lots of vegetables and fruits when available, and a reliance on fresh air, hard work, and staying busy. In addition to these practices, some medicine and herbs were used specifically for prevention. Asafetida, which is a fetid gum resin contained in certain plants, was used as a prophylaxis against contagious diseases before the advent of antibiotics. The asafetida was worn around the neck on a string. Sometimes it was chewed, and sometimes put in a jar with moonshine and the resulting solution was taken.

Sassafras tea and other preparations such as molasses and sulfur were used to purge the blood in the spring in people who were asymptomatic but thought to be in need of a good purging or worming. Catnip tea was used to promote rest and sleep. It was formerly used to break out the hives on newborn babies, which was thought to prevent complications which would result if the hives did not break out.

Family Is the Most Important Thing

For the most part, families made up the primary group for informants in this study. Family members tended to live near each other, often on the same land. Ann described where her children live:

> I had four children. My oldest son is dead. I have a daughter and two sons living. They all live in the Madison section. One of them lives on, well, two of them lives on Glady Fork Road. I mean, my son that passed away, his family still lives on Glady Fork, and my daughter lives on Glady Fork. Yes, and my baby son lives in the Maple Cove on a track of my daddy's land. Then my other son lives in Bird's Eye Cove out in that section. Yes, they all live near me. They can be here in fifteen or twenty minutes.

Families also had a high degree of reciprocal care taking, with the trading off of services and goods being common. Examples include Antique and one of her daughters sharing bushels of fresh vegetables from their gardens; one would give potatoes, and the other cabbage. Brooke's mother assisted her with child care, and Birdie participated in the care of her grandchildren.

Taking care of their own was an important part of this theme. Alicia devoted her life to the care of her daughter, and Lucille's life focused on the care of her husband. Antique, Birdie, Susie, and Tammy had all cared for ailing and elderly family members, both in and out of their homes.

Decisions were made in terms of their effect on the family. Gerri relegated work to a second priority in order to make a good family life for her children. Her devotion to family is expressed in the following vignette:

> Gerri's focus in life was her children and making a good family life for them. She said her parents were not there for her and work came first. Gerri put time with the children ahead of housework or gardening. She said she sometimes stayed up until 1:00 A.M. ironing so she did not have to do it when the children were awake.
>
> Gerri's typical day included child care and some work around the house. The only other person she saw was her husband's mother. She described not having anyone to turn to when she had a problem. Gerri left home only to go to the health department or to the grocery store. Even then her children were her focus, and she made careful preparations in order for the children to be well fed and rested ahead of time.

Antique's husband once pastored a church in rural eastern Tennessee for two years. They made the decision not to relocate because it would disrupt the lives of the children. Therefore, they commuted a distance of nearly one hundred miles at least once a week for two years.

Being able to take care of the family was a reason for taking care of oneself. Birdie talked about taking care of five generations at once. She started to worry about how she could manage when her husband's incapacitated grandmother moved in with them. She went to a Christian counselor who told her that she needed to take some time for herself. Birdie paid her money and never went back. However, she subsequently tried out a different way of coping, which involved taking better care of herself, but it was acceptable because it was framed in terms of being able to be a mother to all those who needed her. Birdie followed the counselor's advice to take time for herself only when it was framed (by herself) in culturally acceptable terms.

The Mother Is at the Center of the Mountain Family

The mother's position is the one of most power in the home. She has tremendous responsibilities, including the health of the family, and she works hard, but she is also the one who is in charge at home.

The mothers in this study did not talk about their work and responsibility in negative terms; their role was never described as a burden. In each case, and in different ways, each informant is a strong woman. They were not doing a job; their families were the focus of their commitment, purpose, and energies.

Determination Is a Mountain Trait

Determination is viewed as a combination of decisiveness, perseverance, and innovative problem solving, and it is the opposite of fatalism, or passive resignation as it is described in the literature.

The informants did seem to be accepting of things over which they had no control, such as a birth defect, low income, or catastrophic illness. However, they were anything but passive in their responses to most situations that came their way. They were persistent in the face of challenges, and the attitude was more of "there has to be a way" rather than "there is no way." Their determination was especially pronounced as it related to the importance of family.

Lucille was told that there was no way she could take care of her husband at home, but with her son's assistance, and despite her own health problems, she has provided optimal care at home which has been evidenced in an improvement rather than a deterioration of his condition. Brooke's primary value was being home as a full-time mother to her children, but she enjoyed working. She found it difficult to stay home, but she has persevered, and now she is very content with the life she has made at home. Antique was caring for her arthritic father who wanted to live independently regardless of his limitations; however, he had difficulty getting over a step into the shower and with dressing. The following vignette illustrates the determination of both Antique and her father:

> Daddy has arthritis from his waist down. It's in his hips. And if there's something Daddy needs to do, he'll find a way to do it. He couldn't get in and out of the shower. I was over there one day and I happened to think about a brick. I told him I was going to bring that brick in here. See his leg is hard for him to maneuver, but by stepping on the brick, he gets over in the shower now. He couldn't get his socks on either, and I was in there cleaning one day and I had a long pair of barbeque tongs. I told my husband I believed Daddy could put his socks on with those. I took those tongs over there and bent them—you know they come out like this and we bent them. Daddy takes those tongs and holds the mouth of the sock open, and then he gets it on his foot and he reaches down and pulls that sock on. It is hard on his socks, but he's got his socks on which he couldn't do by himself before. And I think, you know, where there's a will, there's a way. The determination has to be there, you know, to stay active and not sit down. I believe if something was wrong with me where I just sat down and couldn't go, it would kill me or I'd die faster. Whatever was wrong with me, it would just kill me.

Maggie exhibited her determination in relation to wanting to live independently despite the limitations on her mobility and energy imposed by her illness. She does not drive, but she has a network of family and friends in place who help her out and who meet her social needs. Ann told about having her first heart attack when she was setting a customer's hair in her home shop. She initially had severe angina, but she finished rolling up the woman's hair before she went to the hospital. Susie described being raised to find a way rather than saying that she could not do something. In the following vignette, she describes her determination, including an incident in which she wanted to get a rug out from under one leg of a heavy four-poster bed (after she was eighty):

> A lot of times—now I have had a bladder infection one time. And I sat down and I'd just think—you know I'd put my head down and I'd think—well, that's going to be all right. I've not got it, that's just my imagination. And I'd sit there and dwell on being all right and I'd get all right. But, you know, a lot of things you can't. There is some things you can't talk yourself out of. But I have. I'll tell you what I did one time: I had to lift a bed in there. My rug had got all wadded up, and I was afraid it was going to get a hole cut in it. That was that heavy bed and I tried to lift it and I couldn't scoot that out with my foot. Finally I said, "Well, I know I can!" And I just stood there a few minutes and I just got that bed and I just lifted it right up [laughed]. But I believe in that positive thinking a whole lot.

Intuitive Wisdom and "The Lord Told Me" as Sources of Insight and Guidance

The informants talked about the insights and wisdom which seem to come unbidden to them after they have been faced with a challenge they did not know how to meet. It seems such insights are an extension of their determination, in that the women turned to meditation, prayer, or reflection when solutions to conflicts or problems were not readily apparent. Later, the insight or answer would occur to them. They described this experience in these words: "It just come to me," "The Lord told me," or "I learned to find answers inside myself."

Alicia's daughter was born with a life-threatening birth defect. She describes the Lord telling her that her baby would be all right:

> Well, I put it in the Lord's hands and I had strong faith. And after I had Annie, the Lord told me that she was going to be all right. He's let her be all

> right so far. And I feel that He will take over with her and if it is her time to go then me and Martin would have to accept it then at that time. So, it is in His hands. She's in His hands. I mean, it helped me to be strong and keep holding up and being a Mom like I should to her. And Martin feels the same way too.

In the situation described earlier, Birdie had gone to a Christian counselor when her husband's grandmother moved in with them. She saw the counselor only once because she did not like the advice the counselor gave: to take more care of herself and do less for her family. She prayed for strength to handle the situation and for help to find the way. She felt the Lord guided her to start walking, which she began to do in the morning and in the evenings.

Gerri described being very alone and not having anyone to turn to when she had a problem. She also described herself as being a "heart" person, hurt more on the inside than on the outside. She described an incident that happened when she was pregnant and her pregnant sister was staying with her. Her sister, who did not help out, was one more person to take care of, and Gerri found herself getting more and more tired and unable to sleep. She looked inside herself for an answer and taught herself to start being more assertive. She told her sister that she had to make other arrangements. In the next vignette, Gerri describes listening to her own inner voice:

> I'm healthy. There's not nothing wrong with me, and that's what I'm thankful for. Other than that, I'm happy with myself. More so now than I used to be. I used to put my own self down. I couldn't do nothing. I'd try to show my feelings and I'd go about it the wrong way. There's a part of me that I'll wait and I get this feeling inside me and I go on that feeling. And that's the part that's good. Because every time I do that, it works out. I'm a person that has to think about something. It takes me a while to figure out what's a bothering me and what to do about it. It takes time for me to think about myself and what's my goal. . . . I learned that myself.

When Antique and her husband's adopted daughter first came to live with them at the age of two, she had several behavioral problems, the worst of which was biting herself until she brought blood. Antique took her to doctors and child specialists, but no one could do anything for the child. One day she and her daughter were driving home in traffic, and while stopped at a light, the child bit herself. Antique said it just came to her to bite herself the same way, and she did. Her daughter was upset by Antique's action and told her to stop. At that point Antique told her child that she would not bite herself if the little girl would not bite herself. That was the last time her daughter bit herself.

Implications

The results of this study contribute to the limited body of knowledge about health in Appalachia. Further, the descriptions of Appalachian lifeways in the study challenges some commonly accepted assertions about Appalachians and contributes new understandings to the knowledge about Appalachian culture. The results of this study have several implications for nursing practice, particularly as these relate to preventive care and health promotion.

The centrality of family as a value in Appalachian culture has several implications for nursing. Family members need to be considered and involved in care in order for nursing interventions to be effective, even if the family is not considered the primary client. At a minimum, it is important for nurses to express interest in family members and their well-being. Further, it is important to involve family members in planning care.

In order for nursing intervention to be acceptable to the family, it is necessary to identify and collaborate with the member of the family who is responsible for the health of the family. This person is usually the mother, however, it is possible that this person could be a mother or grandmother who does not live in the same household.

It is important to know the client's role in the family and how changes in the health practices of one member might affect the rest of the family. This is especially true if the mother is the client. Interventions intended to benefit the mother, particularly interventions which could be perceived as placing her needs before those of the family, may need to be framed in terms of their benefit to the whole family.

The tradition of self-care and the cultural values of determination and acceptance of intuitive knowledge have several implications. Of primary importance is that understanding Appalachians in light of these values is a radical departure from the more commonly accepted view of them as fatalistic, unmotivated, ignorant, and resistant to change. This alternative understanding of Appalachians is much more conducive to identifying and working with their strengths. It is critical, therefore, that nurses believe in the capability of their Appalachian clients to know what is healthy for them and to discover what works for them. The combined findings of this study relative to the values of self-care and determination and the use of intuitive processes provide powerful support for the need to collaborate with Appalachian clients in all phases of the nursing process. These findings underscore the importance of Appalachian clients setting their own health goals and of not using directive, authoritarian approaches with them.

Appalachians' religious values have several implications for nursing intervention. Although Appalachians are not homogeneous in their religious beliefs and practices, religion continues to be a dominant influence in their culture. Therefore, spiritual assessment is an important aspect of the health assessment of Appalachians. Some Appalachian religious beliefs may differ from those of nurses, especially nurses who are not from the region. The important implication is the need for nurses to listen to and accept the meaning that Appalachian clients' religious beliefs have to them.

Another implication of religious beliefs is for nursing interventions at the community level. Health teaching and promotion activities need to not directly contradict prevailing beliefs in the community in order to be acceptable. Another implication is that churches may be ideal places to do health promotion and teaching.

The finding of this study that southern Appalachians are more action oriented and less fatalistic than reported in other studies has implications for the way Appalachians define health and their motivation related to health. It follows, then, that it is important for nurses to learn how Appalachian clients define health in order for nursing interventions to be acceptable to them. A related implication is the need to assess the Appalachian client's motivation for health in order to ensure the compatibility of teaching and other interventions.

Health beliefs and practices are learned in a cultural context, and there is evidence to support that informants in this study adhered to many of the traditional practices. Because of cultural change, among other reasons, Appalachian clients can be expected to maintain part, but not all, of the traditional health practices. One illustration of this point is the mountain person who continues to eat a diet high in animal fat, leads a sedentary life-style, and sees no need to change because his ancestors ate the same way and live a long, healthy life.

A related implication for health teaching is the need to frame the proposed changes in terms of the traditional culture rather than the professional frame of reference. One potentially useful approach would be that of comparing present and traditional life-styles, identifying the positive and negative health aspects of both, and working with the client to incorporate more of the health-enhancing traditional ways. To illustrate, information about traditional foods and activities which would reduce blood cholesterol levels and weight gain could be shared with the client.

Another implication related to cultural change is the risk of cultural iatrogenesis, the process whereby people are alienated from their self-care traditions and are turned into passive consumers and objects of medical care (Illich 1976). Self-care is a strong Appalachian tradition which, at an earlier time, was a necessity. Although physicians and other health-care professionals are widely used in western North Carolina and all the informants in this study have received mainstream medical care, self-care remains an important cultural strength on which professional health-care promotion can build.

The increased use of medical care coupled with the denigration of Appalachian culture has the risk of alienating mountain people from their self-care traditions and their reliance on cultural and self knowledge. It is important, therefore, to support the self-care traditions of Appalachians by identifying, valuing, respecting, and supporting their self-knowledge and self-care capabilities.

References

Batteau, Allen. 1990. *The Invention of Appalachia.* Tucson: University of Arizona Press.

Batteau, Allen, and Phillip J. Obermiller. 1983. "Introduction: The Transformation of Dependency." In *Appalachia and America: Autonomy and Regional Dependence,* Allen Batteau (Ed.). Lexington: University Press of Kentucky. Pp. 1–13.

Belcher, J. C. 1962. "Population Growth and Characteristics." In *The Southern Appalachian Region: A Survey,* Thomas R. Ford (Ed.). Lexington: University Press of Kentucky. Pp. 37–53.

Boyle, J. S., and M. N. Counts. 1988. "Toward Healthy Aging: A Theory for Community Health Nursing." *Public Health Nursing* 5(1):45–51.

Branscome, James. 1971. "Annihilating the Hillbilly: The Appalachians' Struggle with American Institutions." *Katallagete: Journal of the Committee of Southern Churchmen* (Winter): 25–32.

Burkhardt, M. A. 1992. "Characteristics of Spirituality in the Lives of Women in a Rural Appalachian Community." *Journal of Transcultural Nursing* 4, no. 2 (Winter): 12–18.

Caudill, Harry M. 1962. *Night Comes to the Cumberlands.* Boston: Little, Brown.

Clark, Mike. 1974. "Education and Exploitation." In *Appalachian Miseducation,* Mike Clark, Jim Branscome, and Bob Snyder (Eds.). Huntington, W.Va.: Appalachian Press. Pp.7–10.

Couto, Richard A., Nancy K. Simpson, and Gale Harris (Eds.). 1995. *Sowing Seeds in the Mountains: Community-based Coalitions for Cancer Prevention and Control.* Washington, D.C.: National Cancer Institute.

Cowan, D. L., G. A. Culley, D. L. Hockstrasser, M. E. Briscoe, and G. W. Somes. 1978. "Impact of a Rural Preventive Care Outreach Program on Children's Health." *American Journal of Public Health* 68:471–76.

Femea, P. L. 1981. "An Exploratory Study of the Relationship Among Religiosity, Sociodemographic Variables, and Preventive Health Attitudes in a Selected Population." Ph.D. dissertation, Catholic University of America.

Fisher, S., and A. L. Paige. 1987. "Women and Preventive Health Care: An Exploratory Study of the Use of Pap Smears in a Potentially High-Risk Appalachian Population." *Women and Health* 11:83–99.

Flaskerud, J. H. 1980. "Perceptions of Problematic Behavior by Appalachians, Mental-Health Professionals, and Lay Non-Appalachians." *Nursing Research* 29:140–49.

Gairola, G., D. Hockstrasser, and L. Garkovich. 1986. "Modern Contraceptive Practice in Appalachia." *American Journal of Public Health* 76(8):100–108.

Goshen, C. E. 1970. "Characterological Deterrents to Economic Progress in People of Appalachia." *Southern Medical Journal* 63:1053–61.

Halverson, L. S. 1987. "Relationships Among Nutrition Knowledge, Attitudes, and Behavior of Appalachian Middle School Children." Ph.D. dissertation, Ohio State University, Columbus.

Hansen, M. M. 1985. "Ten Southern Appalachian Mountain Families: Cultural Determinants of Health-Related Characteristics." Ph.D. dissertation, University of Pittsburgh.

Hansen, M., and L. Resick. 1990. "Health Beliefs, Health Care, and Rural Appalachian Subcultures from an Ethnographic Perspective." *Family and Community Health* 13(1):1–10.

Hardin, S. R. 1990. "Let the Circle Be Unbroken: Health of Elderly Southern Appalachian Widows." Ph.D. dissertation, University of Colorado, Boulder.

Illich, Ivan. 1976. *Medical Nemesis: The Expropriation of Health.* New York: Random House.

Jarvis, M. A., E. W. Chick, R. Six, and E. Wheatley. 1966. Health in a Semi-Isolated West Virginia Community." *Archives of Environmental Health* 13:422–28.

Laffrey, S. C., C. J. Loveland-Cherry, and S. J. Winkley. 1986. "Health Behavior: Evolution of Two Paradigms." *Public Health Nursing* 3(2):92–100.

Leininger, J. 1978. "Culturological Assessment Domains for Nursing Practice." In *Transcultural Nursing: Concepts, Theories, and Practices,* Madeline Leininger (Ed.). New York: John Wiley & Sons. Pp. 85–106.

Nickerson, G. S., and D. L. Hockstrasser. 1970. "Factors Affecting Non-Participation in a County-Wide Tuberculin Testing Program in Southern Appalachia." *Social Science and Medicine* 3:575–96.

Plaut, Thomas, Suzanne Landis, and June Trevor. 1992. "Enhancing Participating Research with the Community Oriented Primary Care Model." *American Sociologist.* 23(4):55–70.

Riffle, K. L., J. Yoho, and J. Sams. 1989. "Health Promoting Behaviors, Perceived Social Support, and Self-Reported Health of Appalachian Elderly." *Public Health Nursing* 6:204–11.

Rowles, Graham. 1991. "Changing Health Culture in Appalachia: Implications for Serving the Elderly." *Journal of Aging Studies* 5(4):375–90.

Shapiro, Henry D. 1978. *Appalachia on Our Mind: The Southern Mountains and Mountaineers in the American Consciousness, 1870–1920.* Chapel Hill: University of North Carolina Press.

Simon, J. M. 1987. "Health Care of the Elderly in Appalachia . . . Subculture of the Appalachian People." *Journal of Gerontological Nursing* 13(7):32–35.

Stekert, E. J. 1970. "Focus on Conflict: Southern Mountain Medical Beliefs in Detroit." *Journal of American Folklore* 83:115–56.

Stephens, Carol C. 1994. "Health Beliefs and Practices of Rural, Southern Appalachian Women from an Ethnographic Perspective." Ph.D. dissertation, University of Alabama, Birmingham.

Tripp-Reimer, Toni, and M. C. Friedl. 1977. "Appalachians: A Neglected Minority." *Nursing Clinics of North America* 12(1):41–54.

Wallack, L., and M. Winkleby. 1987. "Primary Prevention: A New Look at Basic Concepts." *Social Science and Medicine* 25:923–30.

Weller, Jack E. 1965. *Yesterday's People: Life in Contemporary Appalachia.* Lexington: University Press of Kentucky.

Whisnant, David E. 1980. *Modernizing the Mountaineer.* Boone, N.C.: Appalachian Consortium.

Chapter 10

Promoting Wellness among the Eastern Band of Cherokees

Lisa J. Lefler

Working with American Indian communities is a privilege. It is a life experience that brings tremendous joy and challenge. Unfortunately, many non-Indian practitioners who have not grown up in or near American Indian[1] communities, nor had additional training in American Indian studies or anthropology before they begin to practice, may not be prepared to deal with cultural differences relevant to practicing in Indian country. Misunderstandings can easily take place when one is not aware of how reality is shaped and shared in a particular culture. It is also important, however, to point out that American Indian culture is not homogeneous. Cultural beliefs, rituals, and cosmologies vary greatly among the more than five hundred sovereign tribes in the United States. Cultural attitudes and perceptions differ not only inter-tribally but also intra-tribally. In almost all Indian communities, there are individuals who perceive themselves as traditional and others who may feel that most of the "traditional" ways have been lost. To illustrate this, the last section of this chapter will discuss ethnographic data collected among twentieth-century Cherokee healers concerning their approaches and philosophies. The objective of this chapter, therefore, is only to share experiences and beliefs encountered in one southeastern Indian community.

The Eastern Band of Cherokees

Traditionally the Cherokee called themselves A-ni'-yv-wi-ya, the "original people" or "principal people." The word "Cherokee" is thought to be of foreign origin or a derivation of a Choctaw word denoting habitation in caves (Mooney 1932). Today, there are only approximately one thousand Eastern Band Cherokees who speak the native language, which belongs to the Iroquoian family of languages.

The Cherokee kinship consisted of matrilineal clans which, before the invasion of the Europeans and subsequent acculturation, were the core of Cherokee identity and secured integration within society. Sarah Hill notes that "women played complex roles in the matrilineal, matrilocal society that depended on agriculture, gathering, and hunting" (1997:xviii). As indicated in James Axtell's *Indian Peoples of Eastern America,* the "farming tribes, from the Hurons of southern Ontario to the Creeks of Alabama, were largely . . . matrilineal because farming was done by the women who owned the fields and houses, and served as the guardians of tradition and stability" (1981: xvii). With some exceptions, the predominant southeastern Indian matrilineal structure was such that a woman's brother(s) functioned as guide, teacher, and support for her male children, while the mother and her matrilineage functioned in a similar way for her female children. This system provided a variety of adults with whom children interacted for enculturation and socialization.

The Eastern Band of Cherokee Indians (EBCI) make their home today in what is left of the 52,000-plus square miles of the original nation, which covered parts of five states.[2] The core of their homeland is located in the southern Appalachian mountains of western North Carolina and is now identified as the Qualla Boundary. Of the 56,574 acres owned jointly by the tribe, 45,554 make up the Qualla Boundary. The remaining land, most of which does not immediately connect to Qualla, consists of 2,249 acres in nearby Graham County, locally referred to as the Snowbird community; 3,200 acres along a ridge called the 3200-Acre Tract; and 5,571 acres distributed among twenty-six politically unorganized scattered tracts in Cherokee County, North Carolina's westernmost county (Gulick 1960).

Mandatory removal of the Cherokees followed the fraudulent (McLoughlin 1986) Treaty of New Echota in 1835. This took place in the three years following 1835. According to John R. Finger (1984), approximately eleven hundred escaped being removed from North Carolina in 1838. This remnant, along with those few who qualified under federal criteria to farm "citizen reserves," would form the core group from whom the almost thirteen thousand members of the contemporary Eastern Band are descended. Of that number, about 80 percent still reside on tribal land. Falling in line with the demographics of American Indians across the United States, the EBCI are overall younger than their surrounding neighbors, with 42 percent under the age of twenty-five, and about 23 percent being less than fifteen years old (Hipps 1994). With the advent of the tribal casino opening in October 1997, income and employment levels have improved. According to an article from the *Atlanta Journal-Constitution* (Mollison 2003:B3), the "population jumped 28.2 percent in the 1990s . . . [and] annual per capita income rose a hefty 47 percent after inflation to $12,581. The poverty rate of 31.4 percent fell to 23.1 percent. The unemployment rate of 16.8 percent dropped to 8.5 percent."

Even though the casino is now the largest tourist draw in North Carolina, the land and resources in and around the Great Smoky Mountains National Park provides the Cherokees with a "natural draw" for other tourist dollars. Tourism remains "the number one factor affecting the economy of the Cherokee Indian Reservation" (www.ihs.gov 1997).

Culturally Relevant Issues in Promoting Wellness

Factors that can influence how a practitioner approaches health issues among American Indian communities include (1) the practitioner's familiarity with Indian "traditional" values, (2) his or her familiarity with Indian concepts of wellness, (3) stereotypes and/or preconceived ideas of Indian culture that he or she may have been exposed to, (4) the practitioner's understanding of cultural paradigms that challenge the notion of universalized mental health practices, and (5) his or her awareness of health-care resources, both clearly apparent and less visible ones, in the community.

Anthropologists have long been aware of the need to engage in background research, and thus gain foundational knowledge about a specific culture area, before going "into the field." One of the principles that helps those in cross-cultural research maintain objectivity and minimize bias is the notion of cultural relativism. This critical element deters one from ethnocentrism: being quick to judge and/or criticize a group based on the belief that one's own value system is superior. In order to gain the "insider's perspective," one needs to spend time observing and participating in day-to-day activities.

Background reading can certainly assist practitioners in becoming informed about the history of the region and the people. Several classic histories and ethnographies concerning the Eastern Band of Cherokees are available, including J. Mooney's *History, Myths, and Sacred Formulas of the Cherokees* (reprinted 1982); T. Perdue's *Slavery and the Evolution of Cherokee Society, 1540–1866* (1979); W. McLoughlin's *Cherokee Renascence in the New Republic* (1986), *The Cherokees and Christianity, 1794–1870* (1994), and *Cherokees and Missionaries, 1789–1839* (1995); J. R. Finger's *Cherokee Americans* (1993) and *The Eastern Band of Cherokees, 1819–1900* (1984); W. Anderson's edited volume, *Cherokee Removal: Before and After* (1991); S. Neely's *Snowbird Cherokees* (1991); W. H. Gilbert's *Eastern Cherokees* (reprinted 1972); and R. D. Fogelson's *Cherokees: A Critical Bibliography* (1978) and his many articles. Several recent ethnographic projects have also been done among the Eastern Band by Doris Hipps (1994), Margaret Bender (1996), Lisa Lefler (1996), and Sarah Hill (1997).

Anthropologists would also urge individuals preparing for cross-cultural work to take the initiative to learn the indigenous language. Cherokee language courses are available through the local community college and university, both of which have satellite campuses in Cherokee. There are also introductory books and audio tapes available. Having some understanding of the native language can give you tremendous insight into cultural realities. During my time in Cherokee, I had two non-Indian nurses from the area as classmates in Cherokee language classes, and both told me many anecdotes about how understanding the language had helped significantly in their ability to serve the Cherokee patients who came into their unit. Understanding Cherokee can help gain trust and establish rapport with community members, as well as improve your ability to serve.

It is common for newcomers to be noticed and scrutinized in any small, rural community. But with the added element of an oppressive history, it may take even more effort on your part to gain trust. There are several things that can be done to try to build trust and rapport within the community; the most important include being respectful, being of service, and treating people with dignity. These things sound like common sense, but in the past, contact with non-Indians has often been fraught with problems. By researching and realizing the history of Euro-Indian relations, the trauma of boarding schools, the issues that have pervaded Indian communities concerning identity, as well as other life experiences intrinsic to a reservation, the practitioner is positioning him or herself to relate to many of the realities of Indian life.

Most professionals enter an Indian community ready to implement a protocol based on training and education from a middle- or upper-class Western value system. Most successful practitioners with cross-cultural experience will quickly point out the importance of listening and watching, to gain perspective on effective communication strategies and culturally relevant protocol. One of those who has written much in this area is Carl Hammerschlag, author of *The Dancing Healers* (1988) and *The Theft of the Spirit* (1993). His work with American Indian people has taught him, as it has others, to understand that wisdom comes through humility and the willingness to learn. Timothy Thomason contributed a helpful chapter to Atkinson, Morten, and Sue's (1993) *Counseling American Minorities* titled "Counseling Native Americans: An Introduction for Non-Native American Counselors." Other helpful texts are Geri-Ann Galanti's *Caring for Patients from Different Cultures: Case Studies from American Hospitals* (1991), which speaks to a variety of ethnic cultures, inclusive of bibliographic citations concerning American Indians as well as basic concepts of cultural relativism; Day and Weaver's *Health and the American Indian* (1999); and Galloway, Goldberg, and Alpert's *Primary Care of Native American Patients* (1999). For a broader understanding of the history and contextualization of issues in Indian health and health policy, suggested readings include *The Health of Native Americans,* by Kue T. Young (1994); *American Indian Health,* edited by Everette Rhoades (2000); *Medicine Ways: Disease, Health, and Survival Among Native Americans,* edited by Clifford Trafzer and Diane Weiner (2001); *Promises to Keep: Public Health Policy for American Indians and Alaska Natives in the 21st Century,* edited by Mim Dixon and Yvette Roubideaux (2001); *American Indian Population and Recovery in the Twentieth Century* by Nancy Shoemaker (1999); and *Changing Numbers, Changing Needs: American Indian Demography and Public Health,* edited by Gary Sandefur, Ronald Rindfuss, and Barney Cohen (1996).

Cultural Values

As previously mentioned, American Indian people cannot all be pigeonholed into one "type." I cannot emphasize enough that Indian people differ both inter-tribally and intra-tribally. Nevertheless, many ethnographers and counselors have noted some shared values that seem to be foundational to Indian cultures. Among the Cherokees for instance, Gulick (1960 and 1973) found several prominent cultural values, including being nondemonstrative emotionally, controlling interpersonal aggression, being generous, exhibiting the ability to endure pain/hardship, bravery/courage, and a love of humor and practical jokes. Gulick writes about a "continuum of value systems" among the Eastern Cherokee in his classic *Cherokees at the Crossroads* (1960). One concept which he felt particularly important in understanding Cherokee behavior was what Robert K. Thomas referred to as the "Harmony Ethic": "In living from day to day . . . the conservative [traditional Cherokee] tries to avoid giving offense to others and in so doing, he must always wait and see what the others' likes and dislikes are, and . . . perceive what demands are likely to be made of him" (Thomas 1958:137).

Therefore, one may express disagreement "harmoniously," without loud voices or gestures, by merely getting up and leaving the room or avoiding contact all together. On the other hand, if one finds agreement, "harmony" may be expressed via more subtle expressions of service and generosity. This concept allows individuals to maintain the expression of respect and humility, and, as Gulick points out, it is evident that in cases where bad behavior is a problem, Cherokees are more interested in having the behavior modified than in punishment. "The punishment simply compounds the disharmony" (Gulick 1960:136).

Other protocol related to this Harmony Ethic was described by an Indian health practitioner from Cherokee. She said, "One of the things we do is nodding our head in affirmation. It may only mean that we are acknowledging your right to speak, not our agreement. . . . And not making eye contact is cultural as well."

For practitioners, understanding cultural values is important in discerning and appropriately incorporating these paradigms into their approach. DuBray (1985), Clark and Kelly (1992), and Wasinger (1993) are among several practitioners who have written about the American Indian value system and give examples of value concepts. The differences in Western and tribal values include greatly different perspectives of time, space, property, age, and competition, to name a few.

These are important factors to consider in program development, counseling approaches, and medical services, because it is one's cultural value system that determines how decisions are made on a daily basis. Assuming that values are universal is an error that practitioners have historically made in dealing with most ethnic communities in the United States. For example, not all value systems embrace science, competition, and individuality. Instead, it may be that events of nature are sufficient explanations to life's questions and cooperation and group emphasis are more highly valued (DuBray 1985). This is particularly relevant when counseling with individuals from most American Indian communities. It can be beneficial if one understands that an Indian individual may see him or herself as part of a larger, extended system. Indian people, not unlike their rural Appalachian neighbors, value their kin and their community. Carolyn Attneave, a pioneer in counseling protocol with American Indian and Alaska natives, states that

> family ties are usually strong and include extended family members. An aunt or uncle may be a functional parent when absence or alcoholism or other conditions make the biological parent unavailable. A similar problem arises when counselors discover that grandmothers are doing most of the child care, especially for young preschool and elementary school children. While preserving the rights of parents, success with "parents" is not possible without winning the confidence of the grandmother and helping her as well. The elder is always respected, and often his or her accumulated experience has survival value for the counselor as well as the client. (Attneave 1985:139)

This is one of the threads that weaves its way throughout Indian cultures—the value of family. Because these communities are "family-centered," using terms like "co-dependency" may not be culturally relevant. Families are by definition "co-dependent" and have had to be in order to survive. It has been observed that the interdependence of extended families is one reason these families are so resilient. Also, the interdependence of generations of family is clearly evident when working in Indian settings. It may be common, therefore, for children and/or grandchildren to come to work or appointments with a client or employee.

Variables such as these became more evident for me after I established an epidemiological database at a regional Indian adolescent treatment center. For example, a large percentage of adolescents lived with family members other than their biological mother or father. A major issue that counselors had to deal with was the lack of parental support, so necessary for building self-esteem and successful recovery. There were also substantial absences of close family members due to premature deaths and a variety of other circumstances. Thus the traditional "safety net" of family support for Indian children is often not available. Without healthy role models to come home to after treatment, there is a high probability of relapse. How can we expect adolescents to graduate successfully from residential treatment programs, return home, and remain sober living in a family that may be absent and/or continuing to "use"?

Relapse remains an important issue in any aftercare program. For Indian youth, however, it is important to consider the solution from within the

Indian community. By understanding the cultural system of the traditional values, of respect for elders, group cohesion, value of sharing, and strength of the extended family, the center in Cherokee utilized these strengths. They began a program whereby healthy role models or mentors volunteered to sponsor and support youth as they left treatment. The program had significant results, helping to sustain a sobriety rate of 66.7 percent compared to the 45 percent rate for the first year (Lefler 1996). The value of using natural support systems from within Indian communities is substantiated by both the sobriety of those participating and the interest of other tribal communities who are seeking to implement a like model.

Concepts of Wellness

Most Euro-Americans come from a tradition of viewing good health as merely the absence of disease. However, this model is usually insufficient for Indian peoples, who view "health" more holistically. In *Native America: Portraits of the Peoples,* Duane Champagne discusses traditional Indian health practices and cultural views, which include the notion of "interrelatedness between people and their environment and the inclusion of various deities or a great spirit" (1994:803).

Billy Rogers, founder and director of the Native Wellness Institute, has conducted the largest health and wellness conferences in North America for Amerindian peoples. His program's philosophy of wellness is "maximizing individual potential in each of the four dimensions; spiritual, physical, emotional, and mental. Programs are directed at empowerment with proactive approaches to healthy lifestyle changes" (personal communication 1997). His programs reach many Indian people from the United States and Canada. When asked how he addresses such varied groups, he spoke of using symbolism and language recognizable and accepted by most. This includes the use of circles or hoops which are never-ending and multidimensional and significant to most traditional Indian paradigms.

Many in the Cherokee community would agree with the importance of using culturally relevant symbolism in addressing Indian people. Several community members spoke of their journey to "wholeness" or "wellness" as one of overcoming a history of shame and returning to the cycle of ceremony and tradition. One individual spoke of overcoming addiction through the use of the medicine hoop and the spiritual journey which brought balance to her life. Many have incorporated "revitalized" ceremonies such as the use of sweat lodges, healing ceremonies which include "going to the water," and stomp dances (Lefler 1996). Others in the community, however, do not attend these types of ritual and instead attend a Christian service that is more "mainstream."

Regardless of how individuals may engage in ceremony, be it native, Christian, or a fusion of philosophies, most relate to the traditional philosophy that spirituality is inseparable from all other dimensions of life. By presenting information concerning wellness and health in an interconnected and four-dimensional approach, most in the community will associate these concepts with their own experiences and beliefs.

Mental Health Practices Are Often Universalized

It is also important to understand how an individual perceives "healthy" and "normal" within a cultural context. What is seen as deviant or a mental pathology in one culture may be seen as normal in another. Anthropologists have been writing about the cultural inappropriateness of standardizing mental health practices for many years. Behavior and reality are often culturally defined and shaped. What may seem unstable or abnormal in terms of mental health from a Western perspective may not be seen that way from an American Indian perspective.

In Alfred Kroeber's classic article "Psychosis or Social Sanction" (1940), he refers to several examples of states occurring among individuals in American Indian cultures such as possession by a bear spirit, shamanistic possession associated with homosexual or transsexual (two-spirit) phenomena, and persons who believed their disease was associated with communication with a deceased relative.

To present a more pertinent example, there is a phenomenon known throughout many cultures that is known among the Cherokee as the Yunwi Tsunsdi', or "Little People." These little spirits or beings are described in Mooney's (1932) early ethnography, in Fogelson (1982), and, more recently, in a local university class project conducted by Jeannie Reed (1991).

Little People take on many characteristics; they have been described as "helpful and kind-hearted . . . great wonder workers . . . very fond of music, drumming, and dance . . . some may get you lost . . . they may cast a spell . . . be mischievous . . . some aid hunters and fishermen . . . some play practical jokes and hide things from you" (Reed 1991:11). Descriptions of who and what they are may vary some among community members, but the idea that they are and have been valid experiences among the Cherokees usually does not. They are an important part of rich Cherokee heritage and lore, and, as Reed so aptly writes, "perhaps recognizing them and learning from their lessons are steps in the process toward understanding our spirituality as well"

(1991:11). Phenomena such as the Yunwi Tsunsdi' should not be discounted by the practitioner but valued as part of a rich and interesting culture that serves a function in this society.

Stereotyping

> One of the things that has happened in the past is when Indian people go into treatment centers, you know, they're sitting there and they are looking at a non-Indian counselor. And this non-Indian counselor has this fixed idea in their head how treatment should work and how this individual should respond to this certain treatment model. And when there is nothing in the treatment program or organization that the Indian person can connect with, then naturally the individual is going to feel outside, not accepted, not a part of. And not understanding why that conflict is still there. This conflict is, why can't I be who I am. . . . Why is it that I have to change to be acceptable? (Informant, Cherokee 1997)

Stereotypes are generalizations or images created by those who have an agenda. The crisis occurs when those who are being typecast begin to internalize the images that someone else has created. They "give their power away." There has been a long history of Appalachian people, including American Indians, being stereotyped as lazy, drunkards, ignorant, and violent. The history of these stereotypes can be traced back to groups and movements with a vested interest in the creation and perpetuation of these images. Several works relevant to American Indians, including R. F. Berkhofer's *Salvation and the Savage* (1976) and R. Strickland's *Tonto's Revenge* (1997), trace these images and discuss the impact of this labeling mentality.

What has been the effect of multiple generations of oppression, negative stereotyping, and trauma? A 1992 *Journal of the American Medical Association* article suggests:

> Because of the negative stereotyping of American Indians that has been perpetuated throughout the centuries in the literature and the media, other people may have a distorted and negative view of Indian tribes. Furthermore, and most detrimental, many American Indians accept the negative stereotypes. (Lujan 1992)

The research of others integrates the ethnohistorical record of assimilation and destruction of American Indian culture with issues of dual identity (e.g., Berlin 1987 and Kahn 1982). Problems stemming from the clash between the cultural value system of the indigenous population and that of the Europeans have been of considerable interest to many Indian mental health professionals in recent years. One recent ethnographic work, *Disciplined Hearts: History, Identity, and Depression in an American Indian Community*, by Theresa D. O'Nell (1996), demonstrates the importance of understanding mental health issues within the more holistic context of history and culture. Some of these historical issues include the many years of "Indian Policy," which has dictated to them the need for quick and decisive change in the name of "civilizing." This policy has eroded a traditional way of life and has confounded a perspective and philosophy that once offered answers to life's difficult questions. Many social pathologies, including suicide, affect Indian youth, who, because they feel there no longer are answers, cut short their lives and take their questions and frustrations into the next world. Suicide is the second leading cause of death within this adolescent population (U.S. Congress 1990). Practitioners going into an Indian community may need, therefore, to take inventory of their own paradigms concerning Indian people and modify their approach toward intervention models. There are those in Indian communities who may be able to provide assistance in teaching practitioners about traditional paradigms and strategies to make the non-Indian's approach more culturally relevant.

The Not-So-Visible Resources: Healers among the Eastern Band

The final, ethnographic section of this chapter discusses the sometimes less visible sources of healing in the Cherokee community. There have been many changes in the last one hundred years, as is illustrated here, yet it is clear that the use and value of traditional healers to the Cherokees continues.

Since 1887, anthropologists have been interviewing individuals among the North Carolina Cherokees about their medicinal practices. The Qualla Boundary, home of the Eastern Band of Cherokees, like all Indian communities, has undergone tremendous change over the last one hundred years. With changes in life-style, diet, and belief systems come changes in the culture of disease and health intervention. As Indian people resiliently adapt and fuse together traditions of the past with realities of the present, new ideologies about Indian health, healing, and wellness merge with the old.

The nature of the relationship between healing and various types of religious practices and beliefs among the Cherokees has changed over the last one hundred years. This is, to a large degree, because the Cherokee religious landscape has changed. In the late 1800s, James Mooney was able to collect substantial data concerning non-Christian beliefs and practices among the

Eastern Band. Those he found are published in his collections of medicinal formulas and sacred myths (1891, 1900). Ray Fogelson conducted fieldwork in the late 1950s and documented the compatibility of Christianity with some types of traditional non-Christian Cherokee spiritual belief and practice. My fieldwork, conducted during the 1990s, suggests that some Cherokee medicine men and women have moved beyond Christian-Cherokee compatibility and are integrating Christianity, traditional Cherokee beliefs, other tribal practices, the twelve-step philosophy of Alcoholics Anonymous, and even other world religions.

Accounts of traditional healers are usually based on a small number of interviews because practicing medicine men and women prefer a low profile and generally do not engage in direct conversation concerning their practices. For example, Fogelson worked with three individuals. My research includes the responses of four individuals, yet these interviews represent the spectrum of healing beliefs and ritual among the Eastern Band of Cherokees. The term "healer," as used here, includes those who address physical, emotional, and/or spiritual issues. There are also several points to keep in mind when working with the EBCI regarding health issues:

- In Cherokee mythology, plants came to the rescue of human beings. Knowledge of plants indigenous to the region is important.
- A large host (several hundred) of medicinal plants were already known by Cherokees at contact (c. 1500).
- Health is not just defined as the absence of disease. Mind, body, and spirit are interconnected. To treat one is to treat all.
- Location (east, south, west, north), sacred sites (places, water, mountains), and traditional Cherokee songs are important in healing practices.
- There were and are men and women who are considered traditional healers.
- Most EBCI members use traditional approaches and Western medicine in combination.
- Cultural norms about body image are usually not in line with that of the dominant society. "Healthy" can mean heavier. (There were many "lean" years on the Qualla Boundary.)
- Behavior and perceptions of reality are culturally defined and shaped.

Literature on Cherokee Healing

James Mooney's ethnographic fieldwork at the turn of the twentieth century resulted in three important publications, *Sacred Formulas of the Cherokees*

(1891), *Myths of the Cherokee* (1900), and *The Swimmer Manuscript* (1932), edited by Frans Olbrechts. These Bureau of American Ethnology publications were the first to introduce Cherokee concepts of conjuring and healing practices to the English-language-reading public. Mooney's discussion of medicine men suggests that prior to contact, a priestly society of shamans may have existed at Kituhwa, near present-day Bryson City, but that since the mid-sixteenth century, medicine men became more isolated and specialized in their practice (Fogelson 1980). Much of the earlier ethnographic data uses the terms "conjuror," "medicine man," and "shaman" interchangeably. These individuals used ritual and supernatural power and/or knowledge of medicinal plants in their healing tradition.

In the late 1960s, an Oklahoma Cherokee couple, Jack F. Kilpatrick and Anna G. Kilpatrick, also contributed to this genre of medicinal formulae through their "truly staggering collection of Cherokee manuscripts" (Kilpatrick 1997). Subsequently, their son Alan, an American Indian studies professor, published *The Night Has a Naked Soul: Witchcraft and Sorcery Among the Western Cherokee* (1997), a translation of many of those shamanic sacred texts. I asked a local medicine woman how she felt about this most recent publication of Cherokee sacred texts. As she often does when trying to convey an important message, she responded in the form of a parable. She translated the moral of the story and concluded:

> From what I understand, when we use these ceremonies, the only thing we can put out there is the good stuff, 'cause if we don't, it all comes back onto us. It's like the Bible verse says, we reap what we sow. So if we sow negative stuff, then that's what's gonna come back, but if we sow goodness and love, and truth, then it comes back, and I can attest to that. . . . People need to be careful because it could hurt you as much as it could hurt other people.

Twenty-six years after *The Swimmer Manuscript* was published, another anthropologist, Ray Fogelson, appeared in Big Cove, Yellow Hill, Birdtown, and other Cherokee communities to record continuing changes in medicinal and cultural practices (1958, 1980). In a 1980 issue of the *Journal of Cherokee Studies*, Fogelson compares various aspects of conjuring among the Eastern Band of Cherokees of midcentury with that of Mooney's and Olbrechts's accounts.

Twentieth-Century Shamans

In his discussion of the status and organization of conjurors, Fogelson explains that one of his informants views the term "conjuror" as "derogatory and equates it with the practice of 'conjuring against' someone or witchcraft," the term "doctor" being preferable (1980:66). He also refers to a former system whereby there were seven degrees of conjurors, which have dwindled to only one or two degrees at the time of his study. When I asked in the mid-1990s about the prevalence of "conjurors," the response was that there were very few. More recently, in 2003, the answer is still that there are a few, but usually with an insistence that there are some who still practice medicine and that person can use it for good or bad. Conjurors are so designated if they use mysticism in their "conjuring powers" without the use of herbs or plants. One informant quietly spoke the name of an older man who had been widely known for his conjuring abilities. When asked if he was still active, the response was that he had had to move because he had begun to take money from white people for his services. He had been seen as an effective conjuror and known to be able to cure the thrush by blowing in one's mouth. It was also mentioned that he did not have to be near the person to conduct his "magic," and that he became so popular among whites, people would send him their money and request his curative powers from long distances. My consultant said that "the locals stopped going to him 'cause he got uppity. When people start giving you money, everything changes."

Most of those I interviewed frowned upon the use of the term conjuror because the traditional use of this word implies witchcraft and sorcery. There needs to be more ethnographic research that more clearly defines the various categories, but generally speaking, healer, shaman, or medicine man/woman are more commonly used, as well as the Cherokee word *didanvwisgi,* to refer to local healers. A different Cherokee word is used to indicate a modern M.D., *ganakti.* As Fogelson pointed out, many healers specialize in particular types of services. This still seems to be somewhat true, and healers with disparate knowledge will still exchange their knowledge about use of plants, herbs, and medicinal formulas.

As new diseases arise, sometimes healers will be called upon to deliver new or modified traditional services. For example, one of my interviewees told me of an individual who had long ago moved from the community and had sent a message by someone that he was dying of AIDS and wanted to request a "transition ceremony." After a long silence, the elder nodded his head and said that he would send instructions, even though to his knowledge, there was no such long-distance ritual.

One of the healers had received some training from the Keetoowahs of Oklahoma. She stated that her four directions prayer was "taught to me by my teacher in Oklahoma who's a holy man. Some people would call him a medicine man, some would call him a shaman. But he's a simple individual who lives a simple life and when he brings his life into simplicity, that's when wonderful, magical things happen."

The Keetoowahs are considered the religious arm of the western Cherokees. William McLoughlin writes that they began in Oklahoma in the 1850s and were primarily full-bloods who united to represent that which was traditional combined with Christian elements (McLoughlin 1990). Some members of the Keetoowahs have returned to live in western North Carolina. Over the past twelve years or more they have had an influence in the institution of the stomp dance, the bringing of the eternal flame which is central to the stomp dance and ceremonial ground, and other cultural ceremonies in Cherokee.

Ceremonies such as stomp dances, the Green Corn, "going to the water," and use of sweat lodges are all more or less controversial among the Eastern Band of Cherokees. With more than thirty-eight churches located in the area representing nine mostly Protestant denominations, there are some who take the view that traditional shamans are no longer available, and that the ceremonies such as stomp dances and sweat lodges are pagan and not traditionally Cherokee. Interestingly, however, the majority of my consultants attend church regularly and find Christianity compatible with their healing ceremonies. I said to one, "I know you are also Lakota and attend the Sun Dance and participate in ceremony there, and that you conduct sweats and attend stomp dances at home. How do you respond to others who object to the fusion of these belief systems?" Her response:

> The Creator gave different peoples around the world a way of understanding who he is, and I think each belief and way of expressing or using ceremony or these rituals, however you want to describe it, comes from the same place. That simply because there are different names for different ways of doing it that are used by different peoples around the world to get there, to me it's like the poles of a tepee. You gotta have fifteen poles, normally, to put up a tepee. Each pole sits on the ground but they all come together at the top. You need all those poles to complete that tepee. And so when they're all sitting on the ground and they're all pointing in the same direction, they all come together at the top. And so to me that's the different beliefs, each pole can represent. So there's not a more or less than, they're all needed. They're all just as important. And for Indian beliefs, they stand right up there, shoulder-to-shoulder with the rest.

For one of the healers who also identifies as a Christian and uses sweats, the practice is not part of a pan-Indian or inter-tribal identification but is traditionally Cherokee. Fogelson wrote in 1958 that "the majority of Cherokee curative practices may be classified as hydrocentric, since water plays an important part in the therapeutic procedures. In the past, steam baths were taken in small earthen sweat lodges and followed by plunges into a nearby stream, after the proper recitation of prayers for health and long life. This seems to have been a regular ritual that was observed throughout the year, regardless of season. . . . The sweat lodge passed out of existence during the eighteenth century, but the ritual persists in an abbreviated form which now includes only the ceremony and plunge into the stream" (1980:64). Today, however, there has been a revitalization of sweat lodge use. One healer estimated that there were now five or six sweat lodges in Cherokee. I asked one of the medicine women about using the lodges. She responded:

> The sweat lodge I use does come from the Lakota ceremonies, and it faces west. The Cherokees had one that faced the east. Some people are very open to hearing that, and there's others who aren't. One lady said, "My dad told me that we were Cherokee, so whenever I was working out in the west, I might attend some of the ceremonies, but I never involved myself in them simply because I was Cherokee and I didn't feel that I had a right to do that." But my answer to her was that a lot of us goes to churches, so we've accepted that. And that if it works for the people who go to church, then it's okay for us to be involved in other native people's ceremonies, because the Creator only looks at the intent. And so even if we stand on our heads, and say ommmm, same thing.

Much of Fogelson's data regarding Cherokee conjurors still rings true. For example, there are individuals in the community of Cherokee who are seen as herbalists, sought out for their knowledge of medicinal plants only, and others who are looked upon as spiritual advisors, knowledgeable regarding ritual, ceremony, and/or some traditional medicines. Most practice on an individual basis, still engage in renewal rituals in the spring of the year, place great faith in content of dreams, and view illness—both physical and psychological—from a spiritually centered perspective. Even according to an Indian Health Service source, "many of the Cherokee people still practice the old ways of health care using herbs and formulas, either self-administered or with the aid of a medicine man" (www.his.gov 1997).

What has changed in the last one hundred years is the use of stomp dances, the revitalization of sweat lodges, and the fusion of Christian, intertribal, and other ideals in ritual and ceremony. It is not uncommon to hear key phrases or slogans from AA in a sweat lodge or to see what might be associated with Creek or Sioux culture during a ceremony. One will also hear

Christian metaphors and analogies used in describing these rituals, such as the image of Moses' burning bush likened to the eternal flame at a stomp ground.

There is also increased awareness among many service providers of a paradigm discussed by native psychologist and counselor Edurado Duran and Maria Yellow Horse Brave Heart (Duran et al. 1998) regarding intergenerational or historical grief and trauma. Many health and social ills are referred to as the American Indian "Soul Wound" and invoke an understanding of the impact of generations of trauma on Indian families. A group of concerned medical and tribal people among the EBCI, called the Tsalagi Aniyvwiya Dinisdelisgi (Cherokee Indian Helpers) meet to develop a plan to integrate this paradigm that would promote community-wide interventions and education concerning the impact of historical grief (boarding schools, poverty, assimilation policies) on the mental, physical, and spiritual health of their people.

It is through these illustrations that one can see not only a revitalization of traditional culture but also the continued use of medicine men and women during a time of increasing stress and change.

Conclusions

Working as a practitioner in an American Indian community can be a rewarding yet challenging experience. When asked what advice he would give to a "newcomer" in an Indian agency, an Indian counselor responded, "Practitioners should learn to communicate, not only with their clients, but with each other. Listen to each other without being so territorial. Stop, listen, and validate the issues and concerns of the youth. Learn to trust them. By watching the youth, much can be learned about the direction of the community."

Practitioners in the Cherokee community should keep in mind several points in developing service strategies and working toward cultural competency: (1) be mindful of the nonnuclear family system; (2) be aware that American Indians, and specifically Cherokees, are not all alike; (3) be aware of cultural values such as the Harmony Ethic; (4) be mindful that culture shapes experience, as in the example of individuals who may have encountered the Little People; (5) do your homework and be knowledgeable of the history and language; (6) be aware of all relevant community resources, both visible (i.e., hospitals, clinics, and social services) and not so visible (i.e., traditional healers, storytellers, and herbalists); (7) do more listening than talking; and (8) be respectful and treat people with dignity.

Notes

1. I will use the terms "American Indian" and "Indian" in this paper, rather than "native" or "Native American," because these are the words most commonly used among the Eastern Band of Cherokees to designate indigenous people of North America.

2. "Plus square miles" refers to the fact that the Cherokees had land cessions to the United States government that exceeded 125,000 square miles by the early nineteenth century (Thornton 1990:10–12).

3. An earlier discussion of these ideas appeared in R. Bonney and J. A. Paredes's edited volume, *Anthropologists and Indians in the New South* (Tuscaloosa: University of Alabama Press, 2001).

References

Anderson, William L. (Ed.). 1991. *Cherokee Removal: Before and After.* Athens: University of Georgia Press.

Atkinson, Donald R., George Morten, and Derald Wing Sue (Eds.). 1993. *Counseling American Minorities: A Cross-Cultural Perspective.* Madison, Wisc.: Brown & Benchmark Publishers.

Attneave, Carolyn L. 1985. "Practical Counseling with American Indian and Alaska Native Clients." In *Handbook of Cross-Cultural Counseling and Therapy,* Paul Pedersen (Ed.). Westport, Conn.: Greenwood Press. Pp. 135–40.

Axtell, James (Ed.). 1981. *The Indian Peoples of Eastern America.* New York: Oxford University Press.

Bender, Margaret C. 1996. "Reading Culture: The Cherokee Syllabary and the Eastern Cherokees, 1993–1995." Ph.D. dissertation, University of Chicago.

Berkhofer, Robert F. 1976. *Salvation and the Savage.* New York: Atheneum.

Berlin, Irving N. 1987. "Effects of Changing Native American Cultures on Child Development." *Journal of Community Psychology* 15(3):299–306.

Champagne, Duane. 1994. *Native America: Portraits of the Peoples.* Detroit: Visible Ink Press.

Clark, Susan, and Susan D. M. Kelly. 1992. Traditional Native American Values: Conflict or Concordance in Rehabilitation?" *Journal of Rehabilitation* (4/5/6):23–28.

Day, Priscilla A., and Hilary N. Weaver (Eds.). 1999. *Health and the American Indian.* Binghamton, N.Y.: Haworth Press.

Dixon, Mim, and Yvette Roubideaux (Eds.). 2001. *Promises to Keep: Public Health Policy for American Indians and Alaska Natives in the 21st Century.* Washington, D.C.: American Public Health Association.

DuBray, W. H. 1985. "American Indian Values: Critical Factor in Casework." *Social Casework: The Journal of Contemporary Social Work* (1):30–37.

Duran, Eduardo, Bonnie Duran, Maria Yellow Horse Brave Heart, and Susan Yellow Horse-Davis. 1998. "Healing the American Indian Soul Wound." In *International Handbook of Multigenerational Legacies of Trauma*, Yael Danieli (Ed.). New York: Plenum Press. Pp. 341–54.

Finger, John R. 1984. *The Eastern Band of Cherokees, 1819–1900.* Knoxville: University of Tennessee Press.

———. 1993. *Cherokee Americans: The Eastern Band of Cherokees in the Twentieth Century.* Lincoln: University of Nebraska Press.

Fogelson, Raymond D. 1958. "A Study of the Conjuror in Eastern Cherokee Society." Master's thesis, University of Pennsylvania.

———. 1978. *The Cherokees: A Critical Bibliography.* Bloomington: Indiana University Press.

———. 1980. "The Conjuror in Eastern Cherokee Society." *Journal of Cherokee Studies* 5(2):60–87.

———. 1982. "Cherokee Little People Reconsidered." *Journal of Cherokee Studies* (7)2:92–98.

Galanti, Geri-Ann. 1991. *Caring for Patients from Different Cultures: Case Studies from American Hospitals.* Philadelphia: University of Pennsylvania Press.

Galloway, James M., Bruce W. Goldberg, and Joseph S. Alpert (Eds.). 1999. *Primary Care of Native American Patients: Diagnosis, Therapy, and Epidemiology.* Boston: Butterworth-Heinemann.

Gilbert, William H. 1972. *The Eastern Cherokees.* New York: AMS Press.

Gulick, John. 1960. *Cherokees at the Crossroads.* Chapel Hill: Institute for Research in Social Science, University of North Carolina Press.

———. 1973. *Cherokees at the Crossroads. With an Epilogue by Sharlotte Neely.* Chapel Hill: Institute for Research in Social Science, University of North Carolina Press.

Hammerschlag, Carl. 1988. *The Dancing Healers.* New York: Harper-Collins Publishers.

———. 1993. *The Theft of the Spirit.* New York: Simon and Schuster Trade.

Hill, Sarah H. 1997. *Weaving New Worlds: Southeastern Cherokee Women and Their Basketry.* Chapel Hill: University of North Carolina Press.

Hipps, Doris B. 1994. "The Eastern Band of Cherokees: A Study of Their Perceptions of Education and Dropping Out of School." Ed.D. dissertation, University of South Carolina.

Kahn, M. W. 1982. "Cultural Clash and Psychopathology in Three Aboriginal Cultures." *Academic Psychology Bulletin* 4:16–32.

Kilpatrick, Alan. 1997. *The Night Has a Naked Soul: Witchcraft and Sorcery Among the Western Cherokee.* Syracuse, N.Y.: Syracuse University Press.

Kroeber, Alfred. 1940. "Psychosis or Social Sanction." *Character and Personality* 8(3):204–15.

Lefler, Lisa J. 1996. "Mentorship as an Intervention Strategy in Relapse Reduction Among Native American Youth." Ph.D. dissertation, University of Tennessee.

Lujan, Carol C. 1992. "Alcohol-Related Deaths of American Indians," *JAMA* 267(10):1384.

McLoughlin, William G. 1986. *Cherokee Renascence in the New Republic.* Princeton: Princeton University Press.

———. 1990. *Champions of the Cherokees: Evan and John B. Jones.* Princeton: Princeton University Press.

———. 1994. *The Cherokees and Christianity, 1794–1870.* Edited by Walter H. Conser Jr. Athens: University of Georgia Press.

———. 1995. *Cherokees and Missionaries, 1789–1839.* Norman: University of Oklahoma Press.

Mollison, Andrew. 2003. "Cherokees' Casino Hits the Jackpot." *Atlanta Journal-Constitution,* Apr. 27, pp. B1–3.

Mooney, James. 1891. *Sacred Formulas of the Cherokee.* Smithsonian Institution, Bureau of American Ethnology, Seventh Annual Report. Washington, D.C.: GPO.

———. 1900. *Myths of the Cherokees.* Smithsonian Institution, Bureau of American Ethnology, Nineteenth Annual Report, 1897–98. Pt. 1. Washington, D.C.: GPO.

———. 1932. *The Swimmer Manuscript,* Frans Olbrechts (Ed.). Smithsonian Institution, Bulletin 99 of the Bureau of American Ethnology. Washington, D.C.: GPO.

———. 1982. *Myths of the Cherokee and Sacred Formulas of the Cherokees.* Reprinted. Nashville: Charles and Randy Elder-Booksellers.

Neely, Sharlotte. 1991. *Snowbird Cherokees: People of Persistence.* Athens: University of Georgia Press.

O'Nell, Theresa D. 1996. *Disciplined Hearts: History, Identity, and Depression in an American Indian Community.* Berkeley and Los Angeles: University of California Press.

Perdue, Theda. 1979. *Slavery and the Evolution of Cherokee Society, 1540–1866.* Knoxville: University of Tennessee Press.

Reed, Jeannie (Ed.). 1991. *Stories of the YUNWI TSUNDI': The Cherokee Little People.* Cherokee, NC: Cherokee Communications.

Rhoades, Everett R. (Ed.). 2000. *American Indian Health: Innovations in Health Care, Promotion, and Policy.* Baltimore: Johns Hopkins University Press.

Sandefur, Gary D., Ronald R. Rindfuss, and Barney Cohen (Eds.). 1996. *Changing Numbers, Changing Needs: American Indian Demography and Public Health.* Washington, D.C.: National Academy Press.

Shoemaker, Nancy. 1999. *American Indian Population Recovery in the Twentieth Century.* Albuquerque: University of New Mexico Press.

Strickland, Rennard. 1997. *Tonto's Revenge: Reflections on American Indian Culture and Policy.* Albuquerque: University of New Mexico Press.

Thomas, Robert K. 1958. Cherokee Values and World View. Typescript on deposit [NCC CP970.03 T461c pp.6], Microfilmed by the University of North Carolina Library at Chapel Hill.

Thornton, Russell. 1990. *The Cherokees: A Population History.* Lincoln: University of Nebraska Press.

Trafzer, Clifford E., and Diane Weiner (Eds.). 2001. *Medicine Ways: Disease, Health, and Survival Among Native Americans.* Walnut Creek, Calif.: Alta Mira Press.

U.S. Congress. Office of Technology Assessment. 1990. *Indian Adolescent Mental Health.* OTA-H-446. Washington, D.C.: GPO.

Wasinger, Louise. 1993. "The Value System of the Native American Counseling Client: an Exploration." *American Indian Culture and Research Journal. 17(4):91–98.*

www.ihs.gov. 1997.

Young, T. Kue. 1994. The Health of Native Americans: Towards a Biocultural Epidemiology. New York: Oxford University Press.

Part IV

Choosing a Theoretical Paradigm: Application of the Cultural Model in Mental Health Research and Services

Chapters in Parts I, II, and III have all relied on an appreciation of the cultural context in Appalachia. The use of a cultural model for the explanation of human activity leads one to question standard assumptions, models, explanations, and findings because these are likely to be based on a cultural perception of reality which may not coincide with the Appalachian cultural frameworks. As a result, stereotypes and misjudgments can infiltrate assessments, decisions, practices, and policies, rendering them discriminatory and harmful rather than helpful. A cultural model requires investigation of the participants' emic understanding of the meaning of things in order accurately to interpret their ideas, attitudes, and behavior. It also requires developing a holistic approach, encompassing the environmental, historical, cultural, social, economic, and political context within which the emic perspective makes sense. Furthermore, the cultural model is grounded on a comparative method and the assumption that through comparing cultures we can better understand the theoretical significance of cultural similarities and differences.

One outcome of the cultural approach is to question the practitioner's standard theory and practice, for both can incorporate cultural bias. Particularly questionable is the idea of a "value-free" scientific model of understanding the human condition. This approach, sometimes called "positivism," assumes that there is a rational and universalistic way to conceptualize and measure human behavior (Parsons 1949). It assumes that standardized practices can then be developed and applied cross-culturally. While cultural differences may be recognized in the expression of human attitudes and behavior, the "value-free" scientific model nevertheless assumes that these can be studied with a universal "measuring stick" and that cultural groups can be compared and contrasted on the basis of this universal standard. The assumption is that "culture-free" tests, findings, and interpretations are possible.

The rational scientific paradigm is found in all the physical, natural, and social sciences and their applications, including education, social work, public administration, community planning, economic development, and psychological counseling. Perhaps one of the clearest examples of the "value-free" scientific model is in biomedicine (Gordon 1988; Hahn 1995). Biomedicine assumes that the human body is an organism that responds to biological stimuli according to natural laws. Pathology or disease signifies the presence of pathogens that disrupt the normal and healthy biological processes in the body. It is assumed that scientific studies can reveal both the normal and the pathological processes through the application of experimental procedures and measurements. Once understood, corrective allopathic therapies can be developed, tested, and applied to eliminate pathology (primarily through surgery, prescription drugs, and advanced technology) and restore the body to health. The philosophical concept of Cartesian dualism or the idea of the separation of "mind-body" is incorporated into the biomedical model so that only material evidence is considered appropriate and measurable empirically.

When this model is applied to mental illness, biomedical scientists assume that there are mental "diseases" that are universally detectable in human beings and treatable with standardized medications and protocols. It is assumed that the concepts of "normal" and "abnormal" are fixed absolutes that can be defined and identified across cultures. It assumes that "culture-free" tests can be developed to measure the incidence and prevalence of mental diseases in any cultural group. The assumption is that it is possible to develop universal and scientific techniques for the diagnosis and treatment of mental diseases. Moreover, the emphasis is always on organic and biological processes, measures, and outcomes.

The chapters in Part IV are shaped by a cultural model of mental illness that leads authors to question standardized biomedical approaches to the delivery of mental health care and services to Appalachian people. The cultural model assumes that Appalachian people probably define mental illness differently than biomedicine; that certain cultural syndromes (such as "nerves") may not have correlates in biomedicine, that cultural theories explaining the origin of mental illnesses may differ from biomedicine (for example, that alcoholism is a "sin"), that ideas and behaviors have different meanings cross-culturally and that it is therefore unwise and impractical to rely heavily on standardized psychological testing instruments to diagnose mental and emotional problems, that therapists who come from a non-Appalachian cultural background or are trained only in standardized therapeutic interventions may misinterpret cultural cues and misapply therapeutic techniques with Appalachian clients, and that new culturally appropriate therapies might have to be developed to meet the special needs of Appalachian individuals and communities.

For example, in their study of the provision of employee assistance to clients suffering from stress associated with family members' alcohol abuse, Benita Howell and Judith Ivy Fiene discover that Appalachian working women accept both the biomedical disease model and the cultural/religious "sin" model of explaining alcoholism. They also find that women in their study follow a cultural strategy of "guarding family secrets" and are reluctant to acknowledge family alcohol problems publicly. Furthermore, these Appalachian women cope with family stress by disassociating home problems from work (perceived as a completely separate sphere of life that can compensate for bad times at home), by avoiding reliance on co-workers for help, and by relying mostly on independent self-help as a means of coping. Rather than promoting an employee assistance providers' definition of alcohol and stress and its treatment, therefore, Howell and Fiene suggest that Employee Assistance would do better to make available self-help books and referral lists and, if consulted by workers, ensure that counseling is available with a neutral and confidential "outsider" not tied to community social networks. These recommendations make allowances for culturally defined illness, self-diagnosis, and self-treatment within cultural parameters.

In their comparative study of "nerves" in rural and urban Appalachia, Rhoda Halperin and Jennifer Reiter-Purtill find more severe symptoms in the urban sample, which they attribute to greater stress in areas experiencing more rapid culture change, including the often destructive processes of modernization, globalization, migration, and acculturation. They also conclude that the rural sample has more resources, including stable social networks, and that one means of reducing related health-care costs in cities would be to establish more support services for urban migrant communities. From a holistic perspective, then, the mental health status of the Appalachian community can be interpreted as one reflection of its ability and assistance in adapting to a changing cultural context.

Appalachian people have been stigmatized in the popular consciousness as having higher levels of mental disorders, including mental deficiencies and social pathology. Halperin and Reiter-Purtill suggest that biomedicine may have contributed to this perception through the individualized medical treatment of stress-induced syndromes such as "nerves" and the resulting "medicalization of class experience." In their chapter on psychological testing, Susan E. Keefe, Janice L. Hastrup, and Sherilyn N. Thomas suggest that standardized tests also may have contributed to this perception by failing to provide normative data for the Appalachian population whose elevated test scores on a number of MMPI and SCL-90-R scales may be due in part to different cultural boundaries for normalcy. The possible misinterpretation of the elevated Appalachian scores as a sign of greater social pathology contributes to the stereotype by suggesting it is supported by "scientific" evidence.

Furthermore, Keefe, Hastrup, and Thomas conclude that certain personality traits (such as greater "social shyness," a belief in religious sanctions for "sin," and a more "male" orientation for female gender roles) are better interpreted as within the "normal" rather than the "pathological" range in the Appalachian cultural context. At the same time, like Halperin and Reiter-Purtill, Keefe, Hastrup, and Thomas find substantial evidence that there is a relatively high level of psychological stress and a high rate of depression among Appalachians, in whatever way it might be culturally constructed. Both Halperin and Reiter-Purtill and Keefe, Hastrup and Thomas also find evidence that mental illness is more likely to be understood and expressed among Appalachian people in terms of physical rather than mental symptoms, which might further contribute to the medicalization of their mental and emotional problems. These findings call for a more holistic and culturally based appraisal of mental health status and mental health service needs in Appalachian communities.

In the following chapter, Susan Keefe and Susie Greene situate their discussion of mental health therapy in the context of Appalachian cultural values which they point out affect both the therapist's and the client's perception of the therapeutic encounter. They stress the need to incorporate more symbolic, metaphorical, and ritualized techniques with Appalachian people who may not meet the therapist's expectation for more direct and verbal confrontations with emotions and feelings. They also encourage the acknowledgment of evangelical Christian religious beliefs among Appalachian clients, a sensitive issue for therapists trained with a materialist-oriented biomedical model. These recommendations are grounded in the recognition that nonverbal ritualistic and religious/spiritual techniques are common cross-culturally in treating mental illnesses, although they are typically ignored in the biomedical model.

The development of a specific ritual as a rite of passage for at-risk Appalachian adolescent males is the topic of Michael Maloney's chapter. Maloney evaluates the implementation of this ritual in three Ohio counties and recommends more discussion of Appalachian values in the curriculum of the ritual. Values tend to be transmitted to the next generation in Appalachian communities through the cycle of daily social life and normal interaction with parents and other elders. In the context of migration, urbanization, and modernization, where the normal framework of community life has often broken down, rituals must be consciously constructed in order to ensure the successful transition to adulthood. Maloney suggests that the rite of passage program is helpful in creating a positive sense of identity among young Appalachian men, increasing self-esteem and the likelihood of finishing their high school education. In this way, new rituals can contribute to the creation of resources in a community.

References

Gordon, Deborah R. 1988. "Tenacious Assumptions in Western Medicine." In *Biomedicine Examined,* Margaret Locke and Deborah Gordon (Eds.). Dordrecht, Netherlands: Kluwer Academic. Pp. 257–95.

Hahn, Robert A. 1995. *Sickness and Healing: An Anthropological Perspective.* New Haven: Yale University Press.

Parsons, Talcott. 1949. *The Structure of Social Action.* Glencoe, Ill.: Free Press.

Chapter 11

Designing Employee Assistance Programs for Appalachian Working-Class Women: The Alcohol and Stress Research Project

Benita J. Howell and Judith Ivy Fiene

The Alcohol and Stress Research Project was begun in response to an Employee Assistance provider's request for research that would help her understand local patterns of alcohol use and work more effectively with a specific client population, working-class Appalachian women. Expanding employment opportunities in the light-manufacturing and service sectors, coupled with shrinking employment for men in mining, wood industries, and agriculture, has drawn increasing numbers of wives and mothers into "public work" outside of their homes (Beaver 1986).

Potentially, this move into new work roles is stressful for women and their families. Women's new work roles and their status as key wage earners for their households conflict with traditional values and expectations that tied rural Appalachian women firmly to the domestic sphere and extended families with men clearly in charge (Beaver 1979). How, then, do women who are products of this cultural background juggle the competing demands of family and workplace? How do they deal with crises in personal and family life, and how can Employment Assistance Programs (EAPs) in general best support their efforts to maintain effectiveness at work while coping with family and personal problems?

Alcohol abuse is a significant factor in regional social problems as well as domestic issues (Linquist, Cocherham, and Hwang 1999; Willis 1998). Because Appalachia in the past was infamous for moonshining, bootlegging, and violence linked to alcohol, and because alcohol-related problems such as domestic violence and highway accidents and fatalities continue unabated, it is especially important to develop detailed knowledge of drinking patterns and associated values, behaviors, and consequences.

Gender stereotyping, gender segregation, and double standards of behavior are strongly supported by traditional Appalachian values; they have operated with respect to drinking behavior as well as other aspects of family life. Drinking traditionally was a male group activity, often carried on outdoors in conjunction with other male activities such as hunting or on the fringes of social gatherings. Men would drink away from home and hide their drinking from wives and mothers whose fundamentalist religious beliefs might lead them to condemn drinking as sinful (Levine 1980). Women were expected to be abstemious but also to endure and cope with men's drinking and its consequences. EAPs from their inception have equipped themselves to treat employee alcohol abuse; however, new approaches may be needed if these programs are to meet the needs of Appalachian women, who are more likely to be troubled by family members' drinking than to be problem drinkers themselves.

Background and Information Needs

National surveys on Americans' drinking behavior (e.g., Department of Health and Human Services 2002; Johnson et al. 1977; Johnson 1982) and epidemiological research on drinking patterns (e.g., Ferrence 1980; Johnson et al. 1998; McCreary, Newcomb, and Sadava 1999; Robins and Smith 1980; Wilsnack, Wilsnack, and Klassen 1984) suggest that the majority of heavy drinkers and alcoholics are men; women typically drink less frequently than men and consume less alcohol when they drink. The majority of working-class women abstain from drinking altogether, but those who do drink appear to be at risk for problem drinking (Beckman 1975; Greenblatt and Schuckit 1976). Research on women and alcohol has increased since 1980, but the bulk of it has focused on those in treatment for alcoholism (e.g., NIAAA 1980; Schmidt, Klee, and Ames 1990). Comparatively little is known of the sociocultural context of drinking for the general population of adult women who are light or moderate social drinkers. Some researchers interpreted survey data from the late sixties and early seventies as indicating that women's drinking patterns were converging with those of men (NIAAA 1980); however, Ferrence (1980:74–105) questioned the "convergence hypothesis" based on comparison of results from multiple surveys in the United States and Canada. Analyses of survey data also have yielded contradictory predictions regarding which groups of women are most likely to be heavy drinkers. For example, Johnson (1982) reported high rates of problem drinking among married employed women, while Wilsnack, Wilsnack, and Klassen (1984) did not confirm this finding in their analysis of 1981 NORC survey data.

Despite the increasing number of women employed outside the home and suggestions that role conflict between marriage/family and work may increase women's risk for problem drinking (Johnson 1982; Gomberg and Lisansky 1984), the literature on alcohol and the workplace has dealt predominantly with men (e.g., Schramm, Mandell, and Archer 1978; Janes and Ames 1989). Studies of alcohol use by working women have focused on professionals and executives, not working-class women.

EAPs have long been associated with alcohol abuse treatment that combats workers' absenteeism, drinking on the job, and impaired work performance. Certainly, alcohol abuse is a proverbial Appalachian problem of long standing. As we were planning this project, federal statistics were released indicating that for 1988, Tennessee led the nation in alcohol-related arrests (21.4 per 1,000 residents), including driving under the influence, liquor law violations, and public drunkenness (*Knoxville News-Sentinel*, Sept. 23, 1990). Data from the surveys cited previously and our experience with rural Appalachian families would suggest, however, that a large proportion of Appalachian women abstain from drinking alcohol. At first glance, therefore, alcohol abuse counseling would not appear to be a priority need of Appalachian working women. On the other hand, alcohol abuse by family members might be implicated in other problems (e.g., "nerves," abuse of pharmaceuticals, domestic violence) that would bring female clients to the EAP. Men's drinking behavior may well lead to family and relationship problems that cause the women in their households substantial distress and potentially impair their effectiveness on the job. If this is so, then EAPs need to provide appropriate counseling and support for women who are coping with family drinking problems. How can the EAP best help these women deal with other family members' drinking problems—problems that affect the female employees' work performance only indirectly?

The first step in addressing this question must be a needs assessment to learn the incidence and nature of alcohol-related family problems experienced by a cross-section of female employees who are not EAP clients. Systematic data on drinking patterns, associated values, behaviors, and consequences are much needed. Quantitative data is especially necessary, because much of what we think we know about Appalachian drinking patterns (e.g., Edwards 1985) has been constructed anecdotally from travel accounts, oral narrative, written records of court and church proceedings, and also from fictional treatments of family life that resonate with and perpetuate popular stereotypes. There has been far too little systematic investigation outside of a clinical context that would provide reliable data on the incidence and nature of alcohol consumption in the region.

Our survey instrument was designed and administered in collaboration with the EAP program director who encouraged us to undertake this research. Our subjects were female nursing assistants and licensed practical nurses in the regional medical center where this EAP is based.

The survey collected information on personal drinking habits and beliefs about alcohol, family drinking habits (particularly those of mates), and alcohol-related family problems. These parts of the survey were modeled on the Comprehensive Drinker Profile, a clinical assessment tool.[1] The respondents also completed three subscales of the Miller and Smith (1987) Stress Audit, indicating sources of stress they had experienced in the past in their family lives and as individuals.

Survey Administration and Respondents

Because shift scheduling made it impractical for us to meet with workers to explain and administer the questionnaire in person, survey materials were placed in break rooms for nursing assistants and were sent individually to LPNs through the medical center's in-house mail system On advice of the institutional research director, we attempted to reach nursing assistants through the channels usually used for in-service training. The project would be advertised by a written notice from the research director and verbal announcements from supervisors. An audiotaped explanation and packets of questionnaires and consent forms were then placed in break rooms. We made one hundred surveys available for a pool of approximately 150 female nursing assistants, placing ten surveys in each of ten break rooms. Volunteer respondents would have access to these materials on a first-come, first-served basis for two weeks, the length of time needed to rotate through a complete shift pattern. At the end of that time, 23 women had completed and mailed back questionnaires. Discrepancies between the survey plan and what actually happened during administration make the 23 percent response rate difficult to interpret. Some potential respondents did not receive the announcement flyer in advance of the survey period, and only six sets of survey materials remained in the break rooms for the entire two weeks. Additionally, the taped introduction reportedly provoked some negative reactions.

Letters of introduction and surveys were sent directly to each potential respondent in the LPN group. Of 130 questionnaires distributed, 39 (30 percent) were returned sufficiently complete to be used for analysis. Only one respondent indicated that she was a recovering alcoholic. Because the object of this project was to gather information on women not in treatment, that questionnaire was excluded from analysis.

Our sample thus consists of twenty-three nursing assistants and thirty-eight LPNs who voluntarily responded to these administrations of the survey. Of these sixty-one women, 85 percent work full time. Their mean age is forty years. The median length of employment at the medical center is 3.5 years. Sixty-five percent completed twelfth grade, and another 27 percent have one or two years of college. The sample is 90 percent white, 7 percent African American, and 3 percent Native American. Slightly over three-quarters (77 percent) have lived in Tennessee longer than twenty-one years; the same proportion (78 percent) attended the eighth grade in East Tennessee. Two-thirds report that their mother, father, or both grew up in East Tennessee. Only ten women (16.4 percent) have no kinship ties to others in Appalachia or the South. Fifty percent of the sample are Baptist now, and 59 percent were brought up in Baptist churches; 55 percent attend church at least two or three times a month.

Ninety percent of respondents live in the county where the medical center is located or in an adjacent county. Most (63 percent) are living with their husbands, and 86 percent have one or more children living in their households. Single mothers with dependent children account for 11.5 percent of households, while nuclear families and couples living alone account for 61 percent of households. Only 8 percent of households have more than four members.

Findings

We expected that coping with the double load of work responsibilities and traditional duties at home might be especially stressful for nurses because they must assume a caretaker role in both spheres, placing others' needs above their own. We also anticipated that crises provoked by a family member's alcohol abuse would increase the stress of coping with already heavy and conflicting demands from work and family. The data support these hypotheses.

Co-workers, we thought, might provide some support for one another through sharing their experiences in coping with family problems, especially since employees of the regional medical center resided in many different neighborhoods, even different towns and counties, and would be unlikely to know the families involved. They could thus serve as neutral outsiders, sounding boards for one another. This expectation was not borne out, however. Rather, interviews suggest a pattern of guarding family secrets that has important implications for EAP service providers.

Secrecy is a coping mechanism that acts to protect the secret keeper from the anticipated negative opinions of others. It is an effort to avoid being stigmatized for behaviors or qualities that seem, to the secret keeper, to deviate from social expectations. This type of secret keeping concerning behaviors or characteristics of family members has been described in various populations, including women whose partners are infertile (Miall 1986) and women battered by their partners (Fiene 1995). Even in circumstances where poor rural women depend upon one another for assistance, using a neighbor's telephone, for example, they guard family secrets if possible (Fitchen 1981).

As the literature suggested, most of the women who responded to our survey reported that they drank only lightly (34 percent) or not at all (61 percent). However, 8 percent reported that their mates were problem drinkers or alcoholics, and 29 percent reported that their fathers had been problem drinkers or alcoholics. When asked to give a more specific report of alcohol consumption during the past week, 88 percent of the women reported that they had abstained entirely; 10 percent had consumed alcohol on one day; and only 2 percent had consumed alcohol on two days. In contrast, 77 percent of mates were reported to be abstainers, but 9.5 percent had consumed alcohol on four or more days. When asked to report how much alcohol had been consumed, only 5 percent of women who drink reported consuming more than two drinks on one or two days, whereas 11.5 percent of mates consumed alcohol at this rate. No nurse reported consuming alcohol on more than two days during the week, whereas 8 percent of their mates, likely problem drinkers, consumed more than two drinks on five or more days.

The survey included ten statements to assess beliefs about alcohol (table 11.1). Whether or not they consume alcohol or have experienced family prob-

Table 11.1. Beliefs about Alcohol

Beliefs	Average Score	Agree (%)	Strongly Disagree (%)
Not being able to control your drinking is a sign of moral weakness.	3.397	15.5	29.3
Alcoholism is a disease.	1.656	80.3	9.0
Drinking helps people escape from their problems for awhile.	2.869	39.3	24.6
My religion teaches that drinking is a sin.	2.180	62.3	11.5
Drinking is a big cause of family problems for the people I know.	2.459	54.1	19.7
Moderate drinking helps people feel more comfortable in social groups.	3.311	19.7	26.2
There is nothing wrong with moderate drinking.	3.393	26.2	36.1
Respectable women disapprove of drinking.	3.508	27.1	41
Drinking makes men aggressive and prone to get into fights.	2.593	49.2	9.8
Alcohol makes women more relaxed about sex.	3.237	25.4	27.1

Note: N = 61. Mean Likert scale responses: 1 = strongly agree to 5 = strongly disagree.

lems with alcohol, these women subscribe to the medical model, agreeing strongly that alcoholism is a disease, while also affirming that their religion teaches drinking is a sin. Drinking is a big cause of family problems among people they know, and they believe that drinking makes men aggressive and prone to get into fights.

These beliefs can be compared with the experience of the twenty-three women whose mates consume alcohol. Table 11.2 displays the results from survey questions on drinking patterns. Women most often drink at home with mates, on social occasions, or with restaurant meals. Their mates, particularly problem drinkers, consume alcohol under a much broader array of circumstances, more often drinking in taverns or bars and outdoors away from home. These patterns show continuity with traditional conventions of sexual segregation that caused men to prefer consuming alcohol in male groups, outside of women's domestic space. Unfortunately, the current manifestations of this pattern lead to drinking while driving.

Table 11.2. Drinking Patterns of Respondents and Mates Who Consume Alcohol

Habits	Respondents (N = 23) (20 light, 3 moderate drinkers)				Mates (N = 23) (15 light, 4 moderate, 1 problem, 3 alcoholic)			
Drinks Alcohol	Sometimes		Often		Sometimes		Often	
At home	19	82.6%	0	0%	14	60.1%	6	26.1%
At work	0	0%	0	0%	0	0%	2	8.7%
At others' homes	16	69.6%	0	0%	16	69.6%	3	13.0%
Outdoors away from home	11	47.8%	0	0%	15	65.2%	5	21.7%
At social clubs	13	56.5%	1	4.3%	11	47.8%	2	8.7%
At restaurants	18	78.3%	0	0%	19	82.6%	2	8.7%
At social events	17	73.9%	1	4.3%	16	69.6%	2	8.7%
At taverns/bars	11	47.8%	1	4.3%	12	52.2%	4	17.4%
While driving	0	0%	0	0%	5	21.7%	4	17.4%
Alone	8	34.8%	0	0%	9	39.1%	4	17.4%
With one's mate	22	95.7%	0	0%	20	87.0%	3	21.7%
With male friends	12	52.2%	0	0%	15	69.6%	5	13.0%
With female friends	17	73.9%	1	4.3%	4	17.4%	3	13.0%
With male and female friends	19	82.6%	0	0%	18	78.3%	3	13.0%
With strangers	2	8.7%	0	0%	2	8.7%	3	13.0%

The Stress Audit and Sources of Stress

The Stress Audit instrument was developed by Miller, Smith, and Mehler (1986) to help individuals identify stressful situations in their lives as well as physiological, cognitive, and emotional symptoms of stress. The EAP that encouraged our research uses the Stress Audit for clinical assessment as a standard part of initial sessions with new patients. The full assessment of eight situation scales and seven symptom scales is lengthy, so we elected to use only three scales, the sets of questions that measure stress related to family, social roles, and individual issues. We purposely avoided using a fourth scale concerning work/school issues in order to allay concerns on the part of participants or their supervisors that data on the workplace environment and work performance might adversely affect work units or individual employees.

Miller, Smith, and Mehler (1986) provide norms for each scale as a reference benchmark for testers and their clients. Our respondents as a whole scored above the norm on family stress, whether or not drinking problems were an issue. The mean score of 60, compared with the norm of 39, places our average respondent in the eighty-fourth percentile on this scale. However, those with problem drinker parents (usually fathers), and especially those with alcoholic mates, experienced substantially higher levels of family stress. A mean family stress score of 96 places respondents with problem drinker parents or mates in the ninety-eighth percentile on this scale.

Respondents reported substantially less stress in the realms of individual situations and social role performance. The mean score for all respondents was slightly lower than the norm for individual stress (47 compared with 50, or forty-eighth percentile) and substantially lower for social stress (25 compared with 39, or thirty-second percentile). Guidelines for interpreting the Stress Audit note that exceptionally low scores may reflect a tendency to minimize objective stress, a coping strategy that can itself cause problems.

Presumably the Stress Audit was normed for a mixed male and female population. Perhaps women in general would resemble our sample in being more stressed by family problems than by other issues. But it is also possible that our sample of professional "caregivers" (more than women who choose different occupations) become so absorbed by family worries that they pay less attention to stressors that relate to their personal identity and social roles outside of the family.

Frequency data from the Stress Audit reveal the most common stressors. Components of family stress reported by more than two-thirds of respondents related to holidays and family vacations, marital difficulties, disciplinary problems with children, and family conflict over money. Additional sources of family stress that have affected more than half of the respondents include getting married or starting a significant relationship, serious illness in the family, and child-care responsibilities. Most significant for this research, fully 49 percent of respondents report that they have experienced stress from alcohol or drug problems in the family.

The most frequent sources of individual stress (acknowledged by more than two-thirds of respondents) were vacations or travel, feeling unattractive, not having enough time for oneself, not having enough time to get things done, and problems with weight. Over half of the respondents also reported stress related to noticeable aging, lack of personal privacy, difficulty meeting obligations to oneself, and failure to meet personal goals.

The Stress Audit uses a Likert scale to measure degree of stress on a scale from 1 (only slightly stressful) to 5 (extremely stressful). Mean scores indicate that the most stressful family events for those who have experienced them were: death of a close relative (4.219), difficulty meeting obligations to family (3.719), difficulties dealing with other family members (3.683), serious illness in the family (3.657), family conflict over money (3.622), the spouse beginning or stopping work (3.619), and change in the number of arguments with one's spouse (3.615).

The most stressful individual life events were not having enough time to get things done (4.278), change in living conditions (4.143), not having enough time for oneself (4.039), problems with weight (3.900), difficulty meeting obligations to oneself (3.800), and failure to meet personal goals (3.647). Only a minority of respondents indicated that social relationships were stressful, but several events or feelings were sources of considerable stress for the women who did experience them. These included ending old relationships (4.040), feeling unwanted and alone (3.962), having to take special care to maintain relationships (3.655), and feeling excluded from a group (3.609).

Family and individual stress scores are higher for women whose parents and mates are alcoholic or problem drinkers than for their counterparts. Survey questions on problems associated with the mate's drinking reveal much about the extent and specific nature of difficulties these women experience (table 11.3). Roughly one-third of them have experienced serious problems that they attribute to the mate's drinking, including marital problems (43.5 percent), arguments and spousal abuse (39 percent), fights (35 percent), and conflicts with the law (30 percent). Thirty percent also report problems with an adult child's drinking. These women believe that worry about family members' drinking has damaged their own health.

Table 11.3. Reported Effects of Respondents' Drinking and Mates' Drinking

Effects	Respondents' Drinking (N = 23)		Mates' Drinking (N = 23)	
Respondent drinking caused family worry	0	0%	—	—
Mate's drinking causes respondent worry	—	—	6	26.1%
Respondent feels bad about her drinking	2	8.7%	—	—
Gets into fights when drinking	3	13.0%	8	34.8%
Arguments occur when mate drinks	—	—	9	39.1%
Mate is abusive when drinking	—	—	9	39.1%
Drinking has caused problems with mate	2	8.7%	10	43.5%
Friends lost because of drinking	0	0%	3	13.0%
Trouble at work because of drinking	0	0%	2	8.7%
Loss of job because of drinking	0	0%	4	17.4%
Drinking caused neglect of family	0	0%	5	21.7%
Drinking caused neglect of work	0	0%	2	8.7%
Drinking caused conflicts with the law	0	0%	7	30.4%
Drinking caused accidents	0	0%	4	17.4%
Tried to hide drinking from family	3	13.0%	5	21.7%
Have sought help for drinking problem	0	0%	3	13.0%
Hospitalized for drinking problem	0	0%	3	13.0%
Tried unsuccessfully to stop drinking	0	0%	7	30.4%

Follow-up Interviews

In the summer of 1993, Fiene interviewed four women who had participated in the survey and at that time expressed willingness to be interviewed. These interviews took place away from the workplace in her university office. These women were older than the average respondent and had long work histories in nursing. Two of the women were local natives, one was a southerner married to a local man, and the fourth woman and her spouse were northerners. The first three women described numerous stressful life events, including dealing with alcoholic fathers, physical or psychological abuse, mates abusing alcohol, and children who are substance abusers. These women talked freely and gave extensive life narratives. The fourth woman, who was not from the Appalachian region, denied any family problems related to alcohol in her first or second marriage. She seemed more reticent and revealed little personal information.

Interviewees were exposed to the domain of the interview by reading a sheet of questions about their experience with alcohol use in their family and how this had affected their personal and work lives. Then they were asked to begin speaking to a question of their choosing. Interviews lasted from sixty to ninety minutes. They were taped, transcribed, and analyzed for recurring themes and processes. The following sections present the women's insight into what causes them stress, what stress feels like, and successful strategies for coping with stress.

What Causes Feelings of Stress

The women report that stress results when they feel that their personal lives are out of control. These feelings of helplessness come from the recognition that they can do nothing to change the problematic behavior of a significant other, usually a spouse, child, or parent. The subsequent worry and preoccupation about the family member then impairs the woman's ability to go through her daily routines. "I like to be in control. . . . When I was out of control when all of this started with the son [she discovered his substance abuse], it was a miserable time for me," one woman said.

Another woman noted, "As long as I'm organized and can follow my routine, I think I can handle stress pretty well." The unpredictability of the other's behavior emphasizes her lack of control. "It was probably maybe even easier as far as stress goes at that time [when he always drank every day] because you know what to expect . . . because [now] you never know from one day to the other whether you are going to come home [from work] and find him sober or drunk." Also, a partner's behavior may activate feelings and fears from past times when the woman felt helpless or defenseless. One woman commented that when her husband was critical "that used to feed into my terror because I was terrified of men because of the way my father [a physically abusive alcoholic] had raised me."

What Stress Feels Like

"It's like that time when I can't say OK, it's time to go to work now," one woman said. "This goes over here and I go to work. [But] you can't do that. It's like a total. . . . It's mental, it's physical, it's emotional, it's everything. Everything is just a knot and then that's when I can't function." She reported physical symptoms of stress: headaches, teeth clinching, stomach trouble, a gnawing feeling, and emotional symptoms, such as "lazy" feelings, depression, and lowered motivation. One woman was sure that stress exacerbated her chronic illness.

Strategies for Handling Stress

All of the women had developed strategies for dealing with stress and to prevent home stress from affecting work performance. They vividly describe how they disassociate home problems from work. One stayed home when she believed she could not fulfill work functions: "It interfered greatly with me at [work] because of my absences, and because of the stress I would be under. . . . [But] most of the time when I'm at work unless things are extremely bad I can just sort of disassociate and leave all that over here somewhere and just go on with whatever it is I have to do at the moment."

Another woman reported, "When I leave the house to go to work, I get in the car, I become a nurse, you know, becoming nurse all the way to [the] hospital. And when I get in the car, at the end of my shift, I become Mom, or wife, or whatever all the way home and I never take work home and I never take home to work."

The necessity of managing home stress when at work is directly related to the great sense of responsibility the women feel for their work: "I would never put my patient in jeopardy because my mind was not where it should be and I couldn't give my full attention mentally to what I was doing. . . . And [if] I felt that I could not function I would not go. I would rather stay home, and even get fired than to think that I might have made a mistake that cost somebody an extended period in the hospital or even their life. I couldn't deal with that." A woman who worked for many years in the intensive care nursery said,

"I don't allow myself to slough off or put another life in jeopardy just because I have a little bit of a problem."

This strategy means, however, that colleagues at work do not become part of the woman's support network. "I didn't discuss my personal life with co-workers. I didn't want it brought into the work place." And they had not sought out the Employee Assistance Program to address their unhappiness. "In the back of my mind, I've always thought that I should keep . . . psychological stuff and work stuff separate," one woman said.

Some women found other means of handling stress, including the development of self-understanding. The source of insight for two of these women has been self-help books. The women also spoke of using tension-reducing activities that they saw as positive, such as prayer and going fishing. They recognized that they used such negative activities as smoking and overeating to meet the same ends.

Some studies have indicated that working women rely on a network of family and friends for support rather than work-based networks (Gianakos 2002). However, none of the women interviewed reported a supportive network of friends or of extended family members. They felt inhibited in reaching out due to the nature of their family problems. Although the local women spoke of their interactions with local churches, their reticence to acknowledge family problems appeared to keep them at a distance from fellow members.

Discussion

The stories told by women in these interviews underscored and amplified the findings from the Stress Audit component of the survey, particularly the concentration of stress on the family scale. Nuclear family relationships are at the center of these women's lives; when significant others are substance abusers, the women's considerable coping skills are challenged. The interviewees were quite competent women. They had survived abuse and unhappiness, established partnerships, raised children, obtained nursing education after marriage, had long employment records, and expressed very positive feelings about their work. They were more in control of life events than a group of Appalachian battered women whom Fiene (1993) had previously interviewed. But for both groups of women, their families of procreation are their sole source of fulfillment for their emotional needs. They appear to be cut off from other women and organizations by the need to keep family secrets and because they are drained by family and work responsibilities. This isolation from social support was also noted in British women living with alcohol abusing partners (Velleman, Copello, and Maslin 1998).

Implications and Suggestions for Employee Assistance

Family worries do not push work responsibilities into second place in these women's lives. The sense of competence, order, and control they gain from work is extremely important to their self-image, and work satisfaction can be a compensation for bad times at home. However, because they fear any hint that preoccupation with personal problems might undermine the undivided attention nursing demands, and because mental separation of the work and home domains is a coping strategy, these women closely guard the secrets of family life unless and until it is necessary to inform a supervisor of problems.

This presents a dilemma for a health-care facility EAP. While EAP counselors should have an adequate understanding of local cultural mores, beliefs and values, they must stand apart from hospital co-workers in order to be entrusted with client secrets. Who provides EAP counseling can become even more of an issue in rural communities where an EAP employee may appear to be too closely tied to other parts of the community and kinship networks to be trusted.

Despite cultural patterns that favor reticence as a strategy for avoiding conflict (Hicks 1976), interviewees talked freely to Fiene, a sympathetic but neutral outsider. Co-workers, on the other hand, even when they do not know the family members involved, are not treated as neutral outsiders. Not only might they call a troubled woman's competence at work into question (and the women take steps to ensure that personal problems do not impair their work), but confiding in co-workers would violate the strategy of disassociation which has become an effective coping mechanism. For the same reasons, troubled nurses avoid seeking help from their EAP. Despite EAP efforts to publicize and provide comprehensive, confidential counseling services to employees, workers may still associate the EAP with the stigma of mandatory counseling required by employers when inadequate work performance alerts supervisors to problems. Under these circumstances, the EAP will have special difficulties serving these women and their families; however, insights gained from the interviews suggest several strategies for EAP outreach.

First, given the reluctance of employees to use EAP services, EAPs should make greater use of existing employee education formats (speaker series, videos, and printed brochures) to disseminate substantive information which is directed to women. In this case, our survey suggests that family alcohol abuse and associated problems are prevalent enough that it would be worthwhile to distribute unsolicited information on these issues to all women in the medical center work force.

Second, EAPs should analyze the self-help strategies women describe in interviews and build on these wherever possible. Self-help books, for example, have been a valuable resource for helping these women analyze their problems and develop effective coping strategies on their own. EAP counselors could support women in this effort by screening the volumes of good, bad, and indifferent self-help literature on the market and making reading lists of recommended items readily available to all employees.

Finally, employees who want to secure counseling services independently rather than through their EAP need referral lists and information about support groups and other resources available in their locality. This raises a secondary problem of locating needed services and making them accessible to working women, particularly when rotating shift schedules and child-care responsibilities may make it difficult for busy wives and mothers working as nurses to schedule appointments or attend regular group meetings.

The research reported here represents only the initial steps in a collaboration between university-based social scientists and an EAP. Collaboration with an EAP professional led to publishing a summary of findings and implications of the study in a journal read by service providers in this and other parts of the United States (Howell, Fiene, and Woychik 1998). In addition to furnishing background information on a client group and their needs, the interviews suggested that this potential clientele might be reluctant to seek help from the EAP. In line with the recommendation to provide broader education as a preventive mental health service, we suggested that the EAP present our survey results to employees at large. Women who have been silently coping with alcohol-related family problems might then realize that they are not alone; almost half of their co-worker respondents have experienced stress because of alcohol or drug problems in their family; a third have experienced stress because of a mate's problem drinking.

Howell presented the survey results to half a dozen people at an open lunch-time forum at the medical center, but no LPN or nursing assistant attended. The EAP subsequently organized a series of one hour lunch-time discussions related to family life and self-improvement, topics that were thought to have general appeal to workers across the occupational spectrum. Interestingly, the meeting to discuss "Balancing Family and Career" brought no discussants. The two workshops that brought in twelve to fifteen participants were "Improving Your Child's Self-Esteem" and "Male-Female Communication." Attendance was so poor at the first group of meetings that future discussions were canceled. The program director attributed the low attendance at these workshops largely to the inability of employees to take a full hour at a set lunch time. Nursing staff, in particular, do not work on such a schedule.

Two other events at the EAP are noteworthy in light of this study's findings. When another agency of the medical center presented a series of successful workshops on stress reduction, individual workers sought out the presenter and acknowledged workplace stress. They were then referred to the EAP for services. The person delivering these workshops has high visibility and is a well-known physician. Although staff time may be a factor in workshop attendance, it may be important to consider the drawing power of the workshop leader.

The EAP also serviced contracts with rural medical centers, arranging for an on-site counselor on a weekly basis. The counselor in this role was equally adept in communicating with hospital administration and with workers. While she was from the outside, her roots and work experience were also rural. She became a known and trusted person. Financial cutbacks ended the on-site counseling so that workers now access EAP services through telephoning for information and referral to a counselor in their region. Since this change there has been an appreciable drop in EAP utilization rates in these rural medical centers.

In the summer of 1996, the urban medical center eliminated its on-site counseling. Like many corporations and institutions, the medical center elected to contract for services that previously were handled by in-house employees. Removal of counseling services from the workplace is becoming commonplace in our changing mental-health-care environment and may present a further logistical barrier to counseling for working women who are struggling with stress at home (Hartwell et al. 1996). If logistical barriers to service utilization can be overcome, however, counseling provided away from the workplace or the immediate community may be more acceptable than workplace-based mental health services to clients whose secret keeping makes them reluctant to seek help nearby. Such a move will only increase the need for EAP materials to be culturally sensitive and relevant to women's concerns.

Note

1. Sections of the questionnaire were adapted and reproduced by special permission of Psychological Assessment Resources, Inc., 16204 North Florida Avenue, Lutz, Florida 33549, from the Comprehensive Drinker Profile, copyright 1984.

References

Beaver, Patricia D. 1979. "Hillbilly Women, Hillbilly Men: Sex Roles in Rural Agricultural Appalachia. In *Appalachian Women: A Learning-Teaching Guide*, C. Patton-Crowder (Ed.). Knoxville: University of Tennessee Press. Pp. 65–73.

———. 1986. *Rural Community in the Appalachian South,* Lexington: University Press of Kentucky.

Beckman, L. J. 1975. "Women Alcoholics: A Review of Social and Psychological Studies." *Journal of Studies on Alcohol* 36:797–824.

Department of Health and Human Services. Substance Abuse and Mental Health Services Administration. Office of Applied Studies. 2002. *Results from the 2001 National Household Survey on Drug Abuse: Volume 1. Summary of National Findings.* Washington D.C.: U.S. Government Printing Office.

Edwards, G. T. 1985. "Appalachia: The Effects of Cultural Values on the Production and Consumption of Alcohol." In *The American Experience with Alcohol: Contrasting Cultural Perspectives,* Linda A. Bennett and Genevieve M. Ames (Eds.). New York: Plenum. Pp. 131–46.

Ferrence, R. G. 1980. "Sex Differences in the Prevalence of Problem Drinking." *Research Advances in Alcohol and Drug Problems* 5:69–124.

Fiene, Judith Ivy. 1993. "The Appalachian Social Context and the Battering of Women." *Practicing Anthropology* 15(3):20–24.

———. 1995. "Battered Women: Keeping the Secret." *Affilia* 10(2):179–93.

Fitchen, Janet M. 1981. *Poverty in Rural America: A Case Study.* Boulder, Colo.: Westview.

Gianakos, I. 2002. "Predictors of Coping with Work Stress: The Influences of Sex, Gender Role, Social Desirability, and the Locus of Control." *Sex Roles* 46(5/6):149–58.

Gomberg, E. L., and J. M. Lisansky. 1984. "Antecedents of Alcohol Problems in Women." In *Alcohol Problems in Women: Antecedents, Consequences, and Intervention,* Sharon C. Wilsnack and Linda J. Beckman (Eds.). New York: Guilford Press. Pp. 233–59.

Greenblatt, Malton, and Marc A. Schuckit (Eds.). 1976. *Alcoholism Problems in Women and Children.* New York: Grune and Stratton.

Hartwell, T. D., P. Steele, M. T. French, F. J. Potter, N. F. Rodman, and G. A. Zarkin. 1996. "Aiding Troubled Employees: The Prevalence, Cost, and Characteristics of Employee Assistance Programs in the United States." *American Journal of Public Health* 86(6):804–8.

Hicks, George L. 1976. *Appalachian Valley.* New York: Holt, Rinehart & Winston.

Howell, B. J., J. I. Fiene, and J. P. Woychik, J. P. 1998. "Employee Assistance Implications for Appalachian Working Class Women from the Alcohol and Stress Research Project." *Employee Assistance Quarterly* 13(4):55–60.

Janes, C. R., and G. Ames. 1989. "Men, Blue Collar Work and Drinking: Alcohol Use in an Industrial Subculture." *Culture, Medicine and Psychiatry* 13:245–74.

Johnson, F. W., P. J. Gruenewald, J. Treno, and G. A. Taff. 1998. "Drinking Over the Life Course Within Gender and Ethnic Groups: A Hyperparametric Analysis." *Journals of Studies in Alcohol* 59(5):568–81.

Johnson, Paula B. 1982. "Sex Differences, Women's Roles and Alcohol Use: Preliminary National Data." *Journal of Social Issues* 38(2):93–116.

Johnson, P. B., et al. 1977. "U.S. Adult Drinking Practices; Time Trends, Social Correlates and Sex Roles." Santa Monica, Calif.: NIAAA.

Levine, H. G. 1980. "Temperance and Women in 19th Century United States." In *Alcohol and Drug Problems in Women: Research Advances in Alcohol and Drug Problems,* vol. 5, O. J. Lalant (Ed.). New York: Plenum. Pp. 25–67.

Linquist, C., W. C. Cocherham, and S. Hwang. 1999. "Drinking Patterns in the American Deep South." *Journals of Studies on Alcohol* 60(5):663–66.

McCreary, D. R., M. D. Newcomb, and S. W. Sadava. 1999. "The Male Role, Alcohol Use, and Alcohol Problems: A Structural Modeling Examination in Adult Women and Men." *Journal of Counseling Psychology* 46(1):109–24.

Miall, C. E. 1986. "The Stigma of Involuntary Childlessness." *Social Problems* 33(4):268–82.

Miller, L. H., and A. D. Smith. 1987. *Stress Audit.* Brookline, Mass.: Biobehavioral Associates.

Miller, L. H., A. D. Smith, and B. L. Mehler. 1986. *Stress Audit Manual.* Brookline, Mass.: Biobehavioral Associates.

National Institute on Alcohol Abuse and Alcoholism (NIAAA). 1980. *Alcoholism and Alcohol Abuse Among Women: Research Issues.* NIAAA Research Monograph 1. Washington, D.C.: GPO.

Robins, L. N., and E. M. Smith. 1980. "Longitudinal Studies of Alcohol and Drug Problems: Sex Differences." *Research Advances in Alcohol and Drug Problems* 5: 203–32.

Schmidt, C., L. Klee, and G. Ames. 1990. "Review and Analysis of Literature on Indicators of Women's Drinking Problems." *British Journal of Addiction* 85:179–92.

Schramm, Carl J., Wallace Mandell, and Janet Archer. 1978. *Workers Who Drink.* Lexington, Mass.: D. C. Heath.

Velleman, R., A. Copello, and J. Maslin. 1998. *Living with Drink: Women Who Live with Problem Drinkers.* London: Longman.

Willis, S. M. 1998. "Recovering from My Own Little War: Women and Domestic Violence in Rural Appalachia." *Journal of Appalachian Studies* 4(2):255–70.

Wilsnack, R. W., S. C. Wilsnack, and A. D. Klassen. 1984. "Women's Drinking and Drinking Problems; Patterns from a 1981 National Survey." *American Journal of Public Health* 74:1231–38.

Chapter 12

"Nerves" in Rural and Urban Appalachia

Rhoda H. Halperin and Jennifer Reiter-Purtill

> "Never mind," Helen said sharply. "We're fixing to be late, that's all. I'm taking Vonda Louise in to Valleydale to the doctor." She cast this news back over her shoulder as she hurried down the walk. "She's just about out of nerve pills." (Smith 1995:213)

"Nerves," a folk term that refers to a high level of anxiety and depression, is becoming a frequently described culture-bound syndrome in Appalachia (Van Schaik 1988) with counterparts in other parts of the world (Guarnaccia 1993; Guarnaccia et al. 1993; Guarnaccia and Rogler 1999; Davis and Low 1989; Lock 1990; Low 1994; Reiter 1995). The recent and unprecedented inclusion of culture-bound syndromes in the DSM-IV calls attention to the cross-cultural approach suggested in this chapter because it forces both anthropologists and mental health professionals to examine the relationships between Western psychiatric categories and folk illness systems.

Nerves and nerve-like syndromes are beginning to add up to a relatively common and increasingly widespread culture-bound syndrome that seems to be related to experiences of modernization and rapid culture change among migrants and lower-class populations in many parts of the world. This approach is different from most of the discussions of nerves and similar syndromes such as "ataques de nervios," which, until recently, have treated these illnesses more particularistically and labeled them as "culture-bound syndromes,"[1] that is, named psychiatric disorders found in particular cultures. Until recently, the implication has been that these syndromes are idiosyncratic disease entities. Following Van Schaik's (1988) suggestion that the social context is a critical component of nerves and that nerves represents "the medicalization of class experience," this chapter asks the following questions: (1) Is nerves, both in Appalachia and elsewhere, more widespread than the narrow use of the label culture-bound syndrome would suggest? (2) Are the symptoms of "nerves" intensified in urban contexts? (3) If so, how can a holistic, locally based approach to illness management be designed to address the psychosocial/class components of nerves in Appalachia? (4) What are the implications of this holistic approach for understanding nerves and its counterparts in a global framework?

These questions are even more pressing given the fact that culture-bound syndromes are now included in the DSM-IV. This chapter moves in the direction of developing truly cross-cultural approaches to mental health research.

In order to answer these questions, we have taken the following approach. First, we present several urban Appalachian patient cases in which the symptom complexes of nerves and the psychosocial and sociocultural circumstances of nerves sufferers are examined. The following cases are based on our own research in an Appalachian community in Cincinnati.[2] Next, we examine the symptom complexes of nerves and the psychosocial circumstances as these have been described primarily by Van Schaik (1988) for rural Appalachia. Finally, we compare symptom complexes and psychosocial/sociocultural circumstances by (roughly) matching Van Schaik's rural patient cases with our urban Appalachian patient cases.

The data in these cases are presented in the form of summary charts and patient narratives. Table 12.1 provides a summary of the urban patient cases in terms of the symptoms suffered and the psychosocial/sociocultural factors that affect each patient. The cases are arranged in a life-course framework, from oldest to youngest. This framework provides a picture of all life-course stages and an overview of social and cultural issues, especially those related to family support systems. Table 12.2 summarizes Van Schaik's (1988) study of nerves sufferers in rural areas of eastern Kentucky. Finally, table 12.3 compares the symptoms and psychosocial/sociocultural contexts of rural patients to urban patients.

Our arguments/hypotheses are two: (1) the symptoms of nerves are similar in both the rural and urban cases, and (2) the severity of symptoms is greater in the urban context.

The implications of this analysis are potentially far-reaching, not only from the standpoint of improving treatment for patients diagnosed with "nerves" but also from the standpoint of reducing costs of health care. Nerves and similarly labeled psychiatric disorders can be construed as a "medicalization of class experience." If this is true, then the de-medicalization of nerves would reduce the costs of health care after the proper supports are put in place.

Nerves in the City: An Overview

Our urban research derives from two sources: (1) case records at a community health center examined in cooperation with health-center staff who gave their insights into family and community issues, and (2) ethnographic data gathered during five years of fieldwork in the community. During this time, we observed therapy being delivered by both the health center staff and fellow residents of the community. At no time was a formal interview schedule administered. The patients with nerves are a subset of a larger collection of typical patient cases presented to us by health-care providers in this urban community health center. The individuals in this sample either identified themselves as suffering specifically from nerves or were diagnosed with depression. The patients ranged in age from thirteen to sixty-eight.

Table 12.1 presents an overview of symptoms (in the left column) and the psychosocial/sociocultural contexts (in the right column) of patients who suffer from nerves in the urban setting. The males included in this chart are the spouses of nerves sufferers. They exhibit symptoms commonly associated with nerves, but they do not identify themselves as suffering from nerves. Following this figure are detailed narratives of several of the urban patients describing their medical and family histories. For reasons of confidentiality, names and details have been changed to protect the patients' identities.

Urban Narratives

The folk term "nerves" has a variety of manifestations. In some contexts, its symptoms are mild and manageable. In others, the symptoms—principally anxiety, depression—lead to other stress-related diseases such as ulcers, or to the serious psychiatric problems of violence and suicide. The following cases, while not representative of all aspects of nerves, do illustrate some of the cultural contexts within which nerves can be found as well as some of the different life course issues that affect the presentation of nerves. In all of the urban cases, poverty and the presence of welfare are factors in the lives of the patients.

I. Caroline and Gary Reed

Rural to urban migration has hit the Reed family hard. In 1955, they came from rural Ohio to Cincinnati after they could no longer make ends meet on their small tobacco farm. A large family and a series of psychosocial stresses have created serious health problems. The Reed family represents an extreme case of difficulties initiated by rural to urban migration, including domestic violence and substance abuse.

In 1996, Caroline Reed was a sixty-eight-year-old white adult. Her presenting symptoms include a history of chronic back pain, stomach disorders, headaches, and depression. Her husband, Gary, was born in 1925 and died in 1985. Before his death, he had numerous health problems, including high blood pressure, chronic back pain, and heart problems. He suffered from bouts of depression and had long periods of substance abuse (alcohol and prescription drugs).

Family History

Caroline was born in Hamersville, a rural town in Ohio. Both she and Gary are first generation rural to urban migrants. Gary was a bus driver for a number of years until poor health forced him to go on disability. Domestic abuse was a way of life for Gary and Caroline, who admitted that they often "beat each other up" in "knock-down fights."

The Reeds have ten children. One of their daughters, Alicia, is forty-five years old and has a serious alcohol and drug abuse problem. Because of this, Caroline and Gary were forced for several years to care for her three children, one of whom has several learning disorders, including dyslexia and attention deficit disorder. Another daughter, Vickie, was injured in 1985. She too, has a substance abuse problem. Keith, born in 1962, has had a history of cardiac problems. He developed myocardial ischemia at the age of twelve and was treated for a seizure disorder. He passed away in 1988.

Gary and Caroline's daughter, Debby, born in 1956, suffers from low self-esteem and has recovered from several overdoses of hard drugs. She is also known to abuse prescription drugs, which she buys and sells on the streets. She is the victim of domestic abuse by her common-law husband, with whom she has been for over twenty years. She suffers from frequent, incapacitating headaches. Debby has three children, a son and two daughters. Her daughter Cara suffers from epilepsy. Cara and her boyfriend moved to Kentucky and, while there, robbed a Pizza Hut. Cara refuses any treatment for her epilepsy, and she refuses to use birth control.

Debby's other daughter, also named Debby, has a young son. In 1995, she had to take him to Children's Hospital after he fell out of a window while the adults were having a party and were not paying attention. Children's Protective Services was called and considered taking the child away from his mother to be raised by his grandmother. However, they were informed by the social worker that the baby would be better off with his mother.

Clinical Care

Caroline has complained of back pain for a number of years, but its etiology remains unknown. Her peptic ulcer has caused her considerable pain, and several of the nurses describe her as coming to the health center "screaming and cussing." In 1983, she began to vomit blood and subsequently had surgery. She suffers from incapacitating headaches as well as depression and anxiety, which she refers to as suffering from nerves. She has not been treated for these conditions.

Like Caroline, Gary also suffered from depression. He had a serious substance abuse problem and drank heavily every day. He also abused prescription drugs and smoked for forty-three years, despite being constantly short of breath. Gary had dangerously high blood pressure and in 1979 was hospitalized for chest pain. Later that year he had a heart attack. In 1981, he began to receive disability due to a chronically dislocated knee and back pain. His mobility problems worsened in 1982, when his back pain became so severe that he was unable to leave his bed. He died in 1985. Caroline collected a large sum for back Social Security Disability Insurance.

Because of health problems, the Reeds became dependent on the welfare and disability system. There is evidence of widespread substance abuse, domestic abuse, and sexual abuse—Gary was accused by Caroline of having sex with one of their daughters. Given the very high levels of tension in the family, it was difficult for the children to feel any peace. They constantly fought over money and squandered substantial amounts on alcohol and entertainment. Caroline moved to Kentucky in 1996. Her children strongly disapprove of this and believe that "she's leaving us." This separation anxiety has caused further stress for the family.

As first generation rural to urban migrants, the Reeds appear to suffer from a type of situational depression that results when people move to the city. Families from rural areas seek economic opportunities in cities. Once they arrive, however, they are forced to take low paying jobs in which they have little control over their own resources, time, and labor. Thus, when they cannot attain economic success, they experience relative deprivation, anger, and disappointment.

II. Lucy Simpson Rosin and Randy Rosin

Lucy Simpson Rosin represents an extreme case of difficult adaptation to the urban environment. Shortages of cash related to low paying and insecure jobs, access to alcohol on the job, and the difficulties of juggling work and child-care responsibilities all contribute to high levels of stress and morbidity for the entire family, particularly for Lucy.

In 1996, Lucy was a sixty-one-year-old white Appalachian adult. She was born blind in one eye. She has a history of chronic depression and "nerves." She has been hospitalized for depression and has attempted suicide eleven times. Lucy uses both the local health center and hospital. She has a history of respiratory problems, arthritis, and asthma.

Lucy's husband, Randy Rosin, is a sixty-year-old white male. He suffers from cirrhosis of the liver. He was disabled after being shot four times in the abdomen and legs in February 1981. He is now on SSDI (Social Security Disability Insurance).

Family History

Lucy and Randy have lived in the East End most of their lives. Lucy was born in Mount Adams, a formerly Appalachian neighborhood in Cincinnati that is now completely gentrified. Her parents were from Madeira, a town with some farms to the east of Cincinnati. She remembers that her father's parents had an eighty acre farm where she would sometimes spend the summer. Randy's parents were originally from Tennessee and West Virginia. His father worked in the coal mines in West Virginia for many years until he developed black lung disease.

Randy left school in the fifth grade. He worked first for the city and then as a furniture mover before he was shot. Lucy wanted to be a seamstress when she was younger. She now tends bar and collects social security. Her access to alcohol is constant because of her job. She talks about changing jobs so that she will not be tempted to drink.

Randy and Lucy rent a small apartment. The apartment is in poor condition, and the Rosins are forced to turn on the gas burners of the stove in order to provide heat. Moreover, their roof has structural damage and leaks every time it rains. They have tried to patch it, but their landlord refuses to provide the materials.

Lucy and Randy have three children. All three left school before the tenth grade. Vince is thirty years old and lives in Denver. He has been in and out of jail, mostly for minor offenses. He is unmarried and has two sons. Both of the Rosins' daughters, Nan and Colleen, live near their parents. Nan has three daughters from her first marriage and has since remarried. She also works as a barmaid in a local establishment. Colleen is married with five children. She has worked at various jobs, in nursing homes, restaurants, and the local convenience store. She has had to rely on neighbors and friends to "watch" her children, however, and is constantly juggling her domestic responsibilities with her work obligations. She has lost several jobs after taking time off to care for her children when they were ill. In early 1996, she was hospitalized for a nervous breakdown. Her husband has worked at several temporary jobs which often include working the night shift. When he can, he supplements these with odd jobs in landscaping, car repair, and house painting.

Clinical Care

Lucy has had problems with her vision since birth. She was born blind in one eye. She had five surgeries to correct the condition, which kept her out of school until she was seven years old. She now suffers from cataracts. Lucy also has asthma problems and regularly uses an inhaler. In 1981, she was hospitalized for pneumonia. Lucy has a history of chronic depression which she refers to as "nerves." She states that this depression is related to stress concerning her children: "I let things build up."

In late November 1990, she attempted suicide by trying to "slice [her] guts up," for which she needed thirty stitches. Later, she was hospitalized for a month after this suicide attempt. In her last suicide attempt, she drank vodka until she was unconscious. She comes to the health center regularly to talk to the nurses about her "nerves," for which she takes Valium. She has a history of drug abuse. The doctor at the health center has talked to her about trying to quit smoking and sent her to a hospital for pulmonary function testing. She was found to have the beginning signs of cardiac obstructive pulmonary disease (COPD).

Randy uses the liver clinic at a local hospital. He suffers from cirrhosis of the liver. He is supposed to have plenty of fresh fruit and vegetables as well as a low-salt diet. However, he and Lucy are on food stamps, and since they share all resources with their children, they do not have enough money to maintain such a diet. He also has had many health problems related to the shooting. Randy states that the shooting happened when he got into a fight with a neighbor. They were both drunk at the time.

III. Linda Carter

In 1996, Linda Carter was a forty-five-year-old white Appalachian woman who suffers from nerves and substance abuse. She is part of a large family of

Table 12.1. Urban Patient Cases

Case	Symptoms	Psychosocial/Sociocultural Factors
Caroline	Depression/anxiety Headaches Chronic back pain Chronic stomach Disorders (peptic ulcer, needed surgery) Screaming, cussing	68 years old Domestic violence 10 children; many are ill; in trouble with the law Welfare First generation rural/urban migrant
Gary (Caroline's husband)	Depression Substance abuse/ alcoholism High blood pressure Chronic back pain; severe (could not leave bed) Heart problems Short of breath	Deceased Domestic violence Welfare Disabled First generation rural to urban migrant
Lucy	Depression(1 month hospitalized) 11 suicide attempts Respiratory problems (COPD) Asthma Arthritis Cataracts Substance abuse	61 years old Worry over children Poor living conditions Welfare/food stamps
Randy (Lucy's husband)	Depression Drinks heavily Cirrhosis of liver	60 years old Left school in 5th grade Disabled—victim of violent crime Poor living conditions Welfare
Linda	Anxiety, depression Chronic tension and migraine headaches Chest pain Shoulder/back pain Chronic diarrhea Substance abuse Several suicide attempts Malnourished Agitated affect Feels overwhelmed	45 years old Left school after 7th grade Husband alcoholic, abused her, time in prison 5 children, several miscarriages, abortion Many problems with children/ other family members Welfare
Candy	Depression, anxiety, low self-esteem 2 suicide attempts Crying, labile affect Abused by mother's boyfriend	13 years old Mother is heavy drinker, HIV+ Fears losing her community

(Summary of symptoms—women only)

(3) Nervousness/anxiety; (1) Anger; (2) Crying/screaming; (2) Headaches; (2) Trembling; (2) Itching; (2) Gastrointestinal complaints; (2) Insomnia/sleep disorders; (4) Depression; (1) Heart problems/chest pain/high blood pressure; (3) Suicide attempts; (2) Back pain; (2) Substance abuse; (1) Respiratory problems.

rural to urban migrants. Like her father, Linda is a heavy drinker. Like her mother, she became pregnant as an adolescent and feels overwhelmed by her responsibilities to her nuclear and extended families. Her mother and her sister, in particular, are very demanding. She seems always to be caught in a web of emotional and financial obligations that she cannot fulfill. The third generation—Linda's children—seems to be following the pattern of adolescent pregnancy, high anxiety and depression ("nerves"), and early school leaving. Linda's case raises questions about the relationships between social stress and illness.

In her early childhood, Linda lived in a small town in rural Ohio but moved to the city at the age of three. She spent her younger adult years working as a waitress in a small restaurant/bar. She suffers chronically from "nerves," which is often very severe and incapacitating.

Linda's presenting symptoms include a history of chronic headaches, chest pain, and a variety of other somatic complaints which may be linked to her low self-esteem and high levels of anxiety. In the past, she has complained of tension headaches, migraines, shoulder and back pain, and chronic diarrhea. In addition to these, she experiences bouts of depression, which she describes as "nerves," and long periods of abuse of alcohol, street drugs, and prescription drugs. She has tried to kill herself several times.

Family History

Linda was born in 1951 and has eight siblings. Both of her parents were heavy drinkers and, at times, smoked marijuana; they frequently separated but never divorced. Because of his drinking, Linda's father had difficulty holding down a full-time job. He took odd jobs periodically, often working several different jobs in one week. He occasionally took a temporary factory job. In his later years, he lived with Linda but contributed no money to the household. He died in 1985 of liver disease. Just before he died, he was showing signs of dementia.

Linda's mother, Bea, was pregnant with her first child at the age of sixteen. At age sixty-three, she is a heavy smoker and suffers from emphysema. In 1975, she was diagnosed with panic attacks, and often complained of an intense anxiety when she left her house. She feared that she would do something inappropriate in public. In addition, she feels that Linda and her other daughter, Jeanine, impose on her and depend on her too much. At the same time, she becomes angry if they fail to visit her regularly—at least several times per week. She often laments that she has failed her daughters and her son, Herman, because all three have taken drug overdoses. Moreover, she has had considerable trouble dealing with her youngest son, Benny, who has behavioral problems.

Linda left school after completing the seventh grade. At age thirteen, she was treated for pelvic inflammatory disease. Her early years with her husband, Eric, were marred by his alcoholism, his subsequent abuse of her, and his conviction for breaking and entering. He was released from prison in 1978, at which time he took a maintenance job at a school. Together, they have five daughters, though Linda has had several miscarriages and an abortion.

The children have been a consistent source of stress for Linda, who supports the family through Aid to Families with Dependent Children (AFDC). The eldest daughter began bearing children at age fourteen and now has three children. She lives in a neighboring community. Molly, Linda's second child, suffers from low self-esteem and anxiety, which she calls "nerves." Her family describes her as "following in her mother's footsteps." She also smokes heavily and complains frequently of asthma and shortness of breath. Both the eldest daughter and Molly have left school. The children have had a tendency to act out in response to Linda's substance abuse and suicide attempts. Children's Protective Services has consistently been involved in the affairs of the family, although the children have never been removed from the home.

Clinical Care

Linda has been a patient at the health center since 1975. She is malnourished and visits frequently for a variety of complaints. She often looks tense, with an agitated affect, and talks about suffering from "nerves." The nurses at the health center have provided her with regular, but informal counseling. She requests refills for prescriptions of drugs used to treat her recurrent headaches as well as "nerves medication." In 1988, she became very depressed and began to abuse an anti-anxiety agent. She also began to disregard her appearance. She refused to bathe or wear her false teeth. She complained that she had many problems with her children and other family members. She had trouble controlling her children at home, and the children's teachers were concerned about possible attention deficit disorder. These problems became overwhelming for Linda, and they precipitated several suicide attempts. She was referred for counseling at a large psychiatric clinic, but she refused to seek help outside of her community. Her refusal to go to other referred doctors can be understood, in part, as her fear of unfamiliar health-care settings that might discriminate against her for being poor.

Many of Linda's complaints appear to be linked to her significant family responsibilities, both financial and emotional. Her mother and siblings insist that she buy them food, even though she has four girls of her own to feed.

When her sister, Jeanine, had a number of health problems, she expected Linda to take care of her children. These added responsibilities came at the same time Linda felt overwhelmed with the care of her own children. Her husband's conviction and his alcoholism placed additional strain on their relationship.

Linda's physical problems can be understood as her way of coping with anxiety. She requests medication to alleviate her symptoms. By turning her social stress into medical problems, she tries to validate and seek support for her familial problems from the health center staff. The staff members express great sympathy for her, but at the same time, they are frustrated by the sense of helplessness they feel when Linda returns to the health center repeatedly with little or no improvement. Even attempts on the part of the primary care physician to recommend a "counselor" rather than a "psychiatrist" meet with repeated rejections.

IV. Candy Brill

Low self-esteem is the central issue for thirteen-year-old Candy, who is an attractive and intelligent young white Appalachian woman. While her family is supportive to a point, their own problems create only a very weak safety net for her. Candy is constantly fearful of her mother's abusive boyfriend, and her mother is fearful of the health-care system because it might uncover this abusive relationship. As a consequence, Candy does not receive appropriate health care.

Candy's presenting symptoms include a history of depression, anxiety, and low self-esteem. She often mentions that her nerves are bothering her. She has attempted suicide twice. Her family, however, has been reluctant to seek treatment for her.

Family History

Candy was born in 1980 and has three siblings: Jason, age ten, Donny, age six, and Tad, age eight. Her mother, Grace, is a heavy drinker, as are her maternal grandparents, Juanita and Ray Brill. Ray works in a book bindery. Both Juanita and Grace are waitresses. The children spend a great deal of time around the restaurant, which is an important place in the community.

Grace was pregnant with Candy when she was twelve years old. At age twenty-four, Grace learned that she was HIV positive. She constantly teases Candy about the prospects of her becoming pregnant soon. Candy is determined to avoid pregnancy, although she spends enormous amounts of time trying to attract boys by putting on dramatic makeup. She dyes her hair bright blond and constantly changes her hair style. She can be seen walking up and down a major thoroughfare or hanging out with other teens in front of the local recreation center.

Clinical Care

In 1994, Candy was admitted to the hospital after attempting suicide by drinking turpentine and taking pills. Her family swears they will never again agree to hospitalization. They claim she was treated very badly and discriminated against for being poor. About six months after her hospitalization, she began talking again about killing herself. A close friend of the family suspected she was being abused by her mother's boyfriend and that she needed to talk to someone about it. Candy's emotions were labile—at several points in the conversation her eyes filled with tears. She talked about her family, about how important her community is to her—about her worries that the community is slipping away because developers are building houses that the poor cannot afford. She was worried about her brother, Jason, and the kind of trouble he might get into hanging out on the street.

After repeated attempts to urge Candy and her mother to keep the appointment, it became clear that their resistance to the psychiatric clinic was more than a matter of scheduling. A close friend of the family contacted Candy's great grandmother, Mrs. Bird, who lives downtown. "If anyone can get Candy and Grace to do something, it's Mrs. Bird," the friend said. The attempts to contact Mrs. Bird were unsuccessful, however, and Candy never went to the clinic. The underlying issue here was Grace's fear that the social workers and psychiatrists at the clinic would decide that she was a "bad mother" and remove Candy from her household.

The Social Context of "Nerves" in Eastern Kentucky

Van Schaik (1988) administered an interview of open-ended questions to eight women, ranging in age from fourteen to eighty-two years old, in a rural, coal mining region of eastern Kentucky. The questions were based on those developed by Kleinman (1980) for eliciting explanatory models of illness. All eight patients were identified in a community clinic. Six were interviewed at the clinic, and two were interviewed at home. The data from Van Schaik's paper was reorganized and reinterpreted to make it comparable to the urban data which was developed in a holistic community context for understanding individual patients (see table 12.2). Kleinman's explanatory models of illness focus on patients as individuals.

Seven of the eight women had husbands; the eighth was an unmarried fourteen year old. Of the seven husbands, five were stated to be either heavy drinkers or alcoholics, one had a seizure disorder, and the husband of the oldest woman died of Hodgkin's disease, presumably at a relatively young age. In virtually all of the families of these women, there had been at least one, if not several, crisis situations: the death, disappearance, or jailing of a child or some other family member, a serious accident, or a divorce. In one case, a fourteen-year-old girl suffering from nerves had experienced the death of both parents. In the majority of cases, responsibilities for children and the elderly were substantial, but the women, although depressed and anxious, were able to cope in these non-urban settings.

Discussion

For comparative purposes, we have concentrated primarily on those rural cases from Van Schaik's sample and those urban cases that appeared most severe, that is, women with multiple, chronic physical and mental symptoms.

Table 12.2. The Social Context of "Nerves" in Eastern Kentucky

Case	Symptoms	Psychosocial/Sociocultural Factors
Flora	Depression Cannot tolerate waiting Multiple chronic illnesses Lays around and sleeps too much	82 years old Husband died of Hodgkin's disease One stepchild dead; one does not speak to her Has a support/resource system Niece already responsible for elderly parent, cannot care for Flora
Dorothy	High blood pressure Weight gain Insomnia Diarrhea	64 years old Left school at 9 because mother died 11 children cause her worry, hazardous jobs, live far away, frequently ill, or have accidents Husband seriously ill; heavy drinker
Marie	Intense fear of dying Increased/irregular heart rate Increased blood pressure	50 years old Husband left her with 2 small sons Cares for her grandmother Now raising 3 nieces Current husband has seizure disorder Lots of worry in a large family
Clara	Wants to "hurt something"	42 years old Married, 4 children; she does not know where one son is Husband is heavy drinker for 18 years Parents and 2 brothers died within 11 months of each other
Stella	Weight loss Weak and light-headed "Nervous breakdowns" (hospitalized 3 times) Suicidal thoughts	40 years old Married at 14 Worry over son who spent time in jail and daughter who had an abortion at 14 Mother helps support her; can't work because of stroke

Continued on next page

Case	Symptoms	Psychosocial/Sociocultural Factors
Betty	Cannot eat Vomiting, choking, inability to swallow Weight loss Insomnia Fainting, partial loss of consciousness Forgetfulness Cannot tolerate a closed door; claustrophobic?	38 years old First husband killed in mines; heavy drinker, beat her, squandered money 3 children; sons in jail numerous times; daughter repeatedly delinquent Left school at 15 because father ill Second marriage ends in divorce Works at hotels, restaurants, textile plants
Ann	Fear of dying Always tired; complains of having nothing to do Increased heart rate "Smothers" (shortness of breath)	20 years old Husband drank heavily; beat her Divorce after birth of hydrocephalic infant who died Second marriage troubled by in-laws Husband and she are unemployed
Shirley	Stomach pain Dizziness Took 8 pills in suicide attempt	14 years old Both parents deceased Father was mean-spirited Lives with grandmother and neighbor who do not want her

Summary of symptoms of rural nerves sufferers

(5) Feeling nervousness; (2) Being nervous, aggravated; (4) Becoming angry, cursing, and calling names; (3) Crying, screaming; (3) Headaches, often severe; (3) Trembling, shaking, and jerking; cannot hold things or tolerate being still; (3) Itching in hands, feet, back, or "all over"; (4) Gastrointestinal complaints, weight loss; (2) Insomnia; (1) Depression; (3) Heart problems/high blood pressure; (1) Suicide attempts; (1) Back pain; (1) Substance abuse; (1) Respiratory problems; (2) Fainting, dizziness, loss of consciousness; (4) Fight responses

These were arranged in a life course framework (see table 12.3). Two elderly women (Flora and Caroline), four adults (Dorothy, Lucy, Stella, and Linda), and two adolescents (Shirley and Candy) are represented in this sample.

Depression and anxiety are present in some form in all of these women. Depression was either called "depression" or referred to by some other term such as "nervous breakdown." It was also indicated by other symptoms such as insomnia, weight loss, a feeling of anger, or suicidal thoughts/attempts. In addition, headaches and gastrointestinal complaints were frequently mentioned symptoms in both the rural and urban cases, although Van Schaik (1988) fails to systematically specify which women suffered from which symptom.

A comparison of the symptomatology of these rural and urban women appears to indicate that urban women experience more severe symptoms than do rural women. Severity is measured by such factors as length and number of hospitalizations, chronic nature of the illness, and the presence of suicide attempts. For instance, gastrointestinal complaints are common in both rural and urban individuals. However, while the rural women complain of such symptoms as indigestion, diarrhea, and stomach pain, the urban women suffer from chronic diarrhea and chronic stomach disorders such as peptic ulcers. Depression also seems to be more severe in the urban cases, with many more suicide attempts as opposed to the suicidal thoughts of the rural women. The only instance of a suicide attempt among the rural women is in the case of the adolescent Shirley, an unwanted orphan passed among family and neighbors. A final possible indicator of increased severity of symptoms among the urban women is the presence of substance abuse in two of the urban cases but in none of the rural cases (see table 12.3).

Why do the symptoms of nerves appear more severe for urban women than for rural women? In order to understand this pattern, we must look to the psychosocial and sociocultural contexts of the women. Some of these contexts are similar: alcoholic, abusive husbands, and worry over children who are ill, in jail, or victims of accidents. However, a major difference between the two contexts is in the availability of resources. Van Schaik (1988) remarks that Flora has a garden, which could provide relief when cash is short, as well as a family member in close proximity who has offered her assistance. This resource base may act as a buffer to the stresses caused by a lack of necessities and isolation. Caroline, on the other hand, had a somewhat viable subsistence base in the country, consisting of small tobacco farm. However, once subsidies for tobacco were cut, tobacco declined as a cash crop, forcing the family to sell the farm. In the city, Caroline, like many urban individuals, faces the problems of migrants—poverty, unemployment, discrimination,

Table 12.3. Rural and Urban Cases within a Life Course Framework

	Rural	Urban
	Elders	
	Flora (82 years old)	**Caroline** (68 years old)
Symptoms	Diabetes Chronic cystitis Indigestion "Heart trouble" Depression Cannot tolerate waiting Lays around and sleeps too much	Headaches Chronic back pain Chronic stomach disorders (peptic ulcer needed surgery) Depression/anxiety Screaming, cussing
Psychosocial/ sociocultural factors	Husband died of Hodgkin's disease One stepchild dead; the other does not speak to her Has a support/resource Niece already responsible for elderly adult and cannot care for Flora	Domestic abuse, alcoholic husband 10 children, many are ill or in trouble with the law Welfare First generation rural/urban migrant

Continued on next page

	Rural	Urban
	Adults	
	Dorothy (64 years old)	**Lucy** (61 years old)
Symptoms	High blood pressure Weight gain Diarrhea Diabetes Arthritis Cataracts Insomnia	Respiratory problems Asthma Arthritis Depression (1 month hospitalization) Substance abuse 11 suicide attempts
Psychosocial/ sociocultural factors	Left school at 9 because mother died 11 children cause her worry: hazardous jobs, live far away frequently ill or have accidents Husband seriously ill; heavy drinker	Worry over 3 children Poor living condition Welfare/food stamps Disabled, alcoholic husband
	Stella (40 years old)	**Linda** (45 years old)
Symptoms	Weak and light-headed Weight loss "Nervous breakdowns" (hospitalized 3 times) Suicidal thoughts	Chronic tension and migraine headaches Chest pain Shoulder/back pain Chronic diarrhea Malnourished Depression/anxiety Agitated affect Substance abuse Several suicide attempts
Psychosocial/ sociocultural factors	Married at 14 Worry over son who spent time in jail and daughter who had an abortion at 14 Mother helps support her; can't work because of stroke	Left school after 7th grade Alcoholic husband who abused her, served time in prison 5 children, several miscarriages, abortion Many problems with children/other family Welfare
	Adolescents	
	Shirley (14 years old)	**Candy** (13 Years Old)
Symptoms	Stomach pain Dizziness Took 8 blood pressure pills in a suicide attempt	Depression, anxiety, low self-esteem Crying, labile affect 2 suicide attempts
Psychosocial/ sociocultural factors	Both parents deceased Father was mean-spirited Lives with grandmother and neighbor who do not want her	Mother is heavy drinker, HIV+ Losing her community Abused by mother's boyfriend

low income, and poor working conditions—which are exacerbated by poorly formed economic and social resource networks. Such Appalachian migrants "occupy a low status in the stratification hierarchy in urban areas" (McCoy, Trevino, and McCoy 1994). In fact, Caroline, Lucy, and Linda all collect some form of government subsidized welfare.

Another reason for the increased severity of symptoms in the urban women may be that more migrant women work outside of the home than do their rural counterparts. Arrival in the city places new roles on these women. They must "fulfill the traditional roles of homemaker and mother but the urban setting demands some transformation in decision making, in employment, and in marital relationships" (McCoy, Trevino, and McCoy 1994:37). The burden of a double day as well as more conflict with one's spouse are often the result of this transformation. Furthermore, many of these women's socialization and educational experiences have not prepared them to "enter competitive job markets or even [be] given the skills of interacting with the world outside the circle of their immediate acquaintances" (Fiene 1988:77). Men also appear to suffer from nerves. However, Horton (1984) argues that while women suffer from headaches (nerves), men most often suffer from backaches, rendering them incapable of physical activity and thereby releasing them from monotonous and dangerous heavy labor. Men may also turn to alcohol as a source of relief from economic and social stress. Thus, a man may be perceived as an alcoholic rather than a nerves sufferer.

While rural Appalachians, especially women, have many problems, distresses, and difficult circumstances, they often have such resources as small farms or gardens and extended family networks which buffer them from the stresses of living in a cash economy. Van Schaik (1988:88) reports that while nerves leads to nervous breakdowns or thoughts of suicide, "none of these women report being unable to work or fulfill her usual responsibilities because of her nerves." Urban migrants, however, must deal with feelings of anger and powerlessness as well as a loss of autonomy when they are forced to shift to a solely cash-based economy, where they are subject to unstable labor markets and less control over the circumstances of their environment. These conditions become overwhelming and may be somaticized into multiple, often severe illnesses. Thus, while the rural cases presented deal with women who have troubles but are still functional, the urban cases deal with women who are "beyond worry."

Conclusion

In general, at-risk populations for nerves tend to be rural groups undergoing rapid culture change in the forms of migration, industrialization, urbanization, and acculturation. These are global issues. Nerves resembles other culture-bound syndromes around the world, that is, those prevalent in populations undergoing rapid culture change.[3] From the data presented in this study, a continuum of severity of symptoms can be postulated, with individuals from a non-urban setting having the least severe symptoms, followed by greater severity in urban settings. The urban cases are more severe than we would expect to find in a non-urban setting because adaptive systems such as family-based support networks have been destroyed.[4]

Culture change, especially when it involves rural to urban migration, weakens and sometimes destroys social networks for both the migrants and those left behind in increasingly depopulated rural areas. Community breakdown and absence of social support is pathogenic. Generally speaking, individuals who suffer from nerves are members of lower socioeconomic classes who have had their social and economic resources depleted as they come into contact with urban societies.[5] Nerves would not become medicalized in societies where strong social support networks are in place to provide economic and social assistance in times of need, as is done in intact rural communities. However, when such social networks become dismembered through migration or through the stress brought about by culture change, individuals may seek social support and validation for social distress from a physician (Van Schaik 1988; Davis and Guarnaccia 1989).

A holistic, locally based approach to illness management that would address the psychosocial/class components of nerves might be the following. In the urban setting, institutions, both formal and informal, could be put into place in the community to alleviate stress and provide support to community members. Women with small children often suffer from nerves because they are overwhelmed by child-care responsibilities, nutritional stress, and confinement, especially during winter, in small apartments. If there were a community space devoted to children where creativity could be exercised and adults could receive support from members of the community, a great deal of stress could be alleviated. One idea for such a community space came from an East End grandmother who talked about the idea of an imagination center for children and their caretakers. The center might consist only of a simple room with crayons and paper. If the center were next to a food pantry and soup kitchen, nutritional needs might be met while the stigma of using the soup kitchen is reduced by the adjacent imagination center.

Given the widespread occurrence of rural to urban migration and the realties of downward mobility that result from such migration, as well as increased industrialization and the dependency on a low-wage service economy, we can expect the stress of nerves to increase in prevalence.[6] Because there are few studies of the prevalence of nerves or its counterparts, there is a great need for the epidemiologic study of nerves and its counterparts to determine prevalence, incidence, and their correlates over time.

Notes

1. See Simons and Hughes (1985). See also Van Schaik (1988, 1989).

2. These patient cases also appear in Halperin (1998).

3. See also Davis and Low (1989).

4. Susan Keefe (personal communication 1997) has suggested further that within the Appalachian region, nerves might be most prevalent and most severe in coal mining areas such as eastern Kentucky and West Virginia compared to the more agricultural areas of Appalachia due to the greater economic displacement and community breakdown produced by mining.

5. See Guarnaccia, Rubio-Stipec, Canino (1989) for a discussion of general social characteristics of ataques de nervios sufferers.

6. In many urban Appalachian communities, displacement by development and deteriorating houses and infrastructure contribute to the severity of nerves in urban settings. Loss of community can be seen as a major factor in nerves etiology.

References

Davis, Dona, and Peter Guarnaccia. 1989. "Health, Culture, and the Nature of Nerves: Introduction." *Medical Anthropology* 11:1–13.

Davis, Dona, and Setha Low (Eds.). 1989. *Gender, Health and Illness: The Case of Nerves.* New York: Hemisphere Publishing.

Fiene, Judith Ivy. 1988. "Gender, Class and Self-Image." In *Appalachian Mental Health,* Susan Emley Keefe (Ed.). Lexington: University of Press of Kentucky. Pp. 66–80.

Guarnaccia, Peter. 1993. "Ataques de Nervios in Puerto Rico: Culture-Bound Syndrome or Popular Illness?" *Medical Anthropology* 15:157–70.

Guarnaccia, Peter, G. Canino, M. Rubio-Stipec, and M. Bravo. 1993. "The Prevalence of Ataques de Nervios in Puerto Rico: The Role of Culture in Psychiatric Epidemiology." *Journal of Nervous and Mental Disease* 181:159–67.

Guarnaccia, P. J., and L. H. Rogler. 1999. "Research on Culture-Bound Syndromes: New Directions." *American Journal of Psychiatry* 156:1322–27.

Guarnaccia, Peter, Maritza Rubio-Stipec, and Glorisa Canino. 1989. "Ataques de Nervios in the Puerto Rican Diagnostic Interview Schedule: The Impact of Cultural Categories on Psychiatric Epidemiology." *Culture, Medicine, and Psychiatry* 13:275–95.

Halperin, Rhoda H. 1998. *Practicing Community: Class Culture and Power in an Urban Neighborhood.* Austin: University of Texas Press.

Horton, Claire. 1984. "Women Have Headaches, Men Have Backaches: Patterns of Illness in an Appalachian Community." *Social Science and Medicine* 19(6):647–54.

Kleinman, Arthur. 1980. *Patients and Healers in the Context of Culture.* Berkeley and Los Angeles: University of California Press.

Lock, Margaret. 1990. "On Being Ethnic: The Politics of Identity Breaking and Making in Canada, or Nevra on Sunday." *Culture, Medicine and Psychiatry* 14:237–54.

Low, Setha. 1994. "Embodied Metaphors: Nerves as Lived Experience." In *Embodiment and Experience: The Existential Ground of Culture and Self,* Thomas Csordas (Ed.). Cambridge: Cambridge University Press. Pp. 139–62.

McCoy, H. Virginia, Diana Gullett Trevino, and Clyde McCoy. 1994. "Appalachian Women: Between Two Cultures." In *From Mountain to Metropolis: Appalachian Migrants in American Cities,* Kathryn Borman and Phillip Obermiller (Eds.). Westport, Conn.: Bergin and Garvey. Pp. 33–48.

Reiter, Jennifer. 1995. "A Comparative Study of Culture-Bound Syndromes: Ataques de Nervios, Nerves, and Susto." Master's thesis, Department of Anthropology, University of Cincinnati.

Simons, R., and C. Hughes (Eds.). 1985. *The Culture-Bound Syndromes.* Boston: D. Reidel Publishing.

Smith, Lee. 1995. *Saving Grace.* New York: G. P. Putnam's Sons.

Van Schaik, Eileen. 1988. "The Social Context of 'Nerves' in Eastern Kentucky." In *Appalachian Mental Health,* Susan Emley Keefe (Ed.). Lexington: University Press of Kentucky. Pp. 81–100.

———. 1989. "Paradigms Underlying the Study of Nerves as a Popular Illness Term in Eastern Kentucky." *Medical Anthropology* 11:15–28.

Chapter 13

Psychological Testing in Rural Appalachia

Susan E. Keefe, Janice L. Hastrup,
and Sherilyn N. Thomas

Psychological tests are widely used by practitioners in a variety of settings (such as mental health clinics, schools, correctional facilities, etc.) to assess a number of psychological problems in a short period of time (Anastasi and Urbina 1997; Cohen, Swerdlik, and Phillips 1996). The psychological problems examined vary from test to test but often include anxiety, depression, and psychosomatic complaints, as well as more severe psychological disorders such as schizophrenia and bipolar disorder.

As an assessment tool, a psychological test is meaningless without normative information, that is, a summary of the results of giving the test to a representative sample of people (Graham 1990). Normative samples typically are selected to be representative of the larger general population, aiming at appropriate diversity of sexes, races, ages, geographic areas, urban/rural residence, and educational and occupational status. Nevertheless, national norms may not accurately reflect the psychological status of specific populations, such as ethnic minorities or the working poor who are often noted to suffer greater levels of psychological stress. Cockerham (1990), for example, found that individuals with lower socioeconomic status scored higher on measures of psychological distress. Significantly elevated scores on the Minnesota Multiphasic Personality Inventory, or MMPI (Butcher et al. 1989), a widely used test of psychopathology, have been found in studies of African Americans, Native Americans, Asian Americans, and Hispanic Americans (Dana and Whatley 1991; Hoffman, Dana, and Bolton 1985; Okazaki and Sue 1996; Whitworth and Unterbrink 1994).

This chapter addresses the appropriateness of national norms for Appalachia, a relatively poor, rural region exploited by outside economic interests whose people and culture are often described as different from mainstream America. Little research has been done comparing national psychological test norms with norms for cultural minorities other than the major racial and ethnic groups counted by the U.S. Census Bureau. Research with rural children in the southern Appalachian mountains who were screened for psychiatric symptoms suggests prevalence rates that are similar to those of urban children but did not evaluate an adult sample (Costello et al. 1996). In this chapter, we present the results of psychological testing with a representative group of Appalachian adults. Our results should provide clinicians in the region with the ability to better assess the psychological status of their clients using a normative Appalachian population.

Design of the Research

This research grew out of a study conducted by a social-environmental psychologist, Michael Edelstein, who was hired as an expert consultant in litigation involving a rural community in northeastern Tennessee. In order to measure stress in this population, psychological tests were administered to the litigants by Janice L. Hastrup, a licensed clinical psychologist and researcher. After unsuccessful attempts to locate a comparable Appalachian population to serve as a normative sample in the area, Hastrup contacted anthropologist Susan Keefe, who assisted in administering the tests in a rural Appalachian community in western North Carolina.

The administration of such tests is not an easy task in a rural population. The sampling design required a population of 150–200 people, both males and females, ranging in age from twenty to seventy-five, with educational achievement from eight to twelve years on average and otherwise fairly representative of the Appalachian people. Test administration restrictions required gaining compliance from this group of people prior to the testing and then gathering them together at a common time and place.

In rural Appalachia, the most common institutions grouping people together are schools and churches. Both of these presented problems in terms of representative sampling. Adults connected with the schools are typically younger people, and churches in rural Appalachia tend to be relatively small and sectarian, limiting their representativeness. The investigators settled on a third alternative institution: a volunteer fire department. The Appalachian region, like other rural areas, is generally served by volunteer, rather than salaried, fire departments which take responsibility for a bounded area and population. Typically, they are funded in part through county taxes, but these funds are often insufficient and must be supplemented through community fund-raising.

The research team could pay respondents $15 apiece, and this sum was offered as a donation to the volunteer fire department for participating in the research. The local fire chief provided lists of persons living in the district (total population 3,800) to be contacted by a research assistant. An attempt was made to contact all households notifying them of the time and place for testing in the evening at the local elementary school. Those indicating they would be able to participate were called again and reminded of the obligation two days prior to testing. A final sample of 151 was obtained. The resulting total donation of $2,265 was a significant amount of assistance to the local fire department. "That's more than six turkey shoots!" said one firefighter.

The participants ranged in age from eighteen to eighty-three, with an average of forty-five years (standard deviation = 15.2). There were seventy-four men and seventy-seven women, all Caucasian. Their social status on the Hollinghead-Redlich scale (Hollingshead and Redlich 1958) ranged from 14 to 66, with an average of 37.8 (SD = 10.2). The median education was 12 years, with a range from 6 to 20 and a mean of 12.2 (SD = 2.3): 8.6 percent of the group had an eighth-grade education or less; 13.2 percent had attended high school but did not graduate; 30.4 percent were high school graduates; vocational or trade school education was reported by 6.6 percent; and 21.2 percent had attended some college, with an additional 6.6 percent having graduated from college and 3.3 percent reporting some graduate school education.

All of the participants currently lived in Watauga County, North Carolina. They were asked to indicate where they had lived most of their lives. Seventy-four percent said they had lived most of their life in Watauga County. Most of the rest of the participants had lived most of their life in the Appalachian region in general (as defined by the Appalachian Regional Commission

1965). Twenty-three participants (15 percent) said they had lived most of their life outside Appalachia, but six of these people indicated they were born in Watauga or an adjacent county.

Two tests were administered: the Minnesota Multiphasic Personality Inventory (commonly known in the revised form as the MMPI-2) and the Symptom Checklist-90/Revised or SCL-90-R (Derogatis 1994). Caution is observed in the use of both of these tests, which require interpretation in order to be meaningful. In particular, raw scores or counts of certain kinds of questions answered in one direction are considered to be meaningless without normative information. For example, responding in the keyed direction to ten of thirty questions associated with concern about physical symptoms may result in a score which is either (1) higher than normal and more typical of people with a diagnosis of hypochondriasis, (2) normal, that is, typical of the general population, or (3) unusually low compared with the general population.

Both tests provide norms which are designed to represent the U.S. population. However, demographic variables for the MMPI-2 indicate the normative sample of respondents is significantly better educated (45 percent have a college degree), has higher occupational status (52 percent have professional or managerial jobs), and, of course, is generally more likely to be urban dwelling as compared with the general population in Appalachia, which has lower levels of education and occupational status and tends to be rural dwelling. Moreover, of course, the fact that Appalachians are culturally distinctive might affect the validity of their test scores when compared with norms from a non-Appalachian population.

Psychological Testing Instruments

The MMPI-2 is one of the most widely used instruments in testing psychopathology in the United States. The short version consists of approximately four hundred questions answered either "True" or "False." These questions are then scored for three validity scales and ten clinical scales, labeled hypochondriasis (Hs), depression (D), hysteria (Hy), psychopathic deviate (Pd), masculinity-femininity (Mf), paranoia (Pa), psychasthenia (Pt) (anxious, obsessive-compulsive), schizophrenia (Sc), hypomania (Ma), and social introversion (Si). The clinical scales were developed to select out individuals whose responses match those of various clinical groups. For example, an individual who scores high on the D scale is responding to questions in the same way as would someone who is clinically depressed. The actual content of the questions is not interpreted, just the fact that responses are similar. The scores are usually translated into T-scores, which put an emphasis on the extreme scores rather than those in the middle, which in this case would be characterized as "normal." A T-score of 50 represents the average of the population; a T-score of 65 is usually considered to be "abnormal" or a clinically significant elevation, and places one in the top 7 percent of the U.S. population.

Examination of ethnic variation in MMPI and MMPI-2 (revised in 1989) scores has resulted in no consensus as to whether the instrument produces biased profiles for minorities. Conservative reviews in the field find no serious challenge to the validity of MMPI scales for ethnic minorities (Dahlstrom, Lachar, and Dahlstrom 1986; Greene 1987; Hall, Bansal, and Lopez 1999). Yet numerous independent studies find consistent patterns of elevated scores for African Americans (Dana and Whatley 1991), Hispanic Americans (Montgomery and Orozco 1983; Whitworth and Unterbrink 1994), and Native Americans (Hoffman, Dana, and Bolton 1985). The most recent review by Hall, Bansal, and Lopez (1999) suggests that there is still a need for research on psychopathology and ethnicity despite fifty comparative studies focused on African Americans, Latin Americans, and European Americans. Furthermore, level of acculturation is demonstrated to have an effect on scores within an ethnic group (Montgomery and Orozco 1983; Padilla, Olmedo, and Loya 1982). These findings lead to the conclusion that cultural background probably has an impact on MMPI-2 scores and, thus, the possibility that elevated scores may not signify pathology but, rather, genuine ethnic differences. Most of these studies advise using caution in making clinical interpretations based on test results for members of ethnic minority groups.

The only previous study reporting MMPI scores in an Appalachian population also produced results indicating cultural difference was at work. Tellegen et al. (1969) compared test results of members of a serpent-handling church and members of a "conventional" church in a rural county in West Virginia. The results indicated significant differences in T-score averages between members of the two churches, as well as differences by age and sex. But more important, the authors called attention to the overall elevation of the T-scores of both samples. Of seventy-five individual profiles, only forty-four were classified as "normal," while thirty-one (including members of both churches) were classified into neurotic, psychotic, or behavior disorder categories. Rather than dismiss the test results as culturally biased, the authors concede that "the conclusion that both church groups show a high incidence of psychopathology remains . . . tentative" (Tellegen et al. 1969:241). In light of the criticism generated during the last two decades regarding the validity of the MMPI-2 for ethnic minorities, an equally legitimate conclusion might be that T-scores of Appalachian natives should not be uncritically interpreted using scales normed on a non-Appalachian population.

Like the MMPI-2, the SCL-90-R is a self-report inventory designed to screen for psychiatric symptomatology. It includes nine symptom scales: somatization (SOM), obsessive-compulsive (O-C), interpersonal sensitivity (INT), depression (DEP), anxiety (ANX), hostility (HOS), phobic anxiety (PHOB), paranoia (PAR), and psychoticism (PSY), as well as three combination scales which describe more global patterns of psychological distress. Unlike the MMPI-2, the SCL-90-R scales are content relevant. That is, each item within a particular scale was designed to reflect a representative facet of that symptom cluster; for example, the questions within the depression scale were written and designed to be appropriate to the construct of depression. The relevancy of the items was then verified empirically by testing them on psychiatric and nonpsychiatric populations. Scores on the SCL-90-R scales are also expressed in T-scores; in other words, an individual's score on a particular subscale indicates his or her position relative to the normative group where a score of 50 represents the average or a "normal" score.

Unlike the MMPI-2, administration of the SCL-90-R involves having the individual acknowledge not only the presence of a particular symptom, but the severity of that problem. That is, the individual is asked to rate each symptom on a scale ranging from 0 (not at all) to 4 (extremely). The score for each symptom scale thus represents a measure of both its presence and intensity.

Results for a Rural Appalachian Population

Table 13.1 gives the average T-scores for men and women in the Appalachian sample on both the MMPI-2 and the SCL-90-R. Recall that the expected value is 50 and a clinically significant elevation is 65. The observed average scores thus are all in the normal range, but some are distinct from those expected based on the national norms.

MMPI-2

A number of significant differences appear in the average MMPI-2 scores for both men and women. The validity scales L and F did not differ significantly. The K scale scores, however, were somewhat lower for the Appalachian sample for both men, $t(1207) = 5.46, p<.01$ and women, $t(1532) = 5.98, p<.01$. These results suggest less defensiveness in responding for the Appalachian sample. It should be noted that a correction based on K scores is added to some of the clinical scales, to adjust for this one difference based on K scores.

Statistically significant elevations were observed on women's average MMPI-2 scores on the Hs scale, which measures somatic complaints; on the D scale, which assesses depression; and on the Si scale, which is associated with shy, introverted behavior. Thus, these results suggest, first of all, some support for the clinical observation that concerns over bodily symptoms might be more common in Appalachia than nationally (Keefe 1988). The elevation in depression may be reflecting the socioeconomic and educational differences between the rural Appalachian sample, which had a median education of high school graduation as compared with two years of college in the national sample on whom the norms were based. It may also represent what many studies suggest is a higher incidence of depression in Appalachian populations (Keefe and Parsons, this volume; Van Schaik 1988). The elevation on the Si scale, which measures introversion, may reflect an Appalachian or rural cultural style of interaction. The description for this scale indicates that "scores above the mean . . . reflect increasing levels of social shyness, preference for solitary pursuits, and lack of social assertiveness" (Butcher et al. 1989). These traits might be one way of characterizing rural life and the Appalachian "ethic of neutrality" by which people tend to promote peaceful cooperation and avoid conflict in personal relations (Hicks 1976; Keefe 1998).

The Mf scale, a measure of stereotypical masculine-feminine orientation, was also significantly elevated for women. This may reflect the increased independence, self-reliance, and responsibility expected of rural Appalachian women, who often must take on farm chores and household maintenance in everyday life (Beaver 1986). Similar scores have been noted for Hispanic women suggesting that gender role is culturally constructed (Montgomery and Orozco 1983).

For men, the pattern of MMPI-2 scores is similar. Significant elevations were again observed on the D scale (depression) and the Si scale (introversion). The elevation on the Hs scale (somatic complaints) is in the same direction as seen with the women but is not statistically significant. Men also had significantly lower scores on two scales: the Pd scale, which measures social maladjustment and the absence of pleasant experiences, and the Pa scale, which assesses suspiciousness. This is especially notable as it contradicts the stereotype of Appalachian men as being less than law abiding and more suspicious of outsiders. Finally, the score on the Mf scale, which assesses stereotypically masculine and feminine interests, was again different from the U.S. norms and suggested a more traditionally masculine orientation, something one might expect in a rural society where traditionally masculine behaviors are highly valued.

It may be helpful at this point to put these data in a more clinical context. The use of cutoff scores to describe individuals is inevitable in psychological work; generally, test results are seen as generating hypotheses to be explored further in interviews with the individual. A shift in the mean score on a scale can result in many more individuals having scores greater than a traditional cutoff and potentially "pathological," as figure 13.1 shows. Were the results of the rural Appalachian group's scores on the D scale, which measures depression, to be used in a clinical setting, there would be some differences in the numbers of individuals noted as scoring high on this scale. In the U.S. general population, a T-score of 65 would be considered a clinically significant elevation and worthy of follow-up. According to the published U.S. population norms, about 7 percent of people would obtain such a score. Were the same cutoff score of 65 to be used in this rural Appalachian sample, 18 percent of that group would be considered for further evaluation of depression. A similar effect occurs with the Hs scale for concerns about bodily symptoms. In the U.S. population, again, 7 percent would be expected to have scores at or above 65. In this rural Appalachian community, 18 percent of the sample had scores in that range (see fig. 13.1).

SCL-90-R

Table 13.1 indicates a number of significant elevations on the SCL-90-R scales in the Appalachian sample. Both men and women scored significantly higher than the national norms on the Global Severity Index (GSI), which is essentially the average item score across all scales. Not only did this sample rate their symptomatology at a higher average level of severity (PSDI), but they also acknowledged the presence of a slightly greater number of symptoms (PST). Elevations on these global indices reflect slightly higher than average

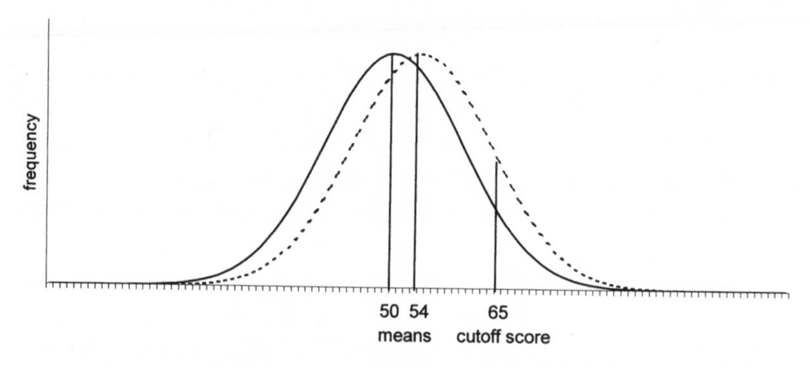

Fig. 13.1. The effect of shifting the mean of T-scores from 50 to 54 is to push an additional 11 percent of people into the pathological category above the 65 cutoff.

Table 13.1. MMPI-2 and SCL-90-R T-Score Averages for Men and Women in the Appalachian Sample

MMPI-2 Scale	Male	Female	SCL-90-R Scale	Male	Female
L	52.3	51.1	GSI	54.1[a]	52.9[a]
F	51.8	51.2	PSDI	54.1[a]	52.9[a]
K	43.0[a]	42.7[a]	PST	50.6	51.6
Hs	52.7	54.4[a]	SOM	54.3[a]	52.6[a]
D	53.1[a]	53.9[a]	O-C	54.4[a]	53.1[a]
Hy	47.9	51.0	INT	53.3[a]	53.1[a]
Pd	47.0	49.8	DEP	54.4[a]	52.2
Mf	40.6[a]	57.6[a]	ANX	53.1	52.3[a]
Pa	47.3[a]	50.3	HOS	51.5	51.6
Pt	52.2	52.6	PHOB	54.7[a]	50.1
Sc	49.2	50.0	PAR	52.2	51.7
Ma	47.6	48.7	PSY	55.5[a]	54.1[a]
Si	56.6[a]	55.1			

[a]Differs from national standardization sample at .05 level of statistical significance.

scores on a number of the symptom scales, which will be discussed individually by gender.

As was observed with the MMPI-2, all of the SCL-90-R average scores fall within normal limits. On the other hand, five of the scores for women are statistically higher than the published norms. They include the SOM scale, which is a measure of somatic complaints. This finding is consistent with the data provided by the MMPI-2, which suggested slightly more emphasis on bodily symptoms. Another elevation occurs on the INT scale, which concerns interpersonal sensitivity. Elevations on this scale are indicative of shyness, introversion, and feelings of uneasiness in public, supporting the MMPI-2 findings, which also indicated a slightly higher level of introversion in the Appalachian sample. Three other significantly elevated scales were not supported by corresponding elevations on the MMPI-2 subscales. They include the O-C scale, which is associated with obsessive-compulsive behaviors, and the ANX scale, which measures anxiety. Finally, a significant elevation was noted on the PSY scale, which is normally associated with psychotic behaviors; however, a perusal of the questions included in this scale suggests that the elevations may be better explained by cultural and religious differences. This will be discussed in depth following a review of the scores for the men in this sample.

Men's average scores on the SCL-90-R in table 13.1 demonstrate some patterns similar to the women. For example, men also have significant elevations on the SOM scale, involving somatization, and the O-C scale, which concerns obsessive-compulsive sensitivity. The Appalachian men also scored significantly higher than average on the DEP scale, which measures depression, corroborating an elevated average score on the D scale for men on the MMPI-2. Another interesting elevation occurs on the PHOB scale, which is labeled "phobic anxiety." This observation is not surprising when one examines the type of questions included in this scale. Three out of the seven items on this scale concern anxieties people may feel when encountering various aspects of city life, including mass transit, crowds, and frightening places or activities. It is very likely that residents of a rural community would acknowledge more uneasiness with these experiences than would an urban sample.

Finally, there are significant elevations for both men and women on the PSY scale, which, as previously mentioned, is associated with psychoticism. The items included in this scale concern various thoughts and feelings that are often experienced by psychotic individuals, for example, feelings of social isolation and magical ideation. Endorsement of these items in the Appalachian sample, however, can be more appropriately interpreted within a cultural or religious context. For example, 33 percent of the Appalachian sample admitted believing that they should be punished for their sins. In the normative U.S. sample, only 17 percent of nonpatient adults acknowledged this belief. Another striking difference occurred on an item that concerned feelings of loneliness when not alone. Twenty-eight percent of the sample endorsed this item, versus only 11 percent of the normative sample. Similarly, 20 percent of the Appalachian residents complained of never feeling close to anyone, in contrast to 10 percent of the normative sample. The feelings of loneliness and isolation reported by the subjects on this scale seem to parallel the MMPI-2 and SCL-90-R data, which suggests a slightly higher level of social introversion and interpersonal sensitivity. Finally, 30 percent of the Appalachian sample admitted fearing that something serious was wrong with their bodies, versus 19 percent in the normative population. Once again, these findings are supported by both the MMPI-2 and the SCL-90-R, which suggested a heavier emphasis by Appalachians on bodily concerns.

Discussion

The results support certain aspects of Appalachian mental health status as reported in the literature, especially the greater psychological distress experienced by people in the region (Looff 1971; Coles 1971). In particular, the increased level of somatic symptoms and the greater incidence of depression in Appalachia noted by many authors is supported by the statistically higher scores (on three out of four gender-specific scores) on these psychological tests. On the other hand, given the extent to which the culture-bound syndrome "nerves" has been discussed in the Appalachian literature (Van Schaik 1988; Halperin and Reiter-Purtill, this volume), it is surprising that symptoms of anxiety are registered higher than the U.S. norm on only one out of four scales. Perhaps this simply supports the argument that "nerves" as conceptualized by Appalachians does not neatly fit into a single psychiatric classification. Finally, there is evidence to support the literature that suggests that certain personality traits (those associated with interpersonal relations, religious attitudes, and gender constructions) are significantly different in Appalachia and suggest a culturally different standard of what is "normal" temperament and behavior. Practitioners are advised to take these differences into account in making their psychological assessments, while at the same time recognizing that the cultural "difference" is relatively small in an empirical sense.

Thus, we take a middle road in our interpretation of the testing results, largely due to the *content* of various items and scales. We acknowledge that real differences in the incidence of pathology may be present in the Appalachian population. This would argue for an increased level of psychological services for adequate mental health care. In other ways, however, our analysis questions certain culture-specific constructions in psychological testing scales which might be invalid for the Appalachian population. These could lead to misinterpretations and misdiagnoses when comparing Appalachian patient profiles to the non-Appalachian scale norms. Therefore, clinicians are urged to interpret scores for Appalachian clients with caution.

References

Anastasi, Anne, and Urbina, Susana. 1997. *Psychological Testing.* 7th ed. Upper Saddle River, N.J.: Prentice-Hall.

Appalachian Regional Commission. 1965. "The Subregions." *Appalachia.* Washington, D.C.: GPO.

Beaver, Patricia D. 1986. *Rural Community in the Appalachian South.* Lexington: University Press of Kentucky.

Butcher, James N., W. Grant Dahlstrom, John R. Graham, Auke Tellegen, and Beverly Kaemmer. 1989. *Minnesota Multiphasic Personality Inventory-2 (MMPI-2): Manual for Administration and Scoring.* Minneapolis: University of Minnesota Press.

Cockerham, William C. 1990. "A Test of the Relationship Between Race, Socioeconomic Status, and Psychological Distress." *Social Science and Medicine* 31:1321–26.

Cohen, Ronald Jay, Mark E. Swerdlik, and Suzanne M. Phillips. 1996. *Psychological Testing and Assessment: An Introduction to Tests and Measurement.* 3d ed. Mountain View, Calif.: Mayfield.

Coles, Robert. 1971. *Migrants, Sharecroppers, and Mountaineers.* Vol. 2 of *Children of Crisis.* Boston: Little, Brown.

Costello, E Jane, Adrian Angold, Barbara J. Burns, Dalene K. Stangl, Dan L. Tweed, Alaattin Erkanli, and Carol M. Worthman. 1996. "The Great Smoky Mountains Study of Youth: Goals, Design, Methods, and the Prevalence of DSM-III-R Disorders." *Archives of General Psychiatry* 53:1129–36.

Dahlstrom, W. Grant, David Lachar, and Leona E. Dahlstrom. 1986. *MMPI Patterns of American Minorities.* Minneapolis: University of Minnesota Press.

Dana, Richard H., and P. R. Whatley. 1991. "When Does a Difference Make a Difference? MMPI Scores and African Americans." *Journal of Clinical Psychology* 47:400–406.

Derogatis, L. R. 1994. *SCL-90R: Symptom Checklist 90-4: Administration, Scoring, and Procedures Manual.* 3d ed. Minneapolis: National Computer Systems.

Graham, J. R. 1990. *MMPI-2: Assessing Personality and Psychopathology.* New York: Oxford University Press.

Greene, Roger L. 1987. "Ethnicity and MMPI Performance: A Review." *Journal of Consulting and Clinical Psychology* 55:497–512.

Hall, Gordon C. Nagayama, Anita Bansal, and Irene R. Lopez. 1999. "Ethnicity and Psychopathology: A Meta-Analytic Review of 31 Years of Comparative MMPI/MMPI-2 Research." *Psychological Assessment* 11:186–97.

Hicks, George L. 1976. *Appalachian Valley.* New York: Holt, Rinehart, and Winston.

Hoffman, Tom, Richard H. Dana, and Brian Bolton. 1985. "Measured Acculturation and MMPI-168 Performance of Native Americans." *Journal of Cross-Cultural Psychology* 16:243–56.

Hollingshead, A. B., and F. C. Redlich. 1958. *Social Class and Mental Illness.* New York: Wiley.

Keefe, Susan Emley (Ed.). 1988. *Appalachian Mental Health.* Lexington: University Press of Kentucky.

———. 1998. "Appalachian Americans: The Formation of 'Reluctant' Ethnics." In *Many Americas: Critical Perspectives on Race, Racism, and Ethnicity,* Gregory R. Campbell (Ed.). Dubuque, Iowa: Kendall/Hunt. Pp. 129–53.

Looff, David H. 1971. *Appalachia's Children: The Challenge of Mental Health.* Lexington: University Press of Kentucky.

Montgomery, Gary T., and Sergio Orozco. 1983. "Mexican-Americans' Performance on the MMPI as a Function of Level of Acculturation." *Journal of Clinical Psychology* 41:208–12.

Okazaki, S., and Stanley Sue. 1996. "Cultural Considerations in the Assessment of Asian Americans." In *Practical Considerations in Clinical Personality Assessment,* James Neal Butcher (Ed.). New York: Oxford University Press.

Padilla, Eligio, Esteban L. Olmedo, and Fred Loya. 1982. "Acculturation and the MMPI Performance of Chicano and Anglo College Students." *Hispanic Journal of Behavioral Sciences* 4:451–66.

Tellegen, Auke, Nathan L. Gerrard, Louise B. Gerrard, and James Neal Butcher. 1969. "Personality Characteristics of Members of a Serpent-Handling Religious Cult." In *MMPI: Research Developments and Clinical Applications,* James Neal Butcher (Ed.). New York: McGraw-Hill. Pp. 221–42.

Van Schaik, Eileen. 1988. "The Social Context of 'Nerves' in Eastern Kentucky." In *Appalachian Mental Health,* Susan Emley Keefe (Ed.). Lexington: University Press of Kentucky. Pp. 81–100.

Whitworth, Randolph H., and Christian Unterbrink. 1994. "Comparison of MMPI-2 Clinical and Content Scales Administered to Hispanics and Anglo-Americans." *Hispanic Journal of Behavioral Sciences* 16:255–64.

Chapter 14

Mental Health Therapy for Appalachian Clients

Susan E. Keefe and Susie Greene

Despite the fact that there are almost two hundred mental health clinics in the Appalachian region and thousands of therapists, both inside and outside of the region, who work with Appalachian clients, little has been written to assist therapists so that they might provide sensitive and culturally relevant services.[1] In this chapter, we provide guidelines for therapists, especially those who are not from the Appalachian region and may not be familiar with its cultural values and meanings.

In generalizing about Appalachian clients, we focus on the modal Appalachian client, that is, the working-class or middle-class white, rural dweller. We recognize that the Appalachian population is diverse, encompassing natives and in-migrant newcomers, racial and ethnic minorities (including African Americans, Native Americans, and Hispanic Americans), and differences by social class and urban/rural residence. These distinctions have an impact on life-styles, cultural values, and cultural identity. Upper-middle-class and urban-dwelling Appalachians, for example, may have largely acculturated to mainstream American values and behavior, especially through the attainment of a college education. Black Appalachians are for the most part urban residents and have had to respond to forces, such as racism and segregation, which have not affected white Appalachians (Keefe and Manross 1999; Turner and Cabbell 1985). And yet, the recommendations to follow may also provide insights for therapists who deal with these populations in that, for example, urbanites may have recently moved to the city from the countryside and black Appalachians share many cultural traits with white Appalachians. [2]

Appalachian Cultural Values

In generalizing about Appalachian clients, we make the assumption that there are cultural values and traits shared by natives of the Appalachian region. It is useful to review some of these in order to put the comments that follow into context. It should be pointed out that Appalachian culture is not totally unique. On the contrary, much is shared with rural southern culture and agrarian life in general. Culture, however, is a pattern of shared ideas and behaviors, and it is the pattern in Appalachia that is unique, not the individual traits.

As mentioned in the introduction to this volume, core Appalachian cultural values include egalitarianism, personalism, familism, a religious world view, a sense of place, and an avoidance of conflict.[3] This pattern of values has emerged out of Appalachia's particular regional cultural history (Keefe, this volume). In addition to these common values, Appalachian people tend to have a separate cultural identity, although there is no single label residents agree upon for people from the region (alternatives include "Appalachian," "mountain people," "country people," and "locals," among others). This group identity becomes especially significant in situations of political competition with groups identified as "outsiders" (Foster 1988; Keefe 1983). It is also an important aspect of individual identity, a fact recognized by the U.S. Census Bureau, which finds increasing numbers of people responding that they are "Appalachian" to the census question regarding ethnic identity.

Egalitarianism is an American cultural value, and it simply tends to be more heightened and applied more broadly in Appalachia (Beaver 1986). In social interaction, people are acknowledged as equals in status, even though it is also understood that there are real status differences within the community. Everyone is expected to be able to have a voice in decision making, and people are sensitive to one another's feelings and ideas. Those in leadership positions try to be nonauthoritarian and self-effacing. People tend to avoid conspicuous consumption or being labeled "big shots." They try to treat each other with respect and to avoid "snobbery" (Fiene 1990). They value hard work but dislike being perceived as "uppity." At the same time, Appalachians value getting an education and making a good living, as long as it is achieved with honesty, modesty, and a continued appreciation of family and the homeplace.

Like southerners in general, Appalachians appreciate and encourage personalism and face-to-face relations (Jones 1994). They are hospitable and smile at strangers on the street. They take time to get to know strangers before trusting them, but once they get to know them, they will be loyal and help out in times of need. Appalachians can be counted upon to keep their word; verbal "contracts" are considered binding. And as in most small-scale societies, Appalachians are honest and fair with those they know.

The family is the fundamental social institution in Appalachia, and familism is the basis for the construction of social relations in general (Beaver 1986; Bryant 1981; Matthews 1965). The Appalachian family structure is different from that of the mainstream in that the Appalachian family includes not only the nuclear family but also the extended family, consisting of parents and grown children and their families. Blood kinship is the strongest basis for social ties, superseding ties with friends, in-laws, or, often, even spouses. Many Appalachians are unfamiliar or ill at ease with strangers and nonkin. Socializing is done mostly (sometimes exclusively) with relatives, although good friends are often incorporated into the family group as fictive kin. Finally, individuals who are estranged from their family tend to suffer dramatically.

Religion pervades the life of mountain people, regardless of whether or not they go to church (Dorgan 1987; McCauley 1995). Most mountaineers read the Bible, self-identify as Christians, and practice personal moral codes based on conservative interpretations of the Bible (disavowing, for example, alcohol, gambling, and profanity). Music preferences of rural Appalachians tend toward country and gospel music, in which religious themes and references are fundamental. Older mountain farmers often still plant and harvest by the "signs" in the *Farmer's Almanac,* based on a supernatural rather than scientific understanding of the world. Prayer is one of the most important ways for individuals to cope with illness, trauma, and overwhelming crises (Keefe 2003). And churches which offer individuals direct access to supernatural power, such as the Pentecostal Church, which believes that members can receive the spiritual gift of the Holy Ghost and thus enjoy a state of holiness on Earth, have significant and growing appeal in a stratified society in which secular power is normally out of reach.

Appalachian natives have a strong sense that the mountains are home. This means that the land is more than mere property to be bought and sold for profit; people have, instead, a mythical and even spiritual bond with the land (Beaver 1986; Hicks 1976). They feel the responsibility of stewardship toward the land, that is, the need to make it productive while protecting and preserving it. The sense of place also involves an appreciation of nature and the natural cycle of life. There is an identification with natural things, and some knowledge of the animals, the birds and insects, and the plants both domestic and wild is expected by people in the mountains. Gardening is enjoyed by most rural Appalachians. Land is significant as property for mountain people in that they hope to inherit it from their parents and pass it on to their children. Land becomes affiliated with families, and the homeplace that is often the location of the family reunion includes not only the house but the grounds and even the farmland of past generations. Appalachian people come to know the land not as a generic but as a specific piece of earth with landmarks and bits of history tied to its meaning. For mountaineers, there is no place like home, and individuals who leave feel homesick for the place as well as the people. Indeed, they may seem to be one in the same.

Finally, like southerners in general, Appalachian people are apt to promote peaceful cooperative relations and avoid conflict at all costs (Hicks 1976; Wagner, this volume). They avoid giving advice directly to nonkin, tending to say something indirectly, such as, "Now, if it were me . . ." (see Puckett, this volume). They are raised with a high regard for manners and etiquette as a means of avoiding personal offense (addressing others as "Sir" or "Ma'am," for example, as a way of indicating respect for others rather than in honor of high status). Children are taught the value of sharing and playing in harmony, and hostile language is discouraged. People are hesitant to criticize others face-to-face, preferring to spread discontent "through the grapevine." Open conflict is an indication that the boundaries of normal behavior have been crossed and that the usual means of dealing with a problem have failed to solve it.

Training Mental Health Professionals for the Region

The training of mental health professionals includes at a minimum the basic concepts of confrontation, intervention, and listening skills (Pipes and Davenport 1990). During training in these areas, the initial emphasis is on "self." What are the blocks to my hearing what the client is saying? How can I "hear" beyond my own fears and questions? It is also a time when the mental health professional is forced to look at the fundamental questions of life: What are my values? What are my beliefs? The therapist is expected to consider how these values and beliefs "play out" in work with individuals (Pipes and Davenport 1990). As in any multicultural clinical setting, the therapist should be prepared for cultural differences and the task of negotiating them in work with Appalachian clients.

The individual therapist is the primary "tool" taken into a mental health situation. This "tool" is the sum total of not only the training models learned but also the values, beliefs, experiences, agendas, and personal circumstances of the therapist. All of these can and do have an impact on the experience of being with and hearing a client. A non-Appalachian therapist can anticipate problems in working with Appalachian clients due to cultural and personal differences, but at the same time, these problems are not insurmountable and they probably will not present the greatest challenge a therapist will face in his or her work. What is important is that a therapist should remember to evaluate how his or her own values may affect work with Appalachian clients. Above all, the therapist should not be quick to make judgments or interpretations or to diagnose illnesses.

It is important to remember that all the skills for listening, confrontation, and/or interventions do not work with all populations (Sue and Sue 1990). A mental health professional is wise to follow some basic guidelines. First, be who you are. If you are unclear about what is being said or about definitions of words, ask for clarification. For example, if a client begins a session by saying he's been "stove up" this week and you are unsure of his meaning, be sure to follow up with a question about it rather than assume it has something to do with a kitchen appliance![4] Often, the therapist is tempted to take on the role of "all-knowing" and thus loses his or her connection with the client as well as with him or herself. Second, learn from your clients. Each client comes with many levels of experience in life. The sharing of their stories is not only a gift but also, in many cases, the opportunity to learn of other ways of being. And third, allow a client his or her own experiences. This assures the client a safety net within which changes can take place. It is unwise for the therapist to make comments, including those beginning "You should" or "You shouldn't." For the therapist to take charge and facilitate the client's experiences makes the experiences those of the therapist and not those of the client (this advice changes, obviously, if the client is a danger to him or herself or to others).

Therapeutic Stumbling Blocks

The following might be encountered as therapeutic stumbling blocks in work with Appalachian clients. Alternative ways of handling these stumbling blocks are offered.

The Goal of Therapy

The client's reason for being present and the mental health professional's goal in therapy might be different. The therapist must ask, Why is the client here? What is the greatest or most pressing need presented? Frequently, rural Appalachians who become clients have serious financial problems. If a client cannot feed her children, she will not be interested in exploring her feelings about this issue. Instead, the client needs and wants a solution to this dilemma. In this instance, it is the obligation of the therapist to offer information about community assistance that might be available and to help guide the client through the maze of programs at hand. Once more immediate problems have been dealt with, other therapy goals might be possible.

In many cases, Appalachian clients present problems with somatic symptoms and they will expect these symptoms to be addressed by the mental health professional. For example, many Appalachian clients conceptualize their problem as "nerves" and expect to be treated with "nerve pills" (see Halperin and Reiter-Purtill, this volume). A cultural syndrome with variable symptoms, nerves provides a meaningful way for Appalachian people to conceptualize and cope with overwhelming life problems. It is also an example of the tendency for Appalachian people to somaticize their emotional problems and, often, to prefer medical treatment to verbal therapy. Rather than countering this cultural knowledge or stigmatizing it as "incorrect," mental health professionals would do well to find ways to work with the client at both the somatic and psychological levels, such as recommending the combination of medication for immediate symptoms as well as exploring alternative ways of coping with or changing life situations.

Therapy Tools

Therapist's Agenda for Process

The therapist typically comes to an interview ready to plunge into the problem at hand. However, in view of the previous discussion of personalism, it will come as no surprise that initially the Appalachian client will expect some socializing before getting down to business. A therapist who is not willing to engage in some sort of sharing at the beginning of an interview will be viewed as aloof and distant. Also, as explained in the discussion of egalitarianism, Appalachian clients tend to view relationships as being between equals and some sharing about self will be expected of the therapist during the interview. Therapists are generally not prepared for this, as personal sharing is discouraged in training. A general rule of thumb is that what the therapist shares should not become the focus of the interview, that is, the therapist should not become the client. Topics open to sharing by the therapist should fit the situation and the relationship established with the client. For example, the counseling session might be opened with a general comment such as "How have you been?" with the expectation of sharing some general comments about the therapist's state of being (e.g., "I've been suffering with a cold this week").

For rural peoples, the pace of life is slower and more deliberate. Therefore, a slower pace in both therapeutic work and speech than one learns in professional training is more acceptable and thus more workable with Appalachian clients. The therapist should never answer for the client, for example, if he or she does not respond quickly enough. Moreover, it is important to remember that slow speech should never be equated with low intelligence.

In the search for a diagnosis, therapists are cautioned to reserve judgment. As multicultural research has demonstrated, the American Psychiatric Association's *Diagnostic and Statistical Manual of Mental Disorders* (1994) is a culturally shaped system of categories whose usefulness in dealing with racially and ethnically distinctive populations is sometimes questionable (Dana 1993; Kirk and Kutchins 1992). Until there is more research, the extent to which Appalachian clients are misdiagnosed is uncertain. As Keefe, Hastrup, and Thomas (this volume) demonstrate, Appalachians score differently than mainstream Americans on the Minnesota Multiphasic Personality Inventory or MMPI-2 (Butcher et al. 1989). In another study by Keefe comparing Appalachian and non-Appalachian client diagnoses in a mental health system, Appalachian clients were likely to be diagnosed differently and as being more severely ill than non-Appalachian clients (Keefe 1988b). This parallels other research on mental health clinic utilization by ethnic minorities who are also perceived as being more abnormal than the white mainstream. This difference in diagnosis may have something to do with measurable differences in symptoms (certainly minorities suffer from greater stress in our society), but it also has to do with differences between cultural systems in distinguishing normal versus abnormal behavior (see Abbott-Jamieson, this volume). Diagnosis is clearly fraught with problems and the wise therapist will proceed with caution.

Verbal Interaction Only

Mental health professionals are trained to use and to expect the use of words by clients. However, in a society where personal worth and family are the basis for reputation, Appalachian people are often reticent to talk about personal or family problems.[5] It is important to be able to use other options for the telling of one's life circumstances and/or life story. While mental health professionals often discourage the telling of stories, particularly if they are long, in doing so they are silencing the client. Appalachian people are known for their oral traditions, and storytelling or folk symbols and proverbs often provide alternative avenues for expressing feelings (see Sawin 2004; Sherrod, this volume). We have already mentioned the Appalachian penchant for gardening, which provides another alternative means for expression. Other options that the therapist might explore include poetry, music, and art. An Appalachian woman, for example, might bring a quilt she has made to a therapy session, and the therapist might inquire about the scraps of material used in the quilt as they are often symbols of parts of her life (e.g., a daughter's graduation dress or a new grandbaby's outfit).

The Assumption of Skills

Language is an important basis for mental health assessment. The Appalachian dialect can be a pitfall for the therapist unfamiliar with the region (see Puckett, this volume). Appalachian clients and mental health professionals may not have the same definitions for words used in casual conversation. An example is the term "sleeping with someone." While this may imply sexual relations to mainstream Americans, it may simply mean co-sleeping in Appalachian families (see Abbott-Jamieson, this volume). It is the mental health professional's responsibility to help clarify the definitions of words and events and not to assume meaning.

Professionals also tend to assume that clients can correctly and immediately name (that is give a verbal definition of) the events and/or feelings they are experiencing. This is not always the case and can be a very dangerous assumption. Using the Myers Briggs Type Indicator as an example, many Introverted and Thinking types tend to go deep within themselves to find the "correct" words and feelings, taking more time than those types who are Extroverted and Feeling. For the former, the feelings or words are there but they may take much longer to access (Myers 1980). The therapist who rushes or assumes often merely pushes the client further into him or herself.

Confrontation

As mentioned in the discussion of values, confrontation is avoided by Appalachian people at all costs. Mental health professionals who try to actively encourage this type of interaction rarely meet with success. Asking a client to just tell someone no or to confront someone with the truth, for example, will certainly fall on deaf ears. In fact, the therapist may be stonewalled because the client does not want to confront the professional about not being confrontational. In addition, a professional who is too blunt will not be heard by clients who are unused to or do not value this style of communication.

More subtle techniques can often achieve the same results. For example, the therapist might ask the client to identify boundaries or the extent of his or her ability to speak the "truth." Once a continuum has been established between what the client feels comfortable saying and that which is "truth," the client can be asked to push his or her limits working in a progressive way. The client might be asked to indicate, for example,

> What would be the hardest thing to say?
> What might be the easiest thing to say?
> Now, what is in between that would not be easy but that you could/would say?

In exploring confrontation, it should be remembered that confrontation may also imply violence. Since Appalachian peoples tend to avoid confrontation, there may not be a recognition of gradations in confrontation by the client or the client's social circle. It is incumbent upon the professional to ensure that the client and therapist share the same definition of confrontation and explore the probable effect of its use.

Religion

Although the southern Appalachian client may not be actively involved in an organized religious group, religion undoubtedly has been an integral part of his or her life experience. In light of the secular training offered in most professional programs, therapists may have difficulty adjusting to the pervasive religious world view of Appalachian natives. Nevertheless, therapists are encouraged to gain an understanding of and to become comfortable with Appalachian religious beliefs, allowing clients to explore spiritual issues if appropriate.[6] In this sense, Bible study groups can serve as professional development for therapists (see Denton and Denton 1994). For many clients, therapeutic steps will be undertaken only when there has been the opportunity for prayer and a personal understanding of the will of God. The client who states, "I will pray about this" at the end of an intense problem-solving session is not devaluing the work done in the session but looking for support for a decision probably already made. The mental health worker does well to connect with the positives of these beliefs.[7]

Silence

Mental health professionals are trained to assume that, in the context of therapy, silence indicates the client is stonewalling. In truth, it can mean several things. First, there is some evidence that Appalachian people are more likely to score higher on social introversion in personality testing and, thus, there may be greater cultural tolerance of silence in Appalachian conversation (see Keefe, Hastrup, and Thomas, this volume). Second, silence may mean the person is going inside him or herself to find the "right" answer, which is a classic Thinking/Feeling difference in Myers Briggs terms. Third, silence may indicate disagreement given the Appalachian unwillingness to confront (as in the admonition "If you can't say anything nice, don't say anything at all"). The therapist must explore and evaluate these alternatives in any therapeutic situation.

Contracts

Since a person's word is taken very seriously in southern Appalachia, it is important to make sure the definitions of expectations are clear and agreed upon. As an example, a mountain man with a severe heart condition was told by his doctor that his diet was to be closely monitored. The man made a verbal contract with his doctor to eat only one biscuit (his favorite) per day. At his next medical checkup, the man's cholesterol was higher than ever, so the doctor asked if the man had kept his word. When the man said that he had, the doctor thought to ask him the size of his biscuit, and it turned out that the man was having his wife make the "one" biscuit in a frying pan!

Clients will expect that mental health professionals will keep their word as well. Appointment times, for example, are expected to be honored. The professional who is consistently late or who breaks appointments will soon be without a client.

Mental Health Services

Planning mental health services in an Appalachian region should take into account the life-styles and cultural values of clients. Rural peoples' working situations often do not fit into the 8:00 A.M. to 5:00 P.M. work day or the fifty-minute session in a centralized clinic that mental health professionals are trained to expect. Professionals need to be flexible with times and options. Satellite clinics should be operated where possible. Natives of the region should be included on planning and advisory boards, and regional organizations must plan to do aggressive recruiting since Appalachians natives may not seek out board positions.

Cultural Differences Encountered in Therapy

Mental health professionals who are not from the region will encounter a number of differences in interaction style, values, and cultural identity when working with Appalachian clients. It is important not to fall into stereotypical thinking in these situations, attaching assorted negative attributes to clients, including those who self-identify as "hillbilly." Professionals should look inside themselves and examine the value that they place on patterns of speech, ways of dressing, and ways of being that are different from their own. Resorting to stereotyping will only impair the professional's ability to "hear" what the client is saying.

Also, genuineness (not to be confused with rudeness) is highly valued in southern Appalachian culture, and a professional who is "playing" at his or her role, such as dressing out of character to fit the culture, will be perceived in a suspicious, nontrusting manner. More value is given by Appalachian natives to the person who lives his or her differences with pride.

Gender

Men and women tend to have gender-defined social spheres in rural Appalachia, men socializing with other men and women with other women. An unmarried man and woman are rarely alone with each other; even courtship is conducted as a family affair in traditional Appalachian society (Beaver 1986). For this reason, a mental health professional who is working with a person of another gender (particularly a female professional working with a male client) needs to address this difference at the beginning of any work together. Male clients are sometimes uncomfortable and, thus, not forthcoming with issues when working with a female therapist. This is particularly true with issues of sexuality.

By addressing this difference and looking at options, this often can become a non-issue. For example, the therapist might address the obvious gender difference at the beginning of the initial interview, giving the client other options, such as selecting a male therapist, a group with other men, and so on. Rather than ignoring or denying the gender difference, it becomes an option and encourages an honest response from the client.

Value of Home and Family

As discussed previously, healthy Appalachian people are generally well integrated into their family and local community (Keefe 1986). Lack of integration into these support systems often leads to the emergence of emotional problems. Successful mental health therapy in such cases will undoubtedly rely upon the reintegration of the individual with their native support system. Encouraging a client to leave, move away, or deny the primacy of the family, on the other hand, will probably be met with silent immobility, even when it is for the safety and/or greater good of the client.

Family-oriented therapy, not surprisingly, has proven successful in Appalachian practice (Cole 1988). Professionals are cautioned that speaking about negative relationships in the family ("talking outside the family") is discouraged in Appalachia, and this may be a roadblock for effective mental health intervention (see Howell and Fiene, this volume). It should be remembered that the extended families in southern Appalachia are a great mental health asset, providing a network of kin who will support their own regardless. This can assist the therapeutic process when tapped appropriately.

Value of the Individual

Individualism is highly valued in Appalachia, but it is constructed differently than in mainstream America, where the right to nonconformity and equal opportunity to compete for the American dream define individuality (Keefe 1998). For Appalachian people, seeing oneself as different from, and particularly as better than, others is undesirable. This can cause problems for the mental health professional who is trained to work with the individual by looking for strengths, skills, and positive traits to increase self-esteem. The mental health professional will need to work to find a balance between building positive self-esteem and allowing the individual to keep his or her "place." One way to think about this is by using the concept of "collective self" which characterizes Appalachian society (see Wagner, this volume). Individual worth may be bolstered by finding ways to contribute to the community as a whole, such as through church work or helping the volunteer fire department.

Blending Two Cultures

Marriages involving an Appalachian and a non-Appalachian partner can be complicated by cultural differences and misunderstandings. In the novel *Raney,* for example, Clyde Edgerton (1985) describes the marriage of Raney Bell, a Free Will Baptist from Bethel, North Carolina, to Charles Sheperd, an Episcopalian from Atlanta, Georgia. Their differences begin with geography and religion and go on to include family, race relations, and language. Once the first glow of love dims into the reality of a relationship as hard work, Raney and Charles must address their differences as equally worthy rather than as one right way and one wrong way. Mental health professionals should be sure to identify the cultural background or birthplace of all family members at the beginning of the interview. Those working with couples in which spouses each have a different cultural background need to assist in the recognition of value differences and increasing tolerance for those differences.

Appalachian natives, especially those who have gained a higher education, are often acculturated, that is, they have adopted many of the values and traits associated with mainstream American life. The process of acculturation is often accompanied by emotional stress as certain aspects of one's culturally constructed self are changed or severed. In one woman's case, the move from a mountain city to Duke University included, in addition to the usual stress associated with life as a college freshman, the added stress of being labeled a "little mountain girl," and so she spent months privately practicing her speech in order to obliterate her mountain dialect and accent. Therapists must be sensitive to their client's place in the acculturation process and how this might complicate mental and emotional problems.

Cultural Identity

People from the mountains often experience lack of self-esteem due to the negative stereotypes that persist regarding their cultural heritage. Mental health professionals are encouraged to stimulate a sense of pride in Appalachian culture and identity. Expressing admiration regarding important cultural values such as familism and personalism is one means of doing this. Promotion of mountain culture can be as simple as playing country music in a clinic waiting room or as complex as assisting a community in saving a local landmark about to be destroyed. What is important is to begin to recognize those goals and values the people deem worthy and then to help facilitate them.

One dimension of a client's problem may have to do with ambiguity regarding cultural identity, that is, a sense of being caught between two different cultures: Appalachian and mainstream American. This often happens among rural middle-class Appalachians who are closely tied to an extended family and a traditional Appalachian culture and yet whose middle-class status draws them into a competitive and consumptive mainstream American life-style and society. Creative ways which build on cultural images can be found to help individuals deal with this identification crisis. In one case, a young woman who is an accomplished musician described how she worked through music to come to terms with her emotional problems and her own identity conflict as a rural mountain woman. She moved from childhood classical piano lessons to high school– and college-level trumpet classes, to an academic appreciation of "mountain music" and learning the guitar, banjo, and dulcimer, and, ultimately, to a reacceptance of the hymns and gospel music of her childhood as well as other mountain styles, such as murder ballads and string band music. Music therapy in the mountains can take an interesting twist!

Conclusion

Work with Appalachian clients requires a recognition of the need for multicultural mental health services. Successful mental health professionals will become aware of and acknowledge the cultural differences between themselves and Appalachian clients. They will foster respect and appreciation for those differences. They will increase their knowledge of native support systems outside the boundaries of the agency. They will respect the individuality of each client. And they will respect and acknowledge their own values, beliefs, and limitations.

Notes

1. For exceptions, see Delaney (1987), Keefe (1988a), and Tripp-Reimer and Friedl (1977).

2. Cultural similarities between blacks and whites in Appalachia bring Turner to describe black Appalachians as "a racial minority within a cultural minority" (Turner 1985:xix).

3. For further discussion of these cultural value patterns, see Keefe (1998).

4. The term "stove up" is a generic term meaning physically ill and incapacitated.

5. For a discussion of personal worth as the basis of reputation in Appalachia, see Beaver (1986). The trait of "silence" in the face of family abuse is addressed by Fiene (1993).

6. For a review of practical implications of Appalachian religious beliefs for mental health professionals, see Humphrey (1988).

7. For a description of the incorporation of spiritual and religious issues in the training of medical professionals in an Appalachian medical school, see Davis (1996).

References

American Psychiatric Association. 1994. *Diagnostic and Statistical Manual of Mental Disorders.* 4th ed. Washington, D.C.: American Psychiatric Association.

Beaver, Patricia D. 1986. *Rural Community in the Appalachian South.* Lexington: University Press of Kentucky.

Bryant, F. Carlene. 1981. *We're All Kin: A Cultural Study of a Mountain Neighborhood.* Knoxville: University of Tennessee Press.

Butcher, James N., W. Grant Dahlstrom, John R. Graham, Auke Tellegen, and Beverly Kaemmer. 1989. *Minnesota Multiphasic Personality Inventory—2: Manual for Administration and Scoring.* Minneapolis: University of Minnesota Press.

Cole, Cynthia. 1988. "Appalachian Family Therapy." In *Appalachian Mental Health,* Susan Emley Keefe (Ed.). Lexington: University Press of Kentucky. Pp. 175–87.

Dana, Richard H. 1993. *Multicultural Intervention Perspectives for Professional Psychology.* Boston: Allyn & Bacon.

Davis, Joel. 1996. "Faith and Medicine." *Now and Then: The Appalachian Magazine* 13, no. 3 (Winter): 15–17.

Delaney, Terry. 1987. "Alcoholism in the Invisible Minority: Some Appalachian Issues." *Alcohol Health and Research World* (Summer): 85–87.

Denton, Roy T., and Martha J. Denton. 1994. "Treating Religious Fundamentalist Families: Therapists' Suggestions from a Qualitative Study." *Human Services in the Rural Environment* 17(3/4):9–14.

Dorgan, Howard. 1987. *Giving Glory to God in Appalachia.* Knoxville: University of Tennessee Press.

Edgerton, Clyde. 1985. *Raney.* Chapel Hill, N.C.: Algonquin Books.

Fiene, Judith Ivy. 1990. "Snobby People and Just Plain Folks: Social Stratification and Rural, Low-Status, Appalachian Women." *Sociological Spectrum* 10: 527–39.

———. 1993. "The Appalachian Social Context and the Battering of Women." *Practicing Anthropology* 15, no. 3 (Summer): 20–24.

Foster, Stephen William. 1988. *The Past is Another Country: Representation, Historical Consciousness, and Resistance in the Blue Ridge.* Berkeley and Los Angeles: University of California Press.

Hicks, George L. 1976. *Appalachian Valley.* New York: Holt, Rinehart and Winston.

Humphrey, Richard A. 1988. "Religion in Southern Appalachia." In *Appalachian Mental Health,* Susan Emley Keefe (Ed.). Lexington: University Press of Kentucky. Pp. 36–42.

Jones, Loyal. 1994. *Appalachian Values.* Ashland, Ky.: Jesse Stuart Foundation.

Keefe, Susan Emley. 1983. "Ethnic Conflict in an Appalachian Craft Cooperative: On the Application of Structural Ethnicity to Mountaineers and Outsiders." In *The Appalachian Experience,* Barry Buxton, Malinda L. Crutchfield, William E. Lightfoot, and Jacqueline P. Stewart (Eds.). Boone, N.C.: Appalachian Consortium Press. Pp. 15–25.

———. 1986. "Southern Appalachia: Analytical Models, Social Services, and Native Support Systems." *American Journal of Community Psychology* 14(5):479–98.

———. (Ed.) 1988a. *Appalachian Mental Health.* Lexington: University Press of Kentucky.

———. 1988b. "An Exploratory Study of Mental Health Service Utilization by Appalachians and Non-Appalachians." In *Appalachian Mental Health,* Susan Emley Keefe (Ed.). Lexington: University Press of Kentucky Press. Pp. 145–58.

———. 1998. "Appalachian Americans: The Formation of 'Reluctant' Ethnics." In *Many Americas: Perspectives on Racism, Ethnicity, and Cultural Identity,* Gregory Campbell (Ed.). Dubuque, Iowa: Kendall/Hunt. Pp. 129–53.

———. 2003. "Religious Healing in Southern Appalachian Communities." In *Southern Heritage on Display: Public Ritual and Ethnic Diversity within Southern Regionalism,* Celeste Ray (Ed.). Tuscaloosa: University of Alabama Press. Pp. 144–66.

Keefe, Susan E., and Jodie D. Manross. 1999. "Race, Religion, and Community: The Demolition of a Black Church." *Appalachian Journal* 26(3):252–63.

Kirk, Stuart A., and Herb Kutchins. 1992. *The Selling of DSM: The Rhetoric of Science in Psychiatry.* Hawthorne, N.J.: Aldine de Gruter.

Matthews, Elmora Messer. 1965. *Neighbor and Kin: Life in a Tennessee Ridge Community.* Nashville: Vanderbilt University Press.

McCauley, Deborah Vansau. 1995. *Appalachian Mountain Religion: A History.* Urbana: University of Illinois Press.

Myers, Isabel. 1980. *Gifts Differing.* Palo Alto, Calif.: Consulting Psychologist Press.

Pipes, Randolph P., and Donna Davenport. 1990. *Introduction to Psychotherapy: Common Clinical Wisdom.* Englewood Cliffs, N.J.: Prentice-Hall.

Sawin, Patricia. 2004. *Listening for a Life: A Dialogic Ethnography of Bessie Eldreth Through her Songs and Stories.* Logan: Utah State University Press.

Sue, Derald, and David Sue. 1990. *Counseling the Culturally Different: Theory and Practice.* New York: John Wiley and Sons.

Tripp-Reimer, Toni, and Mary Cardwell Friedl. 1977. "Appalachians: A Neglected Minority." *Nursing Clinics of North America* 12(1):41–54.

Turner, William H. 1985. "Introduction." In *Blacks in Appalachia,* William H. Turner and Edward J. Cabbell (Eds.). Lexington: University of Kentucky Press. Pp. xvii–xxiii.

Turner, William H., and Edward J. Cabbell (Eds.). 1985. *Blacks in Appalachia.* Lexington: University of Kentucky Press.

Chapter 15

Evaluating a Rite of Passage Program for Adolescent Appalachian Males

Michael E. Maloney

Rites of passage programs as used by social workers in children's homes and other settings are intended as a substitute (or supplement) to what young people in these settings have missed in terms of socialization. What is missing includes a series of orderly "life course transitions" through which youth proceed in traditional societies or even in modern families of some stability. These transitions symbolize and mark key points in the process of becoming a man or woman.

When normal rites of passage are not available to youth, they often invent abnormal ones. In some inner-city urban Appalachian neighborhoods, for example, "going to juvenile" (detention center) or even going to prison has become a rite of passage (Ogilvie and Van Zyl 2001). Getting pregnant may be a rite of passage for young women. In juvenile gangs, commission of murder is an extreme example of an abnormal rite of passage. The assumption of rites of passage programs is that these programs can improve self-concept and a sense of responsibility to self and community (Rite of Passage Experience 2001). The purpose of this article is to explain and evaluate the use of rites of passage programs with adolescent Appalachian males in southern Ohio. A manual was developed in 1992 for use with adolescent males in rural Gallia, Meigs, and Jackson Counties. A formal outside evaluation was conducted, and the program has since been adopted in other rural and urban Appalachian settings. The funding source was not willing to sponsor development of a program specifically for adolescent Appalachian women, saying that they have materials that can be adapted for that population.

In traditional societies, there are processes of socialization to ensure that young men and women proceed from one stage of childhood to another and from childhood to adulthood. When these "passages" are accompanied by a ritual and community acknowledgment, they become "rites of passage." Rites of passage provide permission or opportunity to "move to a higher level of human social and educational development" (Moore et al. 1987:11). The young African engages in fasting and other preparation in a ritual involving the whole village. A Native American male prepares for manhood by engaging in a vision quest. Modern European and American societies, too, have their rites of passage in the form of ceremonies such as baptism, bar mitzvah, confirmation, and graduation (Grimes 2002). Until recently, high school graduation or induction into the army served as major passages to adulthood for young working-class American males. Mahdi, Foster, and Little (1987) believe that the decline of masculine rites of passage since World War II is part of the crisis of our society.

Mahdi and associates believe that most of the rites which used to carry archetypical value in supporting positive masculine ego development have atrophied or vanished altogether due to the evolution of "industrial-urban civilization." Such rituals as remain, moreover, often have more self-congratulatory power for adults than for young men. Rituals such as bar mitzvah and confirmation have no transformative power if the young man goes through the ritual for his parents with little understanding of its meaning. The result for American males is "profound isolation, fear, and the threat of death" (Mahdi, Foster, and Little 1987:137) and a failure to achieve individuation.

Although Van Gennep wrote his classic *The Rites of Passage* in 1909 (reissued in 1960), interest in rites of passage as a tool of social work intervention did not come to full fruition until the 1980s. By then, feminists as well as African American scholars and activists were developing a literature with applications to counseling (Mahdi, Foster, and Little 1987) or other forms of mental health work. Rites of passage manuals were developed for use with African American girls (Moore et al. 1987), African American males (Hare and Hare 1985), and other populations. Other works, while not exactly manuals, explore the concepts of youth development using Africentric and rites of passage concepts (Perkins 1985; Akbar 1991).

Rites of passage programs, in an African American context, are part of a larger effort to develop in black youth and adults an alternative to a racist Euro-centric and self-hating identity. The effort is not to replicate, in whole, elements of traditional African culture, but to apply such basic principles as these:

1. Community elders have a responsibility for helping to train youth to become responsible adults.
2. Youth cannot sufficiently teach themselves to become responsible adults.
3. The socialization of youth must be channeled through institutions that provide them with critical life-sustaining support systems.
4. When the above three principles do not occur, we should not expect our youth to be totally responsible for their actions which are counter productive to the welfare of the community (Perkins 1985:34).

Rites of passage can be seen as one instrument in the development of Africentric theory and practice that includes Robert Williams's notion of "weusi," a Swahili word meaning the collective black mind, "a collective corpus of philosophy, attitudes, preferences, values, beliefs and behaviors which are at once congruous to one another and undergirded by a strong spirited rhythm and African ethos: I am because we are and because we are, therefore, I am" (Williams as cited in Perkins 1985:34).

The Development of a Rites of Passage Program for Adolescent Appalachian Males

It is not surprising that social workers in the field of youth development began to mine the field opened first by anthropologists and mental health professionals. During the 1980s, Africentric rites of passage programs were being promoted by the Cultural Initiatives Division of the Ohio Department of Human Services (DHS). In 1991, Fran Frazier of that division approached me and asked me to work with Gallia County Children's Services to develop a rites of passage program for adolescent Appalachian males in independent living programs in Gallia, Meigs, and Jackson counties in Appalachian Ohio.

Beth Evans, director of Gallia County Children's Services, applied for a grant from the Office of Child Care and Family Services to fund the project.

I was hired as consultant and assigned to work with Russ V. Moore, then director of the Gallia County Children's Home, to develop the program. Evans explained that I was to work closely with Moore to ensure that the end product could be implemented by him and other practitioners. Evans and Moore are both Appalachian, and I saw immediately that they were intent on using an empowerment model that would not leave children's service staff in Appalachian Ohio dependent on outside consultants. Even though my credentials in Appalachian studies and social work applications were recognized and my Appalachian background duly noted, I was still an urban Appalachian from Cincinnati and an outsider to these Appalachian counties. Together, Evans, Moore, and I developed a statement of need to introduce the manual:

> In both rural Appalachia and in urban centers to which Appalachians have migrated many Appalachian communities are in a state of crisis. Since 1940 economic dislocations have forced more than 7,000,000 Appalachians to leave the region. The nature and timing of these dislocations vary greatly from section to section. For example central Appalachia experienced a decline in family farming which hit hardest in the 1940's and 1950's. The decline in demand for coal coupled with automation of the mining industry caused massive unemployment in central Appalachia in the 1953–1965 period. The virtual collapse of the American steel industry had a devastating effect on the Ohio Valley region in the 1970's and 1980's.
>
> The Appalachian Male has had to adapt from a proud and self-sufficient way of life based on strong kinship networks and agriculture and hunting to life in coal camps, mill towns, steel towns, and large industrial centers (often outside his native region). Before the transition from agriculture to manufacturing was complete the American economy began another transition, from manufacturing to a "post industrial" economy based heavily on high technology and service industries.
>
> The effect on some Appalachian communities has been devastating. The extended family has been separated and community life has been weakened. Many Appalachian women have entered the work force and in many cases have become the primary breadwinner. Single parent, usually female headed, families have become common. Teen pregnancy, substance abuse, and crime have reached critical proportions in many rural and urban Appalachian communities. Child abuse and neglect and domestic violence have become common. Appalachian women complain about having to simultaneously hold "public" jobs and care for their husbands (if present at all), children and aging parents.
>
> Appalachian men have experienced massive role displacement. Many men have lost their status as rural mountain patriarchs; their sons have lost their

status as proud producers of coal and steel, and some of the current generation are growing up in weakened family structures without adequate discipline or role models. (Maloney and Moore 1992:1)

Much could be said, of course, about the strength of Appalachian families that has allowed healthy family and community life to survive. In most rural and urban communities, dysfunctional families constitute a small minority of the population. Two important studies provide insight into the adaptability of the Appalachian family to out-migration and deindustrialization: *Mountain Families in Transition* (Schwarzweller, Brown, and Mangalam 1961) and *The Livelihood of Kin: Making Ends Meet the Kentucky Way* (Halperin 1991). Many strong kinship networks have survived in spite of a series of social and economic dislocations. Two articles that discuss the hardships and successes of Appalachians who have had to leave the region to find work are Obermiller and Maloney 1990 and Obermiller and Maloney 2002.

In the preindustrial premigration period of Appalachian history, the Appalachian family was a relatively self-sufficient unit of production and consumption. In this world, the family group (extended family) produced most of the necessities of life: food, shelter, fuel, and clothing. Even toys and recreational activities were largely homemade. The time frame for this "classic" period varied greatly from section to section of the region. On the eastern side of the mountains, which were settled first, the classic period was from the early 1700s to 1820. On the western side, including Appalachian Kentucky and Ohio, which could not be settled until the Shawnee and other Indian tribes were evicted, this period began in the 1780s or 1790s and extended until the 1820s, when such industries as mining and iron works began to appear. In the more remote sections of central and southern Appalachia, the preindustrial period for many extended into the 1940s.

In the agricultural and hunting period the father (and sometimes other adults) was responsible for teaching the boys all they needed to know regarding their environment, work and play. At an early age, boys learned how to care for animals, the identity and use (for food, medicine, toys and crafts) of each plant and tree in the fields and forests. By the age of twelve, the Appalachian male was taught the art of hunting and how to clean and prepare the kill for meals. He learned to plant, cultivate, and harvest a variety of plants. Some of the plants were adopted from the Native Americans.

Although formal rites of initiation were not involved, the learning of skills and the assignment of responsibility was age appropriate and systematic. By the time he was sixteen, the Appalachian boy was considered to be a man. The passage to manhood was sometimes confirmed by allowing the youth to take his first sip of moonshine—under adult supervision. Along the way to manhood there were many small "passages"—getting one's first pocket knife, learning to make a bow and arrow, learning to use an axe to fell a tree, being given one's own hunting rifle. At each step, the boy gained a skill and had adult confirmation of his worth and competency.

Some rites of passage involved the community at large, for example, baptism, marriage, graduation, and entering military service. Appalachian boys were taught respect for elders, respect for girls and women, and a sense of responsibility for younger children. Their way of life was coherent and produced a stable, patriotic, and hard working citizenry. Family solidarity was the centerpiece of the culture. There was sometimes conflict with other families, but in times of need or crisis families would usually pull together as a community, building a barn for a neighbor, for example, or helping a neighbor recover from a flood.

Many of today's Appalachian boys are far removed from the world described above. The depredations of industrialization, industrial decline, and out-migration have weakened family and community structures. Juvenile delinquency, substance abuse, family violence, and family breakup have become all too common. Teen pregnancy is a growing problem in low-income rural and urban areas. Welfare dependency is too common, and youth unemployment is widespread. In many communities, more than half the youth drop out of school before completing high school.

The Appalachian male, all too often, has lost his way. We hear the complaints of Appalachian women that they have too much responsibility. They may have to become the principal breadwinner if the husband cannot find an adequate job. If he leaves, she may be responsible for the care of both children and aging parents. And if the husband is abusive and/or alcoholic, or if the mother is not able to cope, the children may become wards of the state.

Appalachian adolescents moving from foster homes to "independent living" experience their own version of the crisis of the Appalachian male. They tend, for the most part, to insist they have no need for independent living services. They are quick to assert that they can do "just fine" on their own. They say "I already know" what it takes to be independent, "I've been independent for a long time now." This is a typical Appalachian reaction, demonstrating a fiercely independent spirit.

These same adolescents have a sincere need and yearning for "family support" and are usually aware that this is a lacking part of their own lives and will not likely change. They may make every effort to make some family connection, however distant or however harmful. To them, "kin look after their own."

Family, or at least its identification, is a priority concern for a displaced adolescent, especially one who comes from a cultural background that emphasizes the family, however dysfunctional that family may be. The adolescent will not likely express the need for the family connection, but it is ever constant. He believes in self-reliance, but he also believes in family.

The program is designed to address these issues. It will help to fill the need for belonging to a family, yet it will teach the importance of self-reliance as an integral part of manhood. This is the purpose of the Appalachian Rites of Passage Program.

Feelings of abandonment, of being unwanted, experience of an inner void, and fear of close relationships are common for adolescents in foster care. Yet every child has an ethnic identity, however confused and lost it might have become. Participation in a rites of passage program can enable young people to discover their group identity and, in the process, develop a sense of belonging with the youth and adults with whom they share this process of discovery. Such a process can provide a valuable and timely intervention to forestall the carryover of childhood alienation into adult life. In a rites of passage program, an adolescent may discover that although his family life may never be made whole, he is nonetheless worthy of affection, can establish a sense of belonging and self-esteem, and can pass these traits and values along to the family which he will form.

The Appalachian Rites of Passage Program is one response to the crisis of the Appalachian male (which is also a crisis for family and community). The program is designed to replace at least in a small way some of what has been lost in the economic and social upheavals that have weakened rural communities and created migrant ghettos in urban centers.

The program is designed to enable trainers in each community to develop a curriculum suitable to their local target population. A sample curriculum developed for use in Gallia, Jackson, and Meigs Counties in Ohio is also provided. We have also provided a bibliography and resource list on Appalachian culture and history (Maloney and Moore 1992).

In addition to working with the staff of Gallia County Children's Services, I consulted with Moriba Kelsey of the Africentric Personal Development Shop in Columbus, Ohio, and the work of Nathan and Julia Hare (Hare and Hare 1985) and Mafori Moore and her associates (Moore et al. 1987), and then went to work in the field. In consultation with Evans and Moore, and under the watchful eye of the DHS, I developed the program objectives and other parameters for the program. It was decided that the program would last twelve weeks and would not include either a wilderness experience or an elders component. Wilderness experiences and mentoring are fundamental elements of some rites of passage programs, but my client for a variety of reasons did not want these components included. I was asked to help design a training component for those who would implement the program and an overnight retreat for program participants. The program was to be targeted to Appalachian males who were currently in transition from group home or foster care settings to being on their own. The transition period is called "independent living."

The program was intended to address the need among adolescents in custodial care for "family support." It is, to that extent, a substitute for family experience, but the program also helps youth reconnect in some way with their own family history. The overall goal of the program is "to assist adolescent Appalachian males in their transition to manhood."

Objectives

Objectives of the rites of passage program for adolescent Appalachian males include the following:

- To focus youth in the direction of manly commitment, responsibility, and independence.
- To provide youth with an improved sense of self-worth.
- To provide youth with knowledge of their cultural background.
- To provide youth with knowledge of Appalachian regional and local history.
- To provide youth with a sense of belonging in his own culture.
- To provide youth with a sense of belonging in a family-like setting.
- To address the need for youth to establish ties to family, community, and culture.
- To arm youth with negotiation skills to help them deal with negative feedback (cultural barbs and "put-downs").
- To instill an understanding of the necessity for completing a high school education.

Some rites of passage programs focus on sex education, saying "no" to drugs, and other skills related to survival in rural and urban settings. Although the Gallia County curriculum left room for some of these discussions, the client made a decision to make the curriculum very specific to Appalachian culture. The focus is on knowing where you are from, being proud of it, being proud of who you are, and finishing your schooling. And, by the way, you will be made fun of for being Appalachian and here are the skills you will need to deal with the put downs. Children's Service workers in Appalachian Ohio felt strongly that the widespread stereotyping and name calling directed toward Appalachians is a primary reason for low self-esteem among their clients. They felt this issue was more pressing than either substance abuse or teen pregnancy. Feeling better about one's regional heritage was also given a higher priority than learning skills related to Appalachian heritage (e.g., crafts, music, dance). The biggest threats to successful transition to adulthood were thought to be negative images of self, region, and family, lack of connection to community, and the possibility of not completing high school. The objectives, therefore, focus primarily on these concerns.

The Curriculum

The activities proposed in this curriculum outline are designed to address the objectives listed above. Local trainers are to participate in a retreat for the instruction of trainers and then are to adapt the curriculum in consideration of their own talents, local resources, and the needs of the specific target population. This curriculum is designed to include twelve sessions of two hours each. The sessions are to be conducted once a week over a three-month period and can be regarded as preparation for the passage ceremony.

The first session is an orientation, which takes place in an overnight retreat setting. During the session, participants learn how to do a life book (a sort of scrapbook of personal and family experiences). A key component of the retreat is conducted by a clinician, who encourages participants to express emotions and share the pain they are experiencing, thus allowing them to move on with the rest of the programs. The retreat can also include focus on the importance of survival skills and may include rituals developed by the presiding adult.

After the overnight retreat, participants convene weekly for ten to twelve weeks to cover such subjects as Appalachian history and to go on field trips to historic sites in Appalachian Ohio or other parts of Appalachia. There is a unit on local history, one on Ohio history, and a local field trip which might be to a site of importance to Native Americans or other minority cultures in the region. There is a session on dealing with cultural put downs and one on "What does it mean to be an Appalachian man?" A midpoint ceremony acknowledges the accomplishments the youth have made thus far. An appropriate gift is made to each. Further sessions include music and crafts, storytelling, Appalachian and local politics and a community involvement session during which each youth reports on his community service project. The final session is a preparation for the passage ceremony.

The Passage Celebration

The passage celebration is adapted with permission from *Bringing the Black Boy to Manhood* (1985) by Nathan and Julia Hare of the Black Think Tank in San Francisco. The community, including friends, relatives, teachers, and other mentors of the boys, is invited. Grandparents and parents are brought in separately from other kin. The presiding adult directs the activities. An opening processional may include religious or secular music. There follows a ritual in which the presiding adult describes the responsibilities of manhood. Participants then accept the responsibilities and parents or other mentors approve. A word of praise is given by a mentor for each boy, then each boy gives a speech. The presiding adult acknowledges each speech and accepts the participants to manhood. There is a joyous formal exit ceremony. The ritual is followed by a fellowship dinner during which appropriate music and accolades for the boys continue.

The manual includes the following resource material:

- Curriculum Outline
- Passage Ceremony
- Retreat Agenda for Training of Trainers
- Schedule for Orientation Retreat
- Suggested Readings for the Passage Ceremony
- An Appalachian Bibliography and Resource Guide

Adaptation to Local Needs

The Appalachian Rites of Passage Program was developed as a joint effort between an "outside" consultant and local individuals who were then responsible for its implementation. This ensured its applicability to the local situation and that its implementation was feasible. It was expected that agencies wishing to implement this program in other locales would adapt both duration and content to local needs, and this has begun to happen. When urban Appalachians are the target group, there should be one or more sessions on migration to the city and the history of the particular urban Appalachian community. Rural Appalachian youth could also benefit from frank discussions of both the obstacles and opportunities they may face if they have to leave their community to attend college or find work. Other suggested content areas include goal setting, peer pressure (being popular vs. being smart), substance abuse, male sexuality, male/female relationships, suicide and violence reduction, Appalachian religious heritage, and patterns of community cooperation.

Evaluation of the Program

There has been widespread interest in the Appalachian Rites of Passage Program. Gallia County Children's Services has distributed hundreds of copies of the program's manual in response to requests from all over the country. Maloney and Moore have described the material in presentations to social workers in such places as Cincinnati, Columbus, Toledo, and State College, Pennsylvania. There has been no formal effort to determine how many institutions are actually using the program, but Dayton (Ohio) Public Schools recently obtained permission to make sixty copies of the manual. In Columbus, the material has been used at Maryhaven, an adult male day treatment center, but not as a rites of passage program.

The Cultural Initiatives section of the Ohio Department of Human Services, which funded the project, continues to receive requests for the manual and has sponsored at least one workshop (in Toledo) for social workers that included content on the manual.

Russ Moore has worked directly with ten different public and private agencies to implement the program. The total number of youth involved at this point is "about 75–80." The average size of the groups has been seven to eight. According to Moore, coauthor of the manual,

> The response has been good. The program needs to be continuous for at least two months. When it was all over, the participants were saying, "I ain't a hick. I'm an Appalachian." Some of the youth were apologetic about their response to traditional Appalachian music and bluegrass. One response was, "I didn't think I would but I really enjoyed that." We discovered the richness of our heritage and the diversity of our culture. We shucked the stereotype. We included the Indian heritages, did high rope, dialogs, field trips, and canoeing. The trouble makers ended up leading the activities. They got leadership skills, history and cultural awareness and a greater appreciation of their background. There was some improvement in self-esteem. The program has reached hundreds of young men. We have had calls from as far away as Las Vegas and Pennsylvania. It has been used in schools and with males in prison as well as with displaced youth (Moore 1995).

Asked about the different clienteles with which the program has been used, Moore listed independent living, custody, foster care, and at-risk youth. "The program works better," says Moore, "with youth in foster care and custody. At risk kids referred by the courts are tougher to work with." Moore's implementation of the program for youth from three Ohio Appalachian counties was evaluated by John McLaughlin, arts and education consultant from Lexington, Kentucky.

McLaughlin's evaluation included a pre- and post-attitudinal survey that measures changes in participants as a result of participation in the program, interviews, observations, and an ongoing dialog with Russ Moore. The evaluation included two different groups of boys from the Jackson-Gallia-Meigs area of southeastern Ohio. McLaughlin concluded that the program works well in a small group setting and that "the goals of the program are being met" (McLaughlin 1993). Benefits of the program included improvement in self-esteem and improved knowledge of Appalachian culture and feelings about living in the region. Improved ability to express themselves with adults was also seen as a benefit of the program. Other benefits included an increased pride in Appalachian heritage, increased ties to their families, and increased enjoyment of school. In the post test, participants showed a decreased confidence in their leadership and decreased confidence about staying in the region. The evaluator feels these responses may be attributable to a more realistic assessment of their abilities and of the economic opportunities available in depressed counties.

When asked what they liked least about the program, the only item that received more than one response was "being at the retreat with the older (or younger) kids." What they liked best was "getting together with everybody." Other items mentioned favorably included the storyteller, the retreat, going to the Welsh Museum and learning about the history of Appalachia.

When asked what they learned through the program, the most frequently mentioned item was "about Appalachian culture." When asked what changes they would make in the program, responses included nothing, not going to bed so early, more recreational activities and summer camp.

In an interview, McLaughlin commented, "There were real changes in the first group. The curriculum is well constructed." He subscribes to the concept of multiple intelligences and cautions against heavy reliance on lectures. Most of the participants were kinesthetic learners. McLaughlin suggests "more of a foxfire model with hands-on activities" in delivery of the curriculum. "Classes are boring if not hands on. More active learning projects are needed." The age group should not be too wide, he notes, or older kids will pick on the younger ones (McLaughlin 1996).

Are changes needed in the manual? A parallel program needs to be developed for young Appalachian women. But the manual as is very flexible and its users feel free to make adaptations to local needs and program setting. The time frame can be two months or a full year. Moore feels that even a compacted version conducted in one retreat weekend can be very useful (Moore 1996). In Scioto County, Ohio, the sponsor has added a ROPEs program (Rite of Passage Experience 2001). Another has added a camping component in which young men can learn such skills as how to raise a pup, mark a trail, identify plants and their uses, or grow vegetables. A "junior achievement" component could be added to develop entrepreneurial skills. The program already includes material on cultural diversity within Appalachia, but an interracial understanding component could be added. A variation on the camping idea would be to add a wilderness experience more along the lines of that used in some of the Africentric programs. Hands-on activities will vary with the skills of the trainers and the interests of the group.

Incorporating Material on Appalachian Values

In the Africentric rites of passage programs, great stress is placed on values thought to be traditional in African societies. The idea is to provide young people with values that can help them survive and be contributing members of family and society. In the Appalachian program, more content on Appalachian values could be incorporated. In Africentric programs, some use is made of Maulana Karenga's "Nguso Saba," a list of seven values, each with a meaning (table 15.1).

Table 15.1. Nguso Saba

Value	Meaning	Value	Meaning
Umoja	Unity	Nia	Purpose
Kugichagulia	Self-determination	Kuumba	Creativity
Ujima	Collective work and responsibility	Imani	Faith
Ujamaa	Cooperative economics		

The Maloney/Moore manual uses Loyal Jones's list of Appalachian values. There is little point teaching youth about their cultural heritage if we cannot refer them to a set of values that have helped Appalachian people in their journey on this continent. Bob Snyder wrote a thoughtful critique of Jones's book on values in which he suggested that we should not, in teaching Appalachian culture, describe the traits of the subculture as if they were personality traits writ large (Snyder 1995). I would argue that lists of traits should not be used, or if they are, they should be presented as lists of positive stereotypes developed by Appalachians to counter the negative stereotypes so often found in the literature and media presentations. Loyal Jones's and Jack Weller's lists can be presented side by side and discussed. Jones's (1994) book is the best framework we have so far.

Another point that Snyder (1995:258) makes is that we ought to pay some attention not only to the values that Appalachians possess but also to those we *ought* to possess. Writers such as Jones who have talents and interests in the areas of religion and ethics should, says Snyder, abandon the social science model and write as ethicists.

A third point made by Snyder in one of his final writings before his untimely death is that values should not be presented apart from "the conflicted circumstances which they occupy in our lives" (1995:256). They should be presented as part of individual and social conflict. If we teach, for example, that Appalachians have a passion for justice, we should describe times in our history when that sense of justice was threatened or violated. The practice of poaching timber, for example, was not unheard of in the Appalachian past. And there was little justice in the treatment of the Cherokees. Another way in which Snyder expresses his appeal for presenting Appalachian values in historical context is that "when we describe the cultural values of mountain people, we must grasp the facts in which they are embedded" (1995:260).

I think that Snyder is here talking about "the social construction of reality," a phrase often used by progressives to remind us that political and economic practices and oppressive structures often determine cultural practices, not the other way around. "Culture is not values," says Halperin. "Karengi's list can, for example, be mined for *adaptive strategies.* Collective work and responsibility, self-determination (autonomy and control) and control are very important *practices*" (Halperin 1996).

Having said all this, below I list Appalachian values that could be used to counter stereotypes. My list is similar to Jones's (1994) list and is influenced by Karenga's list of African values. It should be pointed out that all traditional societies have certain values. Hospitality, for example, is universal, although customs surrounding it vary greatly. Family centeredness and relations to village, tribe, or clan also have their similarities and differences when we compare societies. And so on. The point is not to come up with a list of what is unique to Appalachian culture, but to be able to discuss commonalties as well as differences with other traditional and modern societies.

Appalachian Values

Egalitarianism

There is a strong belief that fundamentally one man or woman is as good as another or at least can be if he or she tries. Our ancestors violated this value in many ways. Discuss the class system, the virtual extermination of Native Americans, and discuss racism as well as the positive side of race relations in the mountains.

Person Orientation

Appalachians respect the person, not her rank or degrees, care more about helping others than getting ahead, and resent functional relationships such as those required of most interactions in urban society and in bureaucracies. They desire to be respected and to be taken at their word rather than having to prove merit or verify identification. In rural and small-town society, everyone knows everyone; no one is anonymous. Mountain people, however, sometimes violate this value when required by work. The hospital receptionist, for example, cannot get to know personally every patient who comes through. She may, when busy or harassed, be curt, coldly hand people forms to fill out, and tell them to follow the blue line.

Tolerance

In Appalachian communities there is a tendency to judge a person by his behavior, not by his race, family status or social rank, or religion. People are judged by how they conform to their own stated religious beliefs, even if they differ from those of others in the community. This value is violated whenever we prejudge others based on their race, sex, religion, sexual orientation, or other criteria. Prejudice and resentment are often held toward the rich and the powerful, who are thought to violate egalitarian values.

Family Solidarity

Responsibility to one's family comes before career or getting ahead. Going off to college or the army can cause real strain on the individual or family. Family solidarity also affects school attendance and participation in community organization and churches.

Mutual Support

People look out for kin and neighbors who are close enough to be treated like kin. Money, material goods, and services such as auto repair and health care are largely provided within the kin network. The rearing of children is often the responsibility of more than the parents. When parents are unable to take care of the children, other family members may take over. Cash income is supplemented by the goods and services shared within the kin network and neighborhood (Halperin 1996).

Faith

Not all Appalachians are churchgoing, but most have a strong faith in God. For many, this faith is the core of their value system. Although Appalachians belong to a wide variety of churches, the majority are Baptist or Pentecostal.

Their faith stresses the importance of grace and the influence of the Holy Spirit in people's lives (McCauley 1995). It is a religion of the heart more than the head. Obedience to the religious tradition produces a gentleness of spirit and the modesty described by Loyal Jones. We are what we are not because of our superior knowledge or great works but because of God's grace. In her book *Appalachian Mountain Religion,* Deborah McCauley defends the religion of working-class Appalachians and attacks the stereotypes widely held by other Americans toward mountain religion and mountain preachers.

Self-Determination

Like other Americans, Appalachians hold the values of limited government, private property, and the importance of earning one's own living and providing for one's family. Contrary to stereotypes, Appalachians do organize their communities to provide services they regard as essential. They have built their own schools, churches, roads, and bridges. In spite of the depredations of deindustrialization and economic exploitation, the work ethic survives and most people work hard. This value incorporates the values of self-reliance and pride described by Jones.

Creativity

The creativity of mountain people is expressed in many forms, including arts, crafts, and music. As in all traditional cultures, there is a rich tradition of music, dance, storytelling, and folk art. Many Appalachians also contribute to what are often referred to as the fine arts, as distinct from folk art (a distinction some now consider elitist).

Sense of Place

Rural Appalachians, like southerners in general and rural people all over the world, have a strong sense of place. Urban Appalachians and other rural to urban migrants have an attachment to their country places. Places have memories associated with one's own life and the lives of one's ancestors. Places are named after families. Attachment to the home place is strong among Appalachians, and if they are separated from it through migration, they may grieve. Not all Appalachians respect their land enough, we might think, if they allow it to be destroyed by surface mining, but some landowners whose ancestors sold the mineral rights have no choice.

I prepared this list of values to illustrate Snyder's point that none of the existing lists is a matter of science and that we should feel free to use our imagination in describing the core values we believe mountain people to hold.

Any list of values should include respect for self, for family, for women, for the earth, and for community.

Guidelines for Presenting Material on Appalachian Culture

In the previous section, I made an initial response to Bob Snyder's (1995) critique of Loyal Jones book on Appalachian values. Snyder provides a list of guidelines for discussing Appalachian values. The following guidelines adapted from Snyder's should be useful to those who use the Appalachian Rites of Passage manual or otherwise present material on Appalachian culture.

- Do not try to demonstrate the uniqueness of Appalachian culture. Describe it as one of many traditional cultures and be willing to discuss commonalties with other cultures. I think the role of grandmothers is similar in Appalachian and African American cultures, for example.
- Describe the diversity within the culture in a way that describes some of the contributions of all the groups that came into the mountains. One can emphasize the role of Scots-Irish, Anglo-Saxons, and Germans without leaving out Africans or central and southern Europeans in the coal camps and steel mill towns. In Appalachian Ohio, we have two counties where the Welsh heritage is virtually dominant. A brochure titled *What Makes Appalachian Culture Unique?* by the Urban Appalachian council describes the region's diversity: "Appalachian culture is a unique blend of European, Native American, and African elements forged in isolation and over time. The blend of Celtic, Native American, and African influences can be seen in the steps of traditional clogging and can be heard in the old time mountain music, which took on a new sound when combined with the banjo, an African instrument."
- Include material on the cultures of any participants who are not of Appalachian heritage. This will enrich the discussion.
- Tap the material which participants can bring in from their own families and community.
- Be prepared for resistance, in passive or angry form, to the material you have presented. Schoolteachers and social workers who work in oppressive conditions with the poor may have invested heavily in the stereotypes. If they work with people who are "dysfunctional," they may not view your description of Appalachians as recognizable. You may have to listen, discuss class and other diversity within the Appalachian population, or just acknowledge that their experience has been different from yours.

- Explain the fallacy of using a list of traits as a way to get a handle on Appalachian culture. Much more important is to develop an understanding of the situations Appalachians face and their adaptive responses or strategies in coping with situations such as economic exploitation, male dominance, poor school systems, and lack of good jobs.
- Be prepared to discuss issues related to social class and gender and, if necessary, to distinguish these issues from issues of culture. Heavy drinking, for example, may have very little to do with culture and a lot to do with life-cycle stage for working-class men, college students, and so on. In writing about traditions in Appalachian culture, we need to be sensitive to the fact that by current standards some practices were oppressive to women or children. Another concept easily borrowed from the Africentric model is that of capitalizing on the importance of oral tradition in traditional societies and, I would say, among working-class people in general. Program participants should get to talk and they should learn to appreciate the tradition of storytelling in both the Appalachian and scriptural traditions.

Na'im Akbar, in *Visions for Black Men,* recognizes the importance of discipline in transition from boy to man. Discipline is seen as self-control: "Learning to exercise control over one's self is transformation energy. The boy takes his budding rationality and uses it to expand his consciousness" (1991:12). According to Akbar, this "simply means that the process of educating our boys requires that we require of them to tackle real life problems and watch them find solutions" (13).

In rural and urban Appalachian communities, there is no lack of real life problems to tackle. A rites of passage program provides a framework in which adults can provide instruction and guidance to Appalachian males as they make the difficult transition from boyhood to manhood. The program developed for Appalachian Ohio addresses concrete issues such as the lack of jobs for youth, surviving in school, developing community programs for recreation, home repair and chores for the isolated elderly, drugs, teen pregnancy and so on. Young men and women need to be given responsibility for articulating and solving concrete problems. Their adult mentors as well as peers watch and guide as the boy learns responsibility and the discipline that goes with it.

The process of learning discipline used to come naturally as part of life in the extended family and community. At an early age, boys had the opportunity to carry water from the spring, chop wood, hoe corn, or make a sleigh and other toys. As they grew in size, knowledge, and skill, their responsibilities increased and eventually included taking care of animals, tending sick elders and younger children, and sharing food and clothing with other families who had less materially than they did. In today's world, children's work is not needed and they realize this. The effect can be that the development of consciousness is arrested at the level of boyhood. The results can include prison or even early death as well as being unable to exercise responsibility in family and community life. The "community responsibility" component of the rites of passage program is thus a key component.

In conclusion, the Appalachian Male Rites of Passage Program is almost infinitely flexible and can be used to encompass a variety of program concepts, including camping, wilderness experience, self-mastery, community service, and mentoring. It can also be kept fairly simple if there are serious time or money constraints. It can even be used at home as a guide to parents in developing their own program of passages for children or young adults. At its core it is an approach to getting in touch with one's self in the context of family, community, and regional history. Among other things, it is an Appalachian cultural awareness program.

Note

A more complete bibliography is included in "A Rites of Passage Program for Adolescent Appalachian Males" by Michael E. Maloney and Russ V. Moore. For a copy of the manual, write or call:

Beth S. Evans, Director
The Gallia County Children's Services
Courthouse
Gallipolis, Ohio 45631
Telephone: (614) 446-4963

References

Akbar, Na'im. 1991. *Visions for Black Men.* Nashville: Winston-Derek Publishers.

Halperin, Rhoda. 1991. *The Livelihood of Kin: Making Ends Meet the Kentucky Way.* Austin: University of Texas Press.

———. 1996. Interview with author. Mar. 16.

Hare, Nathan, and Julia Hare. 1985. *Bringing the Black Boy to Manhood.* San Francisco: Black Think Tank.

Grimes, Robert L. 2002. *Deeply into the Bone: Re-Inventing Rites of Passage.* Berkeley and Los Angeles: University of California Press.

Jones, Loyal. 1994. *Appalachian Values.* Ashland, Ky.: Jesse Stuart Foundation.

Mahdi, Louise Carus, Steven Foster, and Meredith Little. 1987. *Betwixt and Between: Patterns of Masculine and Feminine Initiation.* LaSalle, Ill.: Open Court.

Maloney, Michael E., and Russ V. Moore. 1992. *A Rites of Passage Program for Adolescent Appalachian Males through Independent Living.* Gallipolis, Ohio: Gallia County Children's Services.

McCauley, Deborah Vansau. 1995. *Appalachian Mountain Religion.* Urbana: University of Illinois Press.

McLaughlin, John. 1993. Program Evaluation for Appalachian Male Rites of Passage Program. Unpublished.

———. 1996. Interview with the author. Jan. 23.

Moore, Mafori, Gwen Akua Gilyard, Karen King, and Nisenga Warfield-Coppock. 1987. *Transformation: A Rites of Passage Manual for African American Girls.* New York: Stars Press.

Moore, Russ V. 1995 and 1996. Interviews with the author. Sept. 5, 1995, and June 17, 1996.

Obermiller, Phillip J., and Michael E. Maloney. 1990. "Looking for Appalachians in Pittsburgh." *Pittsburgh History* (Winter)10:12–24.

———. 2002. "'We Ain't Agoin' Back': A Retrospective Look at Urban Appalachians in Greater Cincinnati." In *Appalachia: Social Context Past and Present* (4th ed.), Phillip J. Obermiller and Michael E. Maloney (Eds.). Dubuque, Iowa: Kendall/Hunt. Pp. 98–103.

Ogilvie, Emma, and Allen Van Zyl. 2001. *Young Indigenous Males, Custody and the Rites of Passage.* Trends and Issues in Crime and Criminal Justice Series. Canberra: Australian Institute of Criminology.

Perkins, Nseni Eugene. 1985. *Harvesting New Generations: The Positive Development of Black Youth.* Chicago: Third World Press.

Rite of Passage Experience™ (ROPE)®. 2001. The Center for the Advancement of Youth, Family and Community Services, Inc.

Schwarzweller, Harry K., James S. Brown, and J. J. Mangalam. 1961. *Mountain Families in Transition.* University Park: Pennsylvania State University Press.

Snyder, Bob. 1995. "The Appalachian Band in the Moral Spectrum." *Appalachian Journal* 22, no. 3 (Spring): 250–61.

Van Gennep, A. 1960 [1909]. *Rites of Passage.* Chicago: University of Chicago Press.

Contributors

Susan Abbott-Jamieson is Lead Social Scientist at NOAA Fisheries Headquarters, Office of Sciences and Technology, Silver Spring, Maryland. She joined NOAA Fisheries (National Marine Fisheries Service) following a twenty-five-year career as a faculty member in the Department of Anthropology at the University of Kentucky. She has carried out major research projects in the areas of psychological anthropology, community studies, and family and household. In addition to earlier research among East African farmer families coping with large-scale economic, social, and cultural change, she has carried out research among Appalachian Kentucky coal mining families in communities coping with widespread structural unemployment because of changes in coal mining technology and natural resource depletion. This work has appeared in over forty publications in professional journals and edited volumes. She is guiding the development of the emerging NOAA Fisheries social science program, which will improve the agency's ability to meet its mission-related research requirements. She also serves as an Adjunct Associate Professor in the Department of Anthropology at the University of Maryland.

Anne B. Blakeney earned her bachelor of science degree in political science at the University of Tennessee and her master of science in occupational therapy at Boston University. She received her Ph.D. in anthropology at the University of Kentucky in 2002. She has taught occupational therapy students for the past twenty years at both the University of North Carolina at Chapel Hill and at Eastern Kentucky University in Richmond, Kentucky.

Charlotte F. Chase, Ph.D., R.N., was an Associate Professor of Nursing at Clinch Valley College of the University of Virginia when she wrote her chapter. She is currently a health care consultant. She has worked as an anthropologist, community health nurse, educator, and researcher with a variety of groups. This has included fieldwork in Mongolia, Poland, and other countries of Eastern and Central Europe during the past twenty years. She has also conducted community health research among Russian-speaking immigrants from Ukraine and Russia to Washington State. She has also worked extensively in Mexico and with Mexican American farm workers in various parts of the United States, including in Virginia, Delaware, Colorado, Texas, and Washington.

Judith Ivy Fiene, MSSW, Ph.D., is Associate Dean, Emeritus at the University of Tennessee College of Social Work. Her interest in the lives of Appalachian women began during her years as a community-based social worker. She is author of *The Social Reality of a Group of Rural Low-Status, Appalachian Women: A Grounded Theory Study* (New York: Garland Press, 1993). She has been active in working with issues of domestic violence in Appalachia and is a member of the Tennessee Domestic Violence State Coordinating Council.

Susie Greene is the Associate Vice Chancellor for Student Development/Dean of Students at Appalachian State University. She has worked at the Appalachian State University Counseling and Psychological Services Center as a therapist and Associate Director, and she maintains a private practice in the community. She is actively involved in community and regional service and professional organizations.

Carol Gross, MSW, is an Associate Professor of Social Work at Appalachian State University. She has practiced as a social worker in rural areas from the Mississippi River to the Atlantic Coast.

Rhoda H. Halperin is Professor of Anthropology at the University of Cincinnati. She is the author of *The Livelihood of Kin: Making Ends Meet the Kentucky Way* (University of Texas Press, 1990). Most recently, she has been working in an urban Appalachian community in Cincinnati and has chronicled this work in *Practicing Community: Class, Culture and Power in an Urban Neighborhood* (University of Texas Press, 1998).

Janice L. (Jan) Hastrup has a Ph.D. in clinical psychology and a master of science in epidemiological research. She is on the faculty of the Department of Psychology at the University of Buffalo. She has consulted on several lawsuits regarding the psychological effects of environmental hazards. She has also conducted research on accuracy of family health history information, beliefs about genetic factors in disease, and methodological problems in science.

Benita J. Howell is Professor of Anthropology at the University of Tennessee–Knoxville. Her long-term interests in economic development and persistence of traditional culture in Appalachia, particularly on the Cumberland Plateau, have included consideration of changing occupational patterns and impacts of women's "public work" on traditional gender roles and family dynamics. She recently published a revised edition of *Folklife Along the Big South Fork of the Cumberland River* (University of Tennessee Press, 2003) and edited *Culture, Heritage, and Conservation in the Appalachian South* (University of Illinois Press, 2002).

Susan E. Keefe is Professor of Anthropology at Appalachian State University. She has served as an expert witness in death penalty cases and has been a consultant for numerous health, mental health, and social service agencies. She coauthored *Chicano Ethnicity* (University of New Mexico Press, 1987) and has edited two volumes, *Appalachian Mental Health* (University of Kentucky Press, 1988) and *Negotiating Ethnicity: The Impact of Anthropological Theory and Practice* (American Anthropological Association, 1989). Her current research examines modernity and Appalachian religion.

Lisa J. Lefler is a medical anthropologist who received her Ph.D. from the University of Tennessee in 1996. She is currently an Adjunct Associate Professor of Anthropology and Cherokee Studies at Western Carolina University. Born in southern Appalachia, her primary research has been related to the social consequences of negative stereotyping and the use of mentors as an intervention strategy for social pathologies among American Indian adolescents. She works fulltime for the Eastern Band of the Cherokee Indians as a behavioral science researcher concerning diabetes prevention and youth.

Michael E. Maloney grew up in Kentucky's Cumberland Plateau and has spent most of his life working with urban and rural Appalachians in Ohio. With Phillip Obermiller, he is coeditor of *Appalachia: Social Context Past and Present*, 4th edition, and the Urban Appalachia section of *The Encyclopedia of Appalachia*. He has served on the boards of several regional organizations and has written extensively about urban Appalachians and Appalachians in Ohio. He is currently involved in work with Catholic Social Services' Appalachian Area Office, the Episcopal Diocese of Southern Ohio, and consulting and training statewide. He staffs the Episcopal Network for Economic Justice. Among programs he has helped establish are the Urban Appalachian Council and the Appalachian Arts Program of the Ohio Arts Council.

Paul Parsons has a bachelor of arts degree in anthropology from Appalachian State University. He currently works as a health technician in Greensboro, North Carolina.

Anita Puckett received her Ph.D. from the University of Texas and is an Associate Professor and Director of the Appalachian Studies Program within the Department of Interdisciplinary Studies, Virginia Polytechnic Institute and State University. She is a linguistic anthropologist who specializes in language and economic relations in coal field areas in Appalachia and is particularly interested in language and materiality and speech and computer technology relations. She is author of *Seldom Ask, Never Tell: Requests and Socioeconomic Relations in Rural Appalachia* (Oxford University Press, 2000).

Jennifer Reiter-Purtill is currently a graduate student in psychology at the University of Cincinnati. She received her bachelor and master of arts degrees in anthropology from the University of Cincinnati with high honors.

Marc Sherrod is an ordained minister in the Presbyterian Church (USA) and served as pastor of the Newland Presbyterian Church in Newland, North Carolina, from 1984 to 1990. He is a graduate of Hampden-Sydney College and Columbia Theological Seminary, and he received a master's degree in Appalachian studies from Appalachian State University in 1991. He is currently a candidate for the doctor of theology degree at the Divinity School of Harvard University.

Carol C. Stephens is an Associate Professor at Western Carolina University, where she serves as the coordinator of the Graduate Nursing Program. She received her doctorate in nursing degree from the University of Alabama at Birmingham in 1994. She has lived in western North Carolina since 1974, and she has taught in the WCU Department of Nursing since 1983. Her clinical experience has primarily been in community and mental health.

Sherilyn N. Thomas has a Ph.D. in clinical psychology and is the director of the Psychological Services Center at the University at Buffalo. She also maintains a private practice in the Buffalo area, specializing in the treatment of anxiety disorders.

MELINDA BOLLAR WAGNER is Professor of Anthropology and an Associate Chair of the Appalachian Studies Program at Radford University in Radford, Virginia. She teaches courses on ethnographic methods and religious and cultural minority groups. She has published ethnographies about the diversity of religion in the United States, *Metaphysics in Midwestern America* (Ohio State University Press, 1983) and *God's Schools: Choice and Compromise in American Society* (Rutgers University Press, 1990), and is currently writing about cultural conservation in the Appalachian region.

Index

Appalachian Cultural Competency was designed and typeset on a Macintosh computer system using InDesign software. The body text is set in 10/13 Minion and display type is set in Formal. This book was designed and typeset by Kelly Gray and manufactured by Thomson-Shore, Inc.

-Paregoric